Royal Air I

C000131520

BOMBER I

IN THE MIDDLE ᴇᴀꜱᴛ ᴀɴᴅ
MEDITERRANEAN

Volume 1: 1939-1942

MIDLAND

An imprint of
Ian Allan Publishing

Royal Air Force

BOMBER LOSSES

IN THE MIDDLE EAST AND MEDITERRANEAN

Volume 1: 1939-1942

DAVID GUNBY & PELHAM TEMPLE

Royal Air Force
Bomber Losses in the Middle East & Mediterranean
Volume 1: 1939-1942

© 2006 David Gunby and Pelham Temple

ISBN (10) 1 85780 234 9
ISBN (13) 978 1 85780 234 4

First published in 2006 by Midland Publishing
4 Watling Drive, Hinckley, LE10 3EY, England
Tel: 01455 254 490   Fax: 01455 254 495
E-mail: midlandbooks@compuserve.com

Midland Publishing is an imprint of
Ian Allan Publishing Ltd.

Worldwide distribution (except North America):
Midland Counties Publications
4 Watling Drive, Hinckley
LE10 3EY, England
Tel: 01455 254 450   Fax: 01455 233 737
E-mail: midlandbooks@compuserve.com
www.midlandcountiessuperstore.com

North American trade distribution:
Specialty Press Publishers & Wholesalers Inc
39966 Grand Avenue, North Branch, MN 55056, USA
Telephone: 651 277 1400   Fax: 651 277 1203
Toll free telephone: 800 895 4585
www.specialtypress.com

Printed in England by Ian Allan Printing Ltd
Riverdene Business Park, Molesey Road
Hersham, Surrey, KT12 4RG

Visit the Ian Allan Publishing website at:
www.ianallanpublishing.com

Contents

Introduction

This volume, and its companion covering the years 1943-1945 that will appear, we hope, in two years' time, are the product of a partnership which began at the farthest possible distance and continued for two years before I, visiting Britain from New Zealand, was able to meet Pel Temple. Having written a history of 40 Squadron, which spent much of the war in the Middle East and Mediterranean, I had turned my attention to 205 Group, the night bomber force in that war theatre, with the intention (still strong) of publishing a history of the Group and its antecedent, 257 Wing. My particular passion was the Wellington. Pel, his interest in the type generated by an article he had read on a 'Lost Squadron', No 211, had developed a like passion for the Blenheim. Put in touch by Errol Martyn, author of the invaluable account of all New Zealanders lost while serving in the RNZAF and Allied air services, *For Your Tomorrow*, we determined to attempt what seemed from the first a task which appeared to us urgently in need of undertaking: a Middle East companion volume or volumes to Bill Chorley's monumental *Bomber Command Losses*.

With Pel working on the day and I on the night bomber squadrons, an approach was made to Midland Counties Publications, to establish whether they were interested in publishing such a work. They were and, buoyed by this, we set about a task about which we knew (and which others including Bill Chorley warned us) would be fraught with difficulty.

So indeed it has been. 'The further from the Air Ministry the worse the record keeping' seems to have been an adage with not a little truth to it, and the problem of inadequate or slipshod record-keeping is of course exacerbated by the confusion which ensued whenever (and it was frequently in 1941-1942) British Commonwealth forces were in retreat. The record-keeping of some of the Blenheim squadrons during the debacle which was the Greek campaign, for instance, was understandably less than perfect, while the operational records of two Blenheim squadrons, 84 and 211, were lost in their entirety when they moved to the Far East, and were engulfed in the disastrously mishandled defence of Malaya, Singapore, the Netherlands East Indies and Burma.

The squadron records of the night bomber squadrons, though in general more complete, were by no means always well-kept, some squadron adjutants seemingly intent more on saving paper and typewriter ribbon than in providing a full record of operational flying. Then, too, there was the problem of squadron detachments to Malta, whether from the United Kingdom or from Egypt, when records might or might not be kept, and if kept, might or might not be substantial and accurate. Similar problems derive from the detachment from Britain to Egypt of flights or individual aircraft from 10, 76 and 109 Squadrons.

When we began, the number of aircraft losses for which we possessed little or no information was perhaps as high as 15%. With persistence, and much help, as well as a little luck, we have, we think, reduced this to something like 5%. Nonetheless, there remain dozens of aircraft for which we can record little or nothing more than the date on which they were struck off charge, if even that. It is our hope that in some cases, at least, there may be survivors who can inform us as to the circumstances surrounding a loss about which we are ourselves at a loss, or those who may be able, from logbooks, letters or diaries, to clear up some of the mysteries which remain.

With errors in the reporting of an aircraft serial, detective work carried out with persistence often results in the discovery of the correct number. With crew names this is often not possible. The dead we have, of course, been able to identify fully and accurately, but others, and particularly the uninjured, may be wrongly identified in any number of ways, including rank, initials, spelling of surname, and even occasionally, the service (that is, RAAF and the like). Again, we hope that information will come to light to enable us to resolve mysteries and correct errors.

The principal sources used in the preparation of the loss tables have been the squadron operational record books (Air Ministry Forms 540 and 541), aircraft movement cards (AM 78) and Aircraft Accident Cards (AM 1180). Despite their (in some cases considerable) limitations, these constitute an invaluable resource, and one which has enabled us from time to time to correct an entry in that other invaluable resource, the Air- Britain Serials Registers compiled by James J Halley MBE. That these are sometimes in error is no reflection on the compiler, but rather a consequence of faulty or inadequate reporting by the authorities in the Middle East, Malta or East Africa.

Where there is a discrepancy between these two major sources, it is shown in the text with the reference to Halley's work indicated by the generic title 'A-B Serials'. The specific volume can be found by reference to the aircraft serial and the list contained in the Bibliography which follows.

As might be expected, the Commonwealth War Graves Commission registers have also been invaluable. They are not infallible, occasionally recording a casualty's unit or date of death wrongly, but they are a rich resource, and we have benefited greatly from their use, and particularly from being able to access records online. It has been our policy throughout to give the rank of the dead as that recorded in the CWGC registers, since official confirmation of promotion often took months to reach a squadron. Thus a member of a crew might be reported as missing in a squadron ORB as Sergeant X, when in fact he had been promoted Flight Sergeant months earlier, and perhaps even further, to

Warrant Officer, but neither he nor the squadron in which he was serving had yet been notified. Where an individual is named in relation to an aircraft loss but was not a casualty, of course, we have often been unable to determine whether the rank given in the ORB, on Aircraft Accident Cards, or other documents, was in fact the rank held at the time of the aircraft loss. Here, as elsewhere, we hope that information will surface to enable us to provide corrections in an appendix to Volume Two.

In the layout of each loss entry we have followed Bill Chorley's example, as, for example, in categorising the circumstance in which the loss occurred. Thus 'Ground' signifies losses of all kinds which occurred on the ground, whether stationary or taxying, but not crashes which occurred on take-off or landing, and 'Unknown' where the nature and purpose of the flight are not known. We have, however, felt the need to introduce several terms to cover specific situations in the Mediterranean and Middle East. Early in the war some aircraft were delivered directly from OTUs or ad hoc units like the '3 Group Training Flight', and are listed as on charge to those units. The vast majority, however, left Britain on charge to Overseas Air Delivery Units. We have accordingly, categorised bombers being flown out to the Middle East for employment there as Delivery Flights. Where, however, a squadron was moving to Malta or Egypt, as did 37 and 38 Squadrons in December 1940, or was relocating from one base to another, we have employed the term 'Relocation Flight'. A 'Transit Flight', by distinction, involved, most frequently, a flight to an advanced landing ground where the aircraft would be refuelled and bombed up in preparation for an operational flight later that day, while a 'Ferry Flight' typically involved a short flight from one base to another, perhaps transporting personnel.

It has sometimes proved impossible to determine the unit with which an aircraft was serving at the time of its loss, and in such cases we have been unable to do more than follow the accident or air movement cards and denote only the location, as (for example) 'Malta' or 'Middle East'. We are aware that in doing so we are certain to have included some losses which we would, were we sure of the unit involved, such as an Air Delivery Unit, or Middle East Training School, have excluded. But it seemed safest, where the unit cannot be determined, to include rather than exclude.

In this connection, too, a note of explanation is needed as to units which were included, and why. The title of this volume proclaims its restriction to bomber losses, pure and simple. But in fact, determining in some instances whether a unit should be included proved very much less than simple. 30 Squadron, for instance, operated both fighter and bomber Blenheims simultaneously from June 1940, and we have, accordingly, included only the Blenheim I losses, not those of the Blenheim IF. A difficult call also had to be made in relation to 14 Squadron, which, after it converted to Martin Marauders in August 1942, operated increasingly in an anti-shipping role. Since the transition was not immediate or complete, however, we have retained 14 Squadron losses to the end of 1942, though they will not feature in Volume Two. With 38 Squadron, on the other hand, which converted one flight from bombing to an anti-shipping role between March and June 1942,

we had as a ready-made cut-off date 1st July, when the remaining bomber crews were posted to other squadrons, and 38 Squadron left 205 Group. This means, of course, that a handful of 38 Squadron losses occurring on anti-shipping operations prior to that date are included, but attempting to decide whether to include on an ad hoc basis seemed simply too problematic. How, for instance, should a loss while mining be designated?

Some explanation also seems required for including, in a volume entitled *Bomber Losses*, losses by special duties squadrons and flights. The decision to include them was made primarily because, from 1941 onwards, but particularly in 1944-45, bomber squadrons themselves were extensively employed on duties such as dropping supplies to partisans which would normally be the responsibility of special duties squadrons. To exclude the latter would, particularly in Volume Two during the heroic Warsaw supply drops, be to obscure the extent of the operation and the sacrifices made in supporting partisan armies. A subsidiary consideration was the fact that, for a considerable period in 1942, 108 Squadron operated a flight of Liberators alongside its Wellingtons, the latter engaged in bombing operations, and the former in partisan supply drops. As with 38 Squadron until the end of June 1942, it would seem pointless to include some 108 Squadron losses and exclude others.

Some comment is also needed relating to the inclusion of two units specialising in radio intelligence, the 109 Squadron detachment and its successor, 162 Squadron. In including these we were influenced by the fact that the Wellingtons of 162 Squadron undertook regular bombing operations when not required for more specialist tasks, and indeed, routinely carried bombs when on radio intelligence operations.

Clearly, then, the term 'Bomber Losses' in *Bomber Losses in the Middle East and Mediterranean* is shorthand. So too, is 'in the Middle East and Mediterranean', since early on we took the decision to include in these two volumes all losses occurring in East Africa, as well as the Middle East proper. We also decided to include here all losses of bomber aircraft en route to the Middle East, whatever route they took, and even if they crashed within minutes of take-off from a base in the United Kingdom. In some few cases this meant an overlap with entries in Bill Chorley's volumes, but again, it seemed better to include, with occasional repetition, than to exclude, with the likelihood that a loss might otherwise never be documented in a volume of this sort.

The order in which the crew of an aircraft is listed follows closely that adopted by Bill Chorley. In day bombers, with a crew of three or four, for the most part, the pilot and observer are followed by the gunner or gunners. With the Wellingtons, until late 1942 carrying a crew of six, the two pilots are followed by the observer, wireless operator and gunners. With the belated introduction in the Middle East of the five-man Wellington crew, second pilots appear only when a newcomer to a squadron is making a 'second dickey' trip, while the bomb aimer is listed after the navigator and wireless operator but before the rear gunner. With Halifax and Liberator crews, the pilot or pilots are followed by the navigator, wireless operator, flight engineer, bomb aimer and gunners. Occasionally, the trades of the crew are not known; this is noted accordingly. When, as is not infrequently the case, only the names of the pilot or pilots are recorded, the existence of other, unidentifiable crew members is indicated by 'crew'. Likewise, passengers whose names are not known are noted as 'passenger' or 'passengers'.

Considerable thought was given to the handling of names, many of which, whether of bases or targets, are of places thoroughly obscure, and now, where traceable, spelt differently. Rather than attempting to update or correct these names, even where, as with Eleusis, in Greece, which is a faulty transliteration of Elevsis, the true name is abundantly obvious, we have chosen rather to retain the original, intervening only to standardise where a name is spelt variously in original documents. This retention of the original version of the

name applies throughout, as with, for example, Tobruk. Replacing this with 'Tubruq' seems pointless in a volume of this sort. With relatively obscure targets, the country in which they are located is named at first citation, but under the name it had at the time, as with, say, Hargeisa, British Somaliland. All bases from which the bombers flew are identified on the set of maps contained in Appendix 1. Landing Grounds are customarily identified in the text both by their number and by name, as for example, LG 29 (Almiriya). Distances, most of them originally in miles, have been given throughout in kilometres.

David Gunby,
August 2006

Acknowledgements

This volume, and its successor, which will detail the losses suffered by bomber and special duties units operating from North Africa and Italy during 1943-45, could not be written without the active support and co-operation of a large number of individuals and organisations. And since so many of the aircraft lost meant also aircrew killed, injured or taken prisoner, it is fitting that our first acknowledgement is the cheerful and unfailing assistance given both authors by Mrs Susan Dickinson of the Air Historical Branch. Where unit records were so often incomplete or confusing, the assistance of the AHB became more than usually crucial. To Susan, and to Sebastian Cox, the Head of the Air Historical Branch, who approved our continued status as researchers, our deepest thanks.

Special acknowledgement should be made here of Jeff Jefford, who generously offered to provide maps showing the bases from which bombers operated in the Middle East. Contained in Appendix 1, these are in a format familiar to those who know Jeff's monumental *RAF Squadrons*. Without the maps, the location of many of the obscure or fleetingly occupied landing grounds, in particular, would have been impossible to indicate adequately.

Our heartfelt thanks, too, to those who have so consistently and generously assisted us in our research. Pel Temple wishes to thank the Royal Air Force Museum, Hendon, and in particular, Graham Warner, whose expertise relating to Blenheims was of the greatest

value, and Ken Smy, without whose many hours of research, willingly given, the entries relating to South African Air Force losses would have been woefully inadequate. David Gunby's thanks go to Hugh Halliday (RCAF casualties), Winston Brent (SAAF personnel), Kevin Mifsud (losses on and around Malta), Bill Chorley, who spent many hours amid his own research into *Bomber Command Losses* identifying Middle East Losses, and relaying information about them to David, and to Col Bill Saavedra USAF (ret'd), of the Air Force History Support Office, Bolling Air Force Base, whose research in United States Air Force archives made as near complete as they are the entries relating to USAAF losses during the period when American units operated under RAF control during the crisis of the summer of 1942.

Above all, David would like to record two great debts of gratitude. The first is to Errol Martyn, friend and co-researcher, who not only gave unstintingly of his time in checking losses involving New Zealand personnel, but also read drafts of the various sections of the book, noting many errors, typographical and otherwise, and suggesting improvements of many kinds. The second debt is to the late Derek Sadler, whose many hours of research into Wellington losses outside the United Kingdom, willingly shared, made the compiling of the Wellington entries in this book so much the easier. Derek's enthusiasm for this project never faltered, even as he fought his last battle with cancer. There is much of him in this book.

Sources and Bibliography

PRIMARY SOURCES
Air Historical Branch:
  Aircraft Accident Cards
  Aircraft Movement Cards

Australian War Museum:
  Roll of Honour Website

Commonwealth War Graves Commission:
  Cemetery and Memorial Registers and website

National Archives Public Record Office, Kew:
  Allied Air Forces Prisoner of War File
  Escape and Evasion Reports
  Squadron and other Operational Record Books

The Aeroplane 1939-46:
  'The Royal Air Force. The Roll of Honour'.

SECONDARY SOURCES & BIBLIOGRAPHY
They Shall Not Grow Old – A Book of Remembrance:
  Les Allison & Harry Hayward; Commonwealth Air
  Training Plan Inc, 1992.

Bristol Blenheim: Theo Boiten; Crowood Press, 1997.

Wellington at War: Chaz Bowyer; Ian Allan, 1982.

Bristol Blenheim; Ian Allan, 1984.

A Gathering of Eagles: J Ambrose Brown; Purnell, 1970.

Eagles Strike: James Ambrose Brown; Purnell, 1974.

*With Courage and Faith – The Story of No 18 Squadron
  RAF:* A Butterworth; Air-Britain, 1989.

*The Distinguished Flying Cross and How it was Won,
  1918-95:* Nick and Carol Carter; Savannah, 1998.

*Wellington Wings – An RAF Officer in the Western
  Desert:* F R Chappell; William Kimber, 1980.

Royal Air Force Bomber Command Losses, Volumes 1-8:
  W R Chorley; Midland Publishing, 1992-2003.

Operation Mercury: M G Comeau MM;
  William Kimber, 1961.

Beam Bombers – The Secret War of No 109 Squadron:
  Michael Cumming; Sutton Publishing, 1998.

The Winged Bomb – The History of 39 Squadron RAF:
  Ken Delve; Midland Counties Publications, 1985.

*Call-Out – A Wartime Diary of Air/Sea Rescue Operations
  at Malta:* Frederick R Galea; Frederick Galea, 2002.

Strike Hard! The Story of 104 (Bomber) Squadron:
  Robert Ginn; 104 Squadron RAF Association, 1990.

*Sweeping the Skies – A History of No 40 Squadron RFC
  and RAF, 1916-56:* D Gunby; Pentland Press, 1995.

RAF Aircraft BA100-BZ999: J J Halley; Air-Britain, 1985.
RAF Aircraft DA100-DZ999; Air-Britain, 1987.

RAF Aircraft EA100-EZ999; Air-Britain, 1988.
RAF Aircraft FA100-FZ999; Air-Britain, 1989.
RAF Aircraft HA100-HZ999; Air-Britain, 1989.
RAF Aircraft L1000-N9999; Air-Britain, 1993.
The K File: The RAF of the 1930s; Air-Britain, 1995.
RAF Aircraft P1000-R9999; Air-Britain, 1996.
RAF Aircraft T1000-V9999; Air-Britain, 1997.
RAF Aircraft W1000-Z9999; Air-Britain, revd edn 1998.
RAF Aircraft AA100-AZ999; Air-Britain, revd edn 2000.

*The Squadrons of the Royal Air Force & Commonwealth
  1918-1988;* Air-Britain, 1988.

Copper Wire: Robert Harding, 2000.

The Flying Camels – The History of 45 Squadron:
  Wg Cdr C G Jefford, 1995.

RAF Squadrons, 2nd edn; Airlife Publishing, 2001.

Aviateurs de la Liberté: Colonel Henri Lafont; Service
  Historique de l'Armée de l'Air. 2002.

For Your Tomorrow, Vol 1: Errol W Martyn;
  Volplane Press, 1998.

Wise Without Eyes – 37 Sqn Royal Air Force 1939-45:
  Kevin Mears; Hooded Falcon Publications, 2005.

The British Air Commission and Lend-Lease:
  K J Meekcoms; Air-Britain, 2000.

Scorpions Sting – The Story of No 84 Squadron RAF:
  Don Neate; Air-Britain, 1994.

*Prisoners of War Naval and Air Forces of Great Britain and
  the Empire, 1939-1945;* HMSO, 1945.
  Reprint by J B Hayward, 1990.

The Halifax File: R N Roberts; Air-Britain, 1982.

The Whitley File; Air-Britain, 1986.

The Battle File: Sidney Shail; Air-Britain, 1997.

Pictorial History of the Mediterranean Air War:
  Christopher F Shores; Ian Allan, 1972.

Dust Clouds in the Middle East; Grub Street, 1996.

Air War for Yugoslavia, Greece and Crete 1940-41: C F
  Shores & B Cull, with N Malizia; Grub Street, 1987.

Malta: The Hurricane Years 1940-41; Grub Street, 1987.

Malta: The Spitfire Year 1942; Grub Street, 1991.

Fighters over the Desert: Christopher F Shores and
  Hans Ring; Arco Publishing, 1969.

The Distinguished Flying Medal Register: Ian Tavender;
  Savannah, 2000.

Per Noctem Per Diem – The History of 24 Sqn SAAF:
  E N Tucker, and P J M McGregor; 24 Squadron
  Album Committee, 1961.

The Bristol Blenheim: G W Warner; Crécy, 2002.

Glossary of Terms

DECORATIONS

AFC	Air Force Cross
AFM	Air Force Medal
BEM	British Empire Medal
CB	Companion of the Order of the Bath
CGM	Conspicuous Gallantry Medal
CMG	Companion of the Order of St Michael and St George
DFC	Distinguished Flying Cross
DFM	Distinguished Flying Medal
DSO	Distinguished Service Order
GC	George Cross
GM	George Medal
MBE	Member of the Order of the British Empire
MC	Military Cross
MiD	Mentioned in Despatches
MM	Military Medal
OBE	Order of the British Empire
TD	Territorial Decoration
VC	Victoria Cross

RANKS

1/Lt	First Lieutenant
2/Lt	Second Lieutenant
A/Cdre	Air Commodore
AC	Aircraftman
AC1	Aircraftman First Class
AC2	Aircraftman Second Class
Adj	Adjutant
Adj-Chef	Adjutant-Chef
Air Mech	Air Mechanic
Air Sgt	Air Sergeant
AM	Air Marshal
AOC	Air Officer Commanding
A/Sgt	Acting Sergeant
AVM	Air Vice-Marshal
Capt	Captain
C-in-C	Commander-in-Chief
Cmdt	Commandant
Cne	Capitaine
CO	Commanding Officer
Col	Colonel
Cpl	Corporal
F/Lt	Flight Lieutenant
F/O	Flying Officer
F/Sgt	Flight Sergeant
Fw	Feldwebel
G/Capt	Group Captain
Gefr	Gefreiter
Hptm	Hauptmann
LAC	Leading Aircraftman
Lt	Lieutenant/Leutnant
Lt Col	Lieutenant Colonel
Lt Cdr	Lieutenant Commander
Maj	Major
Mar	Maresciallo di 1st Classe
Oblt	Oberleutnant
Ofhr	Oberfähnrich
Ofw	Oberfeldwebel
Pfc	Private First Class
P/O	Pilot Officer
Pte	Private
Pvt	Private (USAAF)
Serg	Sergent
Sgc	Sergent Chef
Sgt	Sergeant
Serg Mag	Sergente Maggiore
S/Ldr	Squadron Leader
Slt	Sous-Lieutenant
Sottoten	Sottotennente
S/Sgt	Staff Sergeant
Sub-Lt	Sub-Lieutenant
Ten	Tennente
T/Sgt	Technical Sergeant
Uffz	Unteroffizier
W/Cdr	Wing Commander
W/O	Warrant Officer
W/O1	Warrant Officer First Class
W/O2	Warrant Officer Second Class

ARMED SERVICES

AAIC	Australian Army Intelligence Corps
CT	Caccia Terrestre
FAA	Fleet Air Arm
FAFL	Force Aérienne Française Libre
PAF	Polish Air Force
RA	Royal Artillery
RAAF	Royal Australian Air Force
RAF	Royal Air Force
RAFVR	Royal Air Force Volunteer Reserve
RCAF	Royal Canadian Air Force
RN	Royal Navy
RNZAF	Royal New Zealand Air Force
SAAF	South African Air Force
USAAF	United States Army Air Force
USAF	United States Air Force
USMC	United States Marine Corps

OTHERS

AA	Anti-Aircraft
A-B	Air-Britain
AHB	Air Historical Branch
ALG	Advance Landing Ground
AM	Air Ministry
ASR	Air Sea Rescue

BER   Beyond Economic Repair
Bomb Gp   Bombardment Group
CWGC   Commonwealth War Graves Commission
DBF   Destroyed by Fire
DBR   Damaged Beyond Repair
Esc de Bomb Escadrille de Bombardement
ETA   Estimated Time of Arrival
evd   evaded
FB   Flying Battle (category of damage to
             aircraft)
FB Flt   French Bomber Flight
FF   Free French
Flak   Anti-aircraft fire; acronym from the
             German Fliegerabwehrkanone
Flt   Flight
FTR   Failed to Return
GB   Groupe de bombardement
GC   Groupe de Chasse
GM   Glenn Martin
GMT   Greenwich Mean Time
Gp   Group
GP   General Purpose
GrB   Groupe réservé de bombardement
HMS   His Majesty's Ship
HSL   High Speed Launch
IFF   Identification Friend or Foe
inj   injured
int   interned
JG   Jagdgeschwader
km   kilometre
lb   Pound (weight)
LG   Landing Ground
ME   Middle East
ME Flt   Middle East Flight
mph   miles per hour
MTB   Motor Torpedo Boat
MU   Maintenance Unit
MV   Motor Vessel
NFD   No further details
NJG   Nachtjagdgeschwader
OADF   Overseas Air Delivery Flight
OADU   Overseas Air Delivery Unit
OLG   Operational Landing Ground
Op   Operation
ORB   Operational Record Book
OTU   Operational Training Unit
POW   Prisoner of war
Prov   Provisional
QDM   Call sign for a bearing

RE   Royal Engineers
RSU   Repair and Salvage Unit
SD   Special Duty
SOC   Struck off Charge
SOS   Save our souls (distress message)
Sqn   Squadron
SS   Steam Ship
Stab   Headquarters
Stn   Station
UK   United Kingdom
US   United States
WOp/AG   Wireless Operator/Air Gunner
ZG   Zerstörergeschwader
+   Fatal Casualty

AIRCRAFT DAMAGE CATEGORIES

Cat U   Undamaged, following accident/combat.
Cat A   Damaged, repairable on site by operating
             unit.
Cat Ac   Damaged, repairable on site, but not by
             operating unit.
Cat B   Damaged, repairable at a Maintenance
             Unit, Civilian Repair Depot or manuftrs.
Cat C   Damaged, repairable to ground
             instructional status only.
Cat E   Written off, salvage impossible.
Cat E1   Written off, salvage of components
             possible.
Cat E2   Written off, salvage as scrap possible.
Cat Em   Written off, missing on operational flight.

MESSERSCHMITT Bf or Me ?

The argument about 'Bf' or 'Me' as the prefix for the Messerschmitt 109 and 110 fighters has generally settled upon their being Bayerische Flugzeugwerke (that is, Bf) designs. The German Air Ministry (Reichsluftfahrt-ministerium – RLM) marks the transition from 'Bf' to 'Me' between the unsuccessful Bf 162 Jaguar (whose number was subsequently allocated to the He 162 Volksjäger) and the Me 163 Komet.

All of this was lost on those serving in the British armed forces and aircraft were universally regarded as 'MEs' However, with the benefit of hindsight, for this series types are recorded as Bf 109s and Bf 110s.

Chapter 1

Prelude to War
September 1939 to June 1940

When Britain and France declared war on Germany on 3rd September 1939, it was to be expected that fascist Italy would also enter the conflict, that the personal alliance forged by Hitler and Mussolini would lead to a joint attack on the western democracies. But Mussolini, held off, cautiously waiting to see what might befall. Only when it became clear that the German blitzkreig had shattered the British and French forces, and with it the French will to resist, did Mussolini enter the fray, declaring war on France and Britain on 10th June 1940.

Mussolini's delay was fortunate, in that it gave the Commander in Chief, Middle East, General Sir Archibald Wavell, the opportunity to make modest gains in his land and air strength – modest because Britain was stretched to the limit in meeting its commitments elsewhere – but also unfortunate, in that Britain could by June 1940 no longer rely on its ally, France, to share in the containment, and eventual elimination, of the Italian forces in North Africa. Until France's collapse, the allies' battle plan had involved the exertion of military pressure on Libya and Tripolitania from both the east – Egypt – and the west – Tunisia. With the new French government under Marshal Pétain signing an armistice agreement with both Germany and Italy on 25th June, however, Britain* found itself confronted by the prospect of Italian invasion both of Egypt and, from the Italian colonies of Eritrea, Abyssinia, and Italian Somaliland, of Kenya, Sudan and British Somaliland.

In both sectors Italian superiority in numbers and materiel was immense. In Egypt Wavell had some 36,000 British, Indian and New Zealand troops facing some 215,00 Italian and Italian colonial troops in Libya, while elsewhere some 46,000 troops, scattered through the Sudan, Kenya, British Somaliland, Aden, Palestine and Cyprus, were opposed by more than 200,000 in Italian East Africa.

In the air, Italian superiority, though less overwhelming, was nonetheless massive. In May 1940, when Air Marshal Sir Arthur Longmore took over from Air Marshal Sir William Mitchell as Air Officer Commanding, Middle East, he had, in Egypt and Palestine, a total of just 205 aircraft, of which 96 were bombers (Blenheim I) and bomber-transports (Bombay) to oppose 313 (including 140 bombers) disposed in Libya and the Dodecanese. In East Africa the discrepancy was even worse, with 325 Italian aircraft of all types opposed by a miscellany of types, totalling some 163, including three squadrons of Wellesleys in the Sudan, one and half squadrons of Blenheim Is and 9 Vincents in Aden, and 15 Junkers 86Ks of the South African Air Force in Kenya. Air Marshal Longmore nonetheless felt confident that the discrepancy in numbers and to some extent in quality would, in the event of war, be largely offset by the superior training and morale of the British forces. It was also considered – and was proven to be right – that the Italian maintenance organisation was inferior to that of the RAF and SAAF.

The term should be taken here, as later, as shorthand for British and Imperial forces, since there were under Wavell's command substantial Australian, Indian, New Zealand and later South African units.

11 Sep 1939	30 Sqn P/O F C B Harrison	Blenheim I	K7093 Training Took off 0800, Ismailia/Moascar, on a solo training flight. Landed with the undercarriage retracted. DBR.
13 Sep 1939	47 Sqn Sgt R W T Shelley	Wellesley I +	L2702 Training Took off 0600, Khartoum, to carry out his solo flight on the type. Stalled in circuit, spun and crashed. Buried in Khartoum War Cemetery.
15 Sep 1939	47 Sqn	Vincent	K4673 Unknown SOC as spares.
27 Sep 1939	223 Sqn P/O G O Ross	Wellesley I	L2692 Training Took off Summit on night-flying practice. Overshot on landing and hit Wellesley L2674. DBR.

2 Oct 1939	**113 Sqn** F/Lt J W Dallamore	**Blenheim I**	**L8442**	**Training**

Took off Heliopolis on night-flying practice. One engine failed on take-off, the aircraft crashed and was DBF.

3 Oct 1939	**47 Sqn** Sgt H Lilley	**Wellesley I**	**L2699**	**Training**

Took off 0645, Khartoum, on a solo training flight. Overshot on landing, aircraft swung and undercarriage collapsed. DBR.

16 Oct 1939	**47 Sqn** Sgt J N Owen Sgt Floyd Passenger: A/Sgt L Hutt	**Wellesley I**	**L2700**	**Training**

Took off 0700, Khartoum/Gordon's Tree, on a navigational exercise. Force-landed with engine trouble 40km W of Jebel Aulia, Sudan.

18 Oct 1939	**47 Sqn** P/O F S Holman LAC W Blackshaw	**Wellesley I**	**K7776**	**Unknown**

Took off Khartoum/Gordon's Tree. Undercarriage collapsed on landing. SOC as BER 19.3.40.

	55 Sqn P/O R H Nicolson LAC C H Bartram AC1 T R Sherr AC1 J Rown	**Blenheim I**	**L8673**	**Training**

Took off Ismailia/Moascar for night-flying training. The hydraulics failed with the undercarriage half retracted, and as the pilot was inexperienced on the type, the crew were ordered to abandon the aircraft, which crashed in the desert N of Ismailia.

18 Nov 1939	**8 Sqn** P/O M O Howell P/O R J Melville-Townsend AC1 A U Smith	**Blenheim I** + + +	**L6647**	**Op: Reida al Rasheid**

Took off 0400, Khormaksar, one of four detailed to bomb rebel tribesmen. Turned back with engine trouble and crash-landed 20km N of al-Irqa. The crew escaped unhurt, but were captured and shot by tribesmen. They are buried in Ma'alla Cemetery.

22 Nov 1939	**84 Sqn** F/Lt R A Towgood Crew	**Blenheim I**	**L1380 S**	**Training**

Took off Shaibah for radio formation practice. Retracted the undercarriage by mistake when stationary after landing. DBR.

23 Nov 1939	**14 Sqn**	**Wellesley I**	**L2644**	**Unknown**

SOC, NFD.

	14 Sqn	**Wellesley I**	**L2656**	**Unknown**

SOC, NFD.

	223 Sqn	**Wellesley I**	**L2663**	**Unknown**

SOC, NFD.

24 Nov 1939	**223 Sqn** Sgt V C Durrant	**Wellesley I**	**L2656**	**Unknown**

Took off, Summit. The engine failed during an attempted night landing, and the aircraft was landed with the undercarriage up. SOC.

26 Dec 1939	**49 MU Delivery Flt** Sgt G J C P Bateman LAC P Hodkinson	**Wellesley I**	**L2682**	**Delivery Flight**

Took off Boscombe Down on delivery to the Middle East. Damaged when the aircraft hit telephone wires while trying to land in a field, Angers, France. SOC 21.8.40.

Date	Unit / Crew		Aircraft	Serial / Details	Category
15 Feb 1940	223 Sqn		Wellesley I	**L2669** SOC. NFD.	**Unknown**
19 Feb 1940	45 Sqn F/Lt G J Bush Passengers		Blenheim I	**L8482 W** Took off LG 17 (Fuka Main), and on return crash-landed in a sandstorm. The pilot and five passengers were uninjured.	**Unknown**
28 Feb 1940	47 Sqn Sgt W H C Style		Wellesley I	**L2709** Took off Khartoum/Gordon's Tree. Crashed in a forced-landing near Khartoum at approximately 0800 hrs. SOC.	**Unknown**
13 Mar 1940	211 Sqn P/O C P R Collier LAC C E Thomas	inj inj	Blenheim I	**L1486** Took off LG 105 (El Daba), on night-flying training, but on landing undershot, grazed a railway embankment and crashed. DBR.	**Training**
	211 Sqn P/O E Garrard-Cole		Blenheim I	**L1537** As above: on return crashed in a heavy landing. DBR.	**Training**
27 Mar 1940	14 Sqn F/Lt D C Stapleton DFC AFC Sgt J A Burcher Sgt D Farrell		Blenheim I	**K7752** Took off LG 34 (Aboukir) on an anti-submarine training flight, but hit the windsock mast and crashed. SOC 17.4.40 as BER.	**Training**
4 Apr 1940	36 MU Sgt J A Lewis LAC A R Martin LAC R W E Jordan	+ + +	Wellesley I	**K7740** Took off Boscombe Down on delivery to the Middle East, but in bad weather dived into the sea at Pointe de l'Aiguillon, Vendee, France. All the crew are buried in the l'Aiguillon-Sur-Mer Communal Cemetery.	**Delivery Flight**
	36 MU F/O J D V Porter Sgt R Hawes Sgt A G R Allan	+ + +	Wellesley I	**K7754** Took off Boscombe Down on delivery to the Middle East, but vanished in bad weather off the French coast. All are commemorated on the Runnymede Memorial.	**Delivery Flight**
11 Apr 1940	30 Sqn		Blenheim I	**K7107 B** SOC, NFD.	**Unknown**
	S Sqn P/O A D G Stephenson LAC F J Guest Cpl G G Cumming	+	Vincent	**K4154** Took off 0530 Habbaniyah/Dhibban, to reconnoitre the road between Habbaniyah and Ur. Landed at Hillah LG with engine trouble, and on take-off hit wires and crashed. SOC 3rd July. Cpl Cumming is buried in Habbaniyah War Cemetery.	**Op: Reconnaissance**
24 Apr 1940	8 Sqn F/O P A Nicholas	inj	Blenheim I	**L1544** Took off Khormaksar on night-flying training. Undershot on approach to land, crashed and DBF.	**Training**
12 May 1940	45 Sqn Sgt R H Claxton Sgt N F Smith LAC R J King LAC R C Jobling	+ + inj +	Blenheim I	**L1544** Took off LG 17 (Fuka Main) on a Defence of the Nile Delta training exercise and, lost, flew into a ridge near El Quattara. DBR. The dead are buried in Ismailia War Memorial Cemetery.	**Training**

Chapter 2

The Italian Offensive June to December 1940

In both North and East Africa it was anticipated by the British High Command that the Italians, relying on their superior numbers, would rapidly take the offensive. Instead, they delayed and, when they did advance did so only modestly, in what were essentially defensive moves. In East Africa it was not until July that the Italians moved forward from Eritrea, occupying the town of Kassala, some 12 miles inside Sudan, and then stopping. In the south, a similarly modest advance was made across the border into Kenya, while the only major gain was in British Somaliland, which was occupied after a short struggle, in the course of which the small British, African and Indian force inflicted over 2,000 casualties for the loss of only 250.

In the Western Desert, the British forces began, as soon as war was declared, to patrol offensively, inflicting 3,500 Italian casualties in the period June-September for the loss of only 150 men. Italian morale was considerably lowered, and when, on 13th September, the long-anticipated advance took place, it proved to be as hesitant and limited as in East Africa. The six Italian divisions advanced only 50 miles, to Sidi Barrani, halting there and establishing a chain of defensive forts.

In the air, the Italians proved less hesitant, but nonetheless failed to take advantage of their superiority in numbers, again proving essentially defensively-minded. By contrast, Air Marshal Longmore went on the offensive from the first, concentrating on Italian airfields in an effort to destroy aircraft, fuel and ammunition dumps, and to wreck repair and maintenance facilities. In this he was remarkably successful, with the Blenheim squadrons inflicting such damage that Generale Pinna, reporting on the situation of the Regia Aeronautica, wrote that in the first week the RAF had destroyed a large quantity of food, tyres, engines, spare parts, fuel, and 15 aircraft, and that if the attacks were to continue with the same regularity, the air force would be in a critical condition within a month.

Unfortunately, however, a shortage of aircraft – ten Blenheims were lost in the first three weeks – and of crews meant that the early level of intensity could not be maintained. Consequently, while awaiting the arrival of Blenheim IVs, which had a longer range than the Mk Is in service in the Middle East at the outbreak of hostilities, the daylight bombing raids were scaled back. So too, were the night bombing raids, carried out by 216 (Bomber Transport) Squadron, which had recently re-equipped with the Bristol Bombay. Very rapidly it became clear, in fact, that the Bombays, which with fuselage tanks fitted could reach Benghazi, were more urgently needed in the transport role than as bombers. The decision was thus taken to re-equip 70 (Bomber-Transport) Squadron, equipped with Vickers Valentias, with Wellingtons, and in August 1940 crews flew to Britain to collect their Mk ICs, flying them out to Egypt via Malta. The impact of the single Wellington squadron was immediate, and led to a decision to release 37 and 38 Squadrons from Bomber Command for service in the Middle East. By the end of 1940, therefore, the AOC Middle East had at his disposal three Wellington squadrons.

In East Africa the air war opened with a similarly aggressive policy of daylight attacks on Italian airfields and repair facilities, with fuel and ammunition dumps in Eritrea destroyed, but eleven aircraft were lost by the three Wellesley squadrons (14, 47 and 223) in the first three weeks, and attacks had to be scaled back, since scant reserves of the type were available. From the south the air assault was largely in the hands of the South African Air Force, which deployed (initially) one squadron of Martin Marylands, one of Fairey Battles and one of Junkers 86Ks alongside a small RAF force at Aden, equipped with Blenheim I and Vincent aircraft. Two further SAAF Maryland units were scheduled, but supplies of the Marylands were delayed, and it was not until 12th December that the first of the type was assembled at Takoradi, in Nigeria, for despatch across Central Africa to Egypt.

Supply difficulties also bedevilled the other day bomber units. 14 Squadron converted to Blenheims in September, but the two remaining Wellesley squadrons were rapidly running out of aircraft, since the type was no longer in production, and the reserve in the Middle East was exhausted. The problem was exacerbated when, on 16th October, the Regia Aeronautica carried out a successful dawn attack on 47 Squadron at Gedaref, destroying two Vincents and eight Wellesleys. The situation was little better as regards the Blenheims, since only three squadrons had re-equipped with Blenheim IVs, and the remainder were still flying Mk Is, of which there was a rapidly dwindling reserve.

Further pressure on day bomber resources was caused, in November, by the decision to move three Blenheim squadrons to Greece, to assist the Greeks in their struggle against the invading Italians. 30 Squadron, with Blenheim IVFs, was the first to relocate, followed by 84 and, late in the month, 211 Squadrons. These, assisted by the Wellingtons of 37 and 70 Squadrons, which were detached in Flights to carry out night attacks on Italian bases in Albania and Southern Italy, were of material assistance to the hard-pressed Royal Hellenic Air Force, but their absence in the Western Desert was to be felt in the coming months.

1940 ended optimistically, with a limited British offensive, launched on the night of 7th December, seeing the Italians driven out of Egypt in a week. The greater part of five Italian divisions had been destroyed, with 38,000 prisoners captured at very little cost in men or materiel. In East Africa the position was still relatively static, but preparations were under way for a spring offensive, with a considerably strengthened SAAF presence a key feature of the air support which would be required.

Malta
Malta's war began on 11th June 1940, the day following Italy's entry into the war, with the first of many daylight bombing raids by the Regia Aeronautica. Its first airborne defence consisted of four Gloster Gladiator fighters 'borrowed' from the Royal Navy, supplemented late in June by four Hurricanes, the first of many to be sent to reinforce the island's defences. Swordfish torpedo-bombers followed, and Marylands for photo-reconnaissance, while Malta served as a valuable staging-post for Blenheims and (from September) Wellingtons en route to the Middle East, but the island's offensive capability was fully established only when, in November, the Malta Wellington Flight was formed. Composed of crews from 38 and 115 Squadrons, Bomber Command, flown out from the UK, and operating from Luqa, its purpose was to extend the night bomber offensive to the Italian homeland. On 1st December the unit was reconstituted as 148 Squadron, continuing the attacks on Southern Italy, and particularly ports and airfields.

11 Jun 1940	45 Sqn Sgt P Bower Sgt S G Fox AC1 J W Allison	Blenheim I + + +	L8476	Op: El Adem	Took off 0415, LG17 (Fuka Main), one of eight Blenheims detailed to attack the Italian airfield at dawn. Damaged by flak on the last pass, caught fire and crashed into the sea 24km E of Tobruk. All are commemorated on the Alamein Memorial.
	45 Sqn Sgt M C Thurlow Sgt B A Feldman AC1 H Robinson	Blenheim I + + +	L8519	Op: El Adem	Took off 0415, LG 17 (Fuka Main), detailed as above. Hit by flak and force-landed at LG 02 (Sidi Barrani) and burst into flames. All are buried in the Alexandria (Chatby) Military and War Memorial Cemetery.
	47 Sqn P/O B K C Fuge F/Sgt S A Elsy	Wellesley I pow pow	K7730	Op: Asmara	Took off 0530, Erkowit. Damaged by ground fire and force-landed. The two crew, along with all British and Commonwealth Air Force personnel captured during the East African campaign, were released from Adi Ugri Camp in April 1941.
	113 Sqn F/Lt D A Beauclair W/O H J Owen Sgt J Dobson	Blenheim I pow pow pow	L4823	Op: El Adem	Took off 1415, LG 14 (Maarten Bagush), one of nine Blenheims detailed to attack El Adem airfield. After bombing was attacked by three Italian fighters and shot down in flames 7km E of El Adem. All the crew were badly burned, but walked for eight hours before being captured by an Italian Marine post E of Tobruk.
12 Jun 1940	8 Sqn F/Lt M A Goodwin MiD P/O S W F Palmer Sgt Hannan	Blenheim I	L6654	Op: Assab	Took off 1130, Khormaksar, one of nine detailed to bomb and dive-bomb the airfield. One engine cut and the aircraft belly-landed at Ras Ar LG. DBR.
	223 Sqn F/O G O Ross Cpl R Stevenson	Wellesley I	K7747	Op: Gura	Took off 1130, Summit, one of nine aircraft detailed to bomb hangars and workshops. Damaged by flak and fighters over the target, and crashed on landing at Summit. SOC 7 July as BER.
14 Jun 1940	14 Sqn P/O R P B H Plunkett	Wellesley I +	K7743	Op: Massawa	Took off 1530, Port Sudan, with another aircraft to attack the Acico petrol installation. Seen heading out to sea after bombing, and claimed shot down by Ten Visintini of 412 Squadriglia. The pilot, who was flying the aircraft solo, is commemorated on the Runnymede Memorial.

	45 Sqn F/O J S Davies Sgt G E Negus LAC J K Copeland	**Blenheim I** + + +	**L8524**	**Op: Giarabub** Took off 0730, LG 17 (Fuka Main). Perhaps shot down over the target, where a burnt-out aircraft was seen. All the crew are buried in Halfaya Sollum War Cemetery.
15 Jun 1940	**223 Sqn** P/O P F Willing LAC R Pitt	**Wellesley I**	**L2711**	**Op: Gura** A flare ignited while taxying out to take-off, Summit, to attack Gura airfield, and the aircraft was DBF, the bomb load exploding.
16 Jun 1940	**223 Sqn** P/O M T E Jenkins LAC J J Dixon	**Wellesley I** + +	**L2694**	**Op: Gura** Took off 1635, Summit. Believed shot down by flak. The two crew are commemorated on the Alamein Memorial.
17 Jun 1940	**11 Sqn SAAF** Maj R H Preller SAAF Air Cpl E H Petterson SAAF Air Cpl B N Ackerman, MiD SAAF	**Battle I**	**901**	**Op: Reconnaissance** Took off 1145 Eastleigh, Nairobi, to photograph Italian LGs in the vicinity of Jumba, Jilib and Afmadu, Italian Somaliland. While making a low-level attack on an aircraft at the latter, was hit in the radiator by a single bullet. The aircraft crash-landed 16km from the airfield, and the crew returned to base on foot after 15 days. Maj Preller was awarded an immediate DFC.
18 Jun 1940	**Blenheim Delivery Flt** S/Ldr G A M Pryde DFC Sgt L A Hibbett Sgt A Scott	**Blenheim IV**	**L9263**	**Delivery Flight** En route from Tangmere to Malta via Marignane, Provence. Suffered engine failure on take-off from Marignane and hit a boundary fence. Not repaired before the capitulation of France.
	Blenheim Delivery Flt P/O D S Johnson Sgt K G Walker LAC W H Higgins	**Blenheim IV** + + +	**L9314**	**Delivery Flight** Took off 0630, Tangmere, on delivery to Malta. At 1030 crashed in bad weather, Prunieries, France. The pilot and WOp/Ag died in the crash, and Sgt Walker during removal to hospital. All are buried at Mazargues War Cemetery, Marseilles.
	Blenheim Delivery Flt F/O J McCash Sgt R Micklethwaite AC1 G Harris	**Blenheim IV** + + +	**L9315**	**Delivery Flight** As above. Crashed in bad weather, La Tessone, France. All the crew are buried in Hiesse Communal Cemetery, Charente.
	Blenheim Delivery Flt P/O C W Handley Sgt P D H McGovern LAC J G B Thomas	**Blenheim IV** + + +	**L9317**	**Delivery Flight** As above. Crashed in bad weather, Charroux, France. All are buried in Charroux Communal cemetery, Vienne.
	Blenheim Delivery Flt Sgt M Field Sgt D Murrie AC1 E Pickford	**Blenheim IV** + + +	**L9318**	**Delivery Flight** As above. Crashed in bad weather, Crozon, Finisterre. All are buried at Crozon Communal Cemetery.
	Blenheim Delivery Flt S/Ldr G A M Pryde DFC Sgt L A Hibbett Sgt A Scott	**Blenheim IV** + + +	**L9334**	**Delivery Flight** Took off 1730, Marignane, on the third leg of the flight to Malta. Overshot the island, and on approaching the Tunisian coast crashed into the sea. The pilot and WOp/Ag were killed instantly, and Sgt Hibbett died two days later. Sgt Scott is buried in Medjez-el-Bab War Cemetery. The others are commemorated on the Runnymede Memorial.
	Blenheim Delivery Flt F/Lt J Wilkinson-Bell Sgt A Malcolm Cpl E Blake	**Blenheim IV** + + +	**L9351**	**Delivery Flight** As above. Crashed in bad weather, Soulages, Provence. All are buried at Mazargues War Cemetery, Marseilles.

20-21 Jun 1940	**216 Sqn** F/Lt J B W Smith F/Sgt B T Baker Cpl W C Royle LAC A F Crohill LAC N P Donelly	**Bombay** + + + + pow	**L5850** **Op: El Gubbi** Took off LG 14 (Maaten Bagush). Last seen over the target. The dead are buried in Knightsbridge War Cemetery, Acroma.
24 Jun 1940	**39 Sqn** P/O D G Hunter Sgt R G D Ellis Sgt R Olley	**Blenheim I** +	**L4920** **Op: Diredawa** Took off 1115, Sheikh Othman, one of six aircraft detailed to attack the airfield at Diredawa, Abyssinia. Attacked by Italian CR.42 fighters, and crash-landed 95km NE of Hargeisa, Italian Somaliland. Sgt Olley died of his injuries at the crash site, and is commemorated on the Alamein Memorial. The pilot and observer were assisted by Somalis to reach Allied ground forces.
25 Jun 1940	**47 Sqn** Sgt F A Sanders Cpl G A Battye	**Wellesley I** pow pow	**L2696** **Op: reconnaissance** Took off, Erkowit, to photograph Asmara, Gura, and Mits'iwa, Eritrea. Force-landed near Asmara, reasons unknown, and destroyed by the crew.
26 Jun 1940	**47 Sqn** F/Lt G R Magill LAC J W Davidson	**Wellesley I**	**K7785** **Op: Gura** Took off 0500 Erkowit, to bomb Gura. Undercarriage collapsed on landing because of damaged hydraulics. SOC 17 July as BER.
29 Jun 1940	**113 Sqn** P/O D I Pike Sgt R C Lidstone Sgt J G Taylor	**Blenheim I** pow pow pow	**L8436** **Op: El Gubbi** Took off LG 14 (Maaten Bagush), one of nine aircraft detailed to attack El Gubbi aerodrome, near Tobruk. Three were lost to CR.42 and G.50 fighters, two of them shot down in flames over the Mediterranean, the third last seen damaged near the Libyan-Egyptian border.
	113 Sqn F/Sgt R H Knott Sgt J D Barber LAC J P Toner	**Blenheim I** + + +	**L8522** **Op: El Gubbi** As above. All are commemorated on the Alamein Memorial.
	113 Sqn F/O W R P K Mann Sgt J G Juggins Sgt G K Biggins	**Blenheim I** + + +	**L8447** **Op: El Gubbi** As above. All are commemorated on the Alamein Memorial.
30 Jun 1940	**223 Sqn** Sgt B Poskitt LAC L P Jebb	**Wellesley I** + +	**L2654** **Op: Massawa** Took off 0435, Summit, one of five aircraft detailed to bomb Massawa. The formation was attacked by one CR.32 and two CR.42 fighters, which probably shot this aircraft down. Both are commemorated on the Alamein Memorial.
	Armée de l'Air Slt R Weill Cne J Le Forestier de Vendeuvre Lt J P Berger Slt B Jochaux du Plessix	**Martin 167** + + + +	**GM167** **Defection** Took off 1500, Ber Rèchid, Casablanca, one of three Martins defecting from the Armée de l'Air to RAF Gibraltar. Shot down by Spanish anti-aircraft fire when coming into land at Gibraltar at 1700 hrs. All of the crew were buried in the North Front Cemetery, Gibraltar, but later re-interred in France.

2 Jul 1940	**11 Sqn** F/O J A W Lawrence Sgt H Hill AC1 H T Bowen	**Blenheim I**	**L4924**	**Op: Gura** Took off 0600, Sheikh Othman, to attack Macaaca airfield. The port engine was hit by flak and seized 33km from base, the aircraft crash-landing at Ras Ara, Aden. SOC 3 July.
	47 Sqn P/O C G Bush Sgt J W Davidson	**Wellesley I**	**K7777** + +	**Op: Metemmeh** Took off 0700, Khartoum, to bomb an Italian encampment. Hit by ground fire, crashed just beyond the Post Office, Gallabat, and DBF. The crew were thrown clear in the crash, the pilot dying instantly, and Sgt Davidson the next day. P/O Bush is commemorated on the Alamein Memorial, while Sgt Davidson is buried in the Keren War Cemetery.
3 Jul 1940	**14 Sqn** F/O S G Soderholm MiD Sgt B L Trayhurn F/Sgt J C Dawson	**Wellesley I**	**L2652** + + +	**Op: reconnaissance** Took off 1030, Port Sudan, with two other Wellesleys to reconnoitre coastal Eritrea. Shot down by Ten Visintini of 412 Squadriglia. F/Sgt Dawson is buried in Asmara War Cemetery, the others commemorated on the Alamein Memorial.
8 Jul 1940	**Middle East**	**Wellesley I**	**L2680**	**Unknown** SOC. NFD.
	Middle East	**Wellesley I**	**L8529**	**Unknown** SOC. NFD.
12 Jul 1940	**47 Sqn** Sgt F Nelson Sgt G F Brixton Sgt J Woods	**Wellesley I**	**K8520** + pow pow	**Op: Massawa** Took off Erkowit/ Carthago. Shot down over the target, possibly by Ten Visintini. The pilot is buried in Asmara War Cemetery.
14 Jul 1940	**216 Sqn** Sgt J G Cowlishaw P/O L C Quick Crew	**Bombay**	**L5848**	**Transit Flight** Took off 0545, LG 17 (Fuka Main), for Heliopolis, where the aircraft crashed on landing at 0720. DBR.
14-15 Jul 1940	**216 Sqn** S/Ldr R G Taylor P/O R P J Osborne Cpl E Hazlitt LAC K E Webber LAC G Niven	**Bombay**	**L5815** inj + inj + +	**Op: Tobruk** Took off 1730, LG 17 (Fuka Main), to attack naval storage tanks. Flew into the escarpment 40km S of Mersa Matruh on return. DBF. S/Ldr Taylor and Cpl Hazlitt were both badly burned. The dead are buried in Cairo War Memorial Cemetery.
	216 Sqn Sgt Campbell Sgt Williams Crew	**Bombay**	**L5819**	**Op: Tobruk** Took off 2105, LG 17 (Fuka Main), detailed as above. On return ran out of fuel and force-landed in fog on the SW corner of Lake Mariut. Fired on after landing by Egyptian forces, the crew were taken prisoner but released on proving their identity. DBR.
15 Jul 1940	**8 Sqn**	**Blenheim I**	**L8389**	**Unknown** SOC. NFD.
	55 Sqn F/O M F H Fox Sgt H F A Nicholas Sgt M Klines	**Blenheim I**	**L4820** + + +	**Op: Gazala** Took off 0530, LG 17 (Fuka Main), to bomb Gazala No 1 airfield. On the return flight at very low level the aircraft developed engine trouble, caught fire and crashed near Buq Buq. All are buried at Halfaya Sollum War Cemetery.

	211 Sqn P/O E Garrard-Cole LAC W B Smith AC2 E P F Doolin	**Blenheim I** pow pow pow	**L1491** Took off 0515, LG 105 (El Daba), one of eight detailed to attack Gazala. Force-landed on return near El Adem.	**Op: Gazala**
15-16 Jul 1940	**216 Sqn** Sgt J G Cowlishaw P/O T A Grundy Sgt P D Snowden LAC T Murray LAC M H Winship	**Bombay** + + + + +	**L5848** Took off 2200, LG 17 (Fuka Main).Shot down by a night fighter. LAC Winship, washed ashore near Sollum on 18 July, is buried in Halfaya Sollum War Cemetery; the others are commemorated on the Alamein Memorial.	**Op: Tobruk**
16 Jul 1940	**47 Sqn** Sgt W C H Style Sgt J Clark LAC W Crossland	**Wellesley I** + + +	**L2641** Took off 0930, Erkowit/Carthago. Collided with Wellesley L2675 while under heavy but inaccurate flak fire over Asmara and crashed. All are buried in Asmara War Cemetery.	**Op: Asmara**
22 Jul 1940	**211 Sqn** Sgt G B Smith Sgt R A Steele Sgt G A Sewell	**Blenheim I** + + +	**L6661** Took off 2130, LG 20 (Qotafiah I). Last seen over Sidi Barrani. Sgt Sewell's body washed ashore near Maaten Bagush, and he is buried in the El Daba Military Cemetery. The others are commemorated on the Alamein Memorial.	**Op: El Adem**
23 Jul 1940	**223 Sqn** P/O K H A Ellis DFC Cpl A Cockell Cpl F M Dunn	**Wellesley I**	**L2661** Took off 1015, Summit, one of five aircraft detailed to attack fuel installations. Badly damaged over the target by CR.32 fighters and SOC on return as DBR.	**Op: Massawa**
29 Jul 1940	**11 Sqn** Sgt J J Barry Sgt G J Harnden Sgt A Mackintosh	**Blenheim I** + + +	**L4817** Took off 1115, Sheikh Othman, for a dive-bombing attack. Shot down by flak over the target. All the crew are buried in Asmara War Cemetery.	**Op: Assab and Macaaca**
	223 Sqn P/O J Wallace Cpl F M Dunn Cpl West	**Wellesley I** +	**K8524** Took off 0445, Summit, one of five aircraft detailed. Bombed Massawa because high cloud obscured Asmara, and attacked by Italian fighters, which fatally wounded Cpl Dunn. He is buried at Khartoum War Cemetery. K8524 is not recorded in the ORB after this date. SOC 29.1.41, it was collected from Summit for reduction to produce by 52 RSU on 6.2.1941.	**Op: Asmara**
31 Jul 1940	**47 Sqn** Sgt R S Colvin AC M E Mabey AC Saunders	**Wellesley I**	**K7771** Took off 0500, Erkowit/Carthago, but attacked en route by fighters. The formation turned for home by the coastal route but K7771 was hit by flak from a merchantman, and crashed on landing. SOC as DBR.	**Op: Zula**
1 Aug 1940	**8 Sqn** Sgt J C Franks Sgt J H Thain LAC A T Cumner-Price	**Blenheim I** pow pow pow	**L8406** Took off 1330, Khormaksar, one of six Blenheims detailed for a low-level attack on the airfield at Ghiniele K92. Attacked by CR.32s and shot down by Capt Ricci of 410 Squadrigilia over Ghiniele.	**Op: Ghiniele**

4 Aug 1940	211 Sqn F/Lt G D Jones Sgt P B Dennis Sgt J McIntosh inj	Blenheim I	**L8532** **Op: Bir el Gubbi** Took off LG 20 (Qotafiah I), to bomb Italian motor transport. Heavy opposition was encountered from Italian fighters and Sgt McIntosh was wounded. L8532 was salvaged by 51RSU at Sidi Barrani on 10 August, but SOC 20 September.
5 Aug 1940	8 Sqn P/O R K Felstead + Sgt A D Wright + P/O T McK Mitchell +	Blenheim I	**L8375** **Op: Hargeisa** Took off 1355, Khormaksar, one of six detailed to attack motor transport W of Hargeisa. Shot down by a CR.32 (Sottoten Folcherio) over Hargeisa. All are commemorated on the Alamein Memorial.
6 Aug 1940	11 Sqn Sgt W A M Birt	Blenheim I	**L4911** **Ferry Flight** Took off Sheikh Othman, on a ferry flight to Little Aden. Overshot on a downwind landing, 1710, and hit a sand dune. The aircraft overturned and was DBR.
9 Aug 1940	47 Sqn Sgt R S Colvin DFM Sgt G R Pope + S/Ldr W A Theed	Wellesley I	**K7756** **Op: Gura** Took off 0600, Erkowit/Carthago. Attacked by CR.32 and CR.42 fighters, hydraulics hit and Sgt Pope mortally wounded. The aircraft crashed on landing and was SOC on 26 August as DBR. S/Ldr Theed of HQ 254 Wing was acting as air gunner. Sgt Pope, who died on 11 August, is buried in Khartoum War Cemetery.
10 Aug 1940	8 Sqn F/O A G Curtis + Sgt V H F Witt + LAC H J McLeavy +	Blenheim I	**L8503** **Op: Dhubbato** Took off 1320, Khormaksar, one of three detailed to dive bomb the village of Dhubbato. On the return journey collided with L8506 over the Gulf of Aden, 20km S of Aden. All are commemorated on the Alamein Memorial.
	8 Sqn P/O A J G Bisson + Sgt D J R Wilson + Sgt N F Wilson +	Blenheim I	**L8506** **Op: Dhubbato** As above. All are commemorated on the Alamein Memorial.
11 Aug 1940	45 Sqn	Wellesley I	**L2676** **Unknown** SOC. NFD.
12 Aug 1940	39 Sqn P/O G Rowbotham Sgt E Maltby Cpl L R Pulling	Blenheim I	**L8387** **Op: Tugargon Gap** Took off 0500, Sheikh Othman, to bomb gun emplacements and motor transport. Attacked by CR.42s which rendered the hydraulics unserviceable. Crash-landed at Berbera. The crew were from 11 Sqn.
	39 Sqn F/Sgt B J Thomas DFM Sgt G M Hogan + Cpl J H Wintle	Blenheim I	**L8402** **Op: Hedigale** Took off 0715, Sheikh Othman, to bomb gun emplacements and motor transport. Attacked head-on by CR.42 fighters, the observer being killed and the pilot seriously wounded. Despite this he made a wheels up landing at Berbera. F/Sgt Thomas was awarded an immediate bar to his DFM.
14 Aug 1940	8 Sqn	Vincent	**K4884** **Missing Aircraft Search** Tipped up by a wind gust on landing at Khor Uneira LG. DBR.

	223 Sqn S/Ldr J C Larking DFC Sgt R A Swann Sgt R Whittaker	**Wellesley I**	**K7783** **Transit Flight** Took off 0530, Perim Island, one of 11 Wellesleys relocating to Khormaksar. The engine caught fire and the aircraft was badly damaged in a force-landing in sand dunes near Dar Mujahhar. SOC 27 September.
15 Aug **1940**	**47 Sqn** P/O D M Illsley DFC Crew	**Wellesley I**	**K7757** **Op: Massawa** Took off 0515, Port Sudan, one of five aircraft detailed for a high-altitude attack on the Italian air force and naval base. The aircraft stalled and crashed on landing, 1050 hrs, because the fuel load was unequal in the wing tanks (a problem causing aerodynamic instability for which a modification had been issued: this aircraft had not, however, been modified). DBR.
17 Aug **1940**	**39 Sqn** Sgt T Crehan Sgt D M Keys MiD Sgt A B A Henderson	**Blenheim I**	**L4834** **Op: Reconnaissance** Took off 0530, Sheikh Othman, to reconnoitre around Hargeisa. After completing the reconnaissance, the crew bombed a flak post but the aircraft was hit by return fire which damaged petrol lines. Force-landed in the sea beside the light cruiser HMS *Ceres*, the Blenheim floated long enough for much equipment to be salvaged.
18 Aug **1940**	**8 Sqn** Sgt A T Gay pow LAC E C Clarke + LAC M E Porter +	**Blenheim I**	**L1479** **Op: Nasiye** Took off 0535, Khormaksar, one of three Blenheims detailed to attack Italian motor transport. Shot down in flames by CR.32 fighters, crashing NW of Lfaruug LG, British Somaliland. The pilot bailed out, while LAC Clarke survived the crash, badly burned, to die in hospital at Jijiga on 25 August. He is buried in Addis Ababa War Cemetery, while LAC Porter is commemorated on the Alamein Memorial.
19 Aug **1940**	**14 Sqn** Sgt J A Burcher Sgt G E Dickson Sgt D Farrell	**Wellesley I**	**L2703** **Op: convoy escort** Took off 1350, Port Sudan, to escort a Red Sea convoy. Engine failure forced the pilot to ditch close to the destroyer HMS *Kimberley*, which picked the crew up 10 minutes later.
20 Aug **1940**	**39 Sqn** P/O P E O Jago + Sgt J A Wilson-Law + Cpl J H Wintle +	**Blenheim I**	**L8474** **Op: Diredawa** Took off Sheikh Othman, and shot down over the target by a CR.42 (Capt Santoro, 413 Squadriglia). The three crew are commemorated on Special Memorial E at Diredawa African War Cemetery.
26 Aug **1940**	**114 Sqn** P/O C D Regan pow Sgt W J Paul pow Sgt G H Cluley pow	**Blenheim IV**	**T2058** **Delivery Flight** Took off Thorney Island for Malta. Ran out of fuel and ditched off Pantelleria.
	203 Sqn F/O S C Pendred + F/O MacD Hunter + LAC W Love +	**Blenheim IV**	**L9218** **Op: Assab-Dessie** Took off 0530, Khormaksar, to reconnoitre bridges and attack convoys or other targets. FTR. The three crew are buried in Asmara War Cemetery.
	223 Sqn P/O J C Smitheram + Sgt D F Shaller + Sgt S E Meades +	**Wellesley I**	**K7731** **Op: Asmara** Took off Summit, one of five detailed to attack Asmara. Shot down in flames by Italian fighters. All the crew are buried in Asmara War Cemetery.

26-27 Aug 1940	57 Sqn F/O A B Goldie Sgt R L Dean Sgt F R Conner	Blenheim IV pow pow pow	T2176 **Delivery Flight** Took off 2200, Thorney Island, one of six Blenheims on delivery to Malta. After eight hours flying, and running short of fuel, the pilot made for Lampedusa, where he force-landed the aircraft in a field.
27 Aug 1940	101 Sqn P/O A D McLaren Sgt L D Campbell Sgt J Thomson	Blenheim IV inj + +	T2060 **Delivery Flight** Took off 0117, Thorney Island, for Malta, but crashed into the sea three minutes later when an engine failed. Sgt Thomson is buried in Uphall Cemetery, West Lothian, and Sgt Campbell in Lossiemouth Burial Ground, Moray.
	107 Sqn Sgt J D Hudson Sgt D C B Riddick Sgt D W G Randall	Blenheim IV int int	T2067 **Delivery Flight** Took off Thorney Island on a delivery flight to Malta, but came down in the sea off Tunisia, the crew being interned first there and later in Senegal. Possibly shot down by Vichy French fighters.
	216 Sqn	Bombay	L5849 **Unknown** Lost; NFD (A-B Serials). There is, however, no mention of this loss, or indeed of this aircraft, in the 216 Squadron ORB.
31 Aug 1940	55 Sqn P/O R A Smith Sgt J L Sugden AC1 L Lowe	Blenheim I + + +	L8397 **Op: Tmimi, El Gubbi** Took off 1420, LG 17 (Fuka Main), to bomb airfields at Tmimi or El Gubbi. Turned back with engine trouble and crashed in attempting to land at Mersa Matruh, when turning into the dead engine. The three crew are buried at El Alamein War Cemetery.
	12 Sqn SAAF Lt C J Rosslee SAAF Crew	Ju 86Z-7	653 **Transit Flight** Crashed on Zanzibar after engine failure. NFD.
1 Sep 1940	14 Sqn F/Sgt H N Norris Sgt B M D'Arcy LAC C D Lampard	Wellesley I pow pow +	L2689 **Op: Reconnaissance** Took off 0600, Port Sudan, to carry out a photo reconnaissance of Hamil Island, Dahlak Archipelago. Claimed shot down both by flak and Ten Visintini of 412 Squadriglia. Crash-landed on Hamil Island. LAC Lampard, seriously wounded, died two hours later, and is buried in Asmara War Cemetery.
3 Sep 1940	12 Sqn SAAF Lt R G Donaldson SAAF W/O2 P W Byrnes SAAF Air Mech I D du Plessis SAAF Air Sgt F P du Toit SAAF Air Sgt A A Cusens SAAF Air Sgt J V Pemberthy SAAF Air Sgt C F Maritz SAAF	Ju 86Z-7 + + + + + + +	654 **Op: Yabelo** Took off Nanyuki, refuelling at Marsabit, to attack the main Italian air base at Yabelo. Shot down by flak over the target. All are buried in Nairobi War Cemetery.
4 Sep 1940	211 Sqn S/Ldr A R G Bax Sgt R A Bain AC1 L E C Wise	Blenheim I pow pow pow	L8376 **Op: Derna** Took off 1255, LG 20 (Qotaifyah I), detailed as above. Attacked and damaged by an enemy fighter near Derna, and last seen making for the Libyan coast with one engine dead. Believed to have force-landed near Derna.
6 Sep 1940	14 Sqn F/O T G Rhodes	Wellesley I	L2707 **Training** Took off Port Sudan, but misjudged height in a night landing, 1950, and the undercarriage collapsed; DBR.

	39 Sqn Sgt T Crehan Sgt D M Keys MiD Sgt A B A Henderson	**Blenheim I**	**L8543** **Op: Berbera** Took off 1800, Sheikh Othman, one of three detailed to bomb a disabled SM.79 at Berbera. On landing hit a chance light with its port wing and crashed. DBR.
	84 Sqn	**Blenheim I**	**L8453** **Unknown** SOC; NFD.
	203 Sqn F/Lt W T Ratcliffe Cpl E J Lowther Sgt Scott	**Blenheim IV**	**T2075** **Op: Auase** Developed engine trouble on take-off 0545, Khormaksar, to bomb a bridge at Auase and crashed. DBF.
8 Sep 1940	**FB Flt 1** Adj M R Rolland FAFL + F/O P C de Maismont FAFL pow Cne Chef J Ritoux-Lachaud FAFL + Sgt E Lobato de Faria FAFL +	**Martin 167F**	**82 (AX671)** **Op: reconnaissance** Took off Khormaksar, on a photographic reconnaissance over Moggia, 63km NE of Addis Ababa. Shot down by a CR.42 fighter. The three dead, whose common grave in the Addis Ababa War Cemetery can no longer be located, are commemorated on the Alamein Memorial. Adj Rolland was serving as F/Sgt M R Dinaller, Lt de Maismont as F/O P C Rupert, Cne Chef J Ritoux-Lachaud as F/Lt J M R Montgibaud, and Sgt E Lobato de Faria as F/Sgt N'Guyen-Dzung. FB Flt 1 was attached to 8 Squadron, RAF.
9 Sep 1940	**14 Sqn** F/O T G Rhodes	**Wellesley I**	**K7755** **Air Test** Took off 1445, Port Sudan; the engine cut and the aircraft belly-landed, Port Sudan. DBR.
	11 Sqn SAAF Capt R A Blackwell SAAF pow Air Sgt F S A van Zyl SAAF pow	**Battle I**	**912** **Op: Shasemene** Took off 0900, Archer's Post, landing at Lodwar to refuel before bombing the airfield at Shasamene. Hit by machine gun fire and the engine failed. Crash-landed 13km from the target.
10 Sep 1940	**14 Sqn** P/O J A Ferguson pow P/O J Lynch + Sgt T Conway +	**Wellesley I**	**K7763** **Op: Kassala** Took off 1120, Port Sudan, to bomb Italian motor transport. Shot down in flames by CR.42 fighters. The dead are buried in Keren War Cemetery.
12 Sep 1940	**11 Sqn SAAF** Lt E G Armstrong DFC SAAF + Air Sgt E C Adams SAAF +	**Battle I**	**911** **Op: Shasemene** Took off 0700, Archer's Post, refuelling at Marsabit, to attack the airfield at Shasemene. Shot down by a CR.32 over the target. Both are buried in Addis Ababa War Cemetery.
	11 Sqn SAAF Lt J E Lindsay SAAF pow Air Sgt V P McVicar SAAF pow Air Sgt L A Feinberg SAAF pow	**Battle I**	**913** **Op: Shasemene** Took off 0700, Archer's Post, detailed as above. Shot down by a CR.32 (W/O M Gobbo) over the target. Crash-landed on fire, killing a villager. The crew only escaped lynching when the ammunition began to explode. Air Sgts McVicar and Feinberg were both wounded.
13 Sep 1940	**40 Sqn** P/O G M Goodman pow Sgt C A Hodder pow Sgt E Fletcher pow	**Blenheim IV**	**N3589** **Delivery Flight** Took off Thorney Island for Malta, but a navigational error and shortage of fuel forced the pilot to land on Pantelleria in error. The Regia Aeronautica test-flew the aircraft. There is a photograph of this aircraft in Regia Aeronautica colours in Chaz Bowyer's *Bristol Blenheim*, p72.

14 Sep 1940	**14 Sqn** Sgt J A Burcher Crew	Wellesley I	L2658	**Op: Gura** Hit a fence on take-off, 2005, Port Sudan, because of overload, but managed to jettison the bombs before force-landing. DBR.
15 Sep 1940	**14 Sqn** P/O B J Hyde Crew	Wellesley I	K7764	**Training** Took off, Summit, on the return leg of a training flight, but the undercarriage collapsed on landing, Port Sudan, 1530. SOC 20 September.
16 Sep 1940	**14 Sqn** Sgt B T Hopkins	Wellesley I	L2708	**Ferry Flight** Took off Khartoum on return to Port Sudan after ferrying personnel. The engine lost power and in a heavy landing the undercarriage collapsed. DBR.
	113 Sqn P/O E S Roberts +	Blenheim IV	T2052	**Transit Flight** Took off LG 14 (Maaten Bagush) on a night ferry flight to LG 15 (Maaten Bagush Satellite) with a full bomb load and fuel, ready for operations the following morning. Approaching the aerodrome from the wrong direction, T2052 was fired on by the airfield defences, causing the aircraft to crash on landing at LG 15 at 2030. DBF. The pilot is buried in El Alamein War Cemetery.
	223 Sqn P/O G E Walker + Sgt H L S Price +	Wellesley I	L2664	**Op: Gura** Took off 1445, Summit, one of three aircraft detailed to bomb the aerodrome at Gura. Bad weather was encountered and the flight dispersed. FTR. All are commemorated on the Alamein Memorial.
17 Sep 1940	**47 Sqn** P/O B B Witty	Wellesley I	L2697	**Ferry Flight** Took off Erkowit on a ferry flight to Summit. Overshot on landing and the undercarriage collapsed.
	70 Sqn	Wellington IC	T2830	**Ground** In transit to Egypt. Destroyed by fire, Luqa, after being strafed by Ten Malvezzini. Cpl J G M Davis and AC1 T McCann went into the blazing aircraft and retrieved four Vickers machine guns and ammunition, for which both were subsequently awarded the BEM. SOC 7.4.41.
	211 Sqn Sgt S L Hutt Sgt V Pollard Sgt J Munro	Blenheim I	L6660	**Op: Sidi Barrani** Took off 1240, LG 20 (Qotafiyah I), to attack enemy troop concentrations W of Sidi Barrani. On return at 2045 undershot on landing, bounced, hit a tent and then a car, finally tipping on its nose. DBR.
18 Sep 1940	**113 Sqn** S/Ldr G B Keily DFC AFC pow P/O J S Cleaver + Sgt J Jobson +	Blenheim IV	T2048	**Op: Tmimi** Took off 1600, LG 14 (Maaten Bagush), one of nine detailed. Attacked after bombing by CR.42s, which set the starboard engine on fire. The dead are buried in Knightsbridge War Cemetery, Acroma.
21 Sep 1940	**14 Sqn** F/Lt N G Birks pow Sgt J P Gillhespy pow Sgt J L B Cheyne pow	Blenheim IV	T2061	**Op: Massawa** Took off 1135, Port Sudan, one of three detailed to bomb Otumlo airfield. Hit in the port engine, and force-landed N of Massawa. Sgt Cheyne died of natural causes in captivity on 25 September, and is buried in Asmara War Cemetery.

25 Sep 1940	55 Sqn F/O A S B Godrich Sgt W C Clarke Sgt W H Thompson	Blenheim I + + +	L8394 L Op: Giarabub Took off 1200, LG 17 (Fuka Main), to bomb motor transport at Giarabub Oasis. Shot down by CR.42 fighters 53km N of the target on the return flight. Sgt Thompson bailed out, and his footprints were discovered near the crash site, but he was never found. F/O Godrich is buried in Halfaya Sollum War Cemetery, and the others commemorated on the Alamein Memorial.
	211 Sqn S/Ldr J R Gordon-Finlayson DFC MiD Sgt J Richmond Sgt M Jones	Blenheim I	L8523 Op: Tobruk Took off 1215, LG 20 (Qotafiyah I), to bomb the harbour. The starboard engine caught fire on the return flight but the pilot nursed the aircraft a further 130km to force-land 2.5km W of Qasaba. DBR.
27-28 Sep 1940	57 Sqn F/O A B Goldie Sgt R L Dean Sgt F R Conner DFM	Blenheim IV pow pow pow	T2176 Delivery Flight Took off 2200, Thorney Island, one of six Blenheims on delivery to Malta. After flying for some eight hours the aircraft was running short of fuel and, sighting Lampedusa on his starboard beam, the pilot force-landed there, c.0800, in a field.
30 Sep 1940	45 Sqn S/Ldr G J Bush Sgt J C Usher Sgt J Corney	Blenheim I + + +	L6665 Op: Gura Took off 0700, Wadi Gazouza, one of three detailed. Shot down on the return flight, probably by Ten Visintini of 412 Squadriglia. All are buried in Asmara War Cemetery.
	113 Sqn Sgt L Cater Sgt K H Meadowcroft Sgt B J Shelton	Blenheim IV + + +	T2171 Op: Marawa/Marua Took off 0840, LG 68 (Waterloo), one of nine to bomb landing grounds. Three became separated from the main formation and were attacked by CR.42s N of Tobruk, and T2171 was shot down into the sea. All the crew are commemorated on the Alamein Memorial.
2 Oct 1940	45 Sqn S/Ldr J W Dallamore P/O A G Sheppard Sgt M Mackenzie	Blenheim I + pow +	L8452 Op: Gura and Mai Edega Took off 0230 GMT, Wadi Gazouza, one of three detailed. Shot down over Mai Edega by CR.42s. Both the WOp/Ag and observer bailed out, but only the observer survived to be taken POW. The dead are buried in Asmara War Cemetery.
3 Oct 1940	14 Sqn Sgt J R Taylor	Wellesley I	L2647 Army co-operation exercise Took off Port Sudan to exercise with a mobile radio unit. Overshot on landing, 1110, hit a railway cutting and undercarriage torn off, Port Sudan. DBR.
4 Oct 1940	8 Sqn Sgt C G Loader	Blenheim I	L4903 Training Took off Khormaksar on a night training flight, and undershot on landing, hitting a wall. DBR.
5 Oct 1940	30 Sqn	Blenheim I	K7106 G Op: Patrol Took off Haifa on patrol. Overshot landing and overturned, Haifa. DBR.
10 Oct 1940	47 Sqn Sgt R Shuttleworth	Wellesley I	K7791 Training Took off Erkowit/Carthago on a night-flying training exercise. Lost height on overshoot and crash-landed 4km SE of Carthago, 1750. DBR and SOC 26 October.

11 Oct 1940	**14 Sqn** F/Lt G D Hill	**Blenheim IV**	**T2172** Engine cut on take-off, 0825, Port Sudan; swung and ran into a dyke. DBR.	**Air Test**
	Middle East	**Blenheim IV**	**T2074** DBR in accident. NFD.	**Unknown**
12 Oct 1940	**55 Sqn** P/O M S Singleton Sgt B J Fox Sgt I Brownrigg	**Blenheim I**	**L8530** Took off 1615, LG 17 (Fuka Main) to bomb El Adem aerodrome. Attacked over the target by CR.42s which put the starboard engine out of action and extensively damaged the aircraft. Returned to base but DBR and SOC.	**Op: El Adem**
	223 Sqn P/O G Pelling	**Wellesley I**	**L2686** Took off Summit on a night cross-country training flight. Landed heavily on return, damaging the undercarriage and main spar. SOC 11 November.	**Training**
13 Oct 1940	**45 Sqn** F/O G C B Woodroffe Sgt E B Ryles Sgt A A Meadows DFM P/O L S Roberts	**Blenheim I** + + + +	**L8463** Took off 1145, Wadi Gazouza, one of three Blenheims detailed to bomb a suspected petrol dump. Apparently shot down by fighters. P/O Roberts was the squadron's Intelligence Officer. All are buried in Asmara War Cemetery.	**Op: Gura**
	45 Sqn P/O G A Cockayne Sgt T A Ferris Sgt R W Reader	**Blenheim I** + + +	**L8502** As above. All are buried in Asmara War Cemetery.	**Op: Gura**
16 Oct 1940	**47 Sqn**	**Vincent**	**K4657** Gedaref. One of ten aircraft destroyed in a surprise strafing attack at 0405 by an Italian bomber and eight fighters of 412 Squadriglia.	**Ground**
	47 Sqn	**Vincent**	**K4731** As above.	**Ground**
	47 Sqn	**Wellesley I**	**K7742 T** As above.	**Ground**
	47 Sqn	**Wellesley I**	**K7762** As above.	**Ground**
	47 Sqn	**Wellesley I**	**K7779 C** As above.	**Ground**
	47 Sqn	**Wellesley I**	**K7781 L** As above.	**Ground**
	47 Sqn	**Wellesley I**	**L2650** As above.	**Ground**
	47 Sqn	**Wellesley I**	**L2675** As above.	**Ground**
	47 Sqn	**Wellesley I**	**L2677** As above.	**Ground**
	47 Sqn	**Wellesley I**	**L2688** As above.	**Ground**

17 Oct 1940	11 Sqn SAAF Capt P J Robbertse SAAF Air Sgt P J Lamont SAAF	Battle I	903	Op: Negele

Took off 1840, Archers Post, detailed to attack motor transport. Hit by ground fire and engine failed. Crash-landed 39km W of Marsabit.

18 Oct 1940	55 Sqn P/O E M Metcalfe P/O R Hornby Sgt B J M Noble	Blenheim I	L1538	Op: Sollum and Buq Buq

Took off 1500, LG 17 (Fuka Main), to bomb a military camp S of Sollum and a water tank at Buq Buq. Crashed near Fuka in bad visibility.

18-19 Oct 1940	216 Sqn F/Lt E L Cullimore P/O L C Quick LAC W R York LAC R M Minton LAC J C Perrie	Bombay	+ + + + +	L5816	Op: Benghazi

Took off 1900, LG 17 (Fuka Main). FTR. All are commemorated on the Alamein Memorial.

20 Oct 1940	203 Sqn F/O H M F Barnitt DFC Sgt A J Finch AC2 J W Beaumont	Blenheim IV	+ + inj	T2112	Relocation Flight

Took off 1500, Kamaran, on relocation. An engine cut and the aircraft hit a mosque. DBF. The pilot is buried in the North Point Christian Cemetery, Kamaran, but commemorated on the Maala Memorial, Aden, and the observer, who died next day on board HMS *Defender*, on the Alamein Memorial.

22-23 Oct 1940	223 Sqn Sgt V C Durrant MiD Sgt R M C Edwards Sgt A A Heaney	Wellesley I	+ + +	K7774	Op: Asmara

Took off 1935, Summit, to bomb the aerodrome at Asmara. On return stalled on approach and spun into the ground. All are buried in Khartoum War Cemetery.

26 Oct 1940	14 Sqn F/Lt D C Stapleton DFC AFC Sgt G Bartholomew Sgt D Farrell	Blenheim IV	inj inj inj	T2057	Training

Took off Port Sudan. During bombing practice fired on in error by RAF fighters which mistook the Blenheim for an SM.79. DBR.

27 Oct 1940	113 Sqn F/O P D Squires Sgt Durrant Sgt Hancorn	Blenheim IV	T2068	Op: Benghazi

Took off LG 68 (Waterloo), one of three Blenheims detailed to bomb Benghazi. On return in darkness strayed over Alexandria and was fired on by local flak units. The crew failed to locate base, and bailed out when the fuel was exhausted. The aircraft crashed 20km NW of Wadi Natrun.

30 Oct 1940	115 Sqn P/O A J R Pate DFC Sgt W V Jaggs Sgt W E Elliott Sgt E Fisher Sgt K R Draper	Wellington IC	+ + + + +	T2613	Delivery Flight

Took off Marham for Luqa, but flew into the London balloon barrage and crashed at Iver, Bucks. P/O Pate is buried in Oxford (Wolvercote) Cemetery, Sgt Jaggs in Brookwood Military Cemetery, Sgt Elliott in Carisbrook Cemetery, Sgt Fisher in Hemsworth Cemetery, and Sgt Draper in Uxbridge (Hillingdon) Cemetery.

3 Nov 1940	Wellington Flt Sgt P E Forrester P/O D P Rawlings Sgt T R Wood Sgt D Palmer Sgt A T Smith	Wellington IC	+ + + inj +	R1094	Op: Naples

Lost height after take-off, Luqa, and crashed at Qormi. The aircraft hit walls and houses, the front section ending up in a quarry. The aircraft caught fire. Sgt Smith was rescued, but later died of his injuries. All are buried in Malta (Capuccini) Naval Cemetery.

	Wellington Flt	**Wellington IC**	**T2743**	**Op: Naples**
	Sgt R M Lewin	inj	Failed to gain height after take-off, Luqa, crashing near	
	P/O D R Allen	+	Tal-Handaq. The aircraft caught fire but Sgt Lewin	
	Sgt A Hunter	inj	dragged the unconscious 2nd Pilot clear before the	
	Sgt T Reay	inj	bombs exploded. For this he was awarded the GC. P/O	
	LAC J Hollingworth	inj	Allen is buried in Malta (Capuccini) Naval Cemetery.	

4 Nov	**11 Sqn SAAF**	**Battle I**	**908**	**Op: Negele**
1940	Lt B L Hutchinson SAAF	pow	Took off 0545, Archers Post, and shot down 4km from	
	Air Sgt I S Thorburn SAAF	pow	the target.	
	Air Sgt H G Firth SAAF	pow		

6 Nov	**47 Sqn**	**Wellesley I**	**K7733**	**Op: Metema**
1940	Sgt R M Aldus		Crashed on take-off 0255, Blackdown, detailed to bomb	
	P/O E J Bainbridge		Metemna. SOC 12 November as BER.	
	Wellington Flt	**Wellington IC**	**T2877**	**Unknown**
	P/O A C Hamman		Took off Luqa, and overshot on landing and hit a gun	
	Sgt Kirby		emplacement.	
	Sgt V F Bilborough	inj		
	Sgt R A Coleman	inj		
	Crew			

7 Nov	**70 Sqn**	**Wellington IC**	**T2731**	**Op: Valona**
1940	F/Lt A E Brian	+	Took off Eleusis. Shot down by CR.42s. Sgt Ellam is	
	P/O G R Rawlings	pow	commemorated on Special Memorial E at Phaleron War	
	Sgt G S Wilson	+	Cemetery (buried at the time in Albania – grave now lost),	
	Sgt W Ellam	+	F/Lt Brian and Sgts Wilson and Selley appear on the	
	Sgt W J Mitchell	pow	Alamein Memorial.	
	Sgt J A Selley	+		
	70 Sqn	**Wellington IC**	**T2734**	**Op: Valona**
	Sgt G N Brooks	+	Took off Eleusis. Shot down by CR.42s. Sgts Brooks and	
	Sgt V J Morgan	+	Morgan are commemorated on Special Memorial E at	
	Sgt E R Pitts	+	Phaleron War Cemetery (buried at the time in Albania –	
	Sgt D Philip	+	graves now lost), the remainder on the Alamein	
	Sgt C W Laughton	+	Memorial.	
	Sgt J H Keddie	+		

12 Nov	**216 Sqn**	**Valentia**	**K5605**	**Ground**
1940			Destroyed by strafing CR.42s at LG 14 (Maaten Bagush).	
			Piloted by F/O P A S Baker, this aircraft had, the previous	
			night, carried out the RAF's sole Valentia bombing raid,	
			on troop concentrations at Sidi Barrani. (The only other	
			Valentia bombing raid was carried out on 14-15 August	
			by a SAAF crew, which dropped a home-made bomb,	
			made out of a 45 gallon drum, on an Italian fort on the	
			Kenya-Ethiopia border, causing many casualties.)	

14 Nov	**84 Sqn**	**Blenheim I**	**L1378**	**Op: Koritza**
1940	Sgt W F Sidaway	+	Took off 1445, Menidi/Tatoi, one of three detailed to	
	Sgt C P Hoare	+	attack motor transport and a bridge 5km S of Lake	
	Sgt A J W Friend	+	Ochrid. Fighters were encountered but the cause of the	
			loss is uncertain. All are commemorated on the Alamein	
			Memorial.	
	84 Sqn	**Blenheim I**	**L1389 X**	**Op: Koritza**
	F/Lt A F Mudie	+	Took off 1445, Menidi/Tatoi, detailed as above. It seems	
	F/Sgt E H Lord	+	the aircraft flew into a mountain, perhaps during	
	LAC W J S Chick	+	attempts to evade fighters. All the crew are	
			commemorated on the Alamein Memorial.	

15 Nov 1940	30 Sqn	Blenheim I	L1120	Op: Koritza
	Sgt E B Childs	+	Took off Eleusis, to bomb Italian positions NE of Koritsa.	
	Cpl D Stott	+	Shot down in flames by Italian fighters. The crew were	
	Sgt J D Stewart	+	buried in Albania, but their graves are now lost. They are therefore commemorated on Special Memorial E in Phaleron War Cemetery.	

16 Nov 1940	11 Sqn SAAF	Battle I	916	Op: Reconnaissance
	Lt C A van Vliet DFC SAAF	evd	Took off 0900, Archers Point, refuelling at Lokituang to	
	Air Sgt P J Lamont SAAF	evd	reconnoitre the Todenyang, Kenya - Washa Waha area in	
	Air Sgt E Murphy SAAF	evd	Abyssinia. Damaged by rifle fire and force-landed. The crew evaded and crossed the border into Kenya, where they met a detachment of the King's African Rifles.	

16-17 Nov 1940	37 Sqn	Wellington IC	R3179	Op: Durazzo
	Sgt B W Green	+	Took off Luqa. FTR. Buried at the time in a communal	
	Sgt G A Ross	+	grave at Piroski (?) Monastery, Yugoslavia, all were after	
	Sgt A B Lattimer	+	the war re-interred in Belgrade War Cemetery.	
	Sgt J R Barnes	+		
	Sgt J G D Wilson	+		
	Sgt J G G Butler	+		

	70 Sqn	Wellington IC	T2827	Op: Durazzo
	Sgt J P Palmer-Samborne	+	Took off Tatoi. Overshot the target and flew into a hill,	
	P/O W G Bennett	+	Danilovograd, Yugoslavia, and exploded on impact. All	
	Sgt G B Hawksley	+	five are buried in Belgrade War Cemetery. The aircraft	
	Sgt G Green	+	was carrying an American war correspondent, Ralph	
	Sgt F L Savage	+	Barnes of *The New York Herald Tribune*. His burial place is	
	Passenger: R Barnes	+	unknown.	

17 Nov 1940	47 Sqn	Wellesley I	K7768	Unknown
			SOC. NFD. Last recorded on ops on 18 September.	

19 Nov 1940	45 Sqn	Blenheim I	L8475	Op: Keren
	S/Ldr V Ray		Took off 1220, Wadi Gazouza, to bomb railway buildings	
	Sgt C A Hodder		and an encampment. Badly damaged in a running battle	
	Sgt E Fletcher		with two CR.42 fighters and, though taken on charge by 52 RSU, eventually reduced to salvage and SOC 22.2.41.	

	203 Sqn	Blenheim IV	L9458	Op: Convoy Patrol
	P/O R O Stock Givan	+	Took off 1230, Khormaksar, to patrol convoy BN8. The	
	Sgt F H Banfield	+	pilot lost control in cloud and the aircraft dived into the	
	LAC W R Blackburn	+	sea near Aden. All the crew are commemorated on the Alamein Memorial.	

20-21 Nov 1940	214 Sqn ME Flt	Wellington IC	T2873	Delivery Flight
	S/Ldr N P Samuels DFC	pow	Took off Stradishall for Luqa, but force-landed at Comiso,	
	F/O A J Payne	pow	Sicily. Air Marshal Boyd was en route to Egypt to take up	
	P/O J C Watson	pow	appointment as Deputy Air Officer Commanding,	
	Sgt C W Evans	pow	Middle East.	
	Sgt W Wynn	pow		
	Passengers:			
	A/M O T Boyd CB OBE MC AFC	pow		
	F/Lt J F Leeming	pow		

22 Nov 1940	11 Sqn SAAF	Battle I	927	Op: reconnaissance
	Capt D W Allan SAAF	pow	Took off Archers Post to reconnoitre Kismayu, Afmadow	
	Air Sgt J B Lockwood SAAF	pow	and Gobwen. Shot down by a CR.42 fighter.	
	Air Sgt J L Wright SAAF	pow		

23 Nov 1940	45 Sqn		Wellesley I	L2662	Unknown

SOC, NFD.

24 Nov 1940	211 Sqn		Blenheim I	L8511	Op: Durrazzo
	S/Ldr J R Gordon-Finlayson DSO				
	P/O G Davies DFC MiD				
	P/O A C Geary				

Took off 1030, Menidi. Severely damaged by flak, with one engine stopped and the hydraulics ruptured. Belly-landed on a beach on the S of Corfu. The crew were ferried to the mainland by local fishermen.

25 Nov 1940	38 Sqn		Wellington IC	P9265 F	Ground

Destroyed in a strafing attack, Luqa, while staging through from Marham to Egypt.

26 Nov 1940	14 Sqn		Blenheim IV	R3593	Op: Nefasit
	F/O M MacKenzie				
	Sgt M E F Hitchin				
	Sgt W J McConnell				

Took off 0450, Port Sudan, one of six aircraft detailed to attack the target, 15km E of Asmara. Attacked by CR.42 fighters over the Gulf of Zula, lost an engine, and crash-landed on the coast 13km N of Massawa. S/Ldr Stapleton, the CO, landed beside the crashed Blenheim and retrieved the crew.

	113 Sqn		Blenheim IV	T2067	Op: Bir Sofafi
	F/O D S Anderson	+			
	Sgt G H Lee	+			
	Sgt E S Young	+			

Took off 0710, LG 68 (Waterloo), one of two Blenheims detailed. Sgt Lee is commemorated on the Alamein Memorial, and the other crew members are buried in the Halfaya Sollum War Cemetery.

28 Nov 1940	84 Sqn		Blenheim I	L1385	Op: Durrazzo
	P/O D R Bird	pow			
	Sgt R E Scott	pow			
	Sgt S Davis	pow			

Took off 1155, Menidi/Tatoi, one of nine aircraft detailed. Attacked by Macchi and CR.42 fighters and crash-landed in a dry riverbed near Koritza, Albania. Sgt Scott is reported to have died in captivity, 18.6.41, but does not appear on the CWGC Register.

	OADF		Wellington IC	T2894	Delivery Flight
	W/Cdr C G Hohler	+			
	F/O J A Gray	+			
	Sgt D G Johnson	+			
	Sgt H Hogger	+			
	Sgt J H Jefferies	+			
	Sgt J C Cornish RNZAF	+			

Took off, Luqa, for Egypt before an air raid warning was sounded, and last seen setting course toward a convoy which was being attacked by Italian bombers. All are commemorated on the Runnymede Memorial. Wg/Cdr Hohler (70 Sqn) had gone to the UK to collect one of the first Wellingtons with which the sqn was re-equipping.

29 Nov 1940	47 Sqn		Wellesley I	K7760	Op: Danghila
	P/O E G L Pelling				
	F/O I White				
	Sgt W McCarthy				

Took off 0805, Summit, one of five Wellesleys of 223 Sqn accompanying five from 47 Sqn to attack an Italian camp at Danghila. The engine cut on take-off and the aircraft crash-landed at Sennar. SOC 1 December as BER.

	107 Sqn		Blenheim IV	T2080	Delivery Flight
	P/O A B Smith	int			
	Sgt E Shipley	int			
	Sgt J D Hutchinson	+			

Took off Gibraltar for Malta, and shot down by Vichy fighters off Sidi Ahmed, Tunisia. Sgt Hutchinson is buried in Massicault War Cemetery.

29-30 Nov 1940	214 Sqn ME Flt		Wellington IC	T2893	Delivery Flight
	S/Ldr P J McGinn	inj			
	P/O J A Parker	inj			
	P/O A D Brisbane	inj			
	Sgt R D F Clarke				
	Sgt J Raggenbass	+			
	Sgt C H Bain RNZAF	+			

Took off 0051, Stradishall, for Luqa, but at 0102 crashed at Elmdon, while attempting a forced landing after engine failure. DBF. Sgt Bain is buried at Haverhill, and Sgt Raggenbass in Stockport (Willow Grove) Cemetery. S/Ldr McGinn, like Wg/Cdr Hohler, was from 70 Sqn (see T2894 above).

30 Nov 1940	OADF	Blenheim IV	T2114	**Delivery Flight**
	P/O G Bennett	int	Took off Thorney Island on delivery to the Middle East,	
	Sgt S M Cashman	int	but crash-landed in the Ebro Delta, Spain. Interned, the	
	Sgt E Hannah	int	crew was eventually released, returning to the UK.	

4 Dec 1940	14 Sqn	Blenheim IV	R2770	**Op: reconnaissance**
	F/O T G Rhodes	+	Took off 0430, Port Sudan, to reconnoitre the Damas-	
	Sgt M E F Hitchin	+	Dambe Wadi, between Mai At'al and Ginda, Eritrea.	
	Sgt S C Lewis	+	Believed shot down by CR.42s of 412 Squadriglia. All the crew are commemorated on the Alamein Memorial.	

5 Dec 1940	12 Sqn SAAF	Ju 86Z-7	656	**Op: Moyale and Mega**
	Lt P H Vermeulen SAAF	+	Took off 0905, Nanyuki. Hit by flak over the target. One	
	W/O2 M M Hough SAAF	+	engine cut and the aircraft crashed some 53km S of	
	Air Mech T A O'Cocklin SAAF		Mega. The three who survived remained with the aircraft	
	Air Sgt W Roller SAAF	+	while the other three set off southwards. The remains of	
	F/Sgt J W Armstrong SAAF		the pilot were discovered months later. He and the other	
	F/Sgt A R Ingle SAAF		two dead are commemorated on the Alamein Memorial. A Battle searching for the three lost crew members was itself lost on 11 December.	

6 Dec 1940	30 Sqn	Blenheim I	K7100 V	**Op: Sarande-Valona Rd**
	F/O H P G Blackmore		Took off 1400, Eleusis, to strafe Italian forces. Crash-	
	P/O R K Crowther		landed because of bad weather and shortage of fuel 5km W of Karousadhes, Corfu. SOC 1.2.41.	
	47 Sqn	Wellesley I	K8521	**Op: Bure**
	P/O B B Witty	+	Took off 0815, Sennar, to bomb the village and fort at	
	P/O P A Hunt	pow	Bure. Shot down over the target by a CR.42 fighter. The	
	Sgt G A Bonnar	pow	crew bailed out and were taken prisoner, but P/O Witty, mortally wounded, died on 12 December.	

7 Dec 1940	84 Sqn	Blenheim I	L1381 A	**Op: Valona**
	F/O K Linton		Took off 1220, Menidi/Tatoi, one of six Blenheims	
	P/O A C Dunn		detailed to bomb the harbour at Valona. Crippled by a	
	Sgt R L Crowe		single burst of fire from a CR.42, and crash-landed S of Sarande.	
	84 Sqn	Blenheim I	L8455	**Op: Valona**
	F/Lt L P Cattell MiD	+	Took off Menidi/Tatoi, as above. Shot down over the	
	Sgt H A E Taylor	+	target by CR.42s. All are commemorated on the Alamein	
	Sgt F L Carter	+	Memorial.	
	84 Sqn	Blenheim I	L8457	**Op: Valona**
	Sgt M P Cazalet	+	Took off Menidi/Tatoi, as above. Shot down over the	
	Sgt K J Ridgewell	+	target by CR.42s. The dead are commemorated on the	
	Sgt C R Forster	pow	Alamein Memorial.	
	148 Sqn	Wellington IC	T2838 R	**Op: Castel Benito**
	F/O P W de B Forsyth		Took off 1531, Luqa, attacked by a CR.42 which shot	
	Crew		away the hydraulics; belly-landed, Luqa, at 1916. DBR.	
	211 Sqn	Blenheim I	L1535	**Op: Valona**
	P/O G I Jerdein	+	Took off 1300 Menidi/Tatoi, one of nine detailed to bomb	
	Sgt J E Barber	+	the harbour at Valona. En route in severe weather flew	
	Sgt J Munro	+	into hills near Lamia. All are buried in Phaleron War Cemetery.	
	211 Sqn	Blenheim I	L4926	**Op: Valona**
	F/O P B Pickersgill	+	Took off 1300 Menidi/Tatoi, as above. En route in severe	
	Sgt H Taylor	+	weather flew into hills near Lamia. All are buried in	
	Sgt N A Hallett	+	Phaleron War Cemetery.	

	14 Sqn SAAF Lt B Brain SAAF	**Maryland I**	1601	**Training**

The pilot was taking off from Nakuru on his first solo flight on the type when the Maryland was hit by an Audax which was landing. The Audax penetrated the wing of the Maryland but fell off and was run over when the Maryland throttled back. Crash-landed, the Maryland was DBR and reduced to produce.

---

9 Dec 1940

113 Sqn — **Blenheim IV** — T2073 — **Op: unknown**

P/O J N Owen — inj
Sgt A M Goldfeather — +
Sgt J Crawford — +

Took off LG 68 (Waterloo). The aircraft came down at Sidi Barrani in unknown circumstances. The dead are commemorated on the Alamein Memorial.

3 Group Training Flt — **Wellington IC** — R1246 H — **Delivery Flight**

F/O J W Collins — pow
F/Sgt F J S Steele — pow
P/O P F Walker — pow
Sgt R Ayre — pow
Sgt J A Hunslow — pow
Sgt J F Coombs RNZAF — pow

Took off 0013 Stradishall, for Luqa, but crashed near Rouen in unknown circumstances. The crew bailed out, but were captured within 12 hours. The then W/O Steele was killed when a POW column was strafed by RAF Typhoons on 19 April 1945. He is buried in Berlin War Cemetery.

214 Sqn ME Flt — **Wellington IC** — R1250 R — **Delivery Flight**

F/O C J A G Brain DFC — int
Sgt G E Adams — int
Sgt P J Capon — int
Sgt A E Cook — int
Sgt A B Todd — int
Passenger: P/O R G Brickell — int

Took off 0013, Stradishall, for Luqa. Suffered engine failure and force-landed at Bougie, Algeria, where the crew was interned. P/O Brickell, listed as 'Special Duty Passenger, Air Ministry Works Department', was en route to Crete, to supervise airfield construction.

---

11 Dec 1940

11 Sqn SAAF — **Battle I** — 915 — **Op: Yabelo**

Lt W M P Matthias SAAF
Air Sgt R J van Heerden SAAF

Took off 0630, Archers Post, to attack the airfield at Yabelo. Crash-landed 39km N of base when the engine failed on the return flight.

11 Sqn SAAF — **Battle I** — 918 — **Search and Rescue**

Lt M MacDonald SAAF — +
F/Sgt P C Marais SAAF — +
F/Sgt A Schroeder SAAF — +

Took off Archers Post to search for the Ju 86 missing since 5 December. Crashed and DBF. All the crew are buried in Nairobi War Cemetery.

---

12 Dec 1940

45 Sqn — **Blenheim I** — L8465 — **Op: Sollum**

P/O P C Traill-Smith — +
P/O V D Fry — +
Sgt T O Liggins — +

Took off 0745, LG 20 (Qotafiyah I), to bomb the LG at Sollum. Shot down. All are commemorated on the Alamein Memorial.

RAF Takoradi — **Blenheim IV** — R2790 — **Delivery Flight**

Lt R Roques FAFL
W/O Mirell FAFL
F/Sgt N M Castellain FAFL

Crashed on take-off 1420, Kano, one of four Blenheims of Delivery Flight 15 being flown by French crews to the Free French forces in the Middle East. The undercarriage collapsed and a fire started in the fuselage which eventually engulfed the aircraft.

---

14 Dec 1940

11 Sqn — **Blenheim IV** — L8395 — **Op: Bardia**

Sgt Baleey
Sgt E Maltby
Sgt G W H Ware DFM

Took off 0740, LG 17 (Fuka Main), part of a combined force of 8 Blenheims from 55 Sqn and one from 11 Sqn detailed to bomb Bardia. The formation was attacked over the target by more than 40 CR.42 fighters, and L8395 was badly hit, with the port engine put out of action. Belly-landing at Derawla, near Maaten Bagush, the aircraft was DBR and SOC 6.1.42.

14 Sqn — **Blenheim IV** — T2167 — **Op: Zula Bay**

Sgt B T Hopkins — +

Took off 1420, Port Sudan, to raid aircraft at Zula LG. Last

Sgt J C Hall		+	heard from 25 minutes prior to ETA. FTR. The crew is
Sgt R F Murray		+	commemorated on the Alamein Memorial.

55 Sqn   Blenheim IV   **L8790**   **Op: Bardia**

F/O M S Singleton	+
Sgt E P Chapman	+
Sgt B J Fox	+

Took off 0740, LG 17 (Fuka Main), detailed as for L8395 above. Shot down into the sea. All are commemorated on the Alamein Memorial.

55 Sqn   Blenheim IV   **T1872**   **Op: Bardia**

F/O K H A Ellis DFC
Sgt I Browning
Sgt J E Perkins

Took off 0740, LG 17 (Fuka Main), detailed as for L8395 above. Badly damaged by fighters, with the starboard engine put out of action. DBR.

211 Sqn   Blenheim I   **L8514**   **Op: Valona**

F/Lt L B Buchanan
Sgt Stack
Sgt G Pattison

Took off 0720, Menidi/Tatoi, one of nine Blenheims detailed to bomb Valona. On return force landed at Araxos, 1020, because of fuel shortage, and tipped up. Abandoned in Greece May 1941.

---

15 Dec 1940   **211 Sqn**   Blenheim I   **L1484**   **Unknown**

SOC. NFD.

15-16 Dec 1940   **223 Sqn**   Wellesley I   **L2690   V**   **Op: Gura**

F/O J Wallace
Sgt A Cockell
Sgt W M Perks

Took off 2310, Wadi Gazouza. Attacked over the target by CR.42s and damaged, belly-landing on return with a damaged undercarriage. DBR.

---

16 Dec 1940   **FB Flt 1**   Martin 167F   **GM102 (AX670)**   **Op: reconnaissance**

Adj-Chef Y Trécan FAFL	+
Cne J Dodelier FAFL	+
Sgt Y Michel FAFL	+
F/Sgt R Cunibil FAFL	pow

Took off 0635, Khormaksar, on a photographic reconnaissance and shot down by CR.32 fighters of 410 Squadriglia. Adj-Chef Trécan bailed out but his chute caught on the tailplane. The three dead are commemorated on the Alamein Memorial. W/O Gallipot was the *nom de guerre* of Adj-Chef Y Trécan, F/Lt Boulet of Cne J Dodelier, and F/Sgt Michel of Sgt Y Michel, all formerly of L'Armée de l'Air.

---

17 Dec 1940   **216 Sqn**   Bombay   **L5821**   **Bombing practice**

F/O F A Walton	+
F/O P A S Baker	+
Sgt J O Paul	+
P/O H H J Hobday	+
P/O J C L Hanmer-Strudwick	+
P/O W E Laceby	+
AC2 R Coulson	+

Took off Heliopolis. Stalled and dived into the ground on Suez Road bombing range. All are buried in Cairo War Memorial Cemetery.

---

18 Dec 1940   **30 Sqn**   Blenheim I   **L8462**   **Op: Valona**

F/O S Paget	+
Sgt G Sigsworth	+
Sgt W Tubberby	+

Took off 1000, Eleusis, on offensive reconnaissance, and to bomb the harbour at Valona. Shot down by Italian fighters over the sea 11km W of Sarande. The pilot and observer are commemorated on the Alamein Memorial, while Sgt Tubberby, originally buried in Albania, but whose grave is now lost, is commemorated on Special Memorial E in Phaleron War Cemetery.

---

20 Dec 1940   **113 Sqn**   Blenheim IV   **T2059**   **Op:**

F/O V T H Frith	+
Sgt E M W McKim	+
Sgt G H Lyle	+

Took off LG 68 (Waterloo). FTR. All the crew are commemorated on the Alamein Memorial.

21-22 Dec 1940	**37 Sqn** P/O H A Lax P/O A W Doel RNZAF Sgt J Blyth Sgt J Henderson Sgt Martin P/O R N Ridley	**Wellington IC**	**L7865 W**	**Op: Berka** Took off 2300, LG 09 (Bir Koraiyim), detailed to bomb the airfield at Berka.Reported returning with engine trouble and belly-landed 48km SE of Sidi Barrani; DBF. The crew walked N for several hours to the coastal road. There is a detailed account of this loss in Kevin Mears' *Wise Without Eyes*, pp128-30.
22 Dec 1940	**47 Sqn** Sgt R D Cathcart-Cunnison Sgt F H Taylor Sgt W Schollar	**Wellesley I**	**K7775 N**	**Op: Bure** Took off 1300, Sennar, to bomb troop concentrations, but force-landed 66km SE of Sennar Dam, after compass and cabin light failure. The crew abandoned the badly damaged aircraft and walked for seven hours until they met a tribesman who guided them to a main road, where they obtained a lift. The aircraft was recovered by 52 RSU on 1.1.41, but presumably reduced to spares.
	84 Sqn Sgt A Gordon Sgt Levitt F/Sgt G Furney	**Blenheim I** inj	**L4818**	**Op: Kucove** Took off 0930, Menidi/Tatoi, one of nine aircraft detailed to bomb the Kucove Oilfields. Attacked by G.50 fighters of 1504 Gruppo, CT, and badly damaged, landing at base on one engine. SOC.
	84 Sqn F/O J F Evans Sgt H B Offord Sgt A L Sargeant	**Blenheim I** inj inj +	**L8374**	**Op: Kucove** Took off 0930 Menidi/Tatoi, detailed as above. Damaged by flak and attacked by G.50 fighters of 1504 Gruppo, CT. Sgt Sargeant was killed and the pilot and observer bailed out. F/O Evans was injured when he landed in a farm yard and was kicked by a mule, which broke his thigh. Sgt Sergeant is commemorated on the Alamein Memorial. Positive identification of the aircraft and location of the crash site at Permet, Albania, was made in 1996 by British Embassy staff.
	84 Sqn F/O P F Miles Sgt F G Moir Sgt B A C Brooker	**Blenheim I** + + +	**L8471**	**Op: Kucove** Took off 0930, Menidi/Tatoi, detailed as above. Shot down by G.50 fighters. All are commemorated on the Alamein Memorial.
26 Dec 1940	**211 Sqn** P/O R V Herbert Sgt J B Dunnet Sgt Hughes	**Blenheim I**	**L1482**	**Op: Valona-Himare Rd** Took off 1010, Menidi/Tatoi, to bomb the Valona-Himare Road, and Krioner, Albania. With the hydraulics damaged by enemy fighters, belly-landed at Menidi on return. DBR.
28 Dec 1940	**55 Sqn** F/O K D Potter	**Blenheim I**	**T2178**	**Training** Took off LG 16 (Fuka Satellite) for a night training flight. On approach to land the starboard engine caught fire, a wing dropped, and the aircraft crashed. DBR.
29 Dec 1940	**30 Sqn** F/Lt H D Card RCAF Sgt F Pese Sgt G E Bygrave	**Blenheim I** + + +	**K7104 L**	**Op: reconnaissance** Took off 0845, Eleusis. Shot down into the sea by Serg Zoli of 154 Gruppo CT. Two of the crew were seen to bail out, but did not survive. All are commemorated on the Alamein Memorial.
31 Dec 1940	**211 Sqn** Sgt S L Bennett Sgt W H Tunstall Sgt L R France	**Blenheim I** + + +	**L1540**	**Op: Valona** Took off 1230, Menidi/Tatoi, to bombs woods and buildings S of Valona. Last seen on fire after a fighter attack 27km S of Valona. All are commemorated on the Alamein Memorial.

Chapter 3

Stroke and Counterstroke
January to April 1941

January 1941 promised much. In North Africa the limited attack on the invading Italian army at Sidi Barrani begun on the night of 7th December 1940 had resulted in complete success, with all Italian forces driven out of Egypt in a week. Assuming, rightly, that Italian morale was low, General Wavell decided to strike another blow, though again with limited aims, and on 3rd January 1941 the operation began with an attack on the fortified port of Bardia. This fell three days later, followed on 22nd January by the more important port of Tobruk, where 45,000 prisoners were captured, along with 462 guns and 129 tanks. Emboldened still further, General Wavell gave permission for a further advance by General O'Connor, timed to begin on 12th February, and designed to outflank and destroy Italian forces dug in around yet another port, Derna. When, however, air reconnaissance showed that the Italians were preparing to abandon Derna, and indeed Benghazi, and retreat to Agheila, where it might be possible to block a further advance on Tripoli, the capture of which would mean the loss of Italy's entire North African colonies, General O'Connor planned an encircling move, sending a motorised force, accompanied by tanks, across the interior of Cyrenaica, to cut off the retreating Italians at Beda Fomm. The result was astonishing, a force of 3,000 capturing 20,000 prisoners, 216 guns and 120 tanks.

The way was open to Tripoli, and to the extinction of the Italian empire in North Africa, but at this point the British Government stepped in, at Mr Churchill's initiative, requiring on 12th February the transfer of the bulk of O'Connor's force, together with all his supporting air units, save one fighter squadron, to Greece. This quixotic decision might not have had such a disastrous effect had not it coincided with Hitler's decision to strengthen Italian resistance by sending a small panzer force to North Africa under General Rommel. On 31st March he essayed a small advance against the British front line at El Agheila, and then, meeting little resistance, launched on 2nd April a more ambitious assault which, by 1st April had driven the British back over the border into Egypt, leaving only a small force besieged in Tobruk.

While triumphs were giving place to disasters in North Africa, matters were going much better in East Africa, where the long-awaited spring offensive began in February, with an advance into Italian Somaliland from Kenya. As in Cyrenaica, an Italian collapse resulted, with Kismayu and then, on 25th February, the capital, Mogadishu, captured. The force under General Cunningham then turned inland, into Southern Abyssinia, capturing Jijiga on 17th March, Harar on the 29th, and only a week later, on 6th April, Addis Ababa.

If the southern assault on Mussolini's East African Empire had gone smoothly, however, that from the north into Eritrea was a much tougher proposition. Stalled in the mountains at Keren for 53 days, the attacking force, largely Indian, broke through on 27th March, and the occupation of Asmara on 1st April, and Massawa a week later, ended the Eritrean campaign.

The bomber units supporting the East African campaign were exclusively employed in a tactical role, often involving army co-operation. Those operating in the southern offensive were almost exclusively SAAF squadrons, the bomber component of which consisted of a mixed force of Ju 86s (replaced by Marylands at the conclusion of the East African campaign), Marylands, and Fairey Battles. They were supported, initially from Aden, by RAF units operating Blenheims and Vincents.

On the northern front the squadrons were exclusively RAF, operating Wellesleys and Blenheims, the former (flown by 47 and 223 Squadrons) dwindling so much in number that in late April 223 Squadron converted to Marylands, and moved to Egypt, all remaining Wellesleys now being operated by 47 Squadron.

No heavy bombers operated in East Africa, but in North Africa the Wellington squadrons of 257 Wing, boosted to four by the arrival from Malta of 148 Squadron during March, were tasked with bombing the ports and supply routes of the Axis forces, first Tobruk, then Benghazi and finally, from advanced bases in the desert, Tripoli, each being attacked on a nightly basis.

Malta
The new year, 1941, opened very quietly, but the quiet was deceptive, since in December 1940 Mussolini had accepted a German offer to assist in the neutralisation of Malta, and bomber and reconnaissance units detached from Germany and Norway arrived in Sicily in the first days of the new year, followed in early February by a small but highly experienced unit of Messerschmitt Bf 109s. These units of Fliegerkorps X first made their presence felt in a devastating attack on the aircraft carrier *Illustrious* on 10th January. This was followed up by ferocious attempts to sink the crippled carrier as it was undergoing emergency repairs in Grand Harbour. These failed, but the intense

air attacks continued, with airfields one of the targets. 148 Squadron retaliated, carrying out two particularly successful raids on Catania airfield, headquarters of Fliegerkorps X, destroying some 30 aircraft, and damaging as many again.

From February on, the Axis attacks on Malta intensified, and after losing many Wellingtons to ground attack, including six destroyed and seven damaged in a brief strafing attack on 26th February, the decision was made to evacuate 148 Squadron to Egypt. Luftwaffe attacks did not diminish until April, when in preparation for the invasion of Russia, Operation *Barbarossa*, units were progressively withdrawn from Sicily.

---

1 Jan
1941
Middle East
Blenheim IV
T2076 — Unknown
Lost at Malta en route to the Middle East. NFD.

---

3 Jan
1941
45 Sqn
F/O P J B Griffiths +
Sgt A C Tadhunter +
Sgt C Blackshaw +
Blenheim I
L8479 — Op: Gazala
Took off 0650, LG 20 (Qotafiya 1), one of two Blenheims detailed to attack No 2 Landing Ground. Attacked by a CR.42 fighter on return and shot down in flames 14km off Gazala. The crew is commemorated on the Alamein Memorial.

---

6 Jan
1941
211 Sqn
F/O R D Campbell pow
Sgt J H Beharrell pow
Sgt R Appleyard pow
Blenheim I
L1487 — Op: Valona
Took off 0810, Menidi/Tatoi, to bomb jetties and the foreshore at Valona, and shot down by a G.50bis (Ten L Bassi, 154 Gruppo CT) after bombing, crashing into the sea off the port. All the crew were injured, Sgt Beharrell being rescued by an Italian destroyer, the others swimming ashore, to be captured later.

211 Sqn
F/O L S Delaney +
Sgt V Pollard +
Sgt T A McCord +
Blenheim I
L8536 — Op: Valona
Took off 0810, Menidi/ Tatoi, detailed as above. Badly damaged by flak or fighter fire over the target, but managed to gain the Albanian/Greek border on one engine, hitting boulders and cartwheeling on attempting a crash-landing near the village of Oraiokastron, near Ioannina. All are commemorated on the Alamein Memorial.

6-7 Jan
1941
38 Sqn
Sgt W E Clegg +
Sgt E J Dunton +
Sgt N W Mawby +
Sgt T P Robson +
Sgt P F Wilcock +
Sgt Roberts
Wellington IC
P9293 S — Op: Tobruk
Took off LG 17 (Fuka Main). Damaged by flak and burst into flames while making for Fuka satellite and crashed into the sea off Ishaila Rock, near Sidi Barrani. The rear gunner was picked up by a destroyer. Sgts Robson, Mawby, Dunton are commemorated on the Alamein Memorial, and Sgts Clegg and Wilcock buried in the El Alamein War Cemetery.

---

9 Jan
1941
37 Sqn
Sgt D J Paul
Crew
Wellington IC
N2777 B — Navigation Exercise
Took off Shallufa. The undercarriage collapsed on landing. No details in ORB. SOC 31 January.

---

10 Jan
1941
84 Sqn
P/O I P C Goudge
Sgt I B Croker
Sgt J Wright
Blenheim I
L8501 — Op: Kelcyre-Berat
Took off 1035, Menidi/Tatoi, one of eight Blenheims detailed to attack troop concentrations on the Kelcyre-Berat Road, Albania. Ran out of fuel and crash-landed at Araxos. Presumed lost during the evacuation of Greece.

---

12 Jan
1941
47 Sqn
F/O R J Willitts
Sgt H L Oddy
Sgt A H Paine
Wellesley I
K7728 — Op: Agordat
Took off 1430, Gordon's Tree, to attack the airfield at Agordat. Swung on landing, 2100, and undercarriage collapsed. DBR.

	55 Sqn	**Blenheim IV**	**T2190** **Communication Flight**
	P/O K D Potter	inj	Took off LG 79 to pick up bombs and fuel from LG 17
	Passengers:	inj	(Fuka Main), but in a violent sandstorm was unable to
	AC1 H D Todd		find a place to land, and all bailed out 660km E of its
	LAC Wratton		base, at El Arish, in the Sinai Desert.
	AC2 Stafford		

12-13 Jan	**148 Sqn**	**Wellington IC**	**T2874 W** **Op: Catania**
1941	P/O G K Noble	+	Took off Luqa. Shot down over the target. All are buried
	P/O J Stidolph	+	in Catania War Cemetery.
	Sgt R C Verran	+	
	Sgt J I Wilson	+	
	Sgt S V Hearfield	+	

	148 Sqn	**Wellington IC**	**T2892** **Op: Catania**
	F/O A F A Osborn		Took off Luqa. The aircraft was hit several times and the
	Sgt G C Hall	+	fuel tanks punctured. Ditched 140 miles out to sea near
	Sgt J Reardon	+	HM Trawler *Jade*. The crew was rescued by HSL 107, but
	Sgt Belcher		Sgts Hall and Readon later died of injuries. Both are
	Sgt Digby		buried on Malta: Hall at (Capuccini) Naval Cemetery;
			Reardon at Imtarfa Military Cemetery.

13 Jan	**14 Sqn**	**Blenheim IV**	**T2181** **Ground**
1941	Sgt G E Dickson		Involved in a taxying collision at Port Sudan with
			Blenheim N3557, probably on 13 Jan; SOC the next day.

15 Jan	**38 Sqn**	**Wellington IC**	**N2759 Y** **Op: Benghazi**
1941	S/Ldr F W L Wild		Failed to climb after take-off LG 17 (Fuka Main),
	F/O Harrison		jettisoned bombs safe, but crashed on approach to land,
	P/O Middleton		Fuka.
	Sgt Rosam		
	Sgt Shooter		
	P/O Whyte		

16 Jan	**8 Sqn**	**Blenheim I**	**L8456** **Op: various targets**
1941	F/O K A H Lawrence, MiD	int	Took off 1620, Khormaksar, to bomb targets in Eritrea.
	Sgt W H Tamlin DFM	int	Crashed in a forced landing 3km from the coast at Table
	Sgt A B Houston	int	Cliff, Djibouti. The crew were interned by the French but
			escaped and returned to their squadron on 23 April.

17 Jan	**Takoradi Stn Flt**	**Blenheim IV**	**L9320** **Delivery Flight**
1941	S/Ldr T P Kurdziel PAF		Took off 1010, Takoradi. One of two Blenheims and six
	Sgt Turley		Hurricanes on the first stage of Delivery Flight 27 to the
	Sgt Hughes		Middle East. Bounced on landing at Lagos and the
			undercarriage collapsed. DBR.

20-21 Jan	**14 Sqn**	**Blenheim IV**	**T1868** **Op: Massawa**
1941	Sgt W L Martin		Took off 2230, Port Sudan, to attack searchlights at
	Sgt F J F Adams		Massawa. Unable to distinguish the target so did not
	Sgt K Bamber		bomb. The undercarriage collapsed while landing on
			rough ground, Port Sudan. DBR.

21 Jan	**55 Sqn**	**Blenheim IV**	**T1879** **Op: Tobruk**
1941	F/O F R Bullot	+	Took off 0755, Capuzzo/Amseat No 1, to bomb artillery
	Sgt C H Bartram	+	positions at Tobruk. Four bombs were accidentally
	Sgt D H Clayson	+	released on take-off, two exploding. The port engine cut
			as the aircraft climbed to 35m, then turned to port and
			dived into the ground. The crew is buried at Halfaya
			Sollum War Cemetery.

28 Jan 1941	**38 Sqn**	**Wellington IC**	**T2954**	**Ground**

Badly damaged during an air raid, Luqa; SOC 3 February.

1 Feb 1941	**45 Sqn**	**Blenheim I**	**L6663**	**Unknown**

Lost (A-B Serials). No mention in 45 Sqn ORB. Jefford's history of 45 Sqn, *The Flying Camels*, states that the aircraft was damaged by CR.42s in an attack on Monastir, and that it was still in use in February 1941.

2 Feb 1941	**11 Sqn** Sgt D G Strachan Sgt G Date Sgt R E G Clift AC1 E Bradbury	**Blenheim IV** + + + +	**T2235**	**Transit Flight**

Took off Abu Sueir for Eleusis and missing in icing conditions over the Mediterranean The crew is commemorated on the Alamein Memorial.

	11 Sqn Sgt E H J Thornton Sgt F T Manly Sgt Brown	**Blenheim IV**	**N3580**	**Transit Flight**

Took off Abu Sueir for Menidi/Tatoi, but hit a ridge in a force-landing in bad weather 45km SE of Salonika. The undercarriage collapsed and the aircraft was DBR and abandoned.

	55 Sqn P/O P G Blignaut Sgt H R Rundle Sgt E R W Currie RAAF	**Blenheim IV** + + +	**T2240**	**Op: Marawah**

Took off Capuzzo/Amseat No I to bomb Italian forces escaping by road from Marawah. Shot down by ground fire from the convoy and crashed at Slonta, Libya. The crew is commemorated on the Alamein Memorial.

3 Feb 1941	**38 Sqn**	**Wellington IC**	**P9265**	**Ground**

Destroyed in an air raid, Luqa.

4 Feb 1941	**14 Sqn** F/O M MacKenzie Sgt D Farrell Sgt W J McConnell	**Blenheim IV**	**T2115**	**Op: Keren**

Took off 0800 Port Sudan, one of three detailed to bomb Italian motor transport retreating along the Keren/Asmara road. Attacked in error near the target by Hawker Hurricanes, although correct recognition signals were given. Badly damaged and crash-landed on return when the undercarriage failed to lower. DBR.

	45 Sqn F/Lt J Paine Sgt H C T Holmans Sgt C P Edwards	**Blenheim I** evd + +	**L8538**	**Op: Barce**

Took off Menastir, one of two detailed to bomb a railway line 16km SW of Barce. Shot down in flames by a CR.42 fighter. F/Lt Paine bailed out and helped by local tribesmen returned to his squadron a few weeks later. The dead are commemorated on the Alamein Memorial.

	3 Group Training Flt P/O A L T Todd Sgt T S H Hunter Sgt G J Little Sgt R Player Sgt J Pringle Sgt N Rowell	**Wellington IC** + + + + + +	**R1385**	**Delivery Flight**

Took off Stradishall for Luqa, but failed to arrive. All are commemorated on the Runnymede Memorial. The crew positions of all but P/O Todd and Sgt Hunter are uncertain.

	GRB1 Sgt G Le Calvez FAFL Lt G Claron FAFL Sgt Chef F Devin FAFL	**Blenheim IV** + + +	**T1867**	**Op: Kufra Oasis**

Took off Qunianga, Chad, to bomb Italian positions at Kufra Oasis, but force-landed after navigational difficulties. In 1969 a Libyan border patrol discovered the aircraft and its crew, who were still inside the aircraft, and they were later buried in France.

4-5 Feb 1941	**3 Group Training Flt** Sgt Fadden Sgt Barr Sgt Hunter Sgt Jannay Sgt Porter Sgt Warren	**Wellington IC** inj	**R1386 Y**	**Delivery Flight** Took off Stradishall, 2340, for Luqa. Engine jammed on full throttle; overshot on a third attempt at landing and crashed into a quarry, Luqa.
5 Feb 1941	**84 Sqn** F/Lt R A Towgood Sgt R F Somerville Sgt Atherton	**Blenheim I** + inj	**L4833 U**	**Op: Valone-Tepelen Rd** T/o 0715, Menidi/Tatoi, one of three Blenheims sent to attack motor transport on the Valona-Tepelene road. The port engine failed when coming into land and the aircraft crashed near the boundary fence of Menidi airfield at 0950 hrs. The pilot is buried at Phaleron War Cemetery.
6 Feb 1941	**47 Sqn** P/O A G Leuchars Crew	**Wellesley I**	**K7722**	**Transit flight** Took off 0350, Blackdown, for Kassala, to stand by for operational instructions. Belly-landed in error at 0455. SOC 21 June as BER.
	84 Sqn F/O A N N Nicholson P/O R G C Day Sgt A J Hollist	**Blenheim I** + +	**L1393**	**Op: Tepelene** Took off 1200, Menidi/Tatoi, to bomb Italian forces in the Tepelene area. On return in bad weather ditched at the E end of the Gulf of Corinth. The pilot reached an island in the aircraft's dinghy, eventually returning to base, while Sgt Hollist (commemorated on the Alamein Memorial) was killed in the crash and P/O Day (buried in Phaleron War Cemetery) drowned.
7 Feb 1941	**47 Sqn** F/O R R Helsby P/O E J Bainbridge Sgt A H Paine	**Wellesley I** pow + +	**K8525**	**Op: Adi Ugri Rd** Took off Barentu on reconnaissance and FTR. The two dead are buried in Asmara War Cemetery.
	47 Sqn Sgt E E Blofield Sgt J H Davies Sgt L Bird	**Wellesley I** + + pow	**K7759**	**Op: Adi Ugri Rd** As above. The dead are buried in Asmara War Cemetery.
8 Feb 1941	**14 Sqn** P/O P E Renniker F/O H C P Turney Sgt F G Roy Passenger: P/O T H Scorror	**Blenheim IV** + + + +	**T1818**	**Op: Asmara** Took off 0905, Port Sudan, and hit by flak over the target, crashing and exploding. All on board are buried in Asmara War Cemetery.
9 Feb 1941	**47 Sqn**	**Wellesley I**	**K7713**	**Ground** Destroyed in an air raid by strafing CR.42 fighters, Agordat. SOC 13 February.
	47 Sqn	**Wellesley I**	**L2665**	**Ground** As above.
10 Feb 1941	**78 Sqn** P/O J Wotherspoon Sgt F A Southam Sgt B R Albon Sgt E A Hodges Sgt H J Meddings	**Whitley V** pow pow pow pow pow	**T4167**	**Op: Foggia** Took off Luqa to bomb Foggia as a diversion for Operation *Compass*, a commando raid on a viaduct in Southern Italy. The aircraft suffered engine failure, the crew bailed out over Battipaglia and the pilot force-landed at the mouth of the River Sele.

11 Feb 1941	**47 Sqn** P/O D F O Shelford Sgt K L Burton Sgt Rollinson	**Wellesley I**	K7782	**Transit Flight** Took off Khartoum to fly to the ALG at Agordat for instructions to attack a target near Keren, but the aircraft was struck by a gust of wind on landing, 1420, and the undercarriage collapsed. DBR.
	113 Sqn	**Blenheim IV**	R3917	**Ground** Destroyed in a hangar fire, El Adem, while under repair. SOC 14 February.
13 Feb 1941	**11 Sqn** Sgt L Williams Sgt J F Adamson Sgt O L G Traherne	**Blenheim IV** pow + +	T2166	**Op: Berat** Took off 1330, Larissa, one of six detailed to attack motor transport. The formation was intercepted by G.50 fighters at they approached the target, and T2166 shot down in flames. The pilot and observer bailed out, but only the pilot survived to be taken prisoner. The others are commemorated on the Alamein Memorial.
	11 Sqn P/O J Hutchison Sgt S D Whiles Sgt W T Jackson	**Blenheim IV** + +	T2237	**Op: Berat** As above. Shot down in flames on the return flight. The pilot ordered the crew to bail out, but only the observer could do so before the aircraft crashed into a mountain near Koritza. The dead are commemorated on the Alamein Memorial.
	11 Sqn F/O J V Berggren Sgt N R Powell Sgt H Murphy	**Blenheim IV**	T2347	**Op: Berat** As above. An engine failed and the aircraft force-landed in a field on return to Larissa. Abandoned.
13-14 Feb 1941	**38 Sqn** P/O A B Loveridge Sgt A G McLean P/O R L Pattle Sgt T M Moore P/O F J Leslie Sgt W K Winterbottom	**Wellington IC** + + + + + +	T2742 H	**Op: Scarpanto** Took off 2355, Shallufa. Shot down by flak during an attack on Midi Bay airfield. All are buried in Rhodes War Cemetery.
14 Feb 1941	**113 Sqn**	**Blenheim IV**	R3917 SOC. NFD.	**Unknown**
	223 Sqn F/O P F Willing Sgt G Crowther Sgt P C Benstead	**Wellesley I** + + +	K7788 W	**Op: Mai Edaga** Took off 1808, Wadi Gazouza, to bomb the Caproni plant at Mai Edaga and believed shot down by flak. The crew is commemorated on the Alamein Memorial.
15 Feb 1941	**37 Sqn** F/O A G Wright P/O G S Smith Sgt F J E Hartman Sgt S J Gardner P/O L C Wellman P/O P W Lambert	**Wellington IC** + + + + + +	T2821 T	**Op: Rhodes** Took off 0001, Shallufa. Crashed at Koyceges in the mountains of W Turkey while descending through cloud to make a landfall. All are buried in Haidar Pasha Cemetery, Istanbul.
15-16 Feb 1941	**37 Sqn** Sgt A T H Gillanders Sgt W Hobden Sgt W R Green Sgt A Flockhart Sgt J A McQ MacMillan RNZAF	**Wellington IC** + + pow + pow	T2822 D	**Op: Brindisi** Took off 0145, Menidi. Shot down by flak. The dead are buried in Bari War Cemetery. Sgt McMillan had head injuries.

17 Feb 1941	**37 Sqn** F/O A G W Hough P/O L J Winbolt Sgt J Blyth Sgt J L Baxter Sgt J E Valler P/O G C Muir	**Wellington IC**	**N2757 S** +	**Op: Rhodes** Took off 0001, Shallufa. Force-landed after engine trouble at Tala SW of Cairo. DBF. P/O Winbolt, who was killed in the crash-landing, is buried in Cairo War Memorial Cemetery. There is an account of this loss in Kevin Mears' *Wise Without Eyes*, pp140-141.
18 Feb 1941	**47 Sqn** Sgt G M Keith Sgt Cooper Sgt T Armstrong	**Wellesley I**	**K7723**	**Op: Mogarem** Took off Kassala for the ALG, Agordat, to attack a target in the foothills SW of Mogarem. At 1310 the aircraft crashed in a heavy landing at Agordat. SOC 21 June as BER.
	84 Sqn F/O K Linton P/O A C Dunn Sgt R L Crowe	**Blenheim I**	**L6662**	**Unknown** On take-off, 1515, Menidi/Tatoi, on relocation to Paramythia, L6662 was caught in the slipstream of the leader, the aircraft swung and the undercarriage collapsed. Abandoned on evacuation.
	203 Sqn F/Lt B T Scott Sgt R A Harding Sgt D J Bushnell	**Blenheim IV**	**L9173 V**	**Op: Makale** Took off 0605, Khormaksar, to attack the aerodrome at Makale. Attacked and damaged on the return flight by a CR.42. Crash-landed w/o flaps on return, SOC 17 March.
	203 Sqn S/Ldr A L H Solano Sgt E W A Sutton Sgt R D Rushton	**Blenheim IV**	**T2053** + +	**Op: Makale** Took off 0615, detailed as above and likewise attacked by a CR.42. Crash-landed, after the port engine failed, on the Eritrea-Ethiopia border. Sgt Rushton was found to be dead, but the others set out to walk to Assam, 145km SE. Though they were assisted by friendly tribesmen, S/Ldr Solano collapsed and died eight days later. He and Sgt Rushton are commemorated on the Alamein Memorial.
20 Feb 1941	**38 Sqn**	**Wellington IC**	**L7808**	**Unknown** SOC. NFD.
	211 Sqn P/O J C Cox DFC Sgt W B Stack Sgt Martin	**Blenheim I**	**L8542**	**Op: Berat** Took off Paramythia to bomb Berat. Damaged by G.50 fighters, and abandoned on evacuation, May 1941.
21 Feb 1941	**37 Sqn** F/O A G W Hough F/O R C W Broad F/O A A Scott Sgt J L Baxter Sgt J E Valler P/O G C Muir	**Wellington IC**	**T2575 T** + + + + + +	**Transit Flight** Took off Shallufa for Luqa but blew up about 175km SE of Malta, burning wreckage being reported falling into the sea. All are commemorated on the Alamein Memorial.
	37 Sqn Sgt R Spiller Sgt Milne Sgt McIntyre Sgt Redfern Sgt Bevan P/O Gladwell	**Wellington IC**	**T2607 P**	**Op: Supply drop** The undercarriage collapsed on take-off from a water-logged airfield at Paramythia, when returning to Menidi after a supply-dropping mission to Balli and Korovode.
	84 Sqn Sgt N H Thomas Sgt Oliver P/O T G Corner	**Blenheim I**	**L1379**	**Op: Reconnaissance** Took off 1100, Paramythia, one of nine aircraft from 84 and 211 Squadrons detailed to carry out an offensive reconnaissance of the Bousi-Glava area of Albania. An engine cut on take-off and the undercarriage was raised to stop the aircraft. Abandoned on evacuation, late April.

	RAF Takoradi	Blenheim IV	T2250	Unknown

SOC, Takoradi. NFD.

22 Feb 1941	11 Sqn SAAF	Battle I	926	Op: Reconnaissance
	Lt B S M Hamilton SAAF	+		
	F/Sgt J W Dixon SAAF	+		

Took off 0555, Husseini, to reconnoitre the Lamma Garas-Duduma road, Italian Somaliland, for escaping Italian motor transport. Shot down by Capt Palmera, 110 Squadriglia, the pilot dying in the crash. F/Sgt Dixon was captured by colonial troops and executed. Both are buried in the Nairobi War Cemetery.

23 Feb 1941	11 Sqn	Blenheim IV	T2388	Ferrying personnel
	P/O A D P Hewison	+		
	Sgt J S Dukes	+		
	Passengers:			
	LAC G Bevan	+		
	LAC G W Causer	inj		
	Cpl McCrae			
	AC1 J H McQueen	inj		

Took off 1400, Larissa, for Paramythia, to ferry maintenance personnel on detachment. Encountered severe icing over the Pindus Mountains and, unable to climb out of a ravine near Arta, forcelanded in a riverbed. The aircraft hit a tree and was wrecked. The dead are buried at Phaleron War Cemetery.

24-25 Feb 1941	70 Sqn	Wellington IC	T2891 O	Op: Tripoli
	P/O G H Green	+		
	F/Lt A F Pain	+		
	Sgt R Mead	pow		
	Sgt E Green	pow		
	Sgt A E Limbrick RNZAF	pow		
	LAC G Norker	pow		

Took off Luqa. FTR. The survivors bailed out over Catanzano, and the pilots are buried in Naples War Cemetery. The aircraft was far off course on return, running out of fuel some 375km NW of Malta.

25 Feb 1941	70 Sqn	Wellington IC	T2816 J	Ground

Destroyed in an air raid, Luqa. The 148 Sqn ORB records that six aircraft were burnt out and one was written off after a 50-minute air raid by Ju 87s and Ju 88s.

	148 Sqn	Wellington IC	R1247 M	Ground

As above.

	148 Sqn	Wellington IC	R1381 U	Ground

As above.

	148 Sqn	Wellington IC	R1382 A	Ground

As above.

	148 Sqn	Wellington IC	R1383 V	Ground

As above.

	148 Sqn	Wellington IC	R1384 B	Ground

As above.

	148 Sqn	Wellington IC	T2955 W	Ground

As above.

	OADF	Maryland I	AR743	Delivery Flight
	F/O R J S Wootton			
	P/O G N Bails			
	Sgt Forman			

The pilot lost control on take-off 0435, Tangmere, for the Middle East, the aircraft crashed, and was DBR.

27 Feb 1941	11 Sqn	Blenheim IV	N3579	Op: Valona

Took off Paramythia, detailed to attack the airfield at Valona. Attacked and seriously damaged by CR.42 fighters, on return to Paramythia the aircraft was landed wheels-up because of damage to the hydraulics. DBR.

	11 Sqn	Blenheim IV	T2399	Op: Valona

Took off Paramythia, detailed as above. Also seriously damaged by CR.42 fighters and landed at Paramythia wheels-up. DBR.

---

28 Feb 1941

47 Sqn — Wellesley I — K7739 — **Op: Bure**
Sgt E T Cathcart-Cunison
Crew

Took off Gordon's Tree, but forced by engine failure to land in a maize field 80km S of Sennar. The undercarriage was damaged and the aircraft was SOC in Sep 1941 as BER.

47 Sqn — Wellesley I — K7765 — **Op: Bure**
F/Sgt A F Wimsett — pow
Sgt T W J Hatton DFM — pow
Sgt E Merch-Chammon — pow

Took off Gordon's Tree and refuelled at Sennar. Shot down over Bure by flak.

---

6 Mar 1941

47 Sqn — Wellesley I — K7735 — **Ferry Flight**
P/O R M Aldus
Passenger:
P/O D G Astington

Took off Gordon's Tree to ferry P/O Astington to Agordat. On landing the port undercarriage collapsed, and the aircraft was DBF.

---

7 Mar 1941

37 Sqn — Wellington IC — R3239 T — **Transit Flight**
P/O A De L Thomas — +
Sgt L G Mitchell — +
Sgt H H D Cox — +
Sgt J W Bolton RNZAF — +
LAC J A Casey — +
Passengers:
Cpl J F W Dunn — +
Sgt Allmark
Sgt Calwell
LAC Newham
Sgt R H Jacobs — inj

Took off c.0945, Shallufa, for Menidi. On approach the aircraft was baulked by two Avro Tutors of the Greek Air Force. The pilot opened up the engines to come round again, but the port propeller fell off and the heavily laden aircraft lost height and crashed into a wood at Kyphyssia. Sgts Mitchell and Jacobs and LAC Casey were seriously injured, Mitchell dying the same day and Casey on 18 March. The dead are buried at Phaleron War Cemetery.

---

8 Mar 1941

70 Sqn — Wellington IC — T2733 — **Op: Tripoli**
Sgt Fear
Sgt S S Jenkins
Sgt Kerr
Sgt Watt
Sgt Edwards
Sgt Glancey

Took off 1930, Benina, and DBR in heavy landing in bad weather, El Adem, on return. (Sgt Fear's crew is taken from the ops record of 7 March. The crash card gives Sgt Jenkins as the captain.)

84 Sqn — Blenheim I — L1392 — **Practice Night Flight**
Sgt A Gordon DFM
Sgt F Levitt

Took off Menidi/Tatoi, on a series of night practice flights carried out between 1830 and 2100 hours. The undercarriage collapsed after one of the landings when the aircraft was turned too quickly. Abandoned on the evacuation of the airfield.

RAF Takoradi — Blenheim IV — V5441 — **Delivery Flight**
Sgt Marsh
Sgt Finlay
Sgt J Creighton

Took off Takoradi, as part of Delivery Flight 45 to the Middle East, but left at El Geneina on 6 March when it became unserviceable. Took off from El Geneina on 8 March as part of Delivery Flight 46. but crashed on landing at El Fasher. DBR.

---

9 Mar 1941

8 Sqn — Blenheim I — L8504 — **Op: Diredawa**
S/Ldr T J Hanlon
P/O F H Martin DFC
Sgt D McK Muir — inj

Took off 0745, Khormaksar, one of six aircraft detailed to bomb Diredawa airfield. Damaged by CR.42s over the target, it force-landed on Perim Island, SOC 19 March.

14 Mar 1941	148 Sqn	Wellington IC	T2876 Y	Ferry Flight

14 Mar 1941 — **148 Sqn** — **Wellington IC** — **T2876 Y** — **Ferry Flight**

F/Lt W N Perioli — inj
P/O R O Day — inj
P/O Alexander
Sgt J W Hendry — inj
Sgt W P Corser — inj
Cpl A May — inj
AC S Wood — inj
AC R King — inj

Took off Kabrit to ferry passengers to a conference at Heliopolis, but hit a wall while landing in a dust storm. DBR.

---

15 Mar 1941 — **3 Group Training Flt** — **Wellington IC** — **W5644** — **Delivery Flight**

Sgt R H Alington RNZAF — +
P/O R H F Blandy — +
Sgt K H A Vaughan — +
Sgt H E Meason — +
Sgt C Gillespie — +
Sgt J G Crawford — +
Passenger:
G/Capt D d'H Humphreys — +

Took off Gibraltar for Malta. Shot down by Oblt Muncheberg of 7/JG26 NW of Gozo. He saw the crew getting into a dinghy but they were never found, and were presumed drowned. All are commemorated on the Runnymede Memorial.

---

16 Mar 1941 — **47 Sqn** — **Wellesley I** — **K8527** — **Op: Keren**

P/O A G Leuchars — pow
Sgt S W K English — +
Sgt C W Minn — +

Took off Agordat to attack Italian troop concentrations. Shot down by CR.42s over the target, only the pilot managing to bail out. Sgts English and Minn are buried in Keren War Cemetery.

16-17 Mar 1941 — **37 Sqn** — **Wellington IC** — **R1387 D** — **Op: Tirana**

Sgt D C Murrell — +
P/O D L D Willis — pow
Sgt C G Brett — pow
Sgt S Newman — +
Sgt R L Cherrington — +
Sgt R H Smith — pow

Took off 2030, Paramythia. Shot down in flames by CR.42s near Tirana. Sgts Murrell and Newman were buried in Albania (graves now lost – Special Memorial E in Phaleron War Cemetery). Sgt Cherrington is commemorated on the Alamein Memorial.

17-18 Mar 1941 — **70 Sqn** — **Wellington IC** — **T2732** — **Op: Tripoli**

F/Lt R E Ridgway
F/O Abbott
Sgt Birchall
Sgt Sparks
Sgt Evans
Sgt Carroll

Took off 2230, Benina. Developed engine trouble over target, and overshot landing and hit a drum, Benina, on return. The flarepath was laid out of wind, and not sufficiently cleared of obstacles. DBR.

---

18 Mar 1941 — **47 Sqn** — **Wellesley I** — **K7786** — **Ground**

Destroyed in a strafing attack by CR.32 and CR.42 fighters, Agordat.

55 Sqn — **Blenheim IV** — **T1995** — **Op: Sirte and Mechina**

F/O T O Walker MiD — +
Sgt E P Collingborn — +
Sgt B Lee — +

Took off 0730, Marwa, to reconnoitre the airfields at Sirte and Mechina. Last seen by a Hurricane at 0800 near Benina. The crew is commemorated on the Alamein Memorial.

223 Sqn — **Wellesley I** — **L2695 B** — **Op: Keren**

Sgt L W Bangley
Sgt J Frost
Sgt G R Potter

Took off Wadi Gazouza to bomb Keren. Hit over the target by flak which damaged the hydraulics and pierced a fuel tank. The crew successfully lowered the undercarriage by hand, but the brakes were unserviceable and the aircraft overran the aerodrome and crashed into a ditch. Presumed SOC.

18-19 Mar 1941	**3 Group Training Flt** Sgt A G D Mackay Sgt A L Millington Sgt A R Butler Sgt J W T House Sgt W Ainsbury Sgt S H R Bevan RNZAF	**Wellington IC** pow pow pow pow pow pow	**W5630** **Delivery Flight** Took off 1948, Stradishall, to fly directly to Benina. Encountered cloud over N African coast and, with the radio unserviceable, was unable to get a QDM. Hit by flak and landed in enemy-held territory. The crew, ex-9 Sqn, set fire to the aircraft. (A detailed account of this loss is given in Chaz Bowyer's *Wellington at War*, pp36-43.)
19 Mar 1941	**223 Sqn** P/O E G L Pelling F/O I White Sgt W McCarthy	**Wellesley I**	**L2698 Y** **Op: Keren** Took off 0235, Wadi Gazouza, to bomb enemy positions. On the return flight the engine seized and the aircraft belly-landed 55km S of El Muhena, Sudan. SOC.
20 Mar 1941	**47 Sqn** Sgt A G Brown Sgt H L Oddy Sgt A Sleight	**Wellesley I**	**K7725** **Op: Gondar** Took off 0715, Agordat, to bomb Italian positions at Gondar. On landing, 1015, swung and the undercarriage collapsed. DBR.
22 Mar 1941	**211 Sqn**	**Blenheim I**	**L1490** **Ground** Almost certainly DBR in a strafing attack on Paramythia by MC.200 fighters of 153 Gruppo CT. SOC 10 June.
	211 Sqn	**Blenheim I**	**L8531** **Ground** Set on fire, Paramythia, during a strafing attack as above. The bomb load exploded and the aircraft was destroyed. SOC 5 April.
	211 Sqn	**Blenheim I**	**L8533** **Ground** As above.
25 Mar 1941	**47 Sqn** P/O W S Kennedy DFC Sgt J S Turner DFM Sgt D A German +	**Wellesley I**	**K7715** **Op: Keren** Took off Agordat, to bomb enemy positions. Attacked by two CR.42 fighters the aircraft caught fire, but the pilot extinguished the flames by diving vertically, and nursed the aircraft back to Agordat, where it crashed on landing. SOC 12 April. Sgt German, mortally wounded, died the following day and is buried in Keren War Cemetery.
28 Mar 1941	**203 Sqn** F/O P Moller + Sgt G E Salisbury + Sgt W A L Davidson +	**Blenheim IV**	**T2255** **Op: Awash-Adama** Took off 0705, Khormaksar, on reconnaissance. Brought down by flak near Awash. The crew is commemorated on the Alamein Memorial.
29 Mar 1941	**11 Sqn** P/O P Montague-Bates	**Blenheim IV**	**R2780** **Unknown** Swung on landing at Almyros, and the undercarriage collapsed. The aircraft was abandoned on evacuation.
30 Mar 1941	**84 Sqn** Sgt J M Hutcheson Sgt K J Irwin Sgt J Webb	**Blenheim I**	**L1390** **Op: Ebasan** Took off 1125, Menidi/Tatoi, one of ten aircraft detailed to bomb military buildings at Elbasan. Badly damaged by flak over the target, one engine seizing and the other running erratically. The aircraft crash-landed at Heaolis, 53km S of Koritsa.
	148 Sqn F/O Hartford DFC Crew	**Wellington IC**	**T2890 E** **Op:** Took off from Gambut. An engine cut and on return the aircraft was belly-landed there; awaiting repair, it was burnt on the evacuation of the airfield.

31 Mar 1941	8 Sqn P/O J A Barke DFC Sgt R W Scott Sgt G C Moore	Blenheim I	pow pow +	L8433	Op: Dessie

L8433 — **Op: Dessie**
Took off 1147, Khormaksar, to bomb a petrol dump N of Dessie. Shot down by a CR.32 fighter (Serg Mag Luigi Baron, 412 Squadriglia). The two survivors, both wounded, were released in April. Sgt Moore is buried in Addis Ababa War Cemetery.

OADU — Blenheim IV — **V6434** — **Ground**
Destroyed in an air raid, Luqa.

---

1 Apr 1941 — **55 Sqn** — Blenheim IV — **V5423** — **Op: Reconnaissance**
F/O M S Ferguson +
Lt A Pettigrew RN +
Sgt J W Turner RAAF +
Took off 1525, Marawa, to reconnoitre the Tripoli area. Shot down into the sea SW of Benghazi. The crew were sighted in a dinghy at one point, but could not later be found. Lt Pettigrew was attached to 55 Sqn from 826 Sqn, Fleet Air Arm, serving on HMS *Formidable*. He is commemorated on the Fleet Air Arm Memorial at Lee-on-Solent, while the other two crew members are commemorated on the Alamein Memorial.

84 Sqn — Blenheim IV — **T2382** — **Unknown**
F/Lt D G Boehm +
Sgt K G Lee +
LAC H Jackson +
Crashed at Kiphissia, NE of Athens, and DBF. Cause unknown. All are buried in Phaleron War Cemetery.

113 Sqn — Blenheim I — **L8461** — **Unknown**
Lost. NFD.

---

3 Apr 1941 — **223 Sqn** — Wellesley I — **K7720 S** — **Op: Italian Destroyers**
F/O P D C Thomas DFC
F/O E G H Heath
Sgt N Smith
Took off 1015, Port Sudan, part of a force of Blenheims (14 Sqn) and Wellesleys detailed to attack two Italian destroyers, the *Tigre* and *Pantera*, which were transferring fuel some 20km S of Jeddah. K7720 suffered engine failure over the target and belly-landed on the foreshore near the ships. The crew was rescued by other aircraft from 223 Sqn, the Wellesley being burnt. (see below)

223 Sqn — Wellesley I — **K8530 M** — **Op: Italian Destroyers**
F/Lt W A Wild
Sgt A K T Graham
Sgt W M Perks
Took off 1015, Port Sudan, as above. Landed to pick up crew of K7720 but nosed over while taxying, it was burnt by the crew, who like that of K7720, were rescued by other 223 Sqn aircraft, which landed 7km S of the crash site.

---

4 Apr 1941 — **FF (Bomber) Flt 1** — Blenheim IV — **Z5728** — **Unknown**
Cne G F Lager FAFL
Lost prop and undercarriage jammed; crash-landed E of Sennar

5-6 Apr 1941 — **148 Sqn** — Wellington IC — **R1251 L** — **Unknown**
Sgt J G Broad-Smith
Crew
Engine cut; lost height and belly-landed near Sollum. Destroyed by crew.

---

6 Apr 1941 — **55 Sqn** — Blenheim IV — **L6657** — **Ground**
Destroyed by the army on the evacuation of Gazala North. SOC 22 April.

55 Sqn — Blenheim IV — **T2180** — **Ground**
Destroyed by the army on the evacuation of Gazala North. SOC 22 April.

55 Sqn — Blenheim IV — **T2344** — **Ground**
As above.

	55 Sqn	**Blenheim IV**	**Z5862** **Ground**

55 Sqn   **Blenheim IV**   **Z5862**   **Ground**
Probably destroyed by the army on the evacuation of
Gazala North. SOC 19 April.

113 Sqn   **Blenheim IV**   **L9338**   **Unknown**
Sgt V F McPherson   Overshot landing, Niamata, and ran into a canal.
Crew   Abandoned on evacuation.

113 Sqn   **Blenheim IV**   **T2168**   **Op: Petris**
Sgt K R Price DFM   inj   Took off Niamata. On return at 1930 overshot on landing
Sgt J D Woodcock   inj   and ran into a canal. Abandoned on evacuation.
Sgt J Rooney   inj

3 Group Training Flt   **Wellington IC**   **W5618**   **Delivery Flight**
Sgt R Marr   Took off Stradishall for Malta. Forced by bad weather to
Crew   turn back over France, and stalled and crashed just W of
  Tangmere because of icing.

6-7 Apr   **3 Group Training Flt**   **Wellington IC**   **N2818**   **Delivery Flight**
1941   P/O G T Kimberley RNZAF   +   Took off Stradishall for Malta, but crashed into a hill 5km
Sgt K R Allen   +   E of Ras El Akba, Algeria, while descending through
Sgt H L Williams   +   cloud, presumably to establish its position. All are buried
Sgt R W Fairlamb   +   at Bône.
Sgt R C McCracken   +
Sgt W A Watts   +

7 Apr   **11 Sqn SAAF**   **Battle I**   **906**   **Op: Reconnaissance**
1941   Lt M E James SAAF   +   Took off 0635 Gumbar Dug, detailed with two others to
Air Sgt R C Wallace SAAF   +   reconnoitre Sire, Robe, Bek'oj and Sela. Flying up a
  ravine in the Siri Roti Mountains in bad visibility struck
  the mountainside and exploded. The crew is
  commemorated on the Alamein Memorial.

70 Sqn   **Wellington IC**   **T2995**   **Op: Tobruk**
F/O V R C E Harcourt   Belly landed after engine failure shortly after take-off,
Sgt Moir   Fuka Main. Not repaired; SOC 7 October.
Sgt Pipe
Sgt Burroughs
Sgt Powell
P/O Morris

Chapter 4

Greece, Iraq and Syria
April to July 1941

On 28th October 1940, after the Greek Government rejected Italy's territorial demands, the latter invaded Greece from Albania. Though the initial Italian assault was held, and the Greek army soon took the offensive, driving the Italians back into Albania, the British government, and particularly the Prime Minister, Mr Churchill, pressed the Greek government to accept ground and air support. The Greek Prime Minister, General Metaxas, refused the former, convinced (rightly, as it turned out) that what the British could provide might well provoke German intervention but would prove insufficient to halt a German onslaught. Nonetheless, the offer of air support was accepted, and a small force moved to Greece in early November, this including 30 Squadron with its Blenheim Is and IFs, followed shortly after by 84 Squadron, and late in November by 211 Squadron, also with Blenheim Is. These units carried out daylight raids on targets in Albania, in support of the Greek army, while 70 Squadron Wellingtons operated on detachment from Greek bases to bomb ports in mainland Italy, a task shared, from 1st December, by the newly formed 148 Squadron, based on Malta.

In January 1941 the Blenheim force was strengthened by the arrival of 11 Squadron, while from early February 37 (and later 38) Squadron Wellingtons operated on detachment. The first Blenheim IVs (of 113 Squadron) arrived at the beginning of March, just ahead of the first ground forces, the British government having persuaded the successor to General Metaxas, who died in January, that this was a sound move. It proved precisely the contrary, as on 6th April the Germans invaded in overwhelming force, both on the ground and in the air. By the end of the month the Greek campaign was over, with air and ground forces evacuated either to Crete or to Egypt. The losses in aircraft and crews, particularly by the Blenheim squadrons, were very heavy, with one unit, 113 Squadron, arriving in Greece on 25th March, but losing all its aircraft in a bombing and strafing attack on 15th April. In addition to those destroyed, many damaged aircraft had to be abandoned as the Anglo-Greek armies retreated.

On Crete, in May, the scenario was repeated; a German airborne invasion, begun on 20th May, succeeding at great cost, with a further British evacuation, to Egypt, being completed by 28th May. Once again, the day bomber squadrons suffered heavily in their futile attempt to hinder the invasion forces. May 1941 brought further trouble, this time in Iraq, where intensifying anti-British feeling, encouraged by the Axis victories in Greece and Crete, reached a peak with a coup in which Rashid Ali el Ghailani, a former Prime Minister with strong pro-Axis sympathies, took power. With the prospect of an interruption to its oil supplies looming, Britain took action, General Wavell informing the new government that, in conformity with the terms of the treaty between Iraq and Britain, he intended to land troops in Iraq en route to Palestine. On the 17th the first contingent was airlifted in, and others followed before the end of the month. In retaliation, Rashid Ali surrounded the RAF base at Habbaniyah, outside Baghdad, on 1st May, and the investment of the base, which was to continue for a week, began, Iraqi forces shelling the base, but not attempting a ground assault.

Habbaniyah, being a training station, was equipped with a variety of mostly obsolete aircraft, such as the Fairey Gordon and Hawker Audax, as well as Airspeed Oxfords. A handful of Gladiator fighters, and a solitary Blenheim I comprised the only reasonably modern operational types. With this motley assortment of aircraft, continuous attacks were mounted against the investing infantry and artillery, and reinforced by Wellingtons of 37 and 70 squadrons, operating on detachment from the second RAF base in Iraq, Shaibah, as well as Blenheim IVs of 84 and 203 Squadrons, this forced the Iraqi forces to withdraw. By this time, 8th May, the Iraqi air force had virtually ceased to exist, which was fortunate, since on 12th May there arrived in northern Iraq a Luftwaffe force comprising 14 Messerschmitt Bf 110s, and seven Heinkel He 111H6 bombers. A small contingent of Italian fighters also flew in. They were, however, too late, and deprived of adequate ground support as well as air cover, they rapidly dwindled into insignificance. By the end of May Iraqi resistance had been broken, Rashid Ali fled, and military operations in Iraq ceased.

During the Iraqi insurrection, airfields in Vichy French Syria had been freely used by both German and Italian aircraft en route to Iraq, and had, in consequence been attacked by RAF bombers. The tension this generated was heightened by rumours (unfounded) that airfields in Syria and Lebanon were to be turned over to the Germans, but though the Free French urged an invasion, General Wavell, seeing his first priority a forthcoming offensive in the Western Desert, was unwilling to undertake it. He was overruled by the Chiefs of Staff, the Prime Minister being a proponent of the invasion, and so *Exporter* was planned. The invasion itself did not begin until 8th June, by which time, ironically, all Axis aircraft and personnel had left Syria, but air operations began three days earlier, with a small-scale (and ineffectual) attack on the Royal Dutch Shell oil depot at Beirut. Most of the air fighting during the campaign, which ended with an armistice on 12th July, involved (on the British side) fighter units, but Blenheims of 11, 45 and 84 Squadrons and Wellingtons from 37, 38, 70 and 148 Squadrons, released after Operation *Battleaxe* ground to a halt in the Western Desert, were active.

Meanwhile in East Africa, the destruction of the Italian Empire was proceeding apace. With the capture of Massawa on 8th April, virtually all Eritrea was in Allied hands, while two days earlier Addis Ababa was evacuated by the Italians, enabling Emperor Haile Selassie to return in triumph. Pockets of Italian forces continued to resist, but by the end of July, only Gondar remained in Italian hands, Generale Nasi being surrounded there with 25,000 troops. As earlier, the bulk of the air offensive was undertaken by the SAAF, operating its elderly Ju 86s and Fairey Battles, with support from a Free French unit, GRB1, operating Blenheims, and 47 Squadron, still equipped with Wellesleys. Other bomber units had been withdrawn, as had most of the RAF fighter units, to assist in North Africa.

In North Africa, meanwhile, there had been thrust and counterthrust, but in the end not much change. Besieged in Tobruk, the Australians, later relieved by British units, held off repeated Axis attacks, not being relieved until November, but two attempts were made during the summer to drive Rommel back and relieve the garrison. The first, codenamed Operation *Brevity*, began on 15th May, lasted 36 hours, and after initial success, ended ignominiously in retreat. The second, Operation *Battleaxe*, began on 14th June, and had as its aim driving Rommel back west of Tobruk. Once again initial success gave way to failure as Rommel counter-attacked, and in three days the British forces were back where they had started, having lost 91 tanks to the Germans' 12. Thereafter stalemate ensued, not to be broken until the new British offensive in the autumn.

During this period a by now familiar pattern of activity prevailed, with the four Wellington squadrons bombing ports and airfields, while the day bomber squadrons, the RAF units equipped with Blenheim IVs and the SAAF squadrons with Marylands, focused on targets more closely aligned with the needs of the ground forces, including motor transport, and reconnaissance. On occasions the day bomber units could suffer severe casualties, as in the seven days beginning 21st May, when 14 Squadron lost twelve Blenheims attacking targets in Libya and Crete.

On Malta, meanwhile, the German onslaught continued unabated, with a 148 Squadron detachment operating its Wellingtons only with great difficulty. The decision was thus taken to withdraw the Wellingtons temporarily, and they left on 27th April for Egypt. The same day saw, however, the arrival of 6 Blenheims of 21 Squadron, detached from Bomber Command to operate primarily against Axis shipping. In mid-May they would be reinforced by detachments from 139 and then 82 Squadrons, with the latter being brought up to full squadron strength at the beginning of June. The anti-shipping attacks, which the Blenheims pressed home with great courage, were to prove increasingly costly, as the numbers of the accompanying destroyer-escorts were increased, and flak defences were strengthened. A particularly severe loss was suffered by 110 Squadron Blenheims in an attack on vessels in Tripoli harbour on 9th July, four of the seven aircraft despatched failing to return. Fortunately, during May and June, Luftwaffe units had been gradually withdrawn to Germany in preparation for the invasion of Russia, or to North Africa, in support of General Rommel and the Afrika Korps.

8 Apr 1941	11 Sqn	Blenheim IV	T2247	Op: Strumica-Petric
	P/O R J Coombs		inj	Took off 1230, Almyros, to attack a German motorised
	Sgt C H C Randall		inj	column moving westwards. One engine failed just after
	Sgt L J Macey			take-off and the aircraft force-landed 2km S of the airfield. The pilot was seriously injured.
	55 Sqn	Blenheim IV	T2381	Op: Reconnaissance
	F/Sgt E P C Vignaux		+	Took off LG 145 (Tobruk No 2/El Gubbi West), to
	Sgt R S Browning		+	reconnoitre Benghazi. NFD. The crew is buried in the
	Sgt E J Cook		+	Knightsbridge War Cemetery, Acroma.
	84 Sqn	Blenheim IV	Z5897	Unknown
	S/Ldr H D Jones		inj	Crashed 1330 in a forced landing in bad weather,
	Sgt H Keen			Kereechori. DBF.
	F/O R Trevor-Roper			
	148 Sqn	Wellington IC	Q	Unknown
	Sgt Fennell			Took off El Adem, perhaps on an air test, and the tail
	Crew			wheel collapsed when landing at El Adem. The aircraft was later burnt out when another aircraft ran into it at the end of its landing run. The serial number is uncertain.
9-10 Apr 1941	148 Sqn	Wellington IC	T2952 H	Transit Flight
	F/Sgt H P Adams		+	Took off LG 29 (Almirya) for Malta. Ran out of fuel and
	F/Sgt P Cramp		+	ditched. F/Sgt Cramp and Sgt Sellors are commemorated
	Sgt K W Clifton		+	on the Malta Memorial, the remainder on the Alamein
	Sgt J E Sellors		+	Memorial.
	Sgt J L McNamara RNZAF		+	
	Sgt H L Moody		+	

3 Group Training Flt	**Wellington IC**	W5677	**Delivery Flight**
F/Lt J W E Bridger	pow		
F/O R L Cox	pow		
Sgt D C B Jenkins RNZAF	pow		
Sgt L Hudson	pow		
Sgt J A Collett	pow		
Sgt R J Blackstock RNZAF	pow		
Passenger:			
Gen Carton de Wiart VC CB CMG DSO	pow		

Took off Luqa for Abu Sueir, but ditched off Apollonia on the North African coast after engine trouble. The crew and their passenger, General Carton de Wiart (new head of the British Military Mission to Yugoslavia), swam ashore and were taken prisoner by the Italians. Sgts Blackstock and Hudson, at least, were injured.

---

10 Apr 1941

84 Sqn	**Blenheim IV**	T2164	**Op: Transporting VIP**
P/O J C Eldred			
Sgt A L Loudon	evd		
Sgt A J Acres	evd		
Passenger:			
Greek Army general	inj		

Took off Menidi/Tatoi to fly a Greek general to Sarajevo, Yugoslavia. In bad visibility attempted a forcelanding in a small field at Bar, Montenegro, but crashed. The crew made their way to Cetinje where the injured pilot and observer were admitted to hospital, the pilot being evacuated to Greece a week later by flying boat. Sgts Loudon and Acres evaded capture, making their way through Yugoslavia and Italy, finally reaching Lisbon, whence they were flown back to the UK on 19 June.

11 Sqn SAAF	**Battle I**	909	**Op: Shashemene**
Lt M G T Ferreira SAAF	+		
Air Sgt R Grant SAAF	+		

Took off Gumbar Dug to attack airfields at Shashemene. The crew lost formation in dense cloud and crashed, for reasons unknown, near Deder. The two crew were buried in Addis Ababa War Cemetery.

---

11 Apr 1941

84 Sqn	**Blenheim IV**	L8612	**Op: Monastir Gap**
F/Sgt L Nuttall	+		
F/Sgt A J Neal	+		
Sgt G R Thistle	+		

Took off Menidi/Tatoi, one of six aircraft detailed to bomb German troop concentrations. Shot down by ground fire. The crew is commemorated on the Alamein Memorial.

148 Sqn	**Wellington IC**	T2817 K	**Air Test**
Sgt J K Hutt			
Crew			

Took off Kabrit on an airframe and engine test, but overshot on landing, bounced, and raised the undercarriage to avoid crashing into parked aircraft. DBR.

---

12 Apr 1941

45 Sqn	**Blenheim IV**	Z5894	**Communication Flight**
P/O P J Vincent			
Sgt L E Small			
Sgt D O Cliffe			

Took off LG 170 (Bir el Gubi), for LG 11, Qasaba Damaged by enemy fighters and then became lost in a sandstorm. Force-landed in the desert.

---

13 Apr 1941

211 Sqn	**Blenheim I**	L1434	**Op: Florina**
F/Lt L B Buchanan DFC	+		
S/Ldr L E Cryer DFC	+		
Sgt G Pattison DFM	+		

Took off 1500, Paramythia, one of six detailed to attack German ground units around Florina. The formation was intercepted 20-30km from the target by Bf 109E4 fighters of JG27/6 and all were shot down. F/Lt Buchanan managed to effect a ditching in the SE corner of Lake Prespa. It is believed the pilot and gunner died in an Albanian hospital. All are commemorated on the Alamein Memorial. In 1993 the remains of L1434 were recovered from the lake bed; they are now on display in the Greek Air Force Museum, Athens.

211 Sqn	**Blenheim I**	L1539	**Op: Florina**
F/Sgt A G James			
F/Sgt A Bryce	+		
Sgt A J Waring	+		

As above. Shot down by Fw Krenz. F/Sgt James bailed out at low level and broke his ankle on landing near the lakeside village of Mikrolimni. He managed to reach Larissa and obtained a lift to Athens in a Lysander. This, however, was shot down on take-off by a Bf 109 and F/Sgt James was killed. He and Sgt Waring are commemorated on the Alamein Memorial, while F/Sgt Bryce is buried in Phaleron War Cemetery.

211 Sqn	Blenheim I	L4819	Op: Florina
F/O R V Herbert	+		
W/Cdr P B Coote	+		
F/Sgt W N Young	+		

As above. Shot down by Uffz F Gromotka near the village of Trigonon. The crew is buried in Phaleron War Cemetery. W/Cdr Coote was the RAF Area Commander.

211 Sqn	Blenheim I	L8449	Op: Florina
F/O A C Godfrey			
Sgt J B T O'Neill	+		
F/Sgt J Wainhouse	+		

As above. Shot down by Hauptmann H-J Gelach near the village of Karya. F/O Godfrey managed to bail out and was picked up by an Australian army truck, reaching Larissa on the 14th. Along with F/Sgt James (see L1539 above) he was in a Lysander shot down on take-off by a strafing Bf 109, losing two fingers. He was evacuated later that day to hospital in Athens. The observer and WOp/AG are buried in Phaleron War Cemetery.

211 Sqn	Blenheim I	L8478	Op: Florina
S/Ldr A T Irvine MiD	+		
P/O G Davies	+		
P/O A C Geary DFC	+		

As above. Shot down by Hauptmann Gelach N of the hamlet of Vigla. The crew is buried in Phaleron War Cemetery, Athens. S/Ldr Irvine was the squadron CO.

211 Sqn	Blenheim I	L8664	Op: Florina
F/O C E V Thompson DFC	+		
P/O P Hogarth	+		
F/ Sgt W Arscott	+		

As above. Shot down by Uffz Gromotka near the village of Karya. The crew is commemorated on the Alamein Memorial.

FF (Bomber) Flt 1	Blenheim IV	N3557	Communication Flight
Slt G Grassete FAFL			

Took off 0525 GMT, Gordon's Tree, for Aden, but the pilot retracted the undercarriage prematurely and the aircraft was DBR.

13-14 Apr 1941	38 Sqn	Wellington IC	R1033	Op: Eleusis
	F/O H W S Adams	+		
	P/O A C Holburn	+		
	Sgt C A E Birtles	+		
	Sgt S Miara	+		
	Sgt F G C Downes	+		
	Sgt J M Lowe	+		

Took off 2030, Shallufa. FTR. All are commemorated on the Alamein Memorial.

14 Apr 1941	113 Sqn	Blenheim IV	T2177 V	Supply drop
	F/O G E P Green DFC			
	Sgt W B Gingell DFM			
	Sgt K A Jamieson			

Took off Niamata to drop unfused bombs for New Zealand sappers to use to destroy a bridge. Hit in the port engine and undercarriage by friendly AA fire. The aircraft crash-landed at Niamata and was further damaged in the strafing attack on the airfield the next day (see below). Abandoned on evacuation.

15 Apr 1941	14 Sqn	Blenheim IV	Z5863	Op: Reconnaissance
	P/O I Ormiston	+		
	Sgt A H L Fraser RNZAF	+		
	Sgt E J Smith	pow		

Took off Heliopolis on a reconnaissance of Halfaya-Sollum but FTR. Sgt Smith, wounded, managed to bail out. The others are buried in the Halfaya Sollum War Cemetery.

113 Sqn	Blenheim IV	T2054	Ground

In a strafing attack on Niamata airfield, German fighters eliminated 113 Squadron as a fighting unit, those aircraft not destroyed having to be abandoned when the airfield was evacuated.

113 Sqn	Blenheim IV	T2069	Ground

As above.

113 Sqn	Blenheim IV	T2169	Ground

In a strafing attack on Niamata airfield, German fighters eliminated 113 Squadron as a fighting unit, those aircraft not destroyed having to be abandoned when the airfield was evacuated.

113 Sqn	Blenheim IV	T2182	Ground

As above.

113 Sqn	Blenheim IV	T2186	Ground

As above.

113 Sqn	Blenheim IV	T2216	Ground

As above.

17 Apr 1941

55 Sqn	Blenheim IV	L9322	Unknown

Possibly lost at 1630 on the 5/4/1941 when the landing ground at Derna was strafed and two Blenheims and two Lysanders were so badly damaged that they were destroyed by the army the following day to prevent them falling into enemy hands. SOC 17 April.

55 Sqn	Blenheim IV	T2242	Unknown

SOC. Possibly DBR in the same attack as L9322.

18 Apr 1941

11 Sqn	Blenheim IV	T2348	Op: Kozáni
P/O P Montague-Bates	+		
P/O H R Edge			
Sgt H Murphy	+		

Took off Menidi to attack Axis motor transport near Kozáni. Shot down by a Bf 109E (Oblt A Schmidt of 9/JG77) after attacking a German troop column. The pilot and WOp/AG are commemorated on the Alamein Memorial. P/O Edge made his way to Allied lines.

45 Sqn	Blenheim IV	V5438	Op: El Adem and Bardia
F/O E G Collins	+		
Sgt E J Street	+		
Sgt R H C Crook	+		

Took off LG 17 (Fuka Main) to bomb motor transport at El Adem and between El Adem and Bardia. Shot down over Cyrenaica. Sgt Street is buried in Halfaya Sollum War Cemetery, the others commemorated on the Alamein Memorial.

84 Sqn	Blenheim I	L1391 J	Op: Katerina and Grevena
S/Ldr H D Jones	+		
F/Sgt J Webb	+		
Sgt H Keen	+		

Took off Menidi/Tatoi, one of 14 aircraft detailed to attack enemy forces around Katerina and Grevena. Attacked over Larissa by Bf 110s, pursued out over the Aegean and and eventually ditched. The crew climbed into their dinghy, but while paddling to shore were strafed by the German fighters and killed.S/Ldr Jones is buried in Phaleron War Cemetery, the others commemorated on the Alamein Memorial.

19 Apr 1941

11 Sqn SAAF	Battle I	924	Op: Kembolcha Pass, Dese
Capt J F Britz SAAF	pow		
2/Lt C B Hangar SAAF	pow		

Took off 0845, Gumbar Dug, to attack Italian positions. Hit by ground fire, the aircraft crash-landed at Kembolcha airfield, still in Italian hands. The crew were taken prisoner and held at Dessie until it was recaptured by Allied troops.

RAF Takoradi	Blenheim IV	V5643	Delivery Flight
F/O J R Whelan			
Sgt W A M Dunjey			
Sgt Dyball			

Took off El Geneina, on delivery flight 77 to El Fasher. Both engines cut and the undercarriage collapsed in a forced landing at Kabkabiyah, Sudan. DBR and SOC 9 October.

Date	Sqn	Aircraft	Serial	Op

20 Apr 1941 — **11 Sqn** — **Blenheim IV** — **T2341** — **Ground**
One of four Blenheims of 11 and 211 Squadrons written off after a low-level strafing attack by 10 Bf 109s at 0735.

11 Sqn — **Blenheim IV** — **Z5769** — **Ground**
Probably one of the above. SOC 30 April.

11 Sqn — **Blenheim IV** — **Z5885** — **Ground**
Probably one of the above. SOC 30 April.

21 Apr 1941 — **11 Sqn** — **Blenheim IV** — **N3560** — **Evacuation transport**
P/O A T Darling — inj
Passengers
Took off Menidi to transport 11 Sqn personnel to Crete. A tyre burst on landing at Heraklion, the aircraft swung violently and the undercarriage collapsed. The aircraft was abandoned on evacuation.

24 Sqn SAAF — **Maryland I** — **1626** — **Ferry Flight**
2/Lt B R Haupt SAAF — inj
2/Lt E Coltsman-Cronin SAAF — +
Sgt W J Roscoe SAAF — inj
Sgt C D Herbst SAAF — inj
Took off Khartoum for Wadi Halfa, one of three en route from South Africa to Egypt. A sandstorm was encountered, an engine cut and with the crew unable to locate Wadi Halfa aerodrome, the aircraft crashed nearby. 2/Lt Coltsman-Cronin is buried in the Khartoum War Cemetery.

38 Sqn — **Wellington IC** — **T2993 E** — **Op: Burre**
P/O Slatter
Crew
Took off Fuka. detailed to bomb Benghazi, but bombed Burre instead. SOC. NFD.

22 Apr 1941 — **11 Sqn** — **Blenheim I** — **L1481** — **Op: Evacuation Transport**
Sgt V G Hudson DFM
Took off Heraklion, returning to Greece to evacuate more squadron personnel. Attacked by four Italian CR.42 fighters off Argos, and ditched. The pilot was flying solo.

45 Sqn — **Blenheim IV** — **V5625** — **Op: Benghazi**
F/Sgt W Beverley — +
Sgt R W Gentry — +
Sgt V W J Harrison — +
Took off 0645, LG 17 (Fuka Main), one of three aircraft detailed to bomb Benghazi harbour. Shot down by flak. The crew is commemorated on the Alamein Memorial.

GRB1 — **Blenheim IV** — **Z5727** — **Communication Flight**
F/Sgt J Guillou de Mezillis FAFL — inj
F/Sgt J Bost FAFL — inj
F/Sgt P Robinet FAFL — +
Took off Fort Lamy, Chad, for Khartoum, but suffered mechanical failure and crash-landed in the desert. The pilot was serious injured. F/Sgt Robinet is buried in Moussoro, Chad.

23 Apr 1941 — **55 Sqn** — **Blenheim IV** — **T1873** — **Op: Gazala**
Sgt T Fullarton — +
Sgt H S Latta RNZAF — +
Sgt G McLaren — +
Took off 1114, LG 14 (Maaten Bagush), one of six aircraft detailed to bomb Gazala No 1 Landing Ground. After bombing the formation was intercepted 32km W of Tobruk by two Bf 109s, this aircraft being shot down in flames into the Mediterranean after a running fight of 15 minutes, almost certainly by ObLt Wolfgang Redlich (1/JG27) who claimed two Blenheims in this area. The crew is commemorated on the Alamein Memorial.

24 Apr 1941 — **45 Sqn** — **Blenheim IV** — **T2170** — **Op: Fort Capuzzo**
F/O F W Chadwick
Sgt A Burns
Sgt T Turnbull
Took off 1715, LG 17 (Fuka Main), to bomb motor transport near Fort Capuzzo. Returning at night, the pilot was forced down by cloud, levelling out at 800ft in an attempt to establish his position, but flew into a high ridge at 2215 hrs, approximately 4km S of Mersa Matruh.

	45 Sqn Lt E Jones SAAF P/O L P Bourke RNZAF Sgt S B Whiteley	**Blenheim IV**	**T2174**	**Op: Fort Capuzzo** As above. One engine cut on return and the aircraft crash-landed 8km E of Mersa Matruh.
	OADF Sgt A McVicar Sgt W J Wills Sgt J R Lang	**Blenheim IV** +	**V5584**	**Delivery Flight** Took off Takoradi on delivery flight No 83 to the Middle East. On landing at El Fasher the aircraft was hit by a 'sand devil', the pilot lost control and the aircraft spun into the ground. Sgt McVicar is buried in Khartoum War Cemetery.
25 Apr **1941**	**3 Group Training Flt** F/Lt E F Nind P/O D W Allen Sgt E S Hill Sgt J J Hagen Sgt Dwyer Sgt Culver	**Wellington IC** inj inj inj inj	**T2726**	**Delivery Flight** Took off St Eval for Gibraltar. The crew took a bearing as a course and flew away from Gibraltar. When the error was discovered there was insufficient fuel to reach Gibraltar and the aircraft was ditched.
26 Apr **1941**	**3 Group Training Flt** S/Ldr C F Rodney F/Lt E M Child-Villiers Sgt C S Hunt Sgt C H Burge Sgt H E Herritey Sgt N O Horrocks	**Wellington IC** int int int int int int	**W5652**	**Delivery Flight** Took off Stradishall for Malta. Crashed in a forced landing, Formentara, Balearic Isles, and destroyed by the crew. Sgt Hunt died accidentally during internment. He is buried in the Palma Municipal Cemetery, Majorca. The others were interned until April 1942.
27 Apr **1941**	**47 Sqn** Sgt R J Moore	**Wellesley I**	**K7780**	**Mail Flight** Landed at Kassala with the undercarriage not locked. SOC 12 August.
	203 Sqn F/Lt J C Whittall Sgt S O'Connor Sgt T J Air	**Blenheim IV** + + +	**L9237 S**	**Op: Convoy Escort** Took off 0615, Heraklion, one of three detailed to provide air cover for a convoy off the island of Hydra. A strong Luftwaffe force, comprising Ju 87s, Bf 110s and Bf 109s was encountered, and the aircraft was last seen attacking a Bf 110 and diving steeply away. The crew is commemorated on the Alamein Memorial.
28 Apr **1941**	**15 Sqn** Sgt D S Walsh Sgt P R Herbert Sgt R H P Humphris Sgt L McLean Sgt R W Channer Sgt J Golding	**Wellington IC** int int int int + +	**R1080**	**Delivery Flight** Took off Wyton 2020 for Gibraltar, but ditched out of fuel 40km off Malaga. Sgts Channer and Golding drowned, Channer attempting to save Golding. The others drifted in their dinghy for 10 days before being rescued by a Vichy French ship and interned in Marseilles. Two escaped and were arrested in Spain. The dead are commemorated on the Runnymede Memorial. The Wellington was reported to have floated for at least two days.
	45 Sqn Sgt D Naldrett-Jays Sgt J R Prockter Sgt A W Dann	**Blenheim IV** inj	**T2345**	**Op: Derna** Took off LG 17 (Fuka Main), one of four detailed, with Blenheims of 55 Sqn, to destroy parked Ju 52 transports at Derna. Became lost in low cloud returning at night, and belly-landed 27km S of El Alamein. SOC 10 June.
	45 Sqn P/O B C de G Allan F/Sgt L W Morling Passengers: W/Cdr D V Johnson	**Blenheim IV** + + +	**Z5898**	**Communications Flight** Took off Tobruk to transport passengers back to Egypt, and immediately attacked by five Bf 109 fighters and shot down off the coast. All are commemorated on the Alamein Memorial.

	S/Ldr the Rev J E Cox	+	
	S/Ldr D P Barclay	+	
	P/O S E Beloe	+	
	Capt R W Plowwright	+	

203 Sqn   **Blenheim IV**   **L9044**   **Op: Convoy Escort**
F/O P N Gordon-Hall
Sgt G Poole
Sgt I B Oultram

Took off 0620, Heraklion, to provide air cover for a convoy W of the island of Melos. On joining the convoy at 0704 the aircraft was fired on despite full recognition being followed. The starboard engine caught fire at 0817 and the pilot attempted a return to base but crash-landed 2km N of Retimo at 0850. SOC.

28-29 Apr 1941   **70 Sqn**   **Wellington IC**   **T2727**   **Op: Benghazi**

F/O B S M Jones — +
P/O D R Mitchell — +
Sgt J E McKinley — inj
Sgt S Linton — inj
Sgt C D Ellis — inj
P/O C A Patten — inj
S/Ldr C R Taylor — inj

Took off 1945, Fuka, and on return, after experiencing difficulties in obtaining a bearing, flew into escarpment in low cloud, Sidi Omar; DBF. F/O Jones is commemorated on the Alamein Memorial and P/O Mitchell on the Runnymede Memorial. Sgts Ellis and Linton were seriously injured. P/O Patten walked for a day and a half to get help.

---

29 Apr 1941   **223 Sqn**   **Wellesley I**   **L2668**   **O**   **Unknown**

Last recorded operating with the squadron on 28 January, when it returned undamaged. SOC.

---

30 Apr - 1 May 1941   **148 Sqn**   **Wellington IC**   **W5673**   **Unknown**
Sgt C J Robinson
Crew

A tyre burst on take-off, Fuka Satellite, and on landing the aircraft hit a lorry, the undercarriage collapsed, and the aircraft careered across the aerodrome, hitting a dugout and tyres.

Middle East   **Blenheim IV**   **V5372**   **Unknown**

Lost in Greece. NFD.

---

1 May 1941   **70 Sqn**   **Wellington IC**   **W5670**   **Relocation Flight**
F/Lt J Blackburn
Sgt Sadd
P/O Norledge
Sgt McGregor
Sgt McNicholas
Sgt Chatterton
Passengers

Took off Kabrit for Shaibah but, when the engines lost power, force-landed 30km W of Habbaniyah after jettisoning bombs. The crew and passengers were picked up by another aircraft. Three passengers were slightly injured.

RAF Takoradi   **Blenheim IV**   **V5439**   **Delivery Flight**
F/O R F Milne
Sgt Parker

Took off, Takoradi, as leader of Delivery Flight 89, but short of fuel crashed on force-landing and struck a tree, Kurfi, Katsina Province, Nigeria.

---

2 May 1941   **38 Sqn**   **Wellington IC**   **N2855**   **R**   **Op: Derna & Tobruk**

P/O H W E Lane — +
F/Sgt H C S Thomas — +
Sgt R J Keeper — +
LAC P J Condry — +
LAC R D R Schofield — +

Took off, Shallufa, to attack motor transport near Derna and Tobruk. DBF after landing by the accidental release of a hung-up 40lb bomb. P/O Lane died in hospital on 7 May. All are buried at Ismailia War Memorial Cemetery.

55 Sqn   **Blenheim I**   **L8398**   **Unknown**

SOC, reason unknown.

70 Sqn F/O Anstey Sgt Shaw Sgt Norton Sgt Heywood Sgt Rose	**Wellington IC**	**T2813**	**Op: Habbaniyah** Took off Shaibah to bomb Iraqi forces investing RAF Habbaniyah. Damaged by rifle fire while bombing troop concentrations, forced to land, and eventually destroyed on the ground by Iraqi artillery.
84 Sqn	**Blenheim I**	**L1388 W**	**Ground** Abandoned at Menidi on evacuation. Photographed on the airfield by an Italian photographer on this day.
OADF Sgt R J Fryer Crew	**Wellington IC**	**R3203**	**Delivery Flight** Took off Kemble (?) for Gibraltar, and overshot attempting a flapless landing there, crashing into the sea.

2-3 May 1941	**37 Sqn** P/O L R Hewitt RNZAF inj Sgt G C Chapman inj Sgt I W P Evison RNZAF inj Sgt Chatterley Sgt Wilson Sgt D W Tong RNZAF inj	**Wellington IC**	**R1290 Y** **Op: Benghazi** Took off 1940, Shallufa, and on return ran across the flare-path at Fuka Satellite, and collided with N2855 of 38 Sqn. DBF. Sgts Evison and Tong both suffered burns, the latter seriously, and the two pilots broken or dislocated limbs: all were admitted to hospital.
	38 Sqn	**Wellington IC**	**N2855** **Ground** The aircraft was bombed up and fuelled, Fuka Satellite, but hit by R1290 of 37 Sqn which was landing (see above). DBF.

4-5 May 1941	**37 Sqn** P/O D Paterson pow Sgt A E Richardson pow P/O U Linley pow Sgt T Harris pow Sgt R W Spittles pow Sgt S L G Hughes + Lt G R Haller SAAF pow	**Wellington IC**	**T2615 S** **Op: Benghazi** Took off 2005, Shallufa, but FTR. Sgt Hughes is buried at Benghazi War Cemetery. Lt Haller was serving with 61 Sqn SAAF and his presence on the aircraft is unexplained.
	37 Sqn P/O P T Curry Sgt C S Maxfield Sgt Evans Sgt I McGregor RNZAF Sgt D G Finney + Sgt W H Cox +	**Wellington IC**	**T2983** **Op: Habbaniyah** Struck boundary fence on take-off, Shaibah, crashed and burst into flames. P/O Curry and Sgts Maxfield, Evans and McGregor escaped with slight burns. Sgt Finney was seriously injured but managed to kick a hole in the red-hot geodetic and crawled out (he died on the 9th). Sgt Cox was extricated by three of the crew but was severely burnt and died on the 6th. Sgts Cox and Finney are buried in Basra War Cemetery.
	38 Sqn Sgt N F Dixon RNZAF + Sgt B A Walker RNZAF + Sgt D Rolfe + Sgt L H Harrap + Sgt R S Blackwell + Sgt H O Turner RNZAF +	**Wellington IC**	**W5681** **Op: Benina** Took off Fuka Satellite to bomb Benina Aerodrome, but crashed at El Qasaba on return, and burst into flames. All are buried in the El Alamein Cemetery.

5 May 1941	**37 Sqn** P/O Rash pow Sgt L A Ward pow Sgt D G Campbell + Sgt F C Daniels pow Sgt C Kemp pow Sgt J E Howard pow	**Wellington IC**	**T2711 D** **Op: Raschid Aerodrome** Took off 0220, Shaibah. Hit by ground fire and crash-landed 32km S of Baghdad (near Ctesiphon). Sgt Campbell died in Baghdad hospital of injuries inflicted by Arabs. He is buried in Baghdad (North Gate) War Cemetery. There is a detailed account of this loss in Kevin Mears' *Wise Without Eyes*, pp159-161.

6 May 1941	**Middle East**	**Blenheim IV**	**N3558** Lost in Greece: NFD.	**Unknown**
	Middle East	**Blenheim IV**	**V5424** Lost in Greece: NFD.	**Unknown**

7 May 1941	**8 Sqn**	**Blenheim I**	**L8545** SOC, NFD.	**Unknown**
	113 Sqn	**Blenheim I**	**L8444** Lost in Greece: NFD.	**Unknown**

16 Sqn SAAF   **Ju 86Z-7**   **652**   **Transit Flight**

Lt F H Garrett SAAF	pow
2/Lt P F Dempers SAAF	pow
F/Sgt J Orchard SAAF	pow
Air Sgt C H Buchholtz SAAF	pow
Air Sgt S C Fox SAAF	pow
Air Mech C J Cornelius SAAF	pow

Took off 0730, Addis Ababa, with two other aircraft to report to the ALG at Neghelli, and thereafter to attack Italian positions in woods 2.6km N of Gaddara. En route to Neghelli in 10/10ths cloud, the aircraft ran short of fuel and the pilot landed at Yirga Allem (Dalle) believing it to have been captured. The aircraft bogged down on landing and the crew were captured. It is not clear whether 652 was SOC or not.

OADF   **Wellington IC**   **W5687**   **Delivery Flight**

F/Lt P H Way	
F/Sgt Cleaver	
F/Sgt Andrews	
F/Sgt R Hepple	+
F/Sgt J Richards	+
Sgt W J Griffiths	+

Took off Gibraltar for Malta, but an engine cut, and ditched 22km E of Gibraltar. The dead are commemorated on the Malta Memorial, F/Sgt Richards being listed by the CWGC as of 200 Squadron.

9 May 1941	

84 Sqn   **Blenheim IV**   **Z5865**   **Op: Ar Rutbah**

P/O I C Goudge
Crew

Took off H4, Transjordan, to attack the fort at Ar Rutbah, but shot up and force-landed in the desert 5km W of H3. The crew were uninjured. Presumed SOC.

203 Sqn   **Blenheim IV**   **T2072   M**   **Op: Mosul**

F/O P N Gordon-Hall	pow
Sgt G Poole	pow
Sgt I B Oultram	+

Took off 0520, Habbaniyah/Dhibban, to strafe Luftwaffe aircraft at Mosul airport. Crashed 42km S of Mosul, probably brought down by ground fire. The pilot and observer were captured by the French in Syria, but subsequently released by advancing British forces. Sgt Oultram is buried in Mosul War Cemetery.

11 Sqn SAAF   **Battle I**   **?**   **Unknown**

2/Lt N C Gillies SAAF
F/Sgt I W Balcomb SAAF

Crashed in taking off, Addis Ababa. SOC.

10 May 1941	

14 Sqn   **Blenheim IV**   **T2274**   **Op: Derna**

F/Sgt J R Taylor
Sgt J A A Parker
F/Sgt R F Hall

Took off 1440, LG 21 (Qotafiyah III), to bomb Derna satellite airfield. Intercepted by a CR.42 which over a half hour period inflicted severe damage. One propeller flew off and the other engine cut, the aircraft crash-landing E of Sollum. The crew were unhurt, but killed 11 days later, when the squadron lost five aircraft.

55 Sqn   **Blenheim IV**   **V5514**   **Ferry Flight**

F/O R H Nicolson MiD	+
Sgt J Davison	
P/O J L van Breda	+
F/Sgt H Rhodes DFM	+
F/Sgt J D Duffy	+
F/Sgt R Davies	+
Sgt A T B Hale RAAF	+

Took off LG 95 (Base Landing Ground) with another Blenheim of 55 Sqn to return to the Operational Landing Ground (LG 15, Maaten Bagush). The other machine developed engine trouble and the two landed at LG 28 (Burg-el-Arab), both crews (and two passengers) packing into V5514. En route to Maaten Bagush a severe sandstorm was encountered, and the aircraft turned back

LAC E Buckley		+	to LG 28 where, attempting a landing in poor light, V5514 hit Magister R1974 parked on the airfield boundary, bounced into another Blenheim, broke up and burst into flames. The dead are buried in Alexandria (Chatby) Military and War Memorial Cemetery.

82 Sqn   **Blenheim IV**   V6070   **Delivery Flight**
Believed lost during a ferry flight to Malta, or on Malta. NFD.

203 Sqn   **Blenheim IV**   L9174   D   **Op: Ar Rutbah**
S/Ldr J P D Gethin DFC   +   Took off 1335, H4, Transjordan, one of two detailed to
Sgt E C Crittenden   +   attack Iraqi forces in and around Fort Rutbah. Brought
Sgt L White   +   down by ground fire near the fort, the observer and WOp/AG being killed and the pilot badly burned. He was rescued by the second Blenheim, L9042, and returned to H4, but died later that day. He is buried in Ramleh War Cemetery, and the others in Damascus War Cemetery.

11 Sqn SAAF   **Battle I**   925   **Communications Flight**
2/Lt B H de Swardt SAAF
Passenger
Took off 1100, Gumbar Dug, to fly to Degeh Bur to pick up another member of the squadron. An engine cut on take-off for the return flight, the aircraft crashed and was DBR.

11 May 1941			

55 Sqn   **Blenheim IV**   V5437   **Op: Unknown**
Sgt Hewitt   Took off LG 15 (Maaten Bagush Satellite) and on return
Sgt McCann   crash-landed on the beach near Maaten Bagush with
Sgt R A Stobbs   +   engine trouble. A small bomb, apparently hung up, exploded and the aircraft was destroyed. Sgt Stobbs is buried in the El Alamein War Cemetery.

139 Sqn   **Blenheim IV**   R3885   A   **Delivery Flight**
Sgt M H Farmer   Took off St Eval for Gibraltar. An engine failed as the
P/O J W Moffatt   aircraft approached its destination and the pilot ditched.
Sgt G M Shinnie   A Norwegian ship picked up the crew unhurt.

139 Sqn   **Blenheim IV**   T2134   **Delivery Flight**
Sgt J N Dennis   Took off St Eval for Gibraltar. The aircraft swung and
Sgt Miles   crashed on landing at Gibraltar when the pilot was
Sgt R Waddington   blinded by the late afternoon sun reflecting off objects on
Passenger   the runway, and thought he was about to land in the sea.

12 May 1941			

47 Sqn   **Wellesley I**   K7724   **Mail Flight**
Sgt B Osbourn DFM   On take-off, Asmara, 0523 for Gordon's Tree carrying
Sgt E Dempsey   inj   mail, hit a tree and crash-landed. SOC as BER 7 October.

21 Sqn   **Blenheim IV**   V5461   **Ground**
Destroyed in an air raid, Luqa.

16 May 1941			

45 Sqn   **Blenheim IV**   T2056   **Op: Derna**
F/O J Beveridge   +   Took off 0400, LG 17 (Fuka Main), one of two detailed to
P/O A H Wise RNZAF   +   attack the landing ground at Derna. Heavy ground fire
F/Sgt V J Griffiths   +   was encountered and the aircraft were separated. FTR. The crew are commemorated on the Alamein Memorial.

OADF   **Wellington IC**   T2572   **Delivery Flight**
P/O C F Hart RCAF   int   Took off for Gibraltar, but crash landed on the beach
Sgt I F McManus RAAF   int   5km north of Sao Pedro do Meul, Portugal. The crew
Sgt C J Marshall   int   were briefly interned. Both the aircraft and crew were
Sgt D R Mallett   int   ex-15 squadron.
Sgt D O G Goldfinch   int
Sgt D J Nolan   int

19 May 1941	**45 Sqn** P/O G H M Reuter Sgt H J Cassar Sgt G W Swambo	**Blenheim IV** + + pow	T2179	**Op: Agedabia-Ghemines Rd** Took off LG 17 (Fuka Main), one of five aircraft detailed to strafe motor transport, but seen to crash and burst into flames. P/O Reuter, a Belgian flying under the pseudonym of P/O D Carter, was on his first operational flight with the squadron. The dead are commemorated on the Alamein Memorial.
20 May 1941	**84 Sqn**	**Blenheim IV**	?	**Ground** Destroyed in an attack on Habbaniyah by six Bf 110Ds. A DC-2 and two Valentias of 31 Sqn were also destroyed.
21 May 1941	**14 Sqn** Sgt J F Matetich Sgt A A Sutton Sgt H Jones	**Blenheim IV** + + +	L8874	**Op: Capuzzo - Tobruk Rd** Took off 0355, LG 21 (Qotafiyah III), detailed to attack motor transport and troop concentrations. Shot down by Bf 109E fighters of 1/JG27 near the target. All the crew are commemorated on the Alamein Memorial.
	14 Sqn P/O R F Johnson Sgt M C Fuller F/Sgt A McC Morrison	**Blenheim IV** + + +	T2173	**Op: Capuzzo - Tobruk Rd** Took off 0355, detailed as above, and shot down near the target. All the crew are commemorated on the Alamein Memorial.
	14 Sqn Sgt N W Hoskins F/Sgt H W Easton Sgt W Carver	**Blenheim IV** + + +	Z5979	**Op: Capuzzo - Tobruk Rd** Took off 0355, detailed as above, and similarly lost. All the crew are commemorated on the Alamein Memorial.
	14 Sqn P/O R G Gilmore F/Sgt K J Wilkie Sgt T K Riley	**Blenheim IV** + + +	V5511	**Op: Capuzzo - Tobruk Rd** Took off 0400, detailed as above, and similarly lost. All the crew are commemorated on the Alamein Memorial.
	14 Sqn F/Sgt J R Taylor Sgt J A A Parker Sgt F A Culham	**Blenheim IV** + + +	T2346	**Op: Capuzzo - Tobruk Rd** Took off 0400, detailed as above, and similarly lost. All the crew are commemorated on the Alamein Memorial.
	82 Sqn F/Sgt L H Wrightson P/O K G A Marsh F/Sgt C G Evans	**Blenheim IV** + +	Z6165	**Delivery Flight** Took off Portreath for Malta, but crashed into the Mediterranean 12km N of Gouraya, Algeria. The dead are commemorated on the Alamein Memorial.
	RAF Takoradi Slt Sandre FAFL Crew	**Maryland II**	AH290	**Delivery Flight** Took off Geneina on Delivery Flight 96 to the Middle East. Crashed in forced landing at El Fasher at 1330 hrs when the starboard engine failed through a fuel shortage. DBR.
	RAF Takoradi Lt Y E P H Ezanno FAFL S/Lt P L R Ibos FAFL Sgt Borel FAFL	**Maryland II**	AH293	**Delivery Flight** Took off El Fasher on Delivery Flight 94 from Takoradi. An engine cut on take-off, thought to have been caused by a propeller selection switch being accidentally moved when it caught in the pilot's sleeve. DBR.
22 May 1941	**84 Sqn** Sgt G E Bailey Sgt L E Atkinson RNZAF Sgt F D Round	**Blenheim IV**	T2116	**Op: Leaflet Drop** Took off from Aqir, one of three detailed for a leaflet drop over Syria. On return an engine cut and in landing at Haifa the aircraft overshot and overturned. DBR.
	FF (Bomber) Flt 1 W/O R Jabin FAFL Crew	**Blenheim IV**	T1822	**Op: Dessie** Landing at Gordon's Tree on return from Gondar, a tyre burst and the undercarriage collapsed. SOC.

23 May 1941	8 Sqn	Vincent	K4725	Op: Reconnaissance

8 Sqn   **Vincent**   K4725   **Op: Reconnaissance**
Sgt C G Loader
Undershot on landing and hit a ridge, the undercarriage collapsing, Alula. SOC 3 July.

37 Sqn   **Wellington IC**   T2812   **Night Flying Test**
Sgt R T Spiller — inj
F/Sgt J Newell — +
Sgt Bevan
Took off Shallufa but an aileron malfunction eventually caused the aircraft to become unmanageable, and it struck the ground, broke in half and burst into flames. Sgt Spiller suffered a fractured ankle. F/Sgt Newell is buried at Ismailia War Memorial Cemetery.

45 Sqn   **Blenheim IV**   V5624   **Op: Maleme**
P/O P J Vincent — +
P/O S C Niven RNZAF — +
F/Sgt O B Thompson — +
Took off 1330 LG 17 (Fuka Main), one of four aircraft detailed to bomb Maleme aerodrome. After bombing the aircraft was seen to dive and turn towards the mountains as though taking evasive action. All are commemorated on the Alamein Memorial.

47 Sqn   **Wellesley I**   K8526   **Op: Escort**
Sgt R D Cathcart-Cunnison
Sgt F H Taylor
Sgt W Schollar
Took off Asmara on an escort flight to Dessie, where the aircraft undershot on landing and an undercarriage leg tore off. DBR.

70 Sqn   **Wellington IC**   R1248   **Unknown**
Sgt E Baldwin
Crew
Sank back on take-off and hit the ground, LG 16 (Fuka Satellite). DBF. Or ran out of fuel and landed in the desert, according to Baldwin (Sadler). Not mentioned in the 70 Sqn ORB.

23-24 May 1941

37 Sqn   **Wellington IC**   L7866   R   **Op: Maleme**
Sgt W R Faulkner
Sgt W W Oakley
Sgt H Wheelan
Sgt E N Webb
Sgt S Dawson
Sgt H G W Watkins RNZAF
Took off 2300, Shallufa, to bomb Maleme aerodrome, which had been captured by German forces. High fuel consumption forced the crew to turn back to Crete and land at Heraklion, which was still in RAF hands. Shortly after, while refuelling, L7866 was destroyed by strafing Bf 110s. The crew, unable to be evacuated from Crete, later became POWs.

37 Sqn   **Wellington IC**   T2875   B   **Op: Maleme**
Sgt G E Harris
Sgt Helyar
Sgt Malpas
Sgt Norcross
Sgt Langley
Sgt McCall
Took off 2300, Shallufa. On return, out of fuel, ditched 244km N of Maaten Bagush. Landing alongside HMS *Coventry*, the crew were picked up unharmed.

37 Sqn   **Wellington IC**   T2895   J   **Op: Maleme**
Sgt H J Mew — +
Sgt P Field RAAF — +
Sgt L S Tipper — +
Sgt J Rowe — +
F/Sgt E M Kelsall — +
Sgt P G Marsh — +
Took off 2300, Shallufa. All are commemorated on the Alamein Memorial, Marsh with a CWGC date of death given as 31 March.

24 May 1941

45 Sqn   **Blenheim IV**   Z5766   **Op: Maleme**
Sgt E W McClelland MiD
Sgt H Vipond
Sgt J McGurk
Took off LG 17 (Fuka Main), one of two aircraft detailed to support four Hurricanes on a ground-strafing attack on Maleme airfield. On return an engine cut in a sandstorm and the Blenheim hit a ridge. In the subsequent forced landing, 1.5km S of Sidi Barrani, the undercarriage collapsed. DBR.

25 May 1941	14 Sqn	Blenheim IV	T2003	Op: Maleme
	Sgt H P Jeudwine	+	Took off 1500, LG 21 (Qotafiyah III), to bomb the airfield	
	F/Sgt H Young	+	at Maleme. Shot down by Bf 109 fighters of 5/JG77 over	
	F/Sgt N B Lake	+	Suda Bay. This and the two following aircraft were claimed by Uffz Rudolf Schmidt, while a duplicate claim for one was made by Gefr Horstmann. The crew are commemorated on the Alamein Memorial.	

	14 Sqn	Blenheim IV	T2065	Op: Maleme
	F/Lt R A Green	+	As above. The crew are commemorated on the Alamein	
	P/O A D Browne	+	Memorial.	
	Sgt N P McK Wilson	+		

	14 Sqn	Blenheim IV	V5510	Op: Maleme
	Lt S R E Forrester SAAF	+	As above. Shot down over the Mediterranean by fighters	
	Sgt W A J Fretwell	+	of 5/JG77. The crew are commemorated on the Alamein	
	F/Sgt R F Hall	+	Memorial.	

	24 Sqn SAAF	Maryland II	1608	Op: Maleme
	Lt E G Ford SAAF	pow	Took off LG 16 (Fuka Satellite), to attack Luftwaffe troop transports on Maleme airfield. Attacked by fighters and crashlanded at Tymbaki. Unhurt, the crew joined 71 other officers and men in trying to escape from Crete in a repaired landing craft. They were stopped at sea by an Italian submarine and the officers were told to swim aboard it. While doing so Lt Gill drowned. The others were instructed to return to shore, but led by Sgt McWilliam, who navigated with a 2-inch prismatic compass, they made for Egypt, reaching Mersa Matruh three days later. For this Sgt McWilliam was mentioned in despatches. Lt Gill is commemorated on the Alamein Memorial.	
	2/Lt G L W Gill SAAF	+		
	Sgt D D McWilliam SAAF	evd		
	Sgt T O Muller SAAF	evd		

26 May 1941	45 Sqn	Blenheim IV	T2339	Op: Maleme
	F/Sgt N H Thomas	+	Took off LG 17 (Fuka Main), one of three aircraft detailed	
	Sgt G R Adams	+	to bomb the airfield at Maleme. Attacked over the target	
	F/Sgt G K Grainger	+	and shot down in flames by Bf 109 fighters. Oblt Hoeckner of 6/JG77 claimed three Blenheims and Lt Emil Omert of 9/JG77 one. The crew are buried in Suda Bay War Cemetery.	

	45 Sqn	Blenheim IV	T2350	Op: Maleme
	P/O J Robinson		Took off LG 17 (Fuka Main), detailed as above.	
	Sgt W B Longstaff	+	Navigation problems on the return flight forced the crew to bail out over Cyrenaica. The pilot and WOp/AG were picked up but Sgt Longstaff was never found, and is commemorated on the Alamein Memorial.	
	Sgt A F Crosby			

	45 Sqn	Blenheim IV	V5592	Op: Maleme
	F/O T F C Churcher	pow	Took off LG 17 (Fuka Main), detailed as above. Shot	
	P/O R D May	pow	down over the target by Bf 109 fighters. The crew bailed	
	Sgt H C Langrish	evd	out but only Sgt Langrish evaded capture, to reach the southern coast of Crete and be evacuated on the destroyer HMS *Kandahar*, reaching Egypt on 30 May.	

	12 Sqn SAAF	Maryland II	1627	Ferry Flight
			Took off Nakuru en route to Egypt. At Juba, two B Flight aircraft were damaged, one (1648) in landing (left wing damaged) and the other (1627) in attempting to take off (undercarriage wiped off and engines and airscrews damaged). The port wing of 1627 was then fitted to 1648, the remainder of 1627 being reduced to produce, with the airframe used for training.	

Esc de Bomb 1	**Maryland II**	1607	**Op: Rethimno**
Cmdt G Goumin FAFL		pow	Took off Heliopolis on a supply drop to Allied forces.
Lt P Courcot FAFL		+	After completing the drop the pilot decided to go on to
Adj Chef A Marteau FAFL		pow	strafe Maleme airfield. Brought down by Lt Omert of
Sgt R Lefevre FAFL		pow	8/JG77 for his third kill of the day, the aircraft crash-landed approximately half-way across the island. Esc de Bomb No 1 was attached to 24 Squadron SAAF.

27 May 1941

14 Sqn	**Blenheim IV**	T2338	**Op Suda Bay - Maleme**
F/O M MacKenzie		+	Took off 1430 LG 21 (Quotafiyah III), one of three
Sgt M B Fearn DFM RNZAF			detailed to attack German troop concentrations between
Sgt W J McConnell			Suda Bay and Maleme airfield. One returned with engine trouble, the other two attacked Maleme but became separated and lost on the return flight. Sgts Fearn and McConnell bailed out 80km S of El Daba, over the Qattara Depression and were found, suffering badly from exposure, three days later. F/O MacKenzie survived the crash-landing, as landing strips laid out near the crashed Blenheim indicated, but he was never located and is commemorated on the Alamein Memorial.

14 Sqn	**Blenheim IV**	V5593	**Op Suda Bay - Maleme**
F/O J B Le Cavalier		+	Took off 1430 LG 21 (Quotafiyah III), detailed as above.
Sgt Page			Lost, the aircraft crashed 40km S of Mersa Matruh. Sgts
Sgt C P A Bury		+	Page and Bury bailed out but the latter was found dead close to the crashed aircraft. Sgt Page reached Mersa Matruh on foot. The others are buried in El Alamein War Cemetery.

45 Sqn	**Blenheim IV**	Z5896	**Op: Maleme**
F/O N W Pinnington		+	Took off 0300, LG 17 (Fuka Main) to bomb the airfield at
P/O H F Irving RNZAF		+	Maleme but climbed too steeply after take-off, stalled,
Sgt R J R Martin		+	crashed and caught fire. Sgt Martin was thrown clear, but died two weeks later of his burns. He is buried in the Alexandria (Chatby) War Cemetery, and the pilot and observer in the El Alamein War Cemetery.

55 Sqn	**Blenheim IV**	L9319	**Op: Maleme**
Sgt R B Bale			Took off LG 15 (Maaten Bagush Satellite), detailed to
Sgt A F Wiles DFM			bomb Maleme airfield. Became lost over the desert on
Sgt J Rigby			return and the crew bailed out, rejoining the squadron two days later.

55 Sqn	**Blenheim IV**	T2051	**Op: Maleme**
F/Sgt W L Martin		+	In taking off from LG 15, detailed as above, collided with
Sgt E A Martin		+	another Blenheim and spun into the ground. The crew
Sgt K Bamber		+	are buried in the El Alamein War Cemetery.

55 Sqn	**Blenheim IV**	T2175	**Op: Maleme**
Sgt J H Chesman		+	Took off LG 15, detailed as above, and also became lost
Sgt D G Callender RNZAF		+	on return. The aircraft ran out of fuel and the crew
Sgt R F Lyle		+	elected to attempt a forced landing rather than bail out, and died when the aircraft crashed. All are buried in the El Alamein War Cemetery.

82 Sqn	**Blenheim IV**	V6460	**Op: Anti-shipping**
Sgt E B Inman		+	Took off Luqa, one of six aircraft detailed to attack a large
Sgt K P Collins		pow	Axis convoy making for Tripoli. Brought down by the
Sgt R J Austin		+	explosion of its bombs on one of the ships, only the observer surviving, seriously injured, to be rescued by the Italian destroyer *Cigno*. Sgt Collins' left leg had to be amputated, and he was repatriated in April 1943. The others are commemorated on the Alamein Memorial.

	82 Sqn	Blenheim IV	Z6427 H	Op: Anti-shipping
	F/Lt G M Fairbairn	+		
	P/O P J Higgins	+		
	Sgt S W Kemp	+		

Took off Luqa, detailed as above. Brought down by the explosion of the bombs dropped by V6460. All the crew members are commemorated on the Alamein Memorial.

	211 Sqn	Blenheim IV	V5818	Op: Reconnaissance
	Sgt D V Davis	+		
	Sgt L E Stalder	+		
	F/Lt H Trenholm	+		

Took off 0730, Aqir, on reconnaissance of Vichy French airfields in Syria. Shot down 4km NW of Nerab, near Aleppo by a D.520 fighter of 1/7 (Slt Vuillemin). All are buried in Aleppo War Cemetery.

28 May 1941	203 Sqn	Blenheim IV	T1820	Communications Flight
	P/O J P Tremlett			
	Sgt H E Goodrich			
	Sgt R Hepworth			
	Passenger:			
	AVM J H D'Albiac DSO			

Swung on take-off at Lydda, to transport the AOC Iraq to H4, Transjordan, hitting a steamroller and killing an Arab workman. SOC.

29-30 May 1941	37 Sqn	Wellington IC	L7860 A	Op: Scarpanto
	F/Sgt D D Strickland	+		
	F/Sgt A E Middleton	+		
	P/O W G Dalco RAAF	+		
	Sgt T H Mitchell	+		
	Sgt E Curle	+		
	P/O R E H Nowell	+		

Took off 2300, Shallufa. Fell in flames over the target and crashed on Efialti aerodrome. All are buried in Rhodes War Cemetery.

	37 Sqn	Wellington IC	W5622	Op: Maleme
	Sgt H N Goodall RNZAF	+		
	Sgt J D Decent	+		
	Sgt Higgins	inj		
	Sgt Fraser	inj		
	Sgt Wickham	inj		
	Sgt Buxton	inj		

Collided with W5685 on take-off, Shallufa. The bombs exploded, and the aircraft was DBF. The entire crew was injured, Sgt Decent dying on the 30th and Sgt Goodall on 5 June. Both are buried in Ismailia War Memorial Cemetery.

	37 Sqn	Wellington IC	W5685	Op: Maleme
	F/Sgt J W Kenner	+		
	Sgt J M Milne	+		
	P/O R S C N St John-Spencer	+		
	Sgt J E G Dovey	+		
	Sgt Smith	inj		

Preparing for take-off, Shallufa, the aircraft turned across the flare-path, despite receiving a red light from the aerodrome control pilot, and collided with W5622 which was taking off. W5685 caught fire and the bombs exploded. The dead are buried in Ismailia War Memorial Cemetery.

	38 Sqn	Wellington IC	R1388	Op: Benghazi
	Sgt G Leather	pow		
	Sgt T Morley	pow		
	Sgt C H Martin	pow		
	Sgt J W Mullen	pow		
	Sgt D A Phillipson	pow		

Took off Shallufa to bomb Benghazi harbour, but hit by flak shortly after bombing. With the starboard engine out of action and the port engine beginning to burn, the aircraft was crash-landed about 80km SE of Benghazi. Sgt Mullen suffered a head injury, and two other crew members lesser injuries.

30 May 1941	11 Sqn	Blenheim IV	T2341	Unknown

Lost in 1941. One of some 137 RAF aircraft lost to ground strafing attacks or abandoned on evacuation. Circumstances unknown.

	11 Sqn	Blenheim IV	T2342	Unknown

As above.

	113 Sqn	Blenheim IV	T2183	Unknown

As above.

	113 Sqn	Blenheim IV	T2238	Unknown

As above.

	113 Sqn	Blenheim IV	T2248 **Unknown**

113 Sqn — Blenheim IV — **T2248** — **Unknown**
Lost in Greece, May 1941. One of some 137 RAF aircraft lost to ground strafing attacks or abandoned on evacuation. Circumstances unknown.

211 Sqn — Blenheim IV — **L8466** — **Unknown**
As above.

Middle East — Blenheim IV — **L9300** — **Unknown**
As above.

Middle East — Blenheim IV — **L9342** — **Unknown**
As above.

Middle East — Blenheim IV — **R3918** — **Unknown**
As above.

Middle East — Blenheim IV — **T2390** — **Unknown**
As above.

Middle East — Blenheim IV — **T2391** — **Unknown**
As above.

---

31 May 1941 — **84 Sqn** / Sgt A Gordon DFM + / Sgt G F Humber + / Sgt G Furney DFM + — Blenheim IV — **L9316** — **Op: Reconnaissance**
Took off am, Habbaniyahh/Dhibban and FTR. Shot down near Al Musayib, Iraq, by a French MS.406 fighter. All are buried in Habbaniyah War Cemetery.

---

1 Jun 1941 — **47 Sqn** / Sgt A G Brown / Sgt H L Oddy + / Sgt A Sleight — Wellesley I — **L2710** — **Unknown**
The engine cut shortly after taking off, Asmara, and the aircraft stalled and crashed. The observer suffered a fractured skull and later died. He is buried in Asmara War Cemetery.

---

3 Jun 1941 — **45 Sqn** / P/O S F Champion — Blenheim I — **L8362** — **Unknown**
An engine cut on take-off, Fuka North, and the Blenheim crashed. DBR.

82 Sqn — Blenheim IV — **V5924** — **Ground**
Destroyed in an air raid, Luqa.

139 Sqn / S/Ldr J R Thompson / Sgt W A Hepworth RAAF / Sgt A E Turner — Blenheim IV — **V5460   G** — **Op: Anti-shipping**
Took off 1300, Luqa, one of six Blenheims of 139 Squadron, led by W/Cdr N E W Pepper DFC, on offensive reconnaissance when they came upon a convoy of five merchant ships escorted by four destroyers and four Ju 88s. The first section attacked with delayed-action bombs, but one of these, which had hit an 8,000 ton ammunition ship, exploded just as the second section came in at mast height. The Wing Commander's aircraft, V5860, caught the full blast and disintegrated, while V5460 was badly damaged, and subsequently SOC as DBR.

139 Sqn / W/Cdr N E W Pepper DFC + / Sgt T E Hyde + / Sgt L Pickford pow — Blenheim IV — **V5860   J** — **Op: Anti-shipping**
Took off 1300, Luqa, one of six Blenheims detailed as above, and lost as noted. The pilot is commemorated on the Runnymede Memorial and the observer buried in Tripoli War Cemetery. The WOp/AG was seriously injured and spent a long spell in hospital before being sent to a prisoner of war camp.

GRB1 / F/O C de la Roche Souvestre FAFL + — Blenheim IV — **T1998** — **Op: Ferry Flight**
Took off Fort Lamy for Khartoum, and possibly caught

	Capt L Flury-Hérard FAFL			+	fire in the air, crashing 12km E of the village of Debus
	F/Sgt A Devos FAFL			+	Weiki, Sudan. All are buried at El Fasher.
	Passenger:				
	Cpl J Hugon FAFL			+	

5-6 Jun 1941   **148 Sqn**   **Wellington IC**   T2981   G   **Op: Benghazi**

F/Lt H E Broadsmith — +
P/O P Lane — +
F/Sgt H A Bliss — +
F/Sgt R T Fisher — +
Sgt A Whitworth — +
Sgt S J Millar — +

Took off Kabrit to bomb Benghazi, but on return force-landed at sea 160km N of Sidi Barrani. The crew were located by Sunderland and supplies dropped, but bad weather prevented their being rescued. All are commemorated on the Alamein Memorial.

6-7 Jun 1941   **37 Sqn**   **Wellington IC**   T2917   N   **Op: Benghazi**

F/O McArthur — inj
Sgt Anderson — inj
P/O Camp — inj
Sgt Lamb
Sgt Dovey
Sgt Crook

Took off 2000, Shallufa. Hit by flak and on return ditched N of El Daba. The crew was rescued by Sunderland on 8 June.

8 Jun 1941   **21 Sqn**   **Blenheim IV**   V5996   **Ground**

Destroyed in an air raid, Luqa. A-B Serials gives this as a 21 Sqn aircraft but it was almost certainly a Blenheim being delivered to Egypt by 608 Sqn crews, seven of which were absorbed into 203 Sqn.

RAF Takoradi   **Blenheim IV**   V6129   **Delivery Flight**

Sgt C F Searles
Crew

Took off Takoradi for Lagos, but landing in poor visibility overshot, skidded into a pipeline, and the undercarriage collapsed. DBR.

10 Jun 1941   **55 Sqn**   **Blenheim I**   L1496   **Unknown**

SOC. NFD.

55 Sqn   **Blenheim I**   L8533   **Unknown**

SOC. NFD.

10-11 Jun 1941   **70 Sqn**   **Wellington IC**   W5654   **Op: Benghazi**

Sgt C Muller
Sgt Holland
Sgt Spencer
Sgt Bell
Sgt Ross
Sgt Watkins

Took off 2140, Fuka. On return ran out of fuel while diverting in fog and belly-landed near Fuka after an engine cut while attempting to land.

11 Jun 1941   **82 Sqn**   **Blenheim IV**   Z6426   **Op: Anti-shipping**

S/Ldr M L Watson — +
P/O N C Alers-Hankey — +
Sgt R M Poole — +

Took off Luqa to attack a convoy S of Pantelleria. Hit by flak from the MVs *Tembien* (Italian) and *Wachtfels* (German), the Blenheim hit the mast of the *Tembien*, and crashed into the sea in flames. All are commemorated on the Runnymede Memorial.

15 Sqn SAAF   **Battle I**   902   **Op: Cossa**

Lt E J Steyn SAAF — +
Air Sgt F W Kelly SAAF — +

Took off 1400, Algato, to attack Italian motor transport and troop concentrations 8 to 10km S of Cossa. The aircraft became lost in thick cloud in the mountains and was last seen at 1545, 13km N of Gimma. It was later found crashed in forest at Aggora. The crew are buried in Addis Ababa War Cemetery.

	24 Sqn SAAF 2/Lt A E Halse SAAF	Maryland II	1611	Training
			While taking off, Shandur, to carry out circuits and landings, the Maryland swung, the pilot overcorrected and the undercarriage collapsed. DBR.	
12 Jun 1941	107 Sqn	Blenheim IV	R3610	Unknown
			SOC. AM 78 records the loss as FB, Category E. NFD.	
13 Jun 1941	11 Sqn P/O R J H Lea RAAF Sgt A F S Jones Sgt W C Ferguson	Blenheim IV + + +	Z5891	Op: Reconnaissance
			Took off Aqir on a photo-reconnaissance of Beirut. Shot down by D.520 (Cne Richard) of III/6, Armée de l'Air, and crashed in a small valley 10km N of Litani. The crew are buried in Beirut War Cemetery.	
14 Jun 1941	24 Sqn SAAF Lt E C Newborn SAAF 2/Lt C C Gordon SAAF Air Sgt P W de B Bothma SAAF Air Sgt R E O Giles SAAF	Maryland II pow + + +	1609	Op: Gazala
			Took off pre-dawn, LG 16 (Fuka Satellite), to attack the airfield at Gazala. Shot down by a Bf 109 (Oblt L Franzisket, I/JG27). The pilot bailed out but the rest of the crew perished when the aircraft crashed. They are buried in Knightsbridge War Cemetery.	
15 Jun 1941	11 Sqn Sgt K E Sellars Sgt F T Manly DFM Sgt Edwards	Blenheim IV	R3608	Op: Reconnaissance
			Took off 0615, Haifa, on a photo-reconnaissance of Beirut, Aleppo, Homs and Rayak. Engine trouble necessitated an early return and the aircraft crashed on landing at Haifa, while trying to avoid another aircraft. SOC.	
	38 Sqn Sgt Jones Crew	Wellington IC	P2849	Ferry Flight
			Took off 1930 Shallufa for LG 09, where the undercarriage collapsed during the landing run. DBR.	
	OADU P/O R B Campbell RCAF Sgt J A Proctor RCAF Sgt G H Vickers Sgt G L Cowing RCAF Sgt D S Birtwhistle Sgt E H Parker	Wellington IC + + + + +	N2803	Delivery Flight
			Took off Gibraltar for Malta. Hit a mountain at Souk Ahras, S of Bône, Algeria. The dead are buried in Bône War Cemetery. Sgt Parker, in the rear turret, survived the crash.	
15-16 Jun 1941	OADU Sgt E B Beattie RNZAF Sgt J R Bolton P/O D Cameron RCAF Sgt L B Butler Sgt C R Sanders Sgt F E Drake RNZAF	Wellington IC + + + + + +	R3293	Delivery Flight
			Took off Gibraltar for Malta. Stalled and crashed into the sea near Kalafrana on approach to land at Luqa. Sgt Drake is commemorated on the Runnymede Memorial; the others are buried in Malta (Capuccini) Naval Cemetery.	
16 Jun 1941	84 Sqn F/O E V G Scoones Sgt A McL Blackburn	Blenheim IV inj inj	T2063	Unknown
			Took off Habbaniyahh/Dhibban, on a flight to Mosul, where the aircraft overshot on landing, hit a fire tender, and then barbed wire. DBR.	
	GRB1 F/O J Hirlemann FAFL P/O G Becquart FAFL F/O B Crouzet FAFL Sgt P Grasset FAFL	Blenheim IV + + + inj	T1935	Communications Flight
			Took off Bangui on a comms flight to Brazzaville, but crashed in a forested area 20km SE of Bangui after losing a propeller in a storm. Sgt Grasset and the seriously injured F/O Crouzet (who later died) were rescued by a local village chief, who was alerted by bursts of machine gun fire. The dead were originally buried in Dongou, but the pilot and observer were re-interred in France post-war.	

17 Jun 1941	11 Sqn Sgt V G Hudson DFM — inj Sgt Morton — inj	Blenheim I	V5946	**Op: Homs** On take off Aqir to bomb Homs Airfield, struck by an unknown object, caught fire and was destroyed when the bomb load exploded. Initially reported killed, the crew were later found wandering around the airfield in a dazed state. SOC 21 June.
17-18 Jun 1941	37 Sqn P/O P S Fougere RNZAF Crew	Wellington IC	T2728	**Op: Benghazi** Took off 2030 Abu Sueir. Belly-landed on return. SOC 31.10.43, no doubt by inventory entry.
18 Jun 1941	45 Sqn	Blenheim IV	Z5892	**Unknown** SOC NFD.
19 Jun 1941	82 Sqn Sgt J N Harrison — + Sgt L R MacDonald — + Sgt L N Rowbotham — +	Blenheim IV	T1888	**Op: Anti-Shipping** Took off Luqa, and ditched off Malta returning from a shipping sweep. NFD. All are commemorated on the Malta Memorial.
20 Jun 1941	16 Sqn SAAF ? Lt M S Bryson AFC SAAF — inj	Maryland II	1604	**Training Flight** The pilot was receiving instruction at the time of the crash, 1045 hrs. NFD. The aircraft was DBR.
	OADU Sgt P F Bold — int F/O J D Hall — int Sgt J C Sheridan — int Sgt R H Toshack RCAF — int Sgt W J Poole — int Sgt C G Peak — int	Wellington IC	X3211	**Delivery Flight** Took off Hampstead Norris for Gibraltar. Severe weather, wireless failure and compass problems left the aircraft short on fuel. It was force-landed at Vianda Do Castelo, near Pouva, Portugal. The crew were interned for only a fortnight.
	OADU F/O E I J Bell — int Sgt F M Arnold — int Sgt J A Krause RCAF — int Sgt R Skelton — int Sgt A E Phillips — int Sgt J D Menard RCAF — int	Wellington IC	Z8722	**Delivery Flight** Took off Hamptead Norris for Gibraltar. The wireless was put out of action and the compass affected by an electrical storm. The aircraft ditched out of fuel off Aguilas, Spain, and the crew was interned until March 1942.
20-21 Jun 1941	38 Sqn Sgt C G E Newton — + F/Sgt H Lilley — + Sgt D A Connolly RNZAF — + Sgt H Godfrey — + Sgt G M Barclay — pow F/Lt R W B Rainford — pow	Wellington IC	T2748 K	**Op: Benghazi** Took off 2000, Shallufa, to bomb harbour installations. Messages picked up indicate an engine failed on the return flight. The aircraft crashed approximately 160km E of the target, but no trace was ever found of wreckage or of the four who died, all of whom are commemorated on the Alamein Memorial.
21 Jun 1941	14 Sqn	Wellesley I	L2653	**Unknown** SOC. NFD.
	45 Sqn	Wellesley I	K7778	**Unknown** Damaged in an accident on 9.3.39, but not repaired. SOC.
	105 Sqn Sgt F T J Bryant. — int Sgt P M Thompson — int Sgt D R C Phillips — int	Blenheim IV	Z6453	**Relocation Flight** Took off 1100, Portreath, part of a squadron relocation flight to Luqa via Gibraltar. Fuel blockage problems 200km off the Spanish coast forced the pilot to make for Spain, where a crash-landing was effected on a beach near Cap Finisterre. The crew were interned, initially in Valladolid, where hostility to the Allied cause meant they were at

risk of being lynched, but were returned via Gibraltar to the UK on 12.5.42.

| | Middle East | Blenheim IV | V5929 | Night Flying Test |
| | | | Left Takoradi on or about 6 June. SOC 21 June. NFD. |

| 22 Jun 1941 | 11 Sqn | Blenheim IV | V5591 | Op: Beirut |

F/Lt J A W Lawrence
Sgt H Hill
Sgt H T Bowen DFM — inj

An engine failed on take-off 1220, Aqir, to bomb Beirut harbour. The aircraft crash-landed in an orange grove 2.5km N of Aqir. DBR.

| | 82 Sqn | Blenheim IV | Z6422 | Op: Anti-Shipping |

S/Ldr J Harrison-Broadley — pow
Sgt P L Felton — pow
Sgt S C Thompson — pow

Took off Luqa on a shipping strike against an Axis convoy off the N coast of Lampedusa. Hit in the port engine by flak from the destroyer escorts, the aircraft ditched 2km N of Lampedusa, the crew being rescued by the Destroyer Escort *Orsa*.

| 22-23 Jun 1941 | 37 Sqn | Wellington IC | L7846 J | Op: Benghazi |

Sgt C T Fletcher — +
F/Sgt R Atkin — +
Sgt K Naylor — +
Sgt D A Hinde — +
Sgt J V Rowe — +
F/Sgt J Hood — +

Took off 2030, Shallufa, but unable to locate Benghazi because of cloud and FTR. NFD. All are commemorated on the Alamein Memorial.

| 23 Jun 1941 | 8 Sqn | Vincent | K4664 | Unknown |

F/Lt W D Adams
Crew

Took off Layjun. A tyre burst on landing at Ash Shir, 1130, swung and tipped up. SOC 2 August.

| | 45 Sqn | Blenheim IV | V5440 | Op: Reconnaissance |

P/O S F Champion
P/O L P Bourke RNZAF
Sgt J Bulloch

Took off 1430, Aqir, on reconnaissance over Beirut. Attacked and damaged by four French fighters. On landing a tyre punctured by a bullet caused the aircraft to ground loop and its undercarriage collapse. Believed not repaired.

| 24-25 Jun 1941 | 38 Sqn | Wellington IC | W5628 Y | Op: Benghazi |

P/O R J Cooper
Sgt Pottie
Sgt Ekin-Smyth
Sgt Leisk
Sgt Ritchie
Sgt Mallaby

Took off 2005, Shallufa. Lost a propeller and reduction gear when 48km from Mersa Matruh and crash-landed near Sidi Barrani. DBR.

| 26 Jun 1941 | 47 Sqn | Wellesley I | L2637 | Unknown |
| | | | SOC. NFD. |

| 27 Jun 1941 | 211 Sqn | Blenheim I | L8443 | Unknown |

Suffered engine failure and landed with the undercarriage retracted 26km NE of Wadi Halfa. Presumably not repaired. SOC 20.5.42.

| | 16 Sqn SAAF | Ju 86Z-7 | 641 | Op: Mattu |

Lt A H Pumfrey SAAF
Crew

Took off Algato, one of two Ju 86Z-7s sent to bomb buildings at Mattu. On return crashed on landing at Algato.

| | OADU | Wellington IC | P9277 | Delivery Flight |

P/O C F Butler

Took off, Luqa, for Egypt, but ditched at 0900. NFD.

	Sgt A D Cragg		+	The dead are commemorated on the Runnymede
	P/O L H Campbell-Rogers RCAF		+	Memorial, SOC 8 July.
	Sgt F R Adams			
	Sgt P D Webster			
	Sgt J T Lindsay			

28 Jun **1941**	**203 Sqn** P/O L Harvey P/O H E Jarman RAAF Sgt Macintosh	**Blenheim IV**	**Z9827 Q**	**Op: Anti-shipping** Took off 0225, LG 28 (Burg el Arab), on a search for shipping off the W coast of Crete. Crash-landed LG 106 on return at 0810 hrs. SOC 9.6.42.

29 Jun **1941**	**82 Sqn** Sgt J A Cover RCAF Sgt A T Thomas Sgt R G G Fairweather	**Blenheim IV**	**Z9545 B** + + +	**Op: Tripoli** Took off Luqa, and seen to catch fire and crash in the target area. All of the crew are buried in Tripoli War Cemetery. The target was perhaps shipping attacked the previous day off Tripoli by Marylands of 69 Sqn.

1-2 Jul **1941**	**OADU** Sgt J W Hamborough Sgt S T Flowers RAAF Sgt J E Jamieson RCAF F/Sgt R R Jowett Sgt A Newbould Sgt A J Lassner RCAF F/Sgt H G Simpson	**Wellington IC**	**Z8730** + + + + + + +	**Delivery Flight** Took off 2013, Luqa, for Egypt and came down in the sea. All save Sgt Newbould (buried in El Alamein War Cemetery) and Sgt Flowers (commemorated on the Runnymede Memorial) are commemorated on the Malta Memorial.

2 Jul **1941**	**47 Sqn** Sgt A G Brown F/Sgt S A Elsy F/Sgt D G Barbone	**Wellesley I**	**L2713** + + +	**Op: Gondar** Took off Asmara to bomb Italian positions at Gondar. Shot down over the target by CR.42 fighters (Sergs Mag A Giardina and G Mottet of 410ª Squadriglia). The crew are buried in Asmara War Cemetery.
	84 Sqn Sgt J E Balch Sgt J Wright	**Blenheim IV**	**N6197** + +	**Op: Aleppo** Took off am, Mosul, to bomb Aleppo. Shot down by a D.520 (Lt G C Patin, GC II/3) 106km N of Dayr az Zawr, where it was located, burning, next day by searching 84 Sqn aircraft. The crew is commemorated on the Alamein Memorial.
	84 Sqn F/Lt P R M Williams P/O R Eidsforth Sgt R L Crowe	**Blenheim IV**	**V5629** pow pow pow	**Op: Aleppo** Took off am, Mosul, detailed as above, and also shot down by Lt G C Patin, crash-landing 14km S of Dayr az Zawr. The crew were captured and released by the French when hostilities ended in Syria.
	113 Sqn F/O J P Middlehurst MiD P/O J G Shepherd Sgt J Rooney	**Blenheim IV**	**V5928** + + +	**Op: Derna** Took off 2114, LG 15 (Maaten Bagush Satellite), one of five Blenheims sent to bomb the airfield at Derna. All of the crew are commemorated on the Alamein Memorial.
	24 Sqn SAAF Lt D L Buchanan SAAF Air Sgt D G Malan SAAF Air Sgt E Saks SAAF Air Sgt H H Thomas SAAF	**Maryland II**	**1615** + + + +	**Op: Derna** Took off LG 17 (Fuka Main) on a night bombing raid on Derna, but shot down by flak over the target. All of the crew are commemorated on the Alamein Memorial.

4 Jul **1941**	**84 Sqn** P/O A W Ryan P/O R B Webster F/Sgt L A W Wilkinson	**Blenheim IV**	**T2189** + + +	**Op: Reconnaissance** Took off in the morning from Mosul on a photo reconnaissance mission to Aleppo Airfield. Shot down over Aleppo by an Armée de l'Air Morane MS.406 flown by Adj Chef G Armager of GC 1/7. The pilot bailed out

wounded, but died in captivity six days later. All of the crew are buried in Aleppo War Cemetery.

5 Jul 1941	82 Sqn	Blenheim IV	Z9575	Delivery Flight
	Sgt W E Rand	inj	An engine cut out on take-off Luqa, for Egypt, and the	
	Sgt A D F Murcutt	+	aircraft stalled and crashed near Gudja. DBF. The dead	
	Sgt J Oaten	+	are buried in Malta (Capuccini) Naval Cemetery.	
	Passenger:			
	Cpl W Gape	inj		

7 Jul 1941	148 Sqn	Wellington IC	T2746 R	Op: Aleppo
	F/O F C D Winser	+	Took off Kabrit. On return flew into sand dunes in bad	
	Sgt A Dobson	+	visibility, 64km E of Ismailia, while trying to establish its	
	Sgt F Purnell	+	position. DBF. All but Sgt Beer (commemorated on the	
	F/Sgt L W W Firman	+	Alamein Memorial) are buried in Fayid War Cemetery.	
	Sgt J D Beer	+		
	Sgt J K Callister RNZAF	inj		

	203 Sqn	Blenheim IV	T1988 Y	Op: Anti-shipping
	F/O E C Lane-Sansam DFC		Took off 0545, LG 101, to search for French destroyers	
	P/O R D Lewis DFM		and merchant ships E of Rhodes in the vicinity of Seven	
	Sgt F A Abbott DFM		Capes and Castello Rosso. When both engines failed, the	
			aircraft belly-landed on rough ground on the coast NW	
			of Burg el Arab. DBR.	

8 Jul 1941	113 Sqn	Blenheim IV	V5793	Ground
			Destroyed 0800, at LG 15 (Maaten Bagush Satellite), by Bf 110 fighters.	

9 Jul 1941	110 Sqn	Blenheim IV	Z9533	Op: Tripoli
	Sgt W H Twist	pow	Took off Luqa, one of seven Blenheims detailed to attack	
	Sgt D W Allen	pow	shipping in Tripoli Harbour. Shot down a few km N of	
	Sgt S W Taylor	pow	Tripoli.	

	110 Sqn	Blenheim IV	Z9537	Op: Tripoli
	F/Lt M E Potier	+	Detailed as above. The pilot is buried in Tripoli War	
	P/O T Griffith-Jones	pow	Cemetery.	
	Sgt D H Wythe	pow		

	110 Sqn	Blenheim IV	Z9578	Op: Tripoli
	P/O W H Lowe	+	Detailed as above. The crew is commemorated on the	
	Sgt R E Baird	+	Malta Memorial.	
	Sgt H Lummus	+		

	110 Sqn	Blenheim IV	Z6449	Op: Tripoli
	S/Ldr D H Seale	+	Detailed as above. Last seen ditching. The crew is	
	F/Sgt F B Mulford	+	commemorated on the Runnymede Memorial.	
	F/Sgt W H McDougall	+		

10 Jul 1941	45 Sqn	Blenheim IV	V5509	Op:
			Shot down by Vichy French aircraft near Hammamma. (A-B Serials). Facts doubtful. The aircraft was taken on charge 24 March, but is not mentioned in the sqn ORB thereafter.	

	45 Sqn	Blenheim IV	V5926	Op: Hamah
	Sgt W M Osborne DFM	inj	Took off 1010, Maqueibila, one of twelve aircraft detailed	
	Sgt Martin		to bomb Hamah. Badly damaged when attacked by six	
	Sgt H Garfath	inj	Dewoitine D.520s near Hamah, and crash-landed on return. DBR. The escorting Tomahawks of 3 Sqn RAAF shot down five of the six Vichy French fighters.	

	45 Sqn	**Blenheim IV**	**V5968**		**Op: Beit er Ramal**
	Sgt Stewart		Took off 1605, Maqueibila, one of three aircraft detailed		
	Sgt J A Colway RNZAF		to bomb a crossroads. On landing two 40lb GP bombs,		
	Sgt W Catton		which had hung up in the attack, fell and exploded just		
			prior to touchdown. The aircraft landed safely, but is		
			believed not to have been repaired. SOC 22 December.		

45 Sqn	**Blenheim IV**	**Z6433**		**Op: Hamah**
F/Sgt L T Wilton-Jones	pow	Detailed and lost as V5926 above. The pilot was liberated		
Sgt J C Wimhurst	+	by the 1st Australian Corps when the Vichy French		
F/Sgt D J Lowe	+	surrendered in Syria. Sgt Wimhurst is buried in Beirut		
		War Cemetery and F/Sgt Lowe commemorated on the		
		Alamein Memorial.		

45 Sqn	**Blenheim IV**	**Z6455**	**Op: Hamah**
Sgt D A Cawthen	+	Detailed and lost as above. The crew is commemorated	
F/Sgt K R Cornford	+	on the Alamein Memorial.	
Sgt W D Capewell	+		

45 Sqn	**Blenheim IV**	**Z9547**	**Op: Hamah**
Sgt G M Hardy	+	Detailed and lost as above. One of three shot down by	
Sgt J Newhouse	+	D.520s near Hamah. The dead are commemorated on	
Sgt R Waddington	pow	the Alamein Memorial.	

148 Sqn	**Wellington IC**	**T2975**	**Ground**
		Believed damaged in an air raid, Luqa; SOC 15 August.	
		(Not mentioned in 148 Sqn ORB).	

148 Sqn	**Wellington IC**	**T2980**	**Ground**
		Believed damaged in an air raid, Luqa; SOC 15 August.	
		(Not mentioned in 148 Sqn ORB).	

24 Sqn SAAF	**Maryland II**	**AH352**	**Op: Gazala and LGs**
Lt C W E Blake SAAF		Took off, LG 17 (Fuka Main) one of three Marylands	
Crew		detailed to carry out a night raid on Gazala and the LGs	
		at Tmimi and Martuba. On return the pilot was unable to	
		land at Fuka, which was under enemy attack, attempted	
		to find an alternative airfield, but ran out of fuel and	
		crash-landed, Fuka. DBR.	

12 Jul	**OADU**	**Wellington IC**	**Z8775**	**Delivery Flight**
1941	Sgt E O Townsend	+	Took off 2016, Luqa, for Egypt, but the flaps were	
	Sgt D D P Thomas	+	retracted prematurely and the aircraft crashed and	
	Sgt L F Clay	+	exploded, Safi. All are buried in the Malta (Capuccini)	
	Sgt W J Q Ramsey	+	Naval Cemetery.	
	Sgt R W Askin RNZAF	+		
	Sgt A J Worsfield	+		

13-14 Jul	**38 Sqn**	**Wellington IC**	**N2756 U**	**Op: Benghazi**
1941	F/Sgt J P Wilkins	+	Took off c 1700, Shallufa. FTR. Crews reported burning	
	Sgt F F Clowry RAAF	+	oil on the water outside Benghazi Harbour. The crew is	
	Sgt S M Cashman	+	commemorated on the Alamein Memorial.	
	Sgt W Young	+		
	F/Sgt D Grocott	+		
	F/Sgt A M S Dargie	+		

OADU	**Wellington IC**	**Z8780**	**Delivery Flight**
Sgt D C Haynes	+	Took off Portreath for Gibraltar, but crashed into the sea	
Sgt T V Davies	+	in flames off Espozende Pt, Oporto, Portugal. All are	
Sgt C J Dixon	+	buried in St James Cemetery, Oporto.	
Sgt S J McNeil RCAF	+		
Sgt W B Oakes	+		
Sgt H G Peel RCAF	+		

14 Jul 1941	**110 Sqn** F/Lt C E C Haggitt P/O C D Ramsay P/O F Bennett	**Blenheim IV**	Z9551	**Op: Zuara** Took off, Luqa, to attack Zuara airfield. The brakes failed on landing at Luqa on return, the aircraft overshot and hit a wall. DBR.
	16 Sqn SAAF Lt G E Abbot SAAF Lt D R Wood SAAF Air Sgt W R Wills SAAF Air Sgt P F Hanrahan SAAF Air Sgt E R Scherer SAAF Air Sgt J T Hawkey SAAF	**Ju 86Z-7**	643	**Op: Azezo** Took off Kembolcha, to attack the Italian airfield at Azezo. Hit by anti-aircraft fire over Gondar en route to the target, Lt Abbott made six low-level attacks through heavy machine gun fire until the port engine sustained damage. Knowing that he could not clear the mountains to return to base, he crash-landed 20km SE of Gondar and the crew made its way through enemy territory to Debre Tabor, where they picked up a truck to return to base eleven days later.
17 Jul 1941	**105 Sqn** Sgt G K Williams RNZAF Sgt R E Griffin Sgt N Kay	**Blenheim IV** int int int	Z7366	**Delivery Flight** Took off 1220, Portreath, one of four Blenheims en route to Luqa. Force-landed on the beach at Faro, Portugal, when the aircraft ran out of fuel because an auxiliary fuel pump had broken away from its mounting. The aircraft and crew were interned but escaped on 31 July when taken to Lisbon by the British Consul and placed on the British tramp steamer *Briarwood* which took them to Gibraltar. They arrived back at the squadron's base, Swanton Morley, on 16 August.
	12 Sqn SAAF 2/Lt R A W Blatherwick SAAF P/O A S Middleton RAAF Air Sgt A M Fowler SAAF Air Sgt J S Dunn SAAF	**Maryland II** + + + +	1655	**Gunnery practice** Took off 1130, Shandur, on a gunnery practice flight. A court of enquiry found that the aircraft crashed and was destroyed 4km NE of Suez after it power stalled in an attempt to recover from a dive after testing its front guns. All of the crew are buried at Fayid War Cemetery.
18 Jul 1941	**110 Sqn** W/Cdr T M Hunt DFC F/Sgt F S Thripp Sgt K C Tucker	**Blenheim IV** + + +	Z9582	**Op: Tripoli** Took off Luqa, one of six aircraft detailed to attack a power station. Attacked by an Italian fighter after a successful attack and shot down into the sea approximately 13km from the target c.1430 hrs. All are commemorated on the Alamein Memorial.
19 Jul 1941	**11 Sqn** Sgt E N R Guthrie Sgt D Martin Sgt D A Young Passenger: LAC Davies	**Blenheim IV** inj inj inj	Z5861	**Unknown** An engine cut on take-off from Aqir, and the aircraft crashed and overturned in a ploughed field. DBR.
20 Jul 1941	**OADU** Sgt H J King Sgt A Ryan Sgt W J King	**Blenheim IV**	Z9581	**Delivery Flight** Took off Portreath on delivery to the Middle East, but ran out of fuel in bad weather and force-landed in French Morocco. The crew, having burnt their aircraft, were rescued by a 202 Sqn Swordfish.
	RAF Takoradi Sgt B B Noble P/O Woods Sgt D E Matthews	**Blenheim IV**	V6247	**Delivery Flight** Took off Takoradi on Delivery Flight 161. Undershot landing at Lagos in bad weather and the undercarriage collapsed. DBR.
21 Jul 1941	**OADU** P/O L M Sweeney Crew	**Blenheim IV**	Z7429	**Delivery Flight** Took off Portreath on delivery to the Middle East. Ran out of fuel and crashed at Gibraltar at 1730 hrs.

23 Jul 1941	**110 Sqn** P/O N A C Cathles P/O S G Newborough Sgt B J Child	**Blenheim IV** + + +	**Z7409**	**Op: Anti-shipping** Took off Luqa, to attack merchant shipping in Trapani Harbour, Sicily. The aircraft hit the water twice on the way to the target, carried on to make a successful attack, hitting a ship, but afterwards crashed. No fighters or flak were experienced, the attack being a complete surprise. All three are buried in Catania War Cemetery.
	24 Sqn SAAF Lt J A Williams DSO DFC SAAF Lt L B Bensimon SAAF Sgt H Wilkinson SAAF Sgt E A Myers RAAF	**Maryland II** inj inj	**1656**	**Op: Convoy protection** Took off 2205, LG 17 (Fuka Main). Crossing the coast on return it was hit by enemy anti-aircraft fire and crashed just short of LG 17.
	RAF Takoradi F/O B Pilniak PAF Sgt W J R Hammond Sgt E P P Eden	**Maryland II** inj +	**AH343**	**Delivery Flight** Took off Takoradi, on Delivery Flight 162 to the Middle East. The Maryland crashed when an engine cut on approach to landing at Kuduna, Nigeria.
24 Jul 1941	**110 Sqn** Sgt A J Lee Sgt R Haggett Sgt G Stark	**Blenheim IV**	**Z7410**	**Unknown** A tyre burst on landing and the undercarriage collapsed, Luqa. Presumed DBR in air raids and SOC 18 November.
27-28 Jul 1942	**OADU** Sgt R V Mount P/O D W Garland RNZAF Sgt C W Belcher RNZAF Sgt H C Gibbins Sgt J Templeton RCAF Sgt A MacKie	**Wellington IC** + int int int int int	**X9689**	**Delivery Flight** Took off Gibraltar for Malta, but the starboard engine failed and the propeller flew off. The pilot ordered the crew to bail out and then crash-landed near Lacalle, Algeria. Sgt Mount died of his injuries in hospital and is buried in Bône War Cemetery. His crew were interned in Algeria until 25 November 1942. The crew was ex-214 Squadron.
28 Jul 1941	**14 Sqn** Sgt A Honig Crew	**Blenheim IV**	**Z5770**	**Unknown** Crashed on landing, Nicosia. NFD.
	37 Sqn Sgt A McA Sargent Crew	**Wellington IC**	**W5617**	**Cross country flight** Engine trouble forced the aircraft to land on one engine at Shallufa. The pilot landed well down the runway, overshot the flare-path and the undercarriage collapsed. DBR.
29 Jul 1941	**203 Sqn** Sgt E Langston Sgt H Thompson Sgt J M Munro	**Blenheim IV**	**Z6431 Y**	**Op: Anti-shipping** Took off LG101 to patrol between Crete and Libya. Encountered and unsuccessfully attacked an unidentified submarine. The undercarriage collapsed in a heavy landing at LG 08 (Mersa Matruh).
30 Jul 1941	**84 Sqn** Sgt J W Chambers Sgt G G Bell Sgt Goodwell	**Blenheim IV** inj inj inj	**L9335**	**Training** Took off am, Mosul, on an Army Co-operation Training exercise. Hit a hangar whilst low flying, crash-landed, and DBF. The crew escaped with minor injuries.
	RAF Takoradi Sgt W D Wellwood	**Blenheim IV** inj	**V6498**	**Air Test** Took off Takoradi on an air test but on landing misjudged the approach, landed short of the runway and the undercarriage collapsed. DBR.

Chapter 5

The Axis Repelled
August to December 1941

The failure of the two British offensives, *Brevity* and *Battleaxe*, left the situation in the Western Desert in stalemate. Rommel and his combined German and Italian force were ensconced on the Egyptian border, while further west, in Tobruk, Australian, British, and Indian forces were successfully holding their Axis besiegers at bay. The situation continued thus until September, when Rommel essayed a limited raid, codenamed Operation *Sommernachtstraum*. It failed, and he then turned once more to the problem of Tobruk, planning a new assault on the perimeter. Planned to start on 20th November, it was, however, pre-empted by the major British offensive, Operation *Crusader*, which was launched two days earlier. Aimed at relieving Tobruk, it eventually succeeded in doing so, on the night of 26th November. After a brutal series of attacks and counter-attacks, the Axis forces were driven back by force of numbers, despite inferior generalship (General Auchinleck, C-in-C Middle East, replaced General Cunningham with Major General Ritchie at a crucial point in the battle), retreating to Gazala, though leaving forces invested at Bardia and Halfaya. There, conscious that his weakened force could not long resist the much stronger Eighth Army, he chose to make a further withdrawal, starting on 16th December. Attempts by Eighth Army units to cut him off, as O'Connor's forces had the Italians in January, failed, and by the end of the year the status quo of eleven months earlier had been resumed, with Rommel supposedly crippled, dug in at El Agheila.

During this period the role of the day and night bombers remained much as before, with the night bomber force, now comprising five Wellington squadrons (108 Squadron having been formed in August) undertaking almost nightly what came to be known as the 'milk run' to Benghazi, the principal supply port for the Axis forces. They were also joined, in December, by a small detachment of Fortress Is of 90 Squadron, intended to give the RAF the ability to bomb Tripoli, but these proved ineffective in desert conditions. Losses from enemy action remained relatively light, but those from engine failure in the Pegasus-engined Wellington IC were distressingly frequent, it proving impossible for the IC to maintain height on one engine, even if everything possible was done to lighten the aircraft, and if the non-feathering propeller on the dead engine fell away when, as often happened, the reduction gear sheared. As the autumn gave way to winter, the weather, too, was a hazard, the absence of the navigational aids available to returning Bomber Command crews showing up to particularly disastrous effect on the night of 1st November, when five returning 148 Squadron crews, unable to locate their desert landing ground because of fog, crashed in the desert. No lives were lost, but more than a dozen aircrew were injured, half of them seriously.

The day bomber units, equipped with the Blenheim IV (seven RAF and one Free French squadrons), the Maryland (two SAAF squadrons), and the newly-arrived Douglas Boston (one SAAF Squadron) continued to concentrate on targets immediately behind the front. When adequate fighter cover was provided, losses were generally light, but when caught unescorted, the day bomber units could suffer severely, as did 24 Squadron SAAF, which lost five out of six Bostons in a raid on 9th December, the only survivor returning severely damaged.

Changes were also afoot for two Blenheim squadrons, 45 and 113, which in late December were despatched to the Far East to assist in the defence of Malaya and Singapore.

An unusual operation, and one which initial success led to an attempt to repeat, was the use, on 21st December, of Marylands of 21 Squadron SAAF as a long-range fighter, intercepting far out to sea the Ju 52 transports carrying fuel and other supplies to Rommel's forces. The move was not in itself misjudged, since the Marylands were equipped with four wing-mounted machine guns. But success led to the operation being repeated the next day, despite the misgivings of the squadron commanders, who were convinced that the Luftwaffe would react by sending long-range fighters to protect the Ju 52s. They did, and four Marylands were lost and another badly damaged.

An unusual addition to the Wellington force was a detachment of six aircraft of 109 Squadron, a Bomber Command unit specialising in radio intelligence and counter-measures. Arriving in October, the six aircraft were given the highly dangerous task of flying over enemy territory in daylight, jamming enemy tank radio communications. This, between 20th November and the end of the year, cost the detachment two aircraft shot down and a third severely damaged. The survivors would, in January 1942, be absorbed into what was to become, in March, 162 Squadron.

Meanwhile on Malta, where the departure of the Luftwaffe units had brought a much needed respite, the bomber force had been rebuilt. In the late spring and summer of 1941 five Blenheim squadrons (139, 82, 110, 107 and 105) from 2 Group, Bomber Command, were detached to Malta successively, their task being to disrupt the flow of reinforcements and supplies to the Axis armies in North Africa by attacking ports and shipping. They achieved considerable success, but often at great cost, particularly in low-level attacks on convoys, a squadron at times losing up to half its strength within a fortnight of arrival, mostly to anti-aircraft fire. The night bombers of 38 Squadron, which were detached to Malta between during the summer and early autumn, meanwhile attacked targets in Sicily and mainland Italy, their success leading to the detachment from 3 Group, Bomber Command, in late October, of two Wellington squadrons, 40 and 104, which continued the good work done by 38 Squadron.

Until late November, the level of bombing attacks on Malta remained low, the Regia Aeronautica restricting itself largely to night attacks. So severe was the effect of the attacks on the Axis convoys to North Africa, however, that in late November the Luftwaffe moved Fliergerkorps II back to Sicily, and as December progressed, air raids became heavier and more incessant, the losses of Wellingtons and Blenheims making it difficult to maintain the bombing offensive. Thus nine Wellingtons, including two OADU aircraft staging through to Egypt, were lost in a morning raid on 29 December, and six more would be destroyed on 3 January. Whether offensive operations could be sustained from Malta once more became an issue.

31 Jul - 1 Aug 1941	37 Sqn Sgt D K Taylor Sgt D T Ratcliffe P/O J Prescott Sgt J A Brown Sgt T E Gledhill F/Sgt A L D Barrie	Wellington IC + + + + + +	R1067 A Took off 1930, Shallufa, detailed to bomb harbour installations at Benghazi. On return a message was received that the aircraft was about to come down on the sea near the coast W of Sollum. All are commemorated on the Alamein Memorial.	**Op: Benghazi**
1 Aug 1941	105 Sqn F/Lt A B Broadley P/O A S Ramsay DFC Sgt V R Marsh	Blenheim IV pow + pow	Z9605 U Took off 1540, Luqa, for a shipping strike on two merchant ships in Lampedusa Harbour. The aircraft was hit in the starboard engine by flak and crashed into the sea. P/O Ramsay is buried in Catania War Cemetery.	**Op: Anti-shipping**
	OADU Sgt L D Curtis Sgt A H Geils Sgt J G O'Callaghan Sgt A W Allardice Sgt R E Jones F/Sgt G Prout	Wellington IC inj + + + + +	Z8773 Took off Gibraltar for Malta, but an engine cut, and unable to maintain height the crew ditched in heavy seas off the coast 48km E of Algiers. The dead are commemorated on the Runnymede Memorial. Sgt Curtis was rescued only slightly injured.	**Delivery Flight**
4 Aug 1941	203 Sqn P/O R J Smaile Sgt M G L Hornby	Blenheim IV	V6500 D Took off 2035, LG 101, for night-flying training. On the sixth take-off the pilot retracted the undercarriage prematurely and the aircraft was DBR.	**Training**
5 Aug 1941	24 Sqn SAAF Lt C Clarkson SAAF Sgt C J Fuller RAAF Air Sgt H A Read SAAF Air Sgt G C Green SAAF	Maryland II + + + +	AH354 Took off LG 17 (Fuka Main), to attack Derna. FTR. The bodies of the crew were found and buried on 8 September at Ras el Kanayas, but only that of Air Sgt Read was later recovered. He is now buried in El Alamein War Cemetery; the others are commemorated on the Alamein Memorial.	**Op: Derna**
	Middle East	Blenheim IV	T2188 SOC. NFD.	**Unknown**
8-9 Aug 1941	37 Sqn F/O D F Benbow Sgt W T C Selman P/O Foster Sgt Fowler Sgt Baugh Sgt Buxton	Wellington IC	N2815 L Took off 2105 LG 09. High fuel consumption, caused by the bomb doors not completely closing over the 1,000lb bomb, meant that an engine cut on the return flight. The aircraft was ditched 8km S of Ras El Kenayis and the crew paddled the dinghy to shore in the Daba area.	**Op: Corinth Canal**

	113 Sqn	**Blenheim IV**	**V5990** **Op: Bardia**
	Sgt W R Sands RAAF		Took off 2205, LG 15 (Maaten Bagush Satellite), one of
	Sgt G B Woodroffe RAAF	+	eight Blenheims detailed to attack Gazala No 2 (LG 150),
	Sgt A G Greenlees	+	and gunnery workshops at Bardia. Shot down off Mersa Matruh by RAF night fighters. The dead are commemorated on the Alamein Memorial.
9 Aug **1941**	**16 Sqn SAAF**	**Ju 86Z-7**	**655** **Ground**
	Lt P B Pattison SAAF		The aircraft taxied into a hole on the airfield at Alamata,
	Crew		the undercarriage collapsed, and the aircraft was DBR.
11 Aug **1941**	**105 Sqn**	**Blenheim IV**	**Z7503** **J** **Op: Crotone**
	S/Ldr G E Goode DFC	pow	Took off 1752, Luqa, to attack a chemical works. The
	Sgt N A Nicholls	pow	aircraft was hit in the port engine by flak and force-
	P/O E W Applebee DFM	pow	landed in a field at Cappo delle Colonna, Italy.
12 Aug **1941**	**223 Sqn**	**Wellesley I**	**K7750** **Unknown**
			SOC. The 223 Sqn ORB states that ten of the Squadron's Wellesleys were handed over to 47 Squadron on this date, but since neither this nor the following aircraft appears at any time in 47 Squadron's ORB, it seems likely that neither was in fact transferred, and both were SOC as book entries.
	223 Sqn	**Wellesley I**	**L2648** **F** **Unknown**
			SOC in circumstances as above.
	12 Sqn SAAF	**Maryland II**	**1610** **Unknown**
			Salvaged from Fuka by 52 or 54 RSU on 2.7.41, transferred to 107 MU two days later, and SOC 12 August. NFD.
	24 Sqn SAAF	**Maryland II**	**1616** **Unknown**
			Salvaged by 54 RSU on 2.7.41, transferred to 107 MU two days later, and SOC 12.8.41. NFD.
14 Aug **1941**	**38 Sqn**	**Wellington IC**	**T2989** **F** **Op: Tripoli**
	Sgt W Milligan		Took off 0210, Luqa, but on return landed out of alignment with the flare path. The port wing was raised to clear the control tower and the starboard undercarriage collapsed. SOC 31.10.43 by inventory entry.
15 Aug **1941**	**105 Sqn**	**Blenheim IV**	**Z7522** **E** **Op: Anti-shipping**
	F/O H J Roe	+	Took off 0700, Luqa, to attack a convoy off Bu'ayrat Al
	F/Sgt J D Timms	+	Hasun, Libya. The aircraft hit the mast of one of the ships
	F/Sgt S R Samways	+	and spun into the sea. All are commemorated on the Malta Memorial.
	105 Sqn	**Blenheim IV**	**Z9604** **D** **Op: Anti-shipping**
	P/O P H Standfast	+	Took off, Luqa, detailed as above. Exploded after
	P/O H Sorensen	+	obtaining a hit on one of the tankers in the convoy. The
	Sgt D A D Hoare	+	Pilot and WOp/AG are commemorated on the Malta Memorial while the P/O Sorensen is buried in Tripoli War Cemetery.
	OADU	**Wellington IC**	**X3218** **Ground**
			Damaged in an air raid, Luqa, and SOC.
	Malta	**Wellington IC**	**T2833** **Unknown**
			SOC at Malta, presumably after damage in an air raid.

16 Aug 1941	**223 Sqn** Capt A L Thackwray SAAF	**Maryland II**	**AH332**	**Training** Took off Shandur. While carrying out a practice one-engine landing the pilot lost control and the aircraft spun into the ground, cartwheeled and was wrecked. The pilot, alone on board, sustained only minor injuries.
17 Aug 1941	**203 Sqn** Sgt A Booth P/O L A Smith Sgt E Crossley	**Blenheim IV** +	**Z9552 C**	**Op: Anti-shipping** Took off LG 16 (Fuka Satellite), on an anti-shipping patrol. Both engines cut at low altitude on return and the aircraft ditched in the Mediterranean NW of Sollum Bay, Egypt. The pilot and WOp/AG were rescued but P/O Smith. who was in the nose, was lost when the aircraft broke in half and sank. He is commemorated on the Alamein Memorial.
17-18 Aug 1941	**37 Sqn** Sgt R Gordon Sgt S Harcus RCAF Sgt A Blackmore Sgt L Crump Sgt B Davis Sgt E Tweed	**Wellington IC** pow pow pow pow pow pow	**T2616 K**	**Op: Benghazi** Took off 2124, LG 09, detailed to attack harbour installations at Benghazi. FTR.
18 Aug 1941	**8 Sqn** W/Cdr E Shipley	**Blenheim IV**	**Z6365**	**Unknown** An engine cut on approach to land at Asmara, the aircraft stalled and the undercarriage collapsed. DBR.
	Malta	**Blenheim IV**	**Z6160**	**Unknown** Lost. SOC. NFD.
19 Aug 1941	**14 Sqn** S/Ldr J K Buchanan	**Blenheim IV**	**V5792**	**Unknown** While landing at Habbaniyah at 1100 hrs the aircraft partially stalled after a steep turn and the undercarriage collapsed in a heavy landing. SOC 8 October.
	113 Sqn Sgt N McL Gregor Sgt J R Wallace Sgt S E Miller	**Blenheim IV** + + +	**T2113**	**Bombing Practice** Took off LG 15 (Maaten Bagush Satellite). At 1130 the aircraft's tail hit rocks during recovery from a dive and broke off. The aircraft then crashed into the sea 8km NE of Ras el Kanayas. All of the crew are buried in the El Alamein War Cemetery.
20 Aug 1941	**84 Sqn** Sgt S E Wilton RAAF Sgt S Clough Sgt D S Anderson	**Blenheim IV** inj + inj	**V5443**	**Training** Took off am, Shaibah, on a fighter co-operation training exercise, but stalled in a steep turn at low altitude during fighter affiliation and crashed 33km SW of Shaibah. The observer is commemorated on the Alamein Memorial.
21 Aug 1941	**12 Sqn SAAF** Maj O W B van Ginkel DFC SAAF Lt D H Hillhouse DFC SAAF Sgt R Wells Air Sgt W Graham SAAF	**Maryland II** inj	**1636**	**Op: Menastir** Took off 1730, LG 105 (El Daba), to attack Menastir East Airfield. Attacked on the return journey off Sidi Barrani by two Bf 109 fighters and SOC as BER. Air Sgt Graham was badly wounded.
	12 Sqn SAAF Lt J E M Goodwin SAAF Air Sgt B McD Gerrand SAAF Air Sgt H J Oosthuizen SAAF Air Sgt B E Lea SAAF	**Maryland II** + + + +	**1662**	**Op: Menastir** As above. Attacked and shot down in flames on the return journey at 1900 hrs by Bf 109 fighters 5km E of Sidi Barrani. The crew are commemorated on the Alamein Memorial.

	23 Sqn SAAF	Maryland II	1623	Op: Bardia
	Capt G L Bateman SAAF		Took off LG 17 (Fuka Main), to attack airfields around	
	Lt A S de Burgh-Whyte SAAF		Bardia. Attacked by Bf 109 fighters over the Bay of Sollum.	
	Air Sgt F Joubert SAAF		The pilot flew the burning machine towards land and	
	Air Sgt H F Wiggill SAAF	inj	bailed out only after allowing Air Sgt Joubert (awarded	
			the DFM for his actions) time to rescue Air Sgt Wiggill,	
			severely wounded by gunfire.	

22 Aug	8 Sqn	Blenheim IV	L8518	Unknown
1941	P/O B Fihelly RAAF		A tyre burst on take-off, Kamaran Island, on a flight to	
			Aden, and on landing at Perim Island the aircraft swung	
			and the undercarriage collapsed. DBR.	

	39 Sqn	Blenheim IV	AH361	Op: Reconnaissance
	Sgt C K Berriman RAAF	+	Took off LG 16 (Fuka Satellite), to reconnoitre enemy	
	Sgt H G Waller RAAF	+	lines between Tobruk and the Egyptian frontier. Believed	
	Sgt G M Holstead	+	crashed in Sollum Bay. All are commemorated on the	
	F/Sgt S A McC Crothers	+	Alamein Memorial.	

22-23 Aug	37 Sqn	Wellington IC	N2781	Navigation Exercise
1941	P/O D A Dale	+	An engine cut on take-off at Shallufa, and the aircraft	
	Sgt R G Keen	+	side-slipped into the ground from 300 feet to be DBF.	
	Sgt E McLaughlin	+	All are buried at Suez War Memorial Cemetery.	
	Sgt W H Jones	+		
	Sgt G Mortimer	+		
	Sgt C H T Smith	+		

	37 Sqn	Wellington IC	Z8810 W	Op: Benghazi
	P/O H Liley		Took off 2238, LG 09, to bomb harbour facilities and	
	Sgt Humphrey		shipping, Benghazi. An engine cut on return and the	
	P/O T Treby		aircraft was belly-landed in a maize field 24km NE of	
	Sgt Maddams		Cairo. DBR.	
	Sgt C K Nurse	inj		
	Sgt Stacey			

25 Aug	14 Sqn	Blenheim IV	V5444	Op: Leaflet drop
1941	S/Ldr D M Illsley DFC		Took off 0750, Qaiyara, Iraq, one of 11 aircraft sent to	
	Sgt J H Hibbert		drop leaflets over Teheran. Owing to the duration of the	
	P/O E Burdon DFC		flight, a weak mixture had to be used by the aircraft, two	
			turning back with engine trouble while V5444 also	
			experienced engine trouble and crash-landed in a wadi	
			near Elarjar, just inside the Iraq border. DBR.	

26 Aug	105 Sqn	Blenheim IV	Z7682	Op: Anti-shipping
1941	Sgt R J Scott	+	Took off 1130, Luqa, one of two Blenheims detailed to	
	Sgt W B Healy	+	photograph (and if necessary, bomb) two badly damaged	
	Sgt S G Bastin	+	ships, one E of Kuriat Island, and the other NE of	
			Kerkennah Island. Attacking the latter, Z7682 hit the	
			mast, bursting into flames before crashing into the sea.	
			Sgts Scott and Healy are commemorated on the Malta	
			Memorial, and Sgt Bastin on the Alamein Memorial.	

27 Aug	38 Sqn	Wellington IC	R1180	Unknown
1941	Sgt Gilbert		Hit an obstruction with the tailwheel on take-off, Luqa,	
	Crew		swung on landing and the undercarriage collapsed. DBR.	

	OADU	Wellington IC	N2738	Delivery Flight
	Sgt Scragge		Took off Portreath for Gibraltar. Came into land too high,	
	Crew		lost speed and crashed into an obstacle. DBR.	

OADU	Wellington II	W5569	Delivery Flight
Sgt L A Dyan	inj		
Sgt L F Meyer RCAF	inj		
Sgt H J Ryan			
Sgt R D Stevenson	inj		
Sgt C Desmond	inj		
Sgt H R Teskey RCAF	+		
Passenger: Lt Cdr Longdon			

Took off Portreath for Gibraltar and overshot landing, crashing into Beaufort L5896. Sgt Teskey is buried in Gibraltar North Front Cemetery.

OADU	Blenheim IV	Z7585	Delivery Flight
Sgt D Grant	int		
Sgt R V Dart	int		
Sgt J Bowling	int		

Took off 0915, Portreath, like Z7678 above, and similarly forced by fuel problems to crash-land on the beach at 1500 hrs at Caparica, 14km S of Lisbon. The crew destroyed the Blenheim before they were taken by the maritime police to Lisbon and later that day transferred to a hotel in Caldas da Rainha from which they escaped on 9 September, arriving at Gibraltar on the 11th. All three were back in the UK by 8 October.

OADU	Blenheim IV	Z7678	Delivery Flight
Sgt J B Thompson	int		
Sgt N G Parsons	int		
Sgt R G Martin	int		

Took off 0910, Portreath, in company with aircraft of 107 Squadron on a delivery flight to the Middle East via Gibraltar. The Blenheim suffered from fuel starvation and the pilot landed on the beach at San Jacinto, where the crew burnt the aircraft. Interned by the Portuguese authorities, they escaped with the assistance of British operatives on 9 September along with three other RAF personnel, arriving in Gibraltar on 10 September. Sgts Thompson and Martin returned to the UK in October, but Sgt Parsons flew with another crew from Gibraltar to Malta, whence he was lost on a raid on 19 November.

RAF Takoradi	Maryland I	AH399	Ground

Caught fire at Takoradi shortly after being refuelled, and exploded. Reason unknown. SOC 2 September.

30 Aug 1941	107 Sqn	Blenheim IV	Z7641 C	Op: Licata
	Sgt D J Turner	inj		
	Sgt E J Warmington			
	Sgt G D Robson	inj		

Took off Luqa, but badly damaged by the premature explosion of a previous aircraft's bombs when attacking the target at low level. The explosion destroyed the nose section and flaps, and in landing at Luqa both wings were bent and the undercarriage collapsed. The aircraft was under repair but destroyed by bombing and SOC on 5 September.

12 Sqn SAAF	Maryland II	1648	Transit
Capt T S Fisher SAAF			
2Lt H H Houreld SAAF			
Sgt S C Fox SAAF			
Air Sgt J M Mullineux SAAF			

Took off 1730, LG 105 (El Daba), one of five aircraft that took off for a forward landing ground (LG 02 Sidi Barrani) in preparation for a night attack on Benghazi. The attack was cancelled and 1648 crashed on landing back at LG 105. SOC 3 September.

OADU	Wellington II	W5559	Delivery Flight
Sgt W F Butler	+		
Sgt T P Butterfield	+		
Sgt M H Cope	+		
Sgt D R A Garrick	+		
Sgt D D Todd	+		
Sgt I I Twisleton-Wykeham-Fiennes	+		

Took off Gibraltar for Malta. Shot down in flames by CR.42s 12km S of Lampedusa. All save Sgt Twisleton-Wykeham-Fiennes (commemorated on the Runnymede Memorial) are commemorated on the Malta Memorial. SOC.

OADU	Blenheim IV	Z7583	Delivery Flight
Sgt K E Carey	inj		
Sgt G E Moth	inj		
Sgt C J Brett	inj		

Took off Gibraltar for Malta, but one engine cut, the aircraft lost height and ditched in the sea 106km E of Gibraltar.

30-31 Aug 1941	**38 Sqn** P/O D P C F Mauchlen Sgt J H Joy Sgt S G Shirley-Thomson RNZAF Sgt L G Spilsbury Sgt H J Phillips P/O S J Wrinch	**Wellington IC**	X9737 Z + pow + pow pow pow	**Op: Tripoli** Took off 1730, Luqa, to attack harbour facilities, but brought down near the target. Italian radio claimed an aircraft was shot down in flames by a torpedo boat. The dead are buried in Tripoli War Cemetery.

31 Aug 1941	**113 Sqn** Sgt G L R Sulman Sgt D L Rhodes RNZAF Sgt P Thacker	**Blenheim IV**	T2066 + + +	**Op: Benghazi** Took off 2000, LG 15 (Maaten Bagush Satellite), one of three Blenheims detailed to attack shipping in Benghazi Harbour. Believed shot down by flak in the Harbour area. The crew are commemorated on the Alamein Memorial.
	113 Sqn W/Cdr R H Spencer DFC P/O W J Sears F/Sgt P J R Pratt	**Blenheim IV**	V6136 + + +	**Op: Benghazi** As above, and also believed shot down by flak in the Harbour area. The crew are commemorated on the Alamein Memorial.

31 Aug - **1 Sep** 1941	**148 Sqn** F/Sgt R T Gayer Sgt R J Collier Sgt R T Dodd Sgt G C S Leach Sgt N Jarvis Sgt L G McCormack	**Wellington IC**	Z8791 + + + + + +	**Op: Benghazi** Took off LG Z/LG 208 (Mahsma), detailed to bomb harbour facilities at Benghazi. FTR. The 148 Sqn ORB states that the bodies of Leach, Dodd and McCormack, together with their burnt-out aircraft, were found near Wadi Suissaba, 96km S of Tobruk by Army forward patrols. Their bodies could not, however, be found post-war. F/Sgt Gayer and Sgt Leach are commemorated on the Alamein Memorial, and Sgts Collier, Dodd, Jarvis and McCormack on the Runnymede Memorial.

1 Sep 1941	**8 Sqn** Sgt R S Edwards RAAF Sgt F Harrison Sgt J Cooper Passengers: Mr Oliver Mr Lendrum	**Blenheim I**	L8505 inj inj inj inj inj	**Unknown** Took off Khormaksar but swung, hit the sea and overturned. All aboard were injured, but none seriously. SOC.

4 Sep 1941	**105 Sqn** Sgt W H Wallace Sgt L D Parry Sgt J E Jones	**Blenheim IV**	Z7654 Y + + +	**Op: Crotone** Took off Luqa, to attack a chemical factory at Crotone. One wing was blown off by a direct flak hit over Crotone Harbour, and the aircraft crashed into the harbour. The crew (from 107 Sqn) are buried in Salerno War Cemetery.

5 Sep 1941	**45 Sqn** Sgt C P Melly P/O F L Rippingale MBE Sgt J Halsall	**Blenheim IV**	Z5888 A	**Training** Took off Habbaniyahh/Dhibban, to practice formation flying, but engine failure caused the aircraft to swing on take-off and crash. DBR.
	RAF Takoradi Sgt C W Mott Crew	**Blenheim IV**	Z9536	**Delivery Flight** Took off, Kano, for Maiduguri. On landing there swung off the runway into soft sand and tipped up. DBR.

5-6 Sep 1941	**37 Sqn** F/O R H Wheeler P/O J R Parsons F/O K S Peterson RNZAF Sgt V F Hyatt Sgt F A Leitch Sgt W Hutton	**Wellington IC**	T2512 P + + + + + +	**Op: Derna** Took off 2130, LG 16 (Fuka Satellite), and lost without trace. All are commemorated on the Alamein Memorial.

6-7 Sep 1941	**148 Sqn** P/O J A G Parker Sgt I McP McDonald Sgt R V F Clarke Sgt F W Burrows Sgt E Evans Sgt J O'Brien	**Wellington IC** pow pow pow pow pow pow	**W5683 U** **Op: Benghazi** Took off c.2300, LG Z/LG 208 (Mahsma). FTR.
8 Sep 1941	**12 Sqn SAAF** Lt R H Aitchison SAAF Lt P K J Place SAAF Air Sgt L R Scott SAAF Air Sgt G H Carter SAAF	**Maryland II** inj	**1644** **Op: Reconnaissance** Took off 1305, LG 105 (El Daba), to carry out a high-level reconnaissance of the Sollum Bay area looking for an enemy submarine. The crew then went on to attack the alternative target at Bardia, where flak shot away all but the lateral control. The pilot managed to return to base where he ordered the crew to bale out, Air Sgt Scott breaking a leg on landing. The abandoned aircraft executed two perfect turns before diving into the ground near LG 24.
10 Sep 1941	**8 Sqn** F/O J S Owen P/O B Fihelly RAAF	**Blenheim IV**	**R3894** **Unknown** On landing at Khormaksar the pilot was unable to lower the undercarriage due to failure of the hydraulic system. DBR.
11-12 Sep 1941	**OADU** Sgt E Healey Sgt E D Minshall Sgt D J Farrell Sgt B H Dennis Sgt J G Bell	**Wellington II** + + + + +	**W5596** **Delivery Flight** Took off Hampstead Norris for Gibraltar. Sgt Farrell, washed ashore at Quiberville, France, is buried in Quiberville Cemetery. The others are commemorated on the Runnymede Memorial.
12 Sep 1941	**55 Sqn** W/Cdr R D Welland MiD F/O J Dodds RAAF F/Sgt J W Lucas Passenger: Maj I K Whittaker AAIC	**Blenheim IV** + + + +	**Z9588** **Op: Anti-submarine patrol** Took off 0315, Aqir, on an anti-submarine sweep from Beirut to 13km E of the Suez Canal. A message was received at 0515 indicating that the aircraft was on the return leg of its mission, and ordering four late breakfasts. FTR. All, including the Australian Army Observer, are commemorated on the Alamein Memorial.
	105 Sqn Sgt F B Brandwood Sgt J Miller Sgt A G Mee	**Blenheim IV**	**Z7357 U** **Op: Anti-shipping** Took off Luqa, to attack an Axis convoy of five merchant ships escorted by seven destroyers off the coast of Tripoli. This aircraft was hit by flak from the destroyers, set on fire and ditched about 16km from the convoy. The crew took to the dinghy and were rescued the following day by HM Submarine *Utmost*.
	105 Sqn F/Sgt J Bendall Sgt F K Hindle F/Sgt A Brown	**Blenheim IV** inj	**Z9606 V** **Op: Anti-shipping** Took off Luqa, detailed as above. The aircraft was badly damaged by flak from the destroyers, lost its hydraulics and belly-landed on return to Luqa.
	107 Sqn S/Ldr F R H Charney DFC Sgt S Porteous Sgt D R Harris	**Blenheim IV** + + +	**Z7504 G** **Op: Anti-shipping** Took off Luqa, detailed as above. Hit by flak from the destroyers, the aircraft cartwheeled into the sea in flames. The crew are commemorated on the Malta Memorial.
	107 Sqn Sgt J E Mortimer Sgt D J Reid F/O C D Owen	**Blenheim IV** + + +	**Z9603 F** **Op: Anti-shipping** Took off Luqa, detailed as above. Hit by flak from the destroyers, the aircraft crashed into the sea. The crew are commemorated on the Runnymede Memorial.

13 Sep 1941	8 Sqn Sgt A L Walker AC1 S J Oxley	Vincent + +	K4130 **Unknown** Took off Mukayris but stalled and dived into the ground. Both crew members are buried in Ma' alla Cemetery.

14 Sep 1941	55 Sqn	Blenheim IV	V5927 **Unknown** The undercarriage was retracted in error on landing, Aqir. SOC 4.3.42

	113 Sqn	Blenheim IV	T2184 **Night Flying Test** Last recorded operating with 113 Sqn on 29 November 1940, but perhaps Blenheim Z2184 (not a valid serial), recorded as under salvage by 54 RSU at Habbaniyah, on 3 September. If so, this may be one of two Blenheims lost in the May action against the Iraqis, but unidentified. AM 78 shows T2184 as SOC 1.1.1947 by inventory entry.
	24 Sqn SAAF Lt M Hamm SAAF P/O H Batzofin Air Sgt D J McIntosh SAAF Air Sgt J P Tonkin SAAF	Maryland II + + +	1654 **Op: Sidi Barrani** Took off 1750, LG 17 (Fuka Main), to bomb German tanks and troops in the Sidi Barrani area. Attacked by fighters at 1830 hrs, the aircraft caught fire and blew up, throwing the pilot out, unconscious. He came to in time to open his parachute, landing near some British tanks. The dead are commemorated on the Alamein Memorial.

14-15 Sep 1941	38 Sqn Sgt S J Rane RAAF Sgt D Lyth RAAF P/O MacLean Sgt J C Smith Sgt J F Otten RCAF Sgt A Maxwell	Wellington IC inj inj inj inj inj	X9685 **Op: Tripoli** Took off Luqa to lay mines off Tripoli Harbour. On return the starboard engine cut near Malta and the propeller and reduction gear were lost; crash-landed at Luqa.
	148 Sqn Sgt V V Skerman RAAF Sgt C J Corley RAAF Sgt L W J McCabe Sgt C E Bloor Sgt S A Cameron Sgt F E Gunther	Wellington IC + + + + + +	Z8724 **Op: Benghazi** On take-off from Fuka hit a dispersal pen. Sgt Gunther died of injuries on the16th. All are buried in El Alamein War Cemetery.

17 Sep 1941	105 Sqn F/Sgt J Bendall F/Sgt A Brown Sgt C H Hill	Blenheim IV + + +	P4840 Y **Op: Anti-shipping** Took off 1430, Luqa, one of four Blenheims (three from 105 Sqn and one from 107 Sqn) detailed to attack two 800-ton schooners being towed by a tug at position 35° 15' N, 11° 47' E. The aircraft crashed into the sea when it hit an arrester wire between the masts of one of the schooners. All the crew are commemorated on the Malta Memorial.
	107 Sqn P/O P E C Robinson Sgt B F Brooks Sgt F Burrell	Blenheim IV + + +	Z7755 O **Op: Anti-shipping** Took off 1430, Luqa, detailed as above. The aircraft crashed on the deck of one of the schooners and exploded, possibly having been hit by flak. All the crew are commemorated on the Runnymede Memorial.

21 Sep 1941	148 Sqn	Wellington IC	R1249 **Unknown** Crash landed after an engine fire, Kabrit. (In the 148 Sqn ORB the loss is not mentioned, but the aircraft does not appear in the operational records after the 20th.) SOC 26 September.

22 Sep 1941	105 Sqn	Blenheim IV	Z7423 H	Op: Homs

W/Cdr D W Scivier AFC +
F/Sgt L M Barnett +
F/Sgt B Gray DFM +

Took off 1335, Luqa, to attack Axis army barrack blocks and ammunition dumps at Homs. The aircraft was cut in two when it collided with Blenheim Z9609 of the same squadron and crashed near to the target. All the crew are buried in Tripoli War Cemetery.

113 Sqn   Blenheim IV   V5993   Training

Lt D Thorne SAAF inj
F/O D F Brooks +
Sgt L L Inganni inj
Passenger:
Sub-Lt Bradshaw RN

Took off LG 15 (Maaten Bagush Satellite), on night-flying training. Crashed on approach on return to Maaten Bagush. F/O Brooks is buried in the El Alamein War Cemetery.

OADU   Wellington II   Z8335   Delivery Flight

Sgt R B Hewitt +
Sgt J C Edwards-Cross +
Sgt A J B Hallett +
Sgt G F W Moraes +
Sgt E J Mutton RCAF +
Sgt A R Powell RCAF +

Took off Luqa for Egypt. Missing, presumed lost at sea. All are commemorated on the Runnymede Memorial.

OADU   Wellington II   Z8354   Delivery Flight

P/O R T A McConnochie +
Sgt L C J Marien +
P/O H M Walsh RAAF +
Sgt F J Kemp +
Sgt M W Foxon +
Sgt E Murch +

Took off Hampstead Norris for Gibraltar, but the port engine failed and the aircraft crashed near Abingdon. P/O McConnochie, whose date of death is given as 25 September, is buried at Harwell Cemetery, along with P/O Walsh and Sgt Foxon, Sgt Marien at Leicester City Cemetery, Sgt Kemp at Marton St Paul Cemetery, and Sgt Murch at Hounslow Cemetery.

22-23 Sep 1941   38 Sqn   Wellington IC   Z8776   Op: Tripoli

Sgt R Secomb RAAF +
F/Sgt W F P Brown +
F/Sgt R H Toshack RCAF +
Sgt J C Sheridan +
Sgt W J Poole +
Sgt P F Bold +

Took off Luqa. FTR. Sgt Secomb is buried in Tripoli War Cemetery; the others are commemorated on the Malta Memorial.

23 Sep 1941   84 Sqn   Blenheim IV   L9216   Unknown

Crashed. NFD.

84 Sqn   Blenheim IV   T2427   Unknown

SOC. NFD.

24 Sep 1941   55 Sqn   Blenheim IV   Z6371   Op: Anti-shipping

Sgt W Bain inj
Sgt K A Hepburn RNZAF +
Sgt S E Elsmore inj
Ground staff
Air Mech G J Hicks SAAF +
Air Mech E G Pinnock SAAF inj
Air Mech Looker SAAF inj

Took off 0920, LG 17 (Fuka Main), on an anti-shipping sweep, and landed at LG 02 (Sidi Barrani) at 1125 for re-briefing. Took off at 1232 with instructions to return to LG 02 at 1630, but became lost on return. In attempting a landing in the dark at LG 68 (Waterloo), the pilot misjudged his height and flew into a ridge on approach to a dummy flare-path, hitting a tent and injuring three armourers of 1 Sqn SAAF, one of whom died a few days later. Sgt Hepburn is buried in the El Alamein War Cemetery and Air Mech Hicks in Cairo War Cemetery.

107 Sqn   Blenheim IV   Z9599   Op: Misurata

S/Ldr T J S Warren DFC +
F/O J T Waterfall +
P/O W E Law +

Took off 1405, Luqa, one of two Blenheims detailed to attack transport on the Misurata - Benghazi road. The target was attacked and flak encountered. NFD. All are commemorated on the Malta Memorial.

25 Sep 1941	**8 Sqn** Sgt A G White RAAF Sgt J E Stoddard F/Sgt E V Message	**Blenheim IV** + + +	V6222	**Calibration Exercise**

Took off Khormaksar on a radar calibration exercise. The pilot lost control for reasons unknown and the aircraft crashed in the Gulf of Aden 53km S of Aden. All are commemorated on the Alamein Memorial.

	84 Sqn Sgt C A Brackpool Sgt White Sgt W Miller	**Blenheim IV**	V5578	**Unknown**

On take-off 1315 from Mosul, an engine cut, and the aircraft crashed in a forced landing 4km from Mosul. DBR.

	RAF Takoradi 2/Lt B R McKenzie SAAF	**Blenheim IV**	Z7587	**Air Test**

Took off Takoradi for an engine air test. One of the engines failed, and the aircraft crash landed 5km E of Takoradi. DBF.

	Middle East	**Blenheim IV**	V5878	**Unknown**

Crashed. NFD.

27 Sep 1941	**37 Sqn** F/Lt E E C Tomkins Sgt W T C Selman F/Sgt M V Connolly RCAF Sgt D O McFall Sgt L R Mack Sgt B G Watson	**Wellington IC** + + + + +	R1095 F	**Ground**

At dispersal, LG 09, F/Lt Tomkins left his aircraft to obtain a cushion; while he was away a 250lb bomb exploded and the aircraft was destroyed. The dead are buried at El Alamein War Cemetery.

	37 Sqn Sgt R A Mirre Sgt Haine Sgt Hawkins Sgt Hogg Sgt Palmer Sgt Badman	**Wellington IC** inj	X8684	**Ground**

DBR by the explosion of R1095.

	21 Sqn SAAF Lt A Louw SAAF 2/Lt E W B Fripp SAAF Air Sgt I H McFadyen SAAF Air Sgt R S Daniels SAAF	**Maryland II** pow + + +	1650 G	**Op: Bardia**

Took off 1506 LG 21 (Qotafiyah III), one of nine Marylands detailed, on the second mission of the day, to attack shipping in Bardia Harbour. The crew, on its first operation, was shot down in flames over the sea by two Bf 109s. Two parachutes were seen but only the pilot survived. The dead are commemorated on the Alamein Memorial. Both of the fighters were shot down by Maj J F Britz and his crew, in Maryland 1653 'K', one by the pilot using the front guns and the other by the rear gunners.

27-28 Sep 1941	**108 Sqn** S/Ldr G F Irving F/Sgt T C Fitzgerald RCAF W/O S Howarth F/Sgt W Trotter F/Lt M J Miller F/Sgt E H Keeping	**Wellington IC** + + + + + +	T2729 V	**Op: Rhodes**

Took off 1400, Fayid. A message was sent stating that engine was failing, and that a course was being set for Turkey. It is believed the aircraft ditched close to shore on the S side of Rhodes. All are commemorated on the Alamein Memorial.

28 Sep 1941	**45 Sqn**	**Blenheim IV**	Z9534	**Unknown**

SOC. NFD.

	55 Sqn F/Lt J H Wilson Sgt A F Wiles DFM F/Sgt A E Griffin	**Blenheim IV** + pow +	Z7374	**Op: Bardia**

Took off 0403, LG 17 (Fuka Main), one of three detailed for a low-level attack on a 2,000-ton ship in Bardia Harbour. Believed shot down by flak in the target area, and reported as crashing in flames in the sea. The dead are commemorated on the Alamein Memorial.

55 Sqn	**Blenheim IV**	**V5560**	**Op: Bardia**
Sgt W A Ross	+		
Sgt C I Johnston RNZAF	+		
Sgt E J Sprange	+		

Took off 0407, LG 17 (Fuka Main), detailed as above. After completing the attack V5560 was seen to continue inland at c10 metres. Hit by flak, it crashed into a small house, killing the three crew and several German soldiers. The crew is buried in Halfaya Sollum War Cemetery.

211 Sqn	**Blenheim I**	**K7098**	**Training**
Sgt R J Good RAAF			

The undercarriage was damaged on take-off when the pilot retracted it prematurely, and jammed; crash-landed, Wadi Gazouza. (At the time of the loss 211 Sqn had been designated to set up 72 OTU, but the Sqn had not yet been disbanded.)

Middle East	**Blenheim IV**	**Z6368**	**Unknown**

SOC. NFD.

---

29 Sep 1941	**203 Sqn**	**Blenheim IV**	**Z6445 Y**	**Op: Anti-shipping**
	P/O T R Ruxton	+		
	Sgt R J Young RAAF	+		
	Sgt W B Billingsley-Dooley	+		

Took off 0545, LG 101, on anti-shipping patrol. Almost certainly shot down by a Bf 110 fighter escorting the British tanker, the SS *Tiberio*, which, like the Blenheim crew, it had mistaken for an Italian tanker. The pilot is buried in Khayat Beach Cemetery, Israel, and the observer and WOp/AG are commemorated on the Alamein Memorial.

---

30 Sep 1941	**30 Sqn**	**Blenheim I**	**L4917 B**	**Unknown**

SOC on this date, presumably as an inventory entry relating to an earlier loss, since by this date 30 Sqn was equipped with Hurricanes.

45 Sqn	**Blenheim IV**	**Z7509 S**	**Op: Gambut**
F/O J K Edmonds			
P/O L E Durrant RNZAF			
Sgt K J Chapman			

Took off 1800, LG 16 (Fuka Satellite), one of six detailed to bomb Gambut LG. Landed down-wind at night after the pilot became ill on return, swung and the undercarriage collapsed. DBR.

OADU	**Wellington II**	**Z8353**	**Delivery Flight**
Sgt H M Kennedy			
Sgt W L Smith			
Sgt E L Jackson			
F/Sgt E A Gamble			
Sgt D A MacDonald			
Sgt R L Kitch	+		

Took off Gibraltar for Malta, one of a flight of five, but became separated in heavy rain and low cloud after giving up their map to the flight leader, who did not have one!, Turned south, identified Cap Bon, and turned north for Malta. The port engine cut at 80m and the aircraft crashed into the sea off Cap Bon. Sgt Kitch is commemorated on the Malta Memorial, where his unit is wrongly given as 200 Sqn.

1-2 Oct 1941	**55 Sqn**	**Blenheim IV**	**V6306 R**	**Op: Anti-shipping**
	F/Lt J A Harries	+		
	Sgt L C Wheeler			
	F/Sgt J T Peacock	+		

Took off 1205, LG 17 (Fuka Main). Landed and refuelled at Giarabub and took off at 1630 hrs on an unsuccessful anti-shipping sweep to locate a tanker and three other vessels at 31° 42' N, 18° 42' E. On re-crossing the coast S of Benghazi the pilot strafed and bombed an enemy airfield. The aircraft crashed 33km ESE of Sidi Barrani at about 0030 hrs, after running out of fuel. F/Lt Harries was found near the wrecked aircraft, his parachute unopened, and was buried at a spot 94km on the Mersa Matruh - Sidi Barrani road. He is commemorated on the Alamein Memorial. F/Sgt Peacock is buried in El Alamein War Cemetery.

2 Oct 1941	**Gp Bomb 1** P/O D Neumann FAFL	**Blenheim IV** +	**T1855** **Paratroop Familiarisation Flight** Crashed, possibly because of engine failure at low altitude. The pilot is buried in Demir, Syria.
2-3 Oct 1941	**37 Sqn** Sgt L G Fuller RAAF Crew	**Wellington IC**	**T2508 O** **Op: Benghazi** Swung on take-off, LG 09, burst a tyre and the undercarriage collapsed; DBR.
3-4 Oct 1941	**37 Sqn** F/Lt H J Honour Sgt Jackson Sgt I M Hendricksen RNZAF Sgt G T Price Sgt W Friend Sgt M C F James	**Wellington IC**	**Z8768 V** **Op: Benghazi** Took off 1910, LG 09. An engine caught fire on the return flight. The aircraft was about to ditch 25 metres off the coast at El Dhaba when the port propeller flew off. The crew paddled ashore in their dinghy, three of them slightly injured.
4 Oct 1941	**107 Sqn** Sgt D E Hamlyn Sgt C A Latter RAAF Sgt D Williams	**Blenheim IV** int int int	**V5821** **Op: Zuara** Took off Luqa, Malta. Attacked over the Mediterranean by CR.42 fighters after leaving the secondary target of Zuara airfield, and ditched 96km N of Tripoli at 1430. The crew were picked up near Djerba a few days later. They were released from internment in November 1942, after the invasion of French North Africa.
4-5 Oct 1941	**70 Sqn** Lt C A D Key SAAF P/O W Stewart Sgt A McPhail Sgt R M Shand Sgt W J Logie Sgt A Stewart	**Wellington IC** pow pow pow pow pow pow	**T2828 X** **Op: Benghazi** Took off Fuka, detailed to bomb Benghazi. FTR. Not mentioned in the 70 Sqn ORB.
5 Oct 1941	**148 Sqn** Sgt J K Pickering Sgt R C King Sgt W J Hunter Sgt E E Sparks	**Wellington IC** inj	**Z8733 S** **Communications flight** Took off Kabrit. Engine caught fire; crash-landed 12m W of Burg El Arab; DBF. The crew suffered from shock and abrasions, Sgt Pickering also having 2 broken legs.
7 Oct 1941	**223 Sqn**	**Wellesley I**	**L2705** **Unknown** SOC. NFD.
	12 Sqn SAAF Lt A M C Smith SAAF Air Sgt T A Mitchell SAAF Air Mech L Solomon SAAF Air Sgt J G Inglethorpe SAAF	**Maryland II** + inj	**1638** **Op: Gazala** Took off 0940, LG 105 (El Daba), one of nine Marylands detailed to bomb ammunition dumps at Gazala. Ten minutes after it left the target on a southerly course, four Bf 109 fighters attacked this aircraft over 10 to 12 minutes, by which time the pilot had lost tail trim, the starboard engine had been shut down, the port engine had also sustained damage and both tyres had been punctured. Nonetheless the pilot managed to land at LG 07 (Matruh West), doing a mild ground loop in doing so. WOp/Air Mech Solomon later died of his wounds. He is buried in the El Alamein War Cemetery. SOC or not?
8 Oct 1941	**105 Sqn**	**Blenheim IV**	**Z7367 L** **Unknown** SOC. NFD.

8-9 Oct 1941	**148 Sqn** P/O Cowan P/O W Astell P/O Alexander Sgt Piper Sgt McCurdy	**Wellington II**	**W5594 R**	**Op: Benghazi**

Took off LG 104, detailed to bomb Benghazi harbour and shipping. The port engine failed over the target on the bombing run. The aircraft flew on one engine as far as Sidi Barrani before running into rain and sleet, becoming hard to hold on course. When the other engine began to fail, the aircraft rapidly lost height and landed with the undercarriage up, bounced clear of a sand dune and disintegrated.

9 Oct 1941	**107 Sqn** W/Cdr F A Harte DFC P/O C O Bloodworth F/O T Wewage-Smith Passenger: Lt E E A Talbot RE	**Blenheim IV**	**Z7638** + + + +	**Op: Anti-shipping**

Took off Luqa, on a sweep off the S coast of Italy. At 1440 collided in mid-air with Z7644, crashing at Capo Sant' Allessio. All are buried in Catania War Cemetery.

	107 Sqn F/O N W Walders RNZAF Sgt S Jones Sgt W K Hunting RCAF	**Blenheim IV**	**Z7644** + + +	**Op: Anti-shipping**

Took off Luqa, detailed as Z7638, with which it collided in mid-air. All are buried in Catania War Cemetery.

10 Oct 1941	**203 Sqn** F/O J P Rowntree Sgt J A Edwards RNZAF F/Sgt F W Norton	**Blenheim IV**	**V6493 L** + + +	**Op: Reconnaissance**

Took off LG 101 on reconnaissance from Libya to Crete. A radio signal was received at base from this aircraft giving an ETA of 1730 hrs but nothing further. Possibly lost while low flying when an engine cut. The crew are commemorated on the Alamein Memorial.

11 Oct 1941	**47 Sqn** P/O G W Gordon	**Wellesley I**	**K8529**	**Mail Flight**

Took off Addis Ababa, but crash landed at Adigrat after engine failure. SOC 17 October.

	107 Sqn Sgt A D M Routh Sgt R N Parker Sgt G F McLeod RCAF	**Blenheim IV**	**Z7618** + + +	**Op: Anti-shipping**

Took off Luqa, on an anti-shipping strike in the Gulf of Sirte. At 1404 hrs an Italian convoy consisting of a tanker, the cargo vessel *Priaruggia* and two destroyer escorts, was located and attacked at position 31° 53' N, 15° 43' E. Hit by flak from the *Priaruggia*, Z7618 crashed into the sea. The pilot and observer are commemorated on the Alamein Memorial, and Sgt McLeod on the Malta Memorial.

	107 Sqn F/O R A Greenhill Sgt A MacK Smith Sgt C A Whidden RCAF	**Blenheim IV**	**Z9663** + + +	**Op: Anti-shipping**

Took off Luqa, detailed as above, and, hit in the belly by flak from the *Priaruggia*, Z7618 crashed into the sea after passing over the ship. The pilot and observer are commemorated on the Malta Memorial, and Sgt Whidden who was rescued, died in hospital on 4 November and is buried in Tripoli War Cemetery.

12 Oct 1941	**OADU** Sgt K F Ward Crew	**Wellington II**	**Z8334**	**Delivery Flight**

Took off Portreath for Gibraltar. The port engine failed during the flight, and the aircraft swung on landing at Gibraltar without flaps, the undercarriage collapsing. DBR.

13 Oct 1941	**203 Sqn** F/O G Washington Sgt L R Read RAAF F/Sgt C K Bremner	**Blenheim IV**	**Z9619 M** + + +	**Op: Reconnaissance**

Took off LG 101 to reconnoitre between Libya and Crete. Reported as being shadowed by enemy aircraft, and probably attacked by one of them prior to loss. The crew are commemorated on the Alamein Memorial.

16 Oct 1941	**107 Sqn** F/O S McAllister + Sgt E H Brenton RAAF + Sgt W E Martin RCAF inj	Blenheim IV	Z7511	**Unknown** Took off Luqa. An engine caught fire and the aircraft crashed in circuit, Luqa, and DBF. The dead are buried in Malta (Capuccini) Naval Cemetery.
16-17 Oct 1941	**37 Sqn** Sgt Carver Crew	Wellington IC	T2801 G	**Op: Benghazi** Took off LG 104, 2227, but when only just airborne hit a fuel bowser and crashed. The bowser caught fire but the aircraft did not, although it was a total wreck.
17 Oct 1941	**84 Sqn** Sgt S Owen AC1 J S Wilkinson	Blenheim IV	V6094	**Unknown** On approach to land at Habbaniyah one flap did not lower; the aircraft went into a steep and uncontrollable turn and crashed. DBF.
17-18 Oct 1941	**37 Sqn** Sgt R A Mirre Sgt Mattock P/O J F R Mitchell RCAF Sgt T Penrose Sgt J Blanche Sgt C V Catheralll	Wellington IC	Z8735 N	**Op: Benghazi** Took off 1840, LG 104. Ran out of fuel on return, unable to locate the ALG and crashed in a forced landing 3km SE of Gilal Railway Station. All suffered minor injuries.
19 Oct 1941	**55 Sqn** 2/Lt J N Murphy SAAF + F/O J C MacDonald RAAF + Sgt J J Pender RAAF +	Blenheim IV	Z7416	**Op: Anti-shipping** Took off 1355, LG 17 (Fuka Main), on a sweep NW of Derna. Last sighted W of Derna. FTR. The crew are commemorated on the Alamein Memorial.
20 Oct 1941	**55 Sqn** S/Ldr H G P Blackmore + Sgt W D L Cole RNZAF + Sgt L C Rhoades RAAF +	Blenheim IV	V6228	**Op: Gambut** Took off 0525, LG 17 (Fuka Main), with two others, for high-level bombing raid on Gambut No 1/Main (LG 139). Attacked by four Bf 109s shortly after bombing at 0720, the aircraft gradually lost speed and height and ditched 53km N of Gambut. Lost without trace, crew is commemorated on the Alamein Memorial. Possibly shot down by Ofhr Friedrich Korner (2./JG27), who claimed a kill at 0945.
	84 Sqn	Blenheim IV	V5505	**Unknown** SOC. NFD.
	113 Sqn 2/Lt E H Burr SAAF + Sgt C L Jenkinson RNZAF + Sgt K I Duffin RAAF +	Blenheim IV	V5641	**Op: Gambut** Took off 0710, LG14 (Maaten Bagush), detailed as above. Attacked by enemy fighters just after leaving the target, fell away and not seen again. The crew are commemorated on the Alamein Memorial.
21-22 Oct 1941	**104 Sqn** P/O D Ellis inj F/Sgt R S G Thornton RNZAF inj Sgt E M G Davies + P/O J C Boyers Sgt Bapton RCAF F/Sgt Dixon	Wellington II	Z8411 Z	**Op: Naples** Took off Luqa. On return, failed to put on full flap when landing, overshot and hit an obstruction. Sgt Davies is buried at Malta (Capuccini) Naval Cemetery. Three of the crew suffered injuries.
22 Oct 1941	**18 Sqn** F/Sgt J D Woodburn DFM RCAF + Sgt L Lawson + Sgt G Robinson +	Blenheim IV	Z7898 W	**Op: Homs** Took off Luqa, one of six Blenheims detailed to bomb military barracks at Homs. Following Blenheim Z7802, this aircraft ran into its 40lb bombs, which were fitted with parachutes, and exploded. The crew are buried in Tripoli War Cemetery.

23 Oct 1941	107 Sqn	Blenheim IV	Z9708	Unknown

Damaged its undercarriage on take-off, Luqa, and had to land with the undercarriage partially down. DBR.

23-24 Oct 1941	40 Sqn	Wellington IC	X9912	Relocation Flight
	Sgt J D Paine	+		
	Sgt W D Stuart RNZAF	+		
	Sgt R Jackson	+		
	Sgt C R Eastman	+		
	Sgt B W Nicholls	+		
	Sgt E W Hewitt	+		
	Passengers:			
	Sgt E W Sherwood	+		
	Cpl J B Robinson	+		
	AC1 W A Hodges	+		
	LAC R M Wade	pow		

Took off Alconbury for Luqa, and ditched out of fuel north of Sicily. Sgt Hewitt is buried in Catania War Cemetery, and the others are commemorated on the Runnymede Memorial. LAC Wade was washed ashore unconscious on the coast of Sicily.

	40 Sqn	Wellington IC	X9974	Relocation Flight
	P/O C G R Saunders RCAF	+		
	Sgt H L Steadman RCAF	+		
	P/O A Lodge	+		
	Sgt A N Irving RCAF	+		
	Sgt D Y N Crosby RCAF	+		
	Sgt V J Hale	+		
	Passengers:			
	F/Sgt H Higginson	+		
	Sgt E Beard	+		
	Cpl G I F Davies	+		
	LAC C Robson	+		

Took off Hampstead Norris for Gibraltar, but clipped a boundary fence and lost the pitot tube. The pilot attempted a circuit preparatory to landing, but stalled and crashed. P/Os Saunders and Lodge, Sgts Beard, Crosby, Irving and Steadman are buried at Wyton; Sgt Hale at Crowthorne; F/Sgt Higginson at Leicester (Gilroes) Cemetery; Cpl Davies at Thatcham; and LAC Robson in Warley Congregational Cemetery, Halifax.

---

24 Oct 1941	113 Sqn	Blenheim IV	V6464	Unknown
	Lt V E Wright SAAF			
	Sgt E J Curtis RAAF			
	Sgt K R Hansen RAAF			
	Passenger:			
	Cpl E V Watkins			

An engine cut on take-off from LG 11 (Qasaba); the aircraft was belly-landed on rough ground and DBR.

24-25 Oct 1941	104 Sqn	Wellington II	W5398 D	Op: Tripoli
	Sgt Nichols			
	Crew			

Took off, Luqa, to attack the harbour and shipping at Tripoli. Landed too fast; braked and undercarriage collapsed, Luqa, on return. DBR.

---

25 Oct 1941	107 Sqn	Blenheim IV	Z7704	Op: Zuara-Benghazi Rd
	F/Sgt W T Shaver RCAF	+		
	Sgt A Stanier	+		
	Sgt G L Wincott	+		

Took off Luqa, one of two Blenheims patrolling the Tauza-El He section, searching for targets of opportunity. Crashed 26km E of Tauza at 1350 hrs, believed while low flying. F/Sgt Shaver died of burns on 26 October and Sgt Wincott of severe injuries on the 27th. All are buried in Tripoli War Cemetery.

	OADU	Wellington IC	X9989	Delivery Flight
	P/O P E MacKie			
	F/Sgt C A Bergstein RCAF			
	Sgt L G Lowe RCAF			
	Sgt K S Turner	+		
	Sgt H H Taylor			
	Sgt D G Anderson RCAF	inj		

Took off Harwell for Gibraltar, but failed to gain height because of flap failure and hit an obstruction half a mile from the runway, at Aldworth. Sgt Anderson, seriously injured, died in hospital on 19 November. He is buried in Walberton (St Mary) Churchyard, and Sgt Turner in Harwell Cemetery.

---

28 Oct 1941	OADU	Wellington IC	Z8974	Delivery Flight
	Sgt F V Clayton			
	Crew			

Took off Portreath for Gibraltar. After landing at Gibraltar a gust of wind caused the aircraft to nose over; it was DBR.

29 Oct 1941	OADU Sgt G A Corbett Sgt I A Stark Sgt C Souter	Blenheim IV	Z7843 **Delivery Flight** Took off Gibraltar and landed downwind at Luqa, hitting a wall. DBF. The crew were ex-110 Sqn.

	OADU Sgt A E Belasco P/O D R Lake Sgt D G McG Mayo	Blenheim IV + + +	Z7979 **Delivery Flight** Took off Luqa for Egypt, but ran out of fuel and dived into the sea 13km N of Ras Engla. All are commemorated on the Runnymede Memorial.

29-30 Oct 1941	55 Sqn Lt G C Reid SAAF Sgt H P S Annells RAAF Sgt J K K Browne RAAF	Blenheim IV inj inj	R3660 **Op: Tmimi** Took off 1845, LG 53 (Fuka Point), one of nine aircraft detailed to bomb Tmimi landing ground and dumps. Attacking the target the aircraft was hit either by light flak or a night fighter, which shot away part of the rudder and tail fin, and damaged the elevators. Virtually unable to steer the aircraft the pilot managed to locate the lights of Alexandria where he turned W for 15 minutes. Both engines cut through lack of fuel and the Blenheim ditched at 0055 hrs 180 metres offshore 30km from El Alamein. The crew swam ashore.

	55 Sqn Lt D H Blair SAAF Sgt B P Hoad RAAF Sgt R H Wilson RAAF	Blenheim IV + + +	Z7683 **Op: Tmimi** Took off LG 53 (Fuka Point), detailed as above. NFD. Very bad weather conditions prevailed at the time. All of the crew are commemorated on the Alamein Memorial.

	148 Sqn Sgt T Taranto RAAF P/O D M Elliott RCAF Sgt D H Warner Sgt J I Bramwell Sgt S C Ray Sgt D F Conley	Wellington II + + + + + +	Z8330 S **Op: Candia & Suda Bay** Took off Kabrit to attack shipping off Candia and Suda Bay, but FTR. All are commemorated on the Alamein Memorial.

	148 Sqn F/O N E Canton Sgt D H Townshend Sgt W D Black Sgt S N Bailes Sgt H Brown Sgt R R Rutland	Wellington II pow + + + + +	Z8368 W **Op: Candia & Suda Bay** Took off Kabrit, briefed as above. FTR. On 26 November, news was received that F/O Canton was being sheltered by Cretans, but he was eventually captured by the German occupying force. The dead are commemorated on the Alamein Memorial.

---

30 Oct 1941	21 Sqn SAAF Lt D L Lamont SAAF Lt J J Reyneke SAAF Air Sgt G N Jonas SAAF Air Sgt P A Bleth SAAF	Maryland II pow pow pow pow	1672 B **Op: Benghazi** Took off 1015 hrs LG 75 to bomb Benghazi Harbour. Turning to port to locate the target, this aircraft, leading the third vic, collided with Maryland 1661 'D' and crash-landed. The other aircraft made it back to base.

	OADU F/Sgt J D Graham P/O H J Knight RCAF Sgt I J Bevan	Blenheim IV pow pow pow	Z7782 **Delivery Flight** Took off Gibraltar for Malta. Intercepted and damaged by Italian fighters and crashed-landed on the Sicilian coast between 1330 and 1530.

---

1 Nov 1941	45 Sqn P/O R A Brown F/O J Wright Sgt A Jenkins Passengers: 2/Lt A D Allen SAAF 2/Lt T C Evans SAAF Two others	Blenheim IV	V5435 W **Ferry Flight** On take-off, LG 53, on a ferry flight to Fuka Satellite (LG 16) the starboard tyre burst, the aircraft ground looped and the undercarriage collapsed. DBF. At the time of the crash it is estimated that at least nine personnel, including the crew, were on board.

82 Sqn	**Blenheim IV**	N6146	**Unknown**
		SOC. NFD.	

105 Sqn · **Blenheim IV** · Z6377 N · **Unknown**
AM Form 78 states that the aircraft was SOC on Malta November 1941. Believed DBR in an air raid.

113 Sqn · **Blenheim IV** · Z5907 · **Unknown**
2/Lt C N Summersgill SAAF
P/O G A Gray RAAF — inj
Sgt C J R Stokes RAAF — inj
Sgt Parkinson
Took off LG 15 (Maaten Bagush Satellite). The port engine caught fire and the aircraft crash-landed near Maaten Bagush. Sgt Parkinson was an army passenger.

1-2 Nov 1941

70 Sqn · **Wellington IC** · T2543 · **Unknown**
Sgt Sadd
Sgt Parker
F/O W H Norledge
Sgt McGregor
F/Sgt McNicholas
F/Sgt Cooke
Took off 1030, LG 60. An engine cut on approach, Kabrit, and with no time to lower the undercarriage, the aircraft was belly-landed. SOC 10.5.42

148 Sqn · **Wellington II** · Z8336 K · **Op: Benghazi**
Sgt H W Burr
Crew
Took off 1940, LG 104, detailed to attack Benghazi. Short of fuel and force-landed in fog; swung and the undercarriage collapsed. DBR.

148 Sqn · **Wellington II** · W5556 H · **Op: Benghazi**
Sgt K F D Attwell
Sgt R J Titterington — inj
Sgt W Phillips — inj
Sgt F A Wait — inj
Sgt Grath
Sgt Dossettering
Took off 1910, LG 104, detailed as above. On return force-landed out of fuel in fog 5km SW of LG 104. DBR.

148 Sqn · **Wellington II** · Z8332 C · **Op: Benghazi**
P/O R B Milburn
Sgt M R Knisley RCAF — inj
Sgt H B Cassie RNZAF — inj
Sgt D Hutchison
Sgt W P Griffiths
Sgt R P Morley
Took off 1945, LG 104, detailed as above. On return crashed in a forced landing in fog in the desert 40km SE of Fuka. DBR. All of the crew sustained injuries, but only two were seriously hurt.

148 Sqn · **Wellington II** · Z8348 · **Op: Benghazi**
Sgt Lane RAAF
Crew
Took off LG 104, detailed as above. On return crash-landed in fog 3km W of LG 104. DBR. (The 148 Sqn ORB gives the letter X to both Z8348 and Z8349.)

148 Sqn · **Wellington II** · Z8349 · **Op: Benghazi**
Sgt A P Mayhew
Sgt J Bowman — inj
Sgt Finlay
Sgt J Keenan — inj
Sgt Field
Sgt Wakeham
Took off LG 104, detailed as above. On return crashed in a forced landing in fog, 10km S of LG 103. DBR. Sgts Bowman and Keenan were seriously injured.

2 Nov 1941

45 Sqn · **Blenheim IV** · V6143 T · **Op: Tobruk-Bardia Rd**
Sgt F Scott
Sgt G E Sully — +
Sgt J R Mansfield — +
Took off LG 53, one of five Blenheims detailed to bomb a supply dump on the Tobruk-Bardia Road. On return, attempting to land at LG 53 in dense fog, one wing hit the ground and a hung-up 250lb bomb dropped and exploded. The crew were thrown clear but the observer and WOp/AG died of their injuries. They are both buried in the El Alamein War Cemetery.

2-3 Nov 1941	40 Sqn	Wellington IC	X9763 U	Op: Tripoli
	Sgt G D Colville	+		
	Sgt I R McCalman RAAF	+		
	Sgt H M Forth	+		
	Sgt E D Spry	+		
	Sgt T W Robson	+		
	Sgt J T Ackroyd	+		

40 Sqn Wellington IC X9763 U — Op: Tripoli. Took off Luqa to attack Castel Benito aerodrome, Tripoli, and shot down by Italian night fighters. Sgts Colville and Robson are buried in Tripoli War Cemetery, and the remainder commemorated on the Malta Memorial.

OADU Wellington IC Z1040 — Delivery Flight
Sgt R Wade +
Sgt G E Williamson +
Sgt J G Smith RCAF +
Sgt N Bradley +
Sgt W H Jeffries +
Sgt E A Main +
Took off Gibraltar for Malta between 2040 and 2130. Shot down into the sea by Sottoten Virgilio Vanzan of 10 Gruppo. All are commemorated on the Runnymede Memorial.

OADU Wellington IC X9991 — Delivery Flight
Sgt F Lighthouse
Crew
Took off Gibraltar for Malta. Undershot landing at Luqa, the nose hit a boundary wall and the undercarriage collapsed. One crew member, unidentified, was injured.

4 Nov 1941 223 Sqn Martin 167F AX692 — Training
Lt L L Gordon SAAF
Took off Shandur, to carry out night-flying circuits and landings; undershot the airfield on landing, and crash-landed. The pilot attempted to open up his engines but the port engine did not respond. The accident report found that he had turned the port engine off, instead of the crossfeed on. Several Maryland accidents had happened because of this earlier, and a modification was carried out to eliminate this type of accident. The aircraft, DBR, was ex-Armée de l'Air No 1167.

OADU Blenheim IV T1853 — Delivery Flight
F/Lt T W Horton RNZAF
F/Sgt D H Thrower inj
F/Sgt Howe
Took off Portreath for Gibraltar. A propeller fell off and the aircraft crashed into the sea on approach to Gibraltar.

5 Nov 1941 18 Sqn Blenheim IV Z7801 P — Op: Anti-shipping
Sgt H Vickers +
F/Sgt G A Lowe RCAF +
Sgt A F Daniels +
Took off Luqa, one of eight Blenheims detailed to attack a convoy consisting of two 2-3,000 ton motor vessels and one destroyer, located at position 31° 59' N, 1° 16' E Gulf of Sidra at 1154 hrs. Shot down into the Gulf of Sidra by flak from the escorting destroyer before dropping its bombs. All the crew are commemorated on the Malta Memorial.

18 Sqn Blenheim IV Z7922 A — Op: Anti-shipping
Sgt R J Morris +
P/O P H M Clark +
P/O J J Kelly RCAF +
Took off Luqa, detailed as above, and shot down into the Gulf of Sidra by flak from the motor vessel and escorting destroyer after bombing one of the motor vessels. The pilot is commemorated on the Malta Memorial, and the others on the Runnymede Memorial.

21 Sqn SAAF Maryland II AH392 K — Op: Berka
2/Lt N C Blake SAAF +
2/Lt F R Meintjies SAAF +
Air Sgt P H Clarence SAAF +
Air Sgt L R G Brand SAAF +
Took off 0755, LG 21 (Qotafiyah III), one of six detailed to attack the airfield at Berka. They refuelled at LG 75, taking off at 1140 hrs. Three Italian CR.42s and three German Bf 109s attacked the squadron in a running battle over approximately 20km. The aircraft was seen to catch fire in the port engine and rear gunners' cockpit, crashing near the target at c.1410 hrs. All are commemorated on the Alamein Memorial.

6 Nov 1941	**11 Sqn** Sgt F E Turner RAAF Sgt J S THompson Sgt J C A Bell	**Blenheim IV** inj inj	**T2343** Took off 0118, LG 116, to bomb motor transport workshops at Derna. An engine cut and the aircraft force-landed in the sea near Alexandria.	**Op: Derna**

	148 Sqn P/O H McMaster RAAF Sgt D F Muir AC1 H A Penfold LAC W E Clark RAAF	**Wellington II** + + + +	**Z8365 H** Took off Kabrit on an acceptance test, and stalled on approach. The port engine was feathered, but the pilot turned to port. The aircraft then rapidly lost height, crashed and burst into flames. The two pilots and two ground crew on board were killed. All are buried at Fayid War Cemetery.	**Air Test**

7 Nov 1941	**21 Sqn SAAF** Capt G W Parsons SAAF 2/Lt J H Meyer SAAF Air Sgt P E Methven SAAF Air Sgt L P Stewart SAAF	**Maryland II** pow pow + +	**AH415 G** Took off 0855, LG 21 (Qotafiyah III), one of six Marylands detailed to attack a motor transport garage and repair shops at Derna. Just after bombing the formation was attacked by three Bf 109 fighters. One was shot down by the first flight of Marylands; the others attacked the second flight and concentrated on this aircraft, which was last seen going down between 25 to 40km over the sea northeast of Derna at 1147 hrs, trailing smoke, but with the gunners returning fire. Both are commemorated on the Alamein Memorial.	**Op: Derna**

	OADU P/O R T Hodges P/O W C Craig Crew	**Wellington II**	**Z8352** Took off Gibraltar for Luqa. Landed with one wing low, the aircraft swung, and one engine failed to pick up when the pilot attempted to go around again. Swerved to avoid another aircraft, a tyre burst and the undercarriage collapsed. Still awaiting repair, the aircraft was destroyed in an air raid on 21.4.42.	**Delivery Flight**

8 Nov 1941	**18 Sqn** F/Lt G C Pryor RCAF Sgt D E Mills Sgt T R Buckley	**Blenheim IV** + + +	**Z7895 F** Took off Luqa, one of six Blenheims detailed to attack a convoy of one destroyer and two 2,000 ton motor vessels at position 38° 15' N, 19° 30' E in the Ionian sea 90km W of Kefallonia which had been attacked by 18 Squadron the previous day. Shot down, probably by flak from the destroyer, before bombing. All are commemorated on the Runnymede Memorial.	**Op: Anti-shipping**

	90 Sqn F/O Swanson Crew	**Fortress I**	**AN529 X** Took off Shallufa to attack Benghazi harbour and shipping. Ran out of fuel and force-landed 128km W of Fort Maddelena.	**Op: Benghazi**

	107 Sqn Sgt W A Hopkinson RAAF Sgt I Hamilton Sgt J Gibson	**Blenheim IV** + + +	**V5961** Took off Luqa, to attack a convoy consisting of a destroyer, a merchant vessel and a 3,000-ton motor vessel which was sighted at 1018 hrs. Attacking the motor vessel the aircraft was hit by flak, collided with the mast of a ship and crashed into the sea at 35° 20' N 19° 45' E. All are buried in Phaleron War Cemetery.	**Op: Anti-shipping**

	113 Sqn Sgt J H Moody Sgt A E Hyder Sgt P A Norris	**Blenheim IV** + + +	**Z5867** Took off LG 15 (Maaten Bagush Satellite). Recorded as lost at 0900 hrs. All are commemorated on the Alamein Memorial.	**Unknown**

	223 Sqn	Maryland II	AH334	Training

	223 Sqn	Maryland II	AH334	Training
	W/O2. A R West SAAF	+		
	Air Sgt F H Frolich SAAF	+		
	Air Sgt A F Robertson SAAF	+		
	Air Sgt E F W Hurley SAAF	+		

Took off Shandur, one of two Marylands carrying out a low-level formation training exercise. They flew into a belt of mist but when the leader emerged from the mist no trace could be found of AH334. Later the aircraft was found wrecked near the village of Al-Qazzasin. All are buried in Fayid War Cemetery.

---

10 Nov 1941 · **38 Sqn** · **Wellington IC** · **Z8729 Y** · **Air Test**

Sgt J C Pottie RAAF
Sgt Mostyn
Sgt Leisk
Sgt Mallaby
LAC Holloway
LAC Fisher

Took off Shallufa, 1200. At 250m the port engine cut when the fuel supply was accidentally cut off and the aircraft was crash-landed 5km W of Shallufa. The crew had cuts and bruises; the aircraft was DBR.

11-12 Nov 1941 · **40 Sqn** · **Wellington IC** · **X9765 A** · **Op: Naples**

S/Ldr A D Greer RNZAF — pow
Sgt D Moorey RAAF — pow
Sgt C P Greenhill — +
Sgt J I Henderson RCAF — +
Sgt F G S Fox RCAF — pow
P/O J H S Bebington — +

Took off Luqa to bomb port facilities, Naples. Ditched after engine failure on the return flight. P/O Bebington drowned at that time, and Sgts Greenhill and Henderson when the dinghy overturned in a storm. All three are commemorated on the Malta Memorial. There is a detailed account of this loss in David Gunby's *Sweeping the Skies*, p180.

---

12 Nov 1941 · **55 Sqn** · **Blenheim IV** · **Z9549** · **Op: Anti-Shipping**

P/O T G G Chater — +
P/O A C Johnson RAAF — +
Sgt L T Watson RAAF — +

Took off 1240, LG 17 (Fuka Main), on a shipping sweep NW of Derna. On return at 1830 hrs, the aircraft made a wide circuit on approach and then suddenly crashed and blew up 13km SE of LG 17. All are buried in the Alamein War Cemetery.

12-13 Nov 1941 · **38 Sqn** · **Wellington IC** · **R1139 M** · **Op: Benghazi**

F/O J D Hall — pow
P/O D S Iles — pow
P/O M W Schofield — pow
Sgt G L I Felber — pow
Sgt Robinson — pow
Sgt W A Weaver — pow

Took off LG09. Force-landed on the beach 60km W of Tobruk after engine failure.

148 Sqn · **Wellington II** · **Z8338 Z** · **Op: Benghazi**

F/Sgt J J Watson — +
F/Sgt H O Talty — +
F/Sgt F G Nadeau RCAF — +
Sgt F A Pegram — +
Sgt J Davidson — +
Sgt H Colling — +

Took off LG 104, detailed as above. Presumably shot down into the sea, since Sgt Davidson is buried in Halfaya Sollum War Cemetery, and Sgt Colling in Nicosia War Cemetery. The others are commemorated on the Alamein Memorial.

148 Sqn · **Wellington II** · **Z8340 C** · **Op: Benghazi**

Sgt R E Shears — +
Sgt R A Palmer — +
Sgt H J G Jefferey — +
Sgt W C J Spencer — +
Sgt B A Beeby — +
Sgt R West — +

Took off LG 104, detailed to bomb Benghazi harbour and shipping. FTR. Sgts Palmer, Beeby and West are commemorated on a Special Memorial in Benghazi War Cemetery. The remainder are buried in Benghazi War Cemetery.

---

13 Nov 1941 · **70 Sqn** · **Wellington IC** · **N2811 T** · **Op: Benghazi**

Sgt G A Morley
Sgt Macadam
Sgt Cave

Failed to climb after take-off, LG 60, and crash-landed LG 104. The accident card records that three members of the crew were injured, but not their names.

Sgt Lockley
Sgt Powell
Sgt Slocombe

14 Nov 1941	**47 Sqn** S/Ldr D M Illsley Sgt K V Rann Sgt L J Martin RAAF	**Wellesley I** + inj inj	**L2659** **Op: Adwa** Took off Asmara to search for and (if found) bomb 15 German aircraft rumoured (falsely) to have landed at Adwa 130km S of Asmara. A broken oil pipe caused the engine to seize and the pilot tried to land over a hill 6.5km W of Kilo 148, Adi Quala-Adua road, stalled and crashed. The aircraft was DBR. The pilot is buried in Asmara War Cemetery.

	12 Sqn SAAF Lt R J Stevens SAAF 2/Lt M C Meadows SAAF Air Sgt W Crounkamp SAAF Air Sgt G B Edwards SAAF	**Maryland II** pow pow + pow	**AH287** **Op: Derna** Took off 1125, LG 105 (El Daba), one of nine Marylands detailed to bomb dispersed enemy aircraft on Derna airfield. Bombing took place at 1345 hrs. Intense flak was encountered and AH287, seriously damaged, was last seen at a height of 450m off Marsa Lucch. An Italian radio broadcast reported the aircraft crashed near the target and the crew was captured. Air Sgt Crounkamp is commemorated on the Alamein Memorial. Lt Stevens took part in the Great Escape from Stalag Luft III, was recaptured at Rosenheim and murdered on 29 March 1944. He was cremated at Munich, and his ashes buried in Poznan Old Garrison Cemetery

14-15 Nov 1941	**OADU** Sgt J P Barlow RCAF Sgt Leonard Sgt C C Duncum RNZAF Sgt Welch Sgt B H Cameron RCAF Sgt P Potter RCAF	**Wellington IC** inj	**Z8989** **Delivery Flight** Took off Gibraltar for Luqa, but attacked by CR.42s and ditched 40km SW of Pantelleria. The crew was rescued after 6 hours in their dinghy. Ex-9 Squadron, they joined 40 Squadron on Malta. There is an account of their rescue by HSL 129 in Frederick Galea's *Call-Out*, pp100-101.

15 Nov 1941	**12 Sqn SAAF** Air Sgt J C Middel SAAF Cpl D S van Wyk SAAF Air Mech P J Allen SAAF Air Mech N F Chaplin SAAF Air Mech B J Englebrecht SAAF Air Mech W A D Thomson SAAF Air Mech E W Rafferty SAAF Air Mech E J Whitehead SAAF	**Maryland II** + + + + + + inj inj	**AH350** **Ground** Blew up at LG 105 (El Daba), at approximately 1630. The aircraft had returned from a mission with two hung-up bombs. Maintenance work was being carried out when AH350 caught fire, setting off the two hung-up bombs. The accident report states that the explosion was due to an explosion of petrol vapour in the bomb bay, probably caused by a lighted cigarette or match. Those killed are buried in the El Alamein War Cemetery. SOC 6.4.42.

	21 Sqn SAAF Lt F H Roulston SAAF Lt D Kilcommons SAAF Air Sgt W B Wright SAAF Air Sgt E A Fentonby-Smith SAAF	**Maryland II** + + + +	**AH403** **W** **Op: Gazala** Took off 1250, LG 21 (Qotafiyah III), one of six Marylands detailed to bomb two stores dumps situated about 8km E of Gazala landing ground. Ten minutes after leaving the target the squadron was attacked by two Bf 109F fighters. This aircraft immediately lost height and dived towards the coast pursued by one of the fighters, smoke coming from its starboard engine, and was shot down approximately 40km N of Tobruk. All are commemorated on the Alamein Memorial.

	OADU Sgt F C Banks Sgt D D Lowcock Sgt W A Eaton	**Blenheim IV** +	**Z7887** **Delivery Flight** Took off Gibraltar for Malta. Attacked by fighters en route and crashed at Takali after running through a flooded area. The WOp/AG, who died of wounds received in action, is buried at Malta (Capuccini) Cemetery. The aircraft was DBR.

16 Nov 1941	37 Sqn	Wellington IC	W5626 Q	Op: Bardia

F/O P R Bellamy +
Sgt G Anderson +
P/O J B King +
P/O H A Staszuk RCAF +
Sgt C V Catherall +
Sgt R F Rudee RCAF +

Took off between 0110 and 0300, ALG 09. FTR. All six are commemorated on the Alamein Memorial.

16-17 Nov 1941	148 Sqn	Wellington II	Z8355 B	Op: Benghazi

F/Lt R H Gordon +
F/O P A Bitmead +
F/Sgt A G C Hunter +
Sgt D T Clark +
Sgt R Murphy +
Sgt D F Pickerill +

Took off 2055, LG 104 (Gazala), and brought down by heavy flak, bursting into flames and crashing on or near the aerodrome. All are commemorated on the Alamein Memorial.

17 Nov 1941	8 Sqn	Blenheim IV	V6290	Unknown

P/O D H F Pitt RAAF
Sgt F H Saban
Sgt P K McQuirk inj
LAC E T Darby +
AC2 J P Wright +

Hit a lorry on take-off, Khormsakar, caught fire when airborne and crashed. The crew escaped unhurt, but two airmen in the lorry, which ignored a warning sign, were killed. The bomb-load did not explode but was later detonated. The two airmen are buried at Maala War Cemetery.

	14 Sqn	Blenheim IV	T2241	Unknown

Sgt V C Royals
P/O G L A McKenny
Sgt C C Murfitt inj
F/Sgt R W Chubb +
F/Sgt A L Ellis +
F/Sgt B L Jenkins +

Swung on took off 0630, LG 15 (Maaten Bagush Satellite), in poor visibility and hit a tent, killing three off-duty 14 Squadron aircrew. The crew escaped with only slight injury to the air-gunner, though the aircraft caught fire and the bomb load exploded. The dead are buried in El Alamein War Cemetery.

18 Nov 1941	14 Sqn	Blenheim IV	Z9543	Op: Bir el Baheira

P/O C D Loughlin +
P/O E D Main +
P/O A Franks +

Took off 1010, LG 75, detailed to attack twelve Axis aircraft on the landing ground at Bir el Baheira No 1 (LG 140). FTR. All are commemorated on the Alamein Memorial.

	105 Sqn	Blenheim IV	Z7408	Unknown

SOC. NFD.

	21 Sqn SAAF	Maryland II	AH396 U	Op: Gazala

Lt H D Reid SAAF +
Lt D M Beddy SAAF +
Air Sgt C F B Pappenfus SAAF +
Air Sgt A W Conn SAAF +

Took off 0649, LG 21 (Qotafiyah III), one of nine Marylands detailed to bomb enemy aircraft on Gazala No 2 Landing Ground (LG 150). Circling, at 0915, to locate the target through cloud the squadron was attacked by 12 Messerschmitt Bf 109F and Fiat G.50 fighters. The squadron jettisoned its bombs and sought cloud cover but AH396 was attacked by eight of the fighters and shot down in flames 11km W of Tobruk. All are buried at Knightsbridge War Cemetery, Acroma.

19 Nov 1941	18 Sqn	Blenheim IV	V6060 U	Op: Anti-Shipping

Sgt D W Buck +
F/Sgt D C Newsome RCAF +
Sgt F Thompson +

Took off Luqa, one of six Blenheims despatched on an anti-shipping strike in the Gulf of Sirte. A convoy consisting of the German MV *Spezia* (5,000 tons) the Italian MV *Cadamosto* (2,000 tons) and a small Italian motor sailer, the *Cora*, escorted by a small Italian destroyer, the *Centauro*, was sighted 1445 hrs at position 32° 02' N, 16° 50' E course 270°. Shot down by the *Centauro*. Sgt Buck and F/Sgt Newsome are commemorated on the Malta Memorial and Sgt Thompson on the Alamein Memorial.

18 Sqn	**Blenheim IV**	**V6492 P**	**Op: Anti-Shipping**
Sgt J H Woolman	+		
Sgt R V W Walker	+		
Sgt H Macaulay RCAF	+		

Took off Luqa, detailed as above, and also shot down by the destroyer *Centauro*. All the crew are commemorated on the Malta Memorial.

18 Sqn	**Blenheim IV**	**Z7860 F**	**Op: Anti-Shipping**
Sgt H L Hanson	+		
Sgt G N Parsons	+		
Sgt J S Poulton	+		

Took off Luqa, detailed as above, and FTR. Sgts Hanson and Poulton are commemorated on the Alamein Memorial and Sgt Parsons on Special Memorial E in Tripoli War Cemetery. His body was recovered and he was buried at the time in Sirte Military Cemetery, but his grave has since been lost.

45 Sqn	**Blenheim IV**	**V5943**	**Op: Army Co-operation**
S/Ldr A Hughes			
P/O L E Durrant RNZAF			
F/Sgt D Cliffe			

Took off 1120, LG 75, one of six Blenheims detailed to bomb the battle area at Sidi Rezegh. Shot down by flak and belly-landed in the middle of a tank battle near Sidi Omar. The crew reached British lines and returned to their squadron two days later.

45 Sqn	**Blenheim IV**	**Z7510 C**	**Op: Army Co-operation**
P/O E A Magor RAAF	+		
F/O A J Cain RAAF	+		
Sgt T S MacLiver RAAF	+		

Took off 1120, LG 75, detailed as above. Shot down, location unknown. All the crew are commemorated on the Alamein Memorial.

107 Sqn	**Blenheim IV**	**Z7914**	**Ground**

Overshot on a ground run and crashed into quarry, Luqa.

113 Sqn	**Blenheim IV**	**V5866**	**Unknown**
Sgt J F Hemus	+		
Sgt J B Dewar	+		
Sgt W T Lee RCAF	+		

Crashed on take-off LG 107 (Giarabub), reason unknown. All are buried in Halfaya Sollum War Cemetery.

12 Sqn SAAF	**Maryland II**	**AH319**	**Op: Bardia-Tobruk Rd**
Lt T L Braithwaite SAAF	+		
2/Lt E Clyde-Morley SAAF	pow		
Air Sgt R B Wilkins SAAF	pow		
Air Sgt T B Atkinson SAAF	+		

Took off 1500, LG 76, detailed to attack German troop concentrations along the Bardia - Tobruk road. Shot down by medium flak over the target and crashed 26km NW of Bardia. The dead are commemorated on the Alamein Memorial.

OADU	**Wellington IC**	**X9940**	**Delivery Flight**
• Sgt M H Knowles			
Crew			

Took off Luqa for Fayoum. Ran out of fuel and the undercarriage collapsed in a forced landing 1km SW of Helwan. DBR.

19-20 Nov 1941	**38 Sqn**	**Wellington IC**	**T2991 D**	**Op: Derna LGs and Bardia**
	Sgt F H Lewis RAAF	+		
	Sgt G H Hellyer	+		
	Sgt P Fenn	+		
	Sgt N J Sharpe	+		
	Sgt J V Hamilton	+		
	F/Sgt E Combes	+		

Took off ALG 09. Crashed in a forced landing at El Imayid and blew up. All are commemorated on the Alamein Memorial.

38 Sqn	**Wellington IC**	**Z8711 F**	**Op: Derna LGs and Bardia**
Sgt Swingler RCAF			
Sgt A G Metcalf RNZAF			
P/O McLean			
Sgt Dawson			
Sgt Peak			
Sgt Poole			

Took off ALG 09 between 1945 and 2128. The crew got lost on return and the aircraft, out of fuel, was abandoned near Bahariya Oasis, 250 miles S of Sidi Barrani. The crew set off for the coast and were spotted by a 37 Sqn aircraft and picked up two days later.

20 Nov 1941	**11 Sqn**	**Blenheim IV**	**V6268**	**Op: Army Co-operation**
	P/O P F Smith			
	F/O J R Cockton			
	Sgt Copsey			

Took off 1445, LG 76, to bomb aircraft and motor transport at pinpoint 470401. The aircraft was hit fourteen times by flak over the target and DBR. SOC 24 November.

11 Sqn	**Blenheim IV**	**Z5866**	**Op: Army Co-operation**

P/O J L Loam
P/O R J Ingram RAAF
Sgt B Burnley RAAF — inj

Took off 1445, LG 76, detailed as above. The aircraft was hit by flak over the target, disabling the undercarriage, puncturing the inner petrol tank and damaging the turret. The air-gunner was wounded in the foot by shrapnel and the pilot belly-landed the aircraft on return to LG 76 at 1720 hrs. SOC 24 November.

113 Sqn	**Blenheim IV**	**T2117**	**Unknown**

SOC. NFD.

21 Sqn SAAF	**Maryland II**	**AH302 V**	**Op: Army Co-operation**

Lt R S Haines SAAF — +
Lt M A Vermeulen SAAF — +
Air Sgt L W Balcomb SAAF — +
Air Sgt M R Jack SAAF — +

Took off 1130, LG 76, one of nine Marylands detailed to attack armour and troop concentrations at the crossroads at El Adem on the Tobruk by-pass road. Attacked at 1230 hrs, before they got to the target, approximately 4km SW of El Adem by four Bf 109 fighters led by Lt H A Stahlschmidt of 1/JG27. Five Marylands were lost and DBR on this mission. This aircraft, the third lost, was shot down in flames 26.5km S of El Adem. All are commemorated on the Alamein Memorial.

21 Sqn SAAF	**Maryland II**	**AH305 E**	**Op: Army Co-operation**

Lt E S Corbett SAAF — +
Lt B A Garden SAAF — +
Air Sgt G N James SAAF — +
Air Sgt R G Black SAAF — +

Took off 1130, LG 76, detailed as above. Shot down by Lt H A Stahlschmidt and crashed 6.5km south of El Adem, but not before its gunners had shot down one of the Bf 109 fighters, the first aircraft lost. All the crew are commemorated on the Alamein Memorial.

21 Sqn SAAF	**Maryland II**	**AH387**	**Op: Army Co-operation**

Lt M C E MacDonald SAAF
Lt J H du Plessis SAAF
Air Sgt C D Russell SAAF — inj
Air Sgt K G du Pre SAAF

Took off 1130, LG 76, detailed as above. This aircraft was chased by Lt Stahlschmidt for over 80km; it reached its base severely damaged. Recorded as Cat B damaged, it was sent to a RSU but there is no further record of use and it seems likely that it was reduced to salvage. For his action in saving the life of Air Sgt Russell who had been badly wounded in both legs and whom he saved from falling out of an open hatch, Air Sgt du Pre was awarded the DFM.

21 Sqn SAAF	**Maryland II**	**AH407 M**	**Op: Army Co-operation**

Maj R J Stewart SAAF — +
Lt D Duffus DFC SAAF — pow
Air Sgt W D Tucker SAAF — +
Air Sgt M H Petterson DFM SAAF — +

Took off 1130, LG 76, detailed as above. Shot down by Lt Stahlschmitt, the fourth aircraft lost. Maj Stewart and Air Sgt Tucker are buried in Halfaya Sollum War Cemetery. Air Sgt Petterson is commemorated on the Alamein Memorial.

21 Sqn SAAF	**Maryland II**	**AH409 X**	**Op: Army Co-operation**

Capt J H Eccles SAAF — pow
Lt E A Benzie SAAF — +
Air Sgt F B White SAAF — +
Air Sgt A Friedman SAAF — +

Took off 1130, LG 76, detailed as above. This aircraft was the second shot down, crashing 26.5km S of El Adem. Capt Eccles managed to bale out; the other crew members are commemorated on the Alamein Memorial.

20-21 Nov 1941	**109 Sqn**	**Wellington IC**	**Z8907**	**Op: electronic counter-measures**

F/Sgt H I Wolf RCAF — +
P/O O B Hughes RCAF — +
F/O D J Cruikshank
Sgt D Cross — +
Sgt A Dean — +
Sgt E A Lowther RCAF — +
Passenger:
Lt Col R P G Denman — +

Took off LG 75. FTR. Probably shot down by MC.202 fighters. The body of Sgt Cross was found by 42 Tank Regt. in the burnt-out aircraft, and he was buried nearby. All are now buried in the Halfaya Sollum War Cemetery. Lt Col Denman was a senior War Office specialist in radio countermeasures.

21 Nov 1941	37 Sqn	Wellington IC	Z8720 B	Ground
	LAC A McD Graham		+	
	AC2 H J James		+	
	LAC A L Williams		+	
	Cpl D C Smith		inj	
	AC1 J McLaughlan		inj	
	AC1 P A Dyer		inj	

Sgt Atherstone's aircraft was receiving final inspection at LG 09 prior to take-off when it blew up. The crew were away at the time but three ground crew working on the aircraft were killed outright, AC1 Mclaughlan dying shortly after, and AC1 Dyer (of 38 Sqn) on 24 November. The dead are buried in the El Alamein War Cemetery.

	148 Sqn	Wellington II	W5568	Ground

Destroyed in an air raid, either at Kabrit or LG 104. SOC 24 November.

	223 Sqn	Maryland II	AH368	Unknown

DBR. NFD.

	24 Sqn SAAF	Boston III	W8375 P	Op: Reconnaissance
	Lt G A Chalkley SAAF		+	
	Lt M R Bour SAAF		+	
	Air Sgt A B Le Roux SAAF		+	
	Air Sgt L D Shanley SAAF		+	

Took off LG 112. Crashed near Gambut at 1030 hrs whilst on a reconnaissance of the Sidi Rezegh, Gambut, and Maddalena area with two other Bostons. All are commemorated on the Alamein Memorial.

22 Nov 1941	45 Sqn	Blenheim IV	T2318	Op: El Adem
	Sgt C Melly		pow	
	P/O F L Rippingale		pow	
	Sgt J Halsall		+	

Took off 1230, LG 75, one of six Blenheims detailed, with an escort of Tomahawk fighters, to bomb El Adem airfield. Attacked and shot down by approximately 20 Bf 109F fighters of 1/JG27, which claimed two Blenheims near Gazala, one near Bir Hacheim and one near Bir el Gobi. Sgt Halsall is commemorated on the Alamein Memorial.

	45 Sqn	Blenheim IV	Z6439 Y	Op: El Adem
	W/Cdr J O Willis DFC		+	
	P/O L P Bourke RNZAF		+	
	Sgt M F Carthy		+	

Took off 1230, LG 75, detailed (and lost) as above. All the crew are buried in Knightsbridge War Cemetery, Acroma.

	45 Sqn	Blenheim IV	Z9609	Op: El Adem
	Sgt R Wood		pow	
	Sgt R A Turton RNZAF		evd	
	Sgt S B Whiteley		pow	

Took off 1230, LG 75, detailed (and lost) as above. Sgt Turton spent a fortnight in the desert making his way towards Allied lines, finally being picked up by the 2nd South African Brigade.

	45 Sqn	Blenheim IV	Z7686	Op: El Adem
	P/O C E O'Neill		+	
	Sgt L O Smith		+	
	Sgt K J Chapman		+	

Took off 1230, LG 75, detailed (and lost) as above. All the crew are commemorated on the Alamein Memorial.

	109 Sqn	Wellington IC	X9988	Op: electronic counter-measures
	Sgt R E Nicholson		+	
	Sgt J B Hughes		+	
	F/O D S Jefferies RAAF		+	
	Sgt M A Forrest		+	
	Sgt D Sidebottom		+	
	P/O W A Keogh RCAF		+	

Took off LG 75 FTR. Probably shot down by Italian fighters.

	24 Sqn SAAF	Boston III	W8378	Op: Reconnaissance
	Lt C W E Blake SAAF		pow	
	Lt G A Marshall SAAF		pow	
	Sgt D A Stakemire		pow	
	Sgt J Atkinson		pow	

Took off LG 112, one of two Bostons detailed to reconnoitre the Bir el Gubi - Bir Hacheim area. Shot down by Bf 109 fighters at 1400 hrs between El Adem and Gazala. After belly-landing the burning aircraft the pilot extricated the observer who was trapped in the nose compartment by kicking the perspex in; then despite the heat he and Lt Marshall saved the wounded Sgt Atkinson. The other gunner had bailed out prior to the crash. Lt Blake escaped from an Italian POW Camp and won the Military Cross while working with the Partisans.

23 Nov 1941	OADU Sgt D M Watts RAAF Sgt C G Thompson RAAF Sgt S H Moore Sgt H B Newton RNZAF Sgt A Bain Sgt J W McOmie	Wellington II int int int int int int	Z8432 **Delivery Flight** Took off Portreath for Gibraltar. The port engine seized, and the aircraft force-landed at Portela airport, Lisbon, where it was burnt by the crew. They were repatriated to Gibraltar three weeks later.
23-24 Nov 1941	104 Sqn P/O J Dickenson Crew	Wellington II	W5558 B **Op: Tripoli** Took off Luqa. On return swung on landing in a cross-wind and the undercarriage collapsed when a tyre burst.
24 Nov 1941	40 Sqn	Wellington IC	X9662 **Ground** Blew up at dispersal, Luqa.
	12 Sqn SAAF	Maryland II	? **Ground** Destroyed in a German dive-bombing attack on LG 76, the Maryland is described in the Squadron ORB as 'our Maryland Communication aircraft'.
	24 Sqn SAAF Lt B G Roxburgh SAAF Lt G A Francey SAAF Air Sgt B Van Den Berg SAAF Air Sgt K P Gordon SAAF	Boston III pow pow pow pow	W8384 **Op: Reconnaissance** Took off 0800 LG 112, one of three Bostons detailed to reconnoitre Bir el Gubi - Bir Hacheim - Akramah - El Gubba. Attacked by a Bf 109 fighter and, after a running battle in which an engine was set on fire and the upper gunner had been wounded and his guns shot out of his hands, the pilot finally ordered the crew to bail out. 15 minutes later two German aircraft landed and took the crew to Gazala.
	RAF Takoradi F/Sgt E Lignon FAFL Sgt Milon FAFL Sgt P Hervé FAFL. Passenger: Sgt J Barthélemy	Martin 167 inj inj +	1164 **Delivery Flight** Crashed on take-off Oshogbo, Nigeria, on Delivery Flight 269 from RAF Takoradi to the FAFL Fort Lamy, Chad. Sgt Hervé is buried in Oshogbo, Cemetery. Sgt Barthélemy was a Frenchman serving in the RAF. The aircraft was one of four French contract Martin 167s owned by the French and being returned to them.
24-25 Nov 1941	40 Sqn Sgt T W Parker Sgt E I Cooper F/Sgt M R Chabot RCAF Sgt D R Kelly Sgt G S Stephens Sgt H Whitaker	Wellington IC pow pow + + + +	Z1046 **Op: Benghazi** Took off Luqa. Ditched out of fuel after navigation difficulties caused by radio failure. The survivors spent five days in a dinghy. The dead are commemorated on the Malta Memorial.
25 Nov 1941	14 Sqn Maj E M Lewis SAAF Sgt Johnson Sgt G A Cooke	Blenheim IV	V5573 Z **Op: Army Co-operation** On take-off 1340, LG 75, to bomb motor transport and armoured vehicles 1.5km N of Pin Point 498347, the starboard tyre burst, the aircraft swung and the undercarriage collapsed. DBR.
	113 Sqn	Blenheim IV	Z6438 **Unknown** Hit by light flak; returned to base but DBR. SOC.
25-26 Nov 1941	37 Sqn P/O G E Guthrie RNZAF Sgt G M Goldfinch RNZAF P/O J Mc Taylor Sgt L S Barker RCAF Sgt H Rose Sgt C J Bourner	Wellington IC pow pow pow pow pow pow	Z8798 L **Op: Benghazi** Took off 1845, ALG 09. An SOS was received almost 4 hrs after take-off and the aircraft came down approx 80km E of Benghazi. Sgt Barker died as a POW on 11.3.44, and is buried in Ancona War Cemetery, while Sgt Goldfinch died in an American hospital on 13.4.45, shortly after he was liberated, and is buried in Nedereert War Cemetery.

	37 Sqn	**Wellington IC**	**Z8801 P**	**Op: Benghazi**

Sgt L H Mellor RAAF
Sgt Walker
Sgt S G Bromley RNZAF
Sgt Lumbers
Sgt Webster
Sgt Lindsay

Took off 1900, ALG 09. The aircraft had engine trouble and was returning to base, but gradually lost height and was abandoned 32km W of Mersa Matruh. The crew received only minor injuries, and was located and returned the next day.

148 Sqn — **Wellington II** — **Z8362 K** — **Op: Benghazi**

Sgt J B Starky RNZAF
F/Sgt H B Johnston RCAF   +
Sgt F A M Docker   +
Sgt Bulfront
Sgt Butterfield
Sgt Williams

Engine cut after take-off from LG 60; lost height and crash-landed 7km WNW of the landing ground. The dead are commemorated on the Alamein Memorial.

---

26 Nov 1941

14 Sqn — **Blenheim IV** — **T2428** — **Unknown**

Starboard tyre burst on landing, LG 75. DBR.

47 Sqn — **Wellesley I** — **K7773** — **Mail Flight**

Sgt K D Meares
Passenger

Took off Khartoum to return to Asmara, carrying a passenger. Ran out of fuel and crash-landed 2km from Asmara airfield. SOC 8 December as BER.

113 Sqn — **Blenheim IV** — **Z7446** — **Unknown**

SOC. NFD.

USAAF — **Liberator II** — **AL569** — **Delivery Flight**

Lt E D Reynolds USAAF
Crew

Took off for El Fasher, on the penultimate stage of a delivery flight from Bolling Field to Cairo, but owing to navigational difficulties El Fasher could not be located, and in a night landing at El Obeid the Liberator landed on a shoulder of the runway and was DBR. No injuries were reported. The date is deduced from references in the 108 Squadron ORB, that being the unit designated for re-equipment with Liberators.

26-27 Nov 1941

38 Sqn — **Wellington IC** — **Z8736 Q** — **Op: Derna**

F/O R J Cooper   +
Sgt A D Wren   +
P/O P Eastman   +
Sgt L Peaker   +
Sgt T McNeil   +
F/Sgt G J McKhool RCAF   +

Took off c.1700, LG 09, but FTR. Sent an SOS when a few miles from Derna. Severe electrical storms were reported by other crews. All are commemorated on the Alamein Memorial.

---

27 Nov 1941

47 Sqn — **Wellesley I** — **L2691** — **Mail Flight**

F/O J S S Bazeley   +
Sgt L E Bull RAAF   +

Took off Alomata for Asmara. A wing broke off in turbulence and the aircraft dived into the ground and caught fire 6.5km SW of Debre Sina. Both are buried in Addis Ababa War Cemetery.

84 Sqn — **Blenheim IV** — **N3532** — **Op: Army Co-operation**

Sgt T Ingham-Brown   pow
Sgt L E Atkinson RNZAF   pow
Sgt E F C Maslen   +

Took off 1330, LG 75, to bomb Axis motor transport near El Cascia. Shot down by flak over the target, Ridge 4041. Sgt Maslen is commemorated on the Alamein Memorial.

84 Sqn — **Blenheim IV** — **Z9538** — **Op: Army Co-operation**

Sgt J D McKillop
P/O S G Turner
Sgt Wright

Took off 1330, LG 75, detailed as above, and damaged by flak over Ridge 4041. Belly-landed at base with its hydraulics unserviceable. Not repaired; SOC 18.9.42.

	OADU	**Wellington IC**	**Z9016**	**Delivery Flight**
	P/O J Sharpe RAAF		Took off Gibraltar for Luqa, but failed to gain height and dived into the sea. The probable cause was flap malfunction. One injured, NFD.	
	W/Cdr Griffith			
	Crew			

28 Nov 1941	**11 Sqn**	**Blenheim IV**	**L1317**	**Op: Army Co-operation**
	Lt S Patterson SAAF	pow	Took off 0740, LG 76, one of nine Blenheims detailed to attack German armour on the Tobruk-Bardia Road. Shot down 150m from a German encampment near to the road 13km E of Gambut by a Bf 109 fighter which had seen the Blenheim take off, having just effected an heroic rescue of F/Lt Pringle-Wood and his crew of Z5906 (see below), and Captain H C W Liebenberg (Hurricane Z4065 1 Sqn SAAF) who also had just been shot down, from the middle of the ground battle and amid enemy positions. All survived the crash, although Sgt Bennett had been trapped and injured. P/O Burgan escaped during the night, and after a long trek through the desert he returned to LG 76 on 4 December. Sgt Bennett died in a prisoner of war camp in February 1945, and is buried in Berlin War Cemetery. Capt Liebenberg escaped from a train taking him to Germany at the end of 1943, and managed to reach Allied lines and return to his squadron in 1944. Sgt Collins escaped from Campo 59 (Servigliano) on 14 September 1943 when Italy capitulated.	
	P/O G S Burgan RAAF	pow		
	Sgt J F M Bennett RAAF	pow		
	Capt H C W Liebenberg SAAF	pow		
	F/Lt J Pringle-Wood	pow		
	Sgt N R Powell	pow		
	Sgt B P Collins	pow		

	11 Sqn	**Blenheim IV**	**Z5906**	**Op: Army Co-operation**
	F/Lt J Pringle-Wood		Took off 0743, LG 76, detailed as above. Shot down by ground fire and crashed near the Tobruk-Bardia Rd. (The motor transport identified itself as friendly and then opened fire, shooting this aircraft down). A heroic rescue attempt to recover the crew was made by the pilot of L1317 (see above). This crew was thus shot down twice on the same day.	
	Sgt B P Collins	pow		
	Sgt N R Powell			
	Sgt B P Collins			

	11 Sqn	**Blenheim IV**	**Z7703**	**Op: Army Co-operation**
	F/Sgt R Enticknap	+	Took off 0742, LG 76, detailed as above. Shot down in flames by enemy ground fire, the bomb load exploding on impact. The aircraft crashed near the Tobruk-Bardia Rd 13km E of Gambut. All three crew members are commemorated on the Alamein Memorial.	
	Sgt L M Wishart	+		
	Sgt N E Cooke	+		

	GrB1 Lorraine	**Blenheim IV**	**V6142**	**Op: Tobruk and Gazala**
	W/O R Jabin FAFL	pow	Took off from unknown airfield to bomb Tobruk and Gazala. Shot down in flames E of Gazala by Lt Hans Remmer of 1/JG 27. All were taken prisoner and the pilot and observer, who were injured, were taken to hospital, where F/O Pougin de la Maisonneuve died on 30 November. F/Sgt Jabin was transported to Italy by air where he recovered from his injuries, and then escaped and joined the Italian resistance. The observer is buried in the German War Cemetery, Tobruk. SOC 29 November.	
	F/O C Pougin de la Maisonneuve FAFL	+		
	F/Sgt H Bruneau FAFL	pow		

29 Nov 1941	**104 Sqn**	**Wellington II**	**Z8404 K**	**Op: Benghazi**
	P/O R A A Doherty		Took off Luqa. On return the starboard engine cut; the aircraft overshot landing in poor visibility, Luqa. One crew member was injured.	
	Sgt P Dawson			
	Sgt K Boyce			
	Sgt Ridley			
	F/Sgt Simons			
	Sgt Sproule RCAF			

30 Nov 1941	**RAF Takoradi** F/Lt S Pietrasiewicz PAF F/Sgt R Keyworth Sgt T R Griffiths	**Blenheim IV** + + +	**Z7632** **Delivery Flight** Taking off, Oshogbo, Nigeria, on Delivery Flight 277 to the Middle East, stalled, dived into the ground and exploded. All of the crew are buried in Oshogbo War Cemetery.
30 Nov - **1 Dec** 1941	**37 Sqn** Sgt J C Smith RAAF Sgt T Walsh Sgt J G Alcock Sgt N J Rice Sgt E Hall F/Sgt J Napier	**Wellington IC**	**L7856** **M** **Op: Benghazi** Took off 1913, ALG 09. Ran out of fuel and crashed at Burg El Arab on return. The crew sustained minor injuries.
	148 Sqn P/O W Astell P/O Nixon Sgt W D Shannon Sgt S DeB. Geary Sgt R T Perrin P/O Edmond	**Wellington II** inj inj inj inj	**W5597** **U** **Op: Benghazi** Took off LG 60, detailed to bomb shipping in Benghazi harbour. A 37 Sqn aircraft landed and stayed at the end of the flare path, LG 60, and P/O Astell did not see the aircraft until about to touch down. He attempted to go around again but one wing dropped, hit the ground and was wrenched from its root. The aircraft then swung in and burst into flames. Four crew were badly injured.
1 Dec 1941	**OADU** Sgt G Thomas Crew	**Wellington IC**	**Z9026** **Delivery Flight** Took off Portreath for Gibraltar, but swung on landing and hit a hut on the edge of the runway. DBR.
3 Dec 1941	**11 Sqn**	**Blenheim IV**	**V6496** **Unknown** The undercarriage collapsed on landing, LG 76. DBR.
3-4 Dec 1941	**38 Sqn** Sgt Sebastian Crew	**Wellington IC**	**Z8764** **U** **Op: El Adem Rds** Bursting a tyre on take-off from LG 09, the aircraft swung violently, and the undercarriage collapsed. The port wing hit the ground and the aircraft caught fire. Incendiaries were ignited and the bomb load exploded. DBF.
4 Dec 1941	**45 Sqn** P/O J H Tolman F/O A W Hutton Sgt D S J Harris	**Blenheim IV** + + +	**V5991** **Op: Sidi Rezegh** Took off 1115, LG 75, one of nine Blenheims detailed to attack Axis motor transport. Collided head-on on take-off with Z9572 of FAFL GB Lorraine, whose aircraft were taking off in the opposite direction, each unable to see the other because of a hump in the centre of the LG. V5591 exploded on impact. All are buried in Halfaya Sollum War Cemetery.
	107 Sqn Sgt R G Kidby Sgt L J Burcher Sgt J E Hughes	**Blenheim IV** + + pow	**Z7775** **Op: Anti-shipping** Took off Luqa, one of four Blenheims detailed to attack ferry boats at Messina. Last seen at about 1430 under attack by three Macchi fighters and taking evasive action towards mainland Italy N of Cape Armi. The dead are buried in Catania War Cemetery.
	GB Lorraine Sgt G Fifre FAFL Lt P de Maismont FAFL Sgt H Soulat FAFL	**Blenheim IV** + inj inj	**Z9572** **Op: Sidi Rezegh** Took off LG 75, detailed to attack motor transport at Sidi Rezegh, and collided head-on with V5991 under circumstances described above. Sgt Fifre, serving as Sgt F Freeman RAFVR, was originally buried in the Halfaya Sollum War Cemetery, but has since been re-interred in France.

5 Dec 1941	**114 Sqn** Sgt N Harrison Sgt Noel Sgt Ingram	**Blenheim IV**	**Z7925**	**Delivery Flight** Took off Gibraltar for Malta; undercarriage collapsed in a heavy landing at Luqa. DBR.
	226 Sqn Sgt H C Jewel Crew	**Blenheim IV**	**Z7910**	**Delivery Flight** Took off Gibraltar for Malta. Bounced and stalled in a heavy landing, Luqa; undercarriage collapsed and DBR. Though described as of 226 Squadron, this aircraft was almost certainly on an OADU flight.
5-6 Dec 1941	**40 Sqn** F/O D F Hutt P/O I E Miller P/O A J Pyle Sgt W H Poole F/Sgt T J Arsenault RCAF Sgt L J Abbott RAAF	**Wellington IC** pow pow + + + +	**R1066 K**	**Op: Naples** Took off Luqa, detailed to bomb the docks at Naples. Crashed after a long fight with an Italian CR.42 night fighter (Mar V Patriarcha Ottaviano). The dead are buried in the Salerno War Cemetery.
6 Dec 1941	**GB1 Lorraine**	**Blenheim IV**	**V6495**	**Op: Tobruk** Took off LG 75, and shot down by Bf 109F (Ofw Otto Schulz of 4/JG 27) over Bir el Gobi. Ofw Schulz claimed two Free French Blenheims shot down SE of El Adem at 1228 and 1230: the second was almost certainly V6503.
	GB Lorraine F/O R Sandré FAFL P/O A de Meltcharski FAFL Sgt A Lann FAFL	**Blenheim IV** + + +	**V6503**	**Op: Tobruk** Took off LG 75 and shot down by a Bf 109F flown by Ofw Schulz of 4/JG 27. All are now buried in France.
7 Dec 1941	**24 Sqn SAAF** Lt W N Hollenbach SAAF Sgt P A Grieg Air Sgt C Bran SAAF F/Sgt E B Thomas	**Boston III** + pow + +	**Z2181 R**	**Op: Reconnaissance** Took off 0720, OLG, LG 130, to reconnoitre the El Adem - Akramah road and obtain weather information. Shot down over El Adem by flak. The dead are buried in Knightsbridge War Cemetery, Acroma.
	24 Sqn SAAF Lt A M Kingon SAAF W/O C J Rudge RNZAF Sgt C Lucas Sgt W Hendrick	**Boston III** pow pow pow pow	**Z2202 V**	**Op: Reconnaissance** Took off 0500, ALG, LG 130, detailed as above. Shot down by Ofw Schulz (4/JG27) at 0950 53km S of Tobruk. Lt Kingon crash-landed the Boston, one engine on fire, and was awarded the MBE for the rescue from the burning bomber of the two badly wounded gunners. They were treated in a German hospital at Derna but later liberated by advancing Allied troops. W/O Rudge died in a German POW camp of malnutrition and pleurisy on 6 March 1945 but, since his grave could not later be found, is commemorated on the Alamein Memorial.
	OADU Sgt E G Gittings Sgt J G Scragg Sgt A N Borrow Sgt W W Chisholm Sgt E H Clegg Sgt J S Lewery	**Wellington IC** int int int int int int	**N2814**	**Delivery Flight** Took off Gibraltar for Luqa. The port engine failed and the aircraft was ditched off Algiers, the crew being rescued and interned until November 1942.
8 Dec 1941	**18 Sqn** P/O J A Barclay Sgt H B Lee Sgt W B Allan	**Blenheim IV** + + +	**Z7613 B**	**Op: Catania** Took off Luqa, one of four aircraft (A, N, B & Z) detailed to bomb the aerodrome at Catania. At 1453, en route, flying NW in starboard echelon formation at sea level, a 'Tally Ho' was given by either B or Z when an enemy aircraft was sighted. The aircraft broke formation and B

and Z collided, crashing into the sea. The remaining crews searched fruitlessly, and then returned to base without completing the mission. All are commemorated on the Runnymede Memorial.

	18 Sqn	Blenheim IV	Z9719 Z	Op: Catania
	Sgt W J Cuming	+		
	Sgt R Tollett	+		
	Sgt J H Pilley DFM	+		

Took off Luqa, detailed as above, and lost in collision with V5465. All are commemorated on the Runnymede Memorial.

9 Dec 1941	14 Sqn	Blenheim IV	T2064 Z	Op: Bum bah
	Sgt H S Grimsey			
	Sgt J H Pilley DFM	+		
	P/O L A D Speller			
	Sgt P B Martell			

Took off 1150, LG 75, detailed to bomb Axis motor transport on the Derna-Mersa Matruh road. Unable in poor visibility to locate the target, the crew bombed a flak position at Bum Bah. On return the base could not be located, and the crew abandoned the aircraft near LG 75 when it ran out of fuel. They then walked back to base.

9-10 Dec 1941	148 Sqn	Wellington II	Z8333 M	Op: Derna and Gazala
	F/O D L Skinner	+		
	Sgt H Freeman	+		
	Sgt C E Newman	+		
	Sgt N Maddox	+		
	Sgt R M D McLeod	+		
	Sgt J Marsland	+		

Took off LG 60, detailed to bomb motor transport. FTR. All are commemorated on the Alamein Memorial.

10 Dec 1941	24 Sqn SAAF	Boston III	Z2170	Op: Bir el Gubbi
	Lt G Genis SAAF	+		
	Lt D McPherson SAAF	inj		
	Sgt R E L Bowerman	+		
	Sgt D C M Ross	+		

Took off 1025, OLG, LG 130, one of six detailed to attack German ground positions and armour. Shot down E of Bir Hacheim en route to the target by a Bf 109 (Fw Franz Elles 2/JG27), exploding on striking the ground. Lt Genis and Sgt Bowerman are buried in Knightsbridge War Cemetery, Acroma, and Sgt Ross is commemorated on the Alamein Memorial. 24 Squadron lost five of the six aircraft sent on this mission, in an action ironically labelled 'the Boston Tea Party' in the squadron history.

	24 Sqn SAAF	Boston III	Z2182	Op: Bir el Gubbi
	Capt F W Goch SAAF	+		
	Lt H M Raw SAAF			
	Air Sgt B A S Delaney SAAF	+		
	Air Sgt M V Clulee SAAF	+		

Took off OLG, LG 130, detailed as above, and shot down 15km E of Bir Hacheim by Hptm Erich Gerlitz (2/JG27). Air Sgt Delaney is buried in Knightsbridge War Cemetery, Acroma, while the Pilot and Air Sgt Clulee are commemorated on the Alamein Memorial.

	24 Sqn SAAF	Boston III	Z2187	Op: Bir el Gubbi
	Lt J A Williams SAAF			
	Lt B G Alexander SAAF	+		
	2/Lt R A Joiner SAAF	inj		
	Air Sgt D Newell SAAF	inj		

Took off OLG, LG.130, detailed as above, and shot down near Bir Hacheim by Lt Willi Kothmann (2/JG27), who was badly wounded by return fire. Lt Alexander is commemorated on the Alamein Memorial.

	24 Sqn SAAF	Boston III	Z2191	Op: Bir el Gubbi
	Lt B Middleton-Stewart SAAF			
	F/O E M Harding RAAF	+		
	Air Sgt J H van Dyk SAAF	+		
	F/Sgt J Handley	+		

Took off OLG, LG 130, detailed as above, and shot down 15km E of Bir Hacheim by Ofw Hermann Forster (2/JG27). The intercom failed and only the pilot bailed out before the aircraft exploded. Those killed are commemorated on the Alamein Memorial.

	24 Sqn SAAF	Boston III	Z2201	Op: Bir el Gubbi
	Lt D R Haupt SAAF	inj		
	Lt L B Bensimmon SAAF	+		
	Air Sgt V StC Black SAAF	+		
	Air Sgt L E Venter SAAF	inj		

Took off OLG, LG 130, detailed as above, and shot down by Lt Friedrich Korner (2/JG27) en route to the target. All but Lt Bensimmon bailed out, but the pilot was injured in doing so, and Air Sgt Black was killed by enemy fire as he descended. He is buried in Knightsbridge War Cemetery, Acroma, while Lt Bensimmon is commemorated on the Alamein Memorial.

	OADU F/Lt H A H Watts Crew	**Wellington II**	**Z8434** **Delivery Flight** On take-off, Gibraltar, for Luqa the port wing hit a light object. No injuries. SOC 1/1/47, by inventory entry.

11 Dec 1941

11 Sqn — **Blenheim IV** — **Z7797** — **Op: Derna**
S/Ldr C F Darbishire +
Sgt J C B Webster – —— –+
F/Sgt L J Macey +

Took off 1015, LG 76, detailed to bomb the aerodrome at Derna if there was sufficient cloud cover. Shot down over Bomba Bay at 1145 by a Bf 109 (Ofw Albert Espenlaub, 1/JG27). All are commemorated on the Alamein Memorial.

18 Sqn — **Blenheim IV** — **Z7802   Q** — **Op: Argostoli Harbour**
F/Lt E G Edmunds DFC RNZAF +
Sgt S E Hedin DFM +
Sgt M J Mills +

Took off Luqa, one of three Blenheims detailed to bomb shipping. Probably shot down by flak encountered in the harbour area from both ships and harbour installations. All are buried in Phaleron War Cemetery.

21 Sqn SAAF — **Maryland II** — **AH344   Y** — **Op: patrol**
Lt W L Wood SAAF +
2/Lt D Harris SAAF +
Air Sgt M Greenberg SAAF +
Air Sgt M J Fleming SAAF +
2/Lt A H M Moolman SAAF pow

Took off LG 76, as No 2 in the second of four pairs of Marylands sent at intervals to patrol an area over the Mediterranean Sea about 53km N of Derna to intercept German Ju 52s ferrying fuel from Crete to Appolonia. Shot down by return fire and crashed 1.5km N of Gazala. All the crew are commemorated on the Alamein Memorial. Lt Moolman was a fighter pilot from 94 Sqn RAF.

12 Dec 1941

11 Sqn — **Blenheim IV** — **Z7909** — **Op: Derna**
2/Lt R I Burrage SAAF +
Sgt N G S Drummond RAAF +
F/Sgt D Martin +

Took off 1000, LG 76, detailed to bomb Derna Airfield if there was sufficient cloud cover. FTR. All the crew is commemorated on the Alamein Memorial.

55 Sqn — **Blenheim IV** — **Z5908** — **Op: Anti-shipping**
F/Sgt J H L Thompson +
Sgt R T Quilter +
Sgt R T Morris +

Took off 0635, LG 17 (Fuka Main), detailed to locate an enemy motor vessel with a cruiser escort. At 0900 hrs in position 33° 15' N, 23° 02' E they were attacked by a Bf 110, possibly from 8/ZG26. The Blenheim was caught in the first burst of fire and crashed into the sea. All are commemorated on the Alamein Memorial.

55 Sqn — **Blenheim IV** — **Z9595** — **Op: Anti-shipping**
F/O C H Anderson +
Sgt D A Bruton +
Sgt J Evans +

Took off 0700, LG 17 (Fuka Main), one of two Blenheims detailed to carry out an anti-shipping sweep of Derna. Survived two attacks by a Bf 110 at position 32° 30' N 22° 00' E, continuing the sweep, but at 1024, 20km N of Cape Aamer, F/O Anderson broke formation and turned to land, but crashed into the sea. The crew, seconded from 8 Sqn, are commemorated on the Alamein Memorial.

113 Sqn — **Blenheim IV** — **V5588** — **Op: Patrol**
2/Lt C N Summersgill SAAF +
F/O J A Galvin RAAF +
Sgt L L Purves RAAF +

Crashed at Giarabub, 1500, reason unknown. All the crew are buried in Halfaya Sollum War Cemetery.

12 Sqn SAAF — **Maryland II** — **1622** — **Op: Patrol**
Lt W G Parsons SAAF +
2/Lt W G Carthew SAAF +
Air Sgt D A Chalmers SAAF +
Air Sgt G J De Klerk SAAF +

Took off 1030, OLG LG 110, detailed to locate and destroy Ju 52 transports carrying mechanics and petrol from Maleme to Appolonia. Shot down c.1330 by Ofw Otto Polenz (8/ZG26). All are commemorated on the Alamein Memorial.

12 Sqn SAAF — **Maryland II** — **AH405** — **Op: Patrol**
Maj T S Fisher SAAF +
Lt S Goldfoot SAAF +
Air Sgt S Radomsky SAAF +
Sgt B Gray +

Took off 1030, OLG LG 110, detailed as above, and also shot down c.1330 by Ofw Polenz. All are commemorated on the Alamein Memorial.

21 Sqn SAAF		**Maryland II**	**AH289 B**	**Op: Patrol**
Lt T L Parry SAAF	+			
Sgt G M Hart RAAF	+			
Sgt W J Dillon RAAF	+			
Air Sgt J E Phelps SAAF	+			

21 Sqn SAAF   **Maryland II**   **AH289   B**   **Op: Patrol**
Lt T L Parry SAAF   +
Sgt G M Hart RAAF   +
Sgt W J Dillon RAAF   +
Air Sgt J E Phelps SAAF   +

Took off 0800, LG 76, with No 1614, forming one of four pairs of Marylands sent at half-hour intervals to locate, 50km N of Derna, and destroy Ju 52 transports ferrying mechanics and petrol from Maleme to Appolonia. The Marylands were carrying bombs, which were to be dropped on the Ju 52s, which had been using a water-hugging tactic the previous day. Shot down by either Uffz Gunther Wegmann or Oblt Fritz Schulze in Bf 110s of 8/ZG26, each of whom claimed a Maryland shot down. All the crew are commemorated on the Alamein Memorial.

21 Sqn SAAF   **Maryland II**   **1614   G**   **Op: Patrol**
Capt F C Ramsay SAAF
2/Lt Nicholson SAAF   inj
Air Sgt R T Hutchinson SAAF
Air Sgt N C Scott-Winlow SAAF

Took off 0800, LG 76, detailed as above. Badly damaged by return fire from three of the Ju 52 transports and force-landed at Tobruk, where, with no facilities to repair it, it had to be written off.

21 Sqn SAAF   **Maryland II**   **1661   D**   **Op: Patrol**
Maj M H Fowler SAAF   +
Lt M A Oberholzer SAAF   +
Air Sgt F R Viljoen SAAF   +
Air Sgt J J Hattingh SAAF   +

Took off 0900, LG 76, detailed as above. Last seen heading for Tobruk pursued by two Bf 110 fighters. Presumed shot down either by Uffz Wegmann or Oblt Schulze (see above). All of the crew are commemorated on the Alamein Memorial.

12-13 Dec 1941   **OADU**   **Wellington IC**   **Z9038**   **Delivery Flight**
Sgt P W Todd
Crew

Took off Gibraltar for Luqa. Attacked by enemy aircraft 24km E of Cap Bon, and force-landed at Luqa. Presumably not repaired. SOC 11.3.42.

OADU   **Wellington IC**   **Z1163**   **Delivery Flight**
Sgt S R Bottomley   +
Sgt M F J Boulton   +
Sgt E L Harvey   +
Sgt E P Jackson   +
Sgt T Brunyee   +

Crashed in the sea on night take-off, Gibraltar, and exploded; the cause was obscure, but possibly flaps-up was selected instead of undercarriage. The crew is buried in Gibraltar North Front Cemetery.

---

13 Dec 1941   **18 Sqn**   **Blenheim IV**   **Z7858   M**   **Op: Anti-shipping**
Sgt F W Jury
Sgt T L G Black
Sgt D J Mortimer

Took off Luqa, one of six Blenheims detailed to attack shipping in Argostoli Harbour, Kefalonia, where there were anchored three motor vessels and five 'Navigatori' class destroyers. Attacked on the return flight and after a 66km chase by a Bf 109 (Lt Herbert Hass), ditched near Malta with its port engine on fire. The crew were rescued by a Maltese fishing boat. See Frederick Galea's *Call-Out*, p104.

37 Sqn   **Wellington IC**   **N2780   E**   **Op: Derna**
Sgt Carver
F/O A L Davis   inj
P/O W A Tanner RCAF   +
Sgt W L Pointing   +
Sgt Pearson
Sgt H J Bluck   inj

Took off 0001-0105, LG 09, detailed to attack motor transport near Derna. Damaged by flak over the target and force-landed in the sea off Sidi Barrani on return. Four of the crew (two injured) reached the shore in the dinghy the next afternoon. P/O Tanner and Sgt Pointing were last seen swimming strongly for shore. They are commemorated on the Alamein Memorial.

55 Sqn   **Blenheim IV**   **V6291**   **Op: Anti-shipping**
F/Lt G Pelling   +
P/O J H Strong DFM   +
Sgt E M Lindsay RAAF   +

Took off 1150, El Gubbi, one of nine aircraft detailed for a combined high- and low-level attack on destroyers and motor vessels in Navarin Bay. Shot down by a Bf 109 (Ofw Karl Heinz Bendert of Stab II/JG27 V6291) 8-10km NE of Timimi. All the crew are commemorated on the Alamein Memorial.

	70 Sqn	**Wellington IC**	X9686 Z — **Op: Derna**
	F/O K C Kitto	+	Took off 0130, Kabrit, detailed as for N2780 above, but
	Sgt A O Hawkes	+	shot down at 0400, crashing near Martuba, S of Derna.
	F/Sgt D G Pettet RCAF	+	All are buried at Knightsbridge War Cemetery, Acroma.
	Sgt E R G Lewis	+	
	Sgt B J Williams	+	
	F/Sgt W H J Milner RNZAF	+	

	107 Sqn	**Blenheim IV**	Z7368 — **Op: Anti-shipping**
	Sgt R D Gracie	+	Took off Luqa, one of six Blenheims detailed as Z7858
	F/Sgt A P McLean RCAF	+	above. Shot down by flak or when attacked by a single
	F/Sgt J S A Calderwood RCAF	+	Macchi fighter on patrol at the time. All are buried in
			Phaleron War Cemetery.

	107 Sqn	**Blenheim IV**	Z7800 — **Op: Anti-shipping**
	Sgt A J Lee	pow	Took off Luqa, detailed and shot down as above.
	Sgt R Haggett	pow	
	Sgt A J Comeau RCAF	pow	

	Malta	**Blenheim IV**	Z7988 — **Unknown**
			DBR in an accident. SOC, 19 December. NFD.

13-14 Dec **1941**	**40 Sqn**	**Wellington IC**	X9993	**Op: Minelaying**
	Sgt G H Easton RNZAF		Took off Luqa. While minelaying off Benghazi, the	
	Sgt C N Hardman		hydraulics were damaged by flak, and with flaps,	
	Sgt G A Little RCAF		undercarriage and bomb doors down the aircraft flew to	
	Sgt F H Cochrane	inj	Tobruk, where it crash-landed. The crew was returning	
	Sgt K R Blackhurst		to Luqa by Sunderland on 22 December when it was	
	Sgt A E Boorman		attacked and crippled by Bf 110s, force-landing in the sea.	
			Sgt Hardman was killed, and Sgt Boorman, who manned	
			the Sunderland's rear turret when the Sunderland's	
			gunner was mortally wounded, slightly wounded. Sgt	
			Hardman is commemorated on the Alamein Memorial.	
			There is a detailed account of this incident in David	
			Gunby's *Sweeping the Skies*, p193 footnote 3.	

14 Dec **1941**	**14 Sqn**	**Blenheim IV**	Z5860 O	**Op: Derna**
	Sgt F W Dennis RAAF	+	Took off 0530, LG 75, and landed at LG 144 (El Adem)	
	F/Sgt W R Campbell RCAF	+	at 0635 hrs to collect a fighter escort which never	
	Sgt J A Redfern	+	materialised. Took off from El Adem at 1100 hrs to bomb	
			targets of opportunity. FTR. All of the crew are	
			commemorated on the Alamein Memorial.	

	84 Sqn	**Blenheim IV**	Z5981 — **Op: Damah**
	Sgt C A Brackpool		Took off LG 75, but force-landed 'in the Blue' (that is, the
	Crew		desert), according to a rudimentary ORB written after the
			84 Sqn ORB was lost in the Far East. SOC 30 December.

	OADU	**Blenheim IV**	Z7958 — **Delivery Flight**
	Sgt E S Waine	inj	Took off Gibraltar for Malta, but baulked on approach to
	Sgt D H Phillips	inj	land at Luqa by another aircraft. Opened up to go round
	Sgt G Taylor		again, but both engines cut through lack of fuel. The
			aircraft force-landed in a field near Luqa village. DBR.

17 Dec **1941**	**14 Sqn**	**Blenheim IV**	V6461 B — **Op: Army Co-operation**
	Sgt T N Archer RAAF		Took off LG 75, for LG 144 (El Adem), for a briefing. Both
	Sgt Brown		engines cut as it turned to land at El Adem and it crashed
	Sgt Guy		and burst into flames. All the crew extricated themselves
			safely before the bomb load exploded.

	107 Sqn	**Blenheim IV**	Z9804 — **Op: Sorman and Zuara**
	P/O F H W Keene	pow	Took off Luqa, one of two Blenheims detailed to attack
	Sgt C T Small	pow	motor transport between Sorman and Zuara. Crashed

Sgt J Pickup		+	3km E of Zuara at 1150 hrs. Sgt Pickup is buried in Tripoli War Cemetery.

21 Sqn SAAF   **Maryland II**   **AH381**   **Op: Barce**
Lt R A Henwick SAAF
Lt G B Smith
Sgt Wieldon
Air Sgt S A Balfour SAAF

Took off 0927, LG 76, one of nine Marylands from 12 and 21 Sqns SAAF detailed. On return, landing at 1300, a tyre burst and the aircraft overturned. DBR.

---

18 Dec 1941

14 Sqn   **Blenheim IV**   **V6183**   U   **Ferry Flight**
F/Lt H K Keck RAAF
P/O L R Farrow RCAF
Sgt M German

Took off LG 75, in transit to a forward landing ground at LG 144 (El Adem) for briefing on troop concentrations W of Mechili. An engine failed, and the aircraft landed undercarriage up. Originally categorised as repairable, it was SOC 1.4.42.

---

19 Dec 1941

14 Sqn   **Blenheim IV**   **V6508**   **Ferry Flight**
P/O S F Lawson RAAF
P/O C K Goodwin RAAF
Sgt Alexander

Took off LG 75, in transit to a new base at LG 139 (Gambut No 1/Main), the undercarriage collapsing in a heavy landing. It was not repaired and the airframe only was salvaged, 23.12.42.

40 Sqn   **Wellington IC**   **X9992**   **Ground**
Set on fire during an air raid and DBR, Luqa. SOC 2.1.42.

40 Sqn   **Wellington IC**   **Z9029**   **Ground**
Destroyed in an air raid, Luqa.

104 Sqn   **Wellington II**   **Z8351**   **Op: Tripoli**
F/Lt W Knight
Crew

Took off, Luqa. On return, in poor conditions, landed on the wrong side of the Luqa flare path, which had been reduced by bomb damage to a single line of lights. The port wheel struck a tractor and the undercarriage collapsed. DBR. SOC 15.1.42

12 Sqn SAAF   **Maryland II**   **1630**   **Op: Benghazi**
Lt R E Stanford SAAF   pow
2/Lt P C De Meillon SAAF   +
Air Sgt S R Galloway SAAF   +
Air Sgt A Kahn SAAF   +

Took off 0955 OLG LG 110, one of nine Marylands from 12 and 21 Sqns detailed to attack German airfields at Barce, Benina, and Berka. Few aircraft were seen on Barce airfield so the Marylands attacked Benina. Immediately afterwards four Bf 109F fighters attacked and 1630 was shot down SSE of Benina by Hptm Erich Gurlitz of 2/JG 27. The dead are commemorated on the Alamein Memorial.

19-20 Dec 1941

70 Sqn   **Wellington IC**   **T2987**   O   **Op: Benina**
Capt L N Evans SAAF   +
Sgt J F Lilies   +
S/Ldr H Parkinson   +
F/Sgt D E Webb   +
P/O H D Grey   +
F/Sgt E E Nelson RCAF   +

Took off c.2145, LG 60. Shot down by flak, Benina. All are buried in Benghazi War Cemetery.

70 Sqn   **Wellington IC**   **Z8728**   U   **Op: Benina**
W/Cdr W A A de Freitas DFC   +
Sgt H H Brown   +
F/Sgt C M Complin RCAF   +
Sgt R S Prior   +
Sgt M Hogarth   +
P/O D Woodcock   +

Took off c.2145, LG 60. On return an engine cut, and the aircraft crashed in a forced landing, Bir el Garanis; DBF. All are commemorated on the Alamein Memorial.

20 Dec 1941	**45 Sqn** Sgt G T Bennett Sgt H C Nullis Sgt H W Twydell	**Blenheim IV**	**V5948 X** Took off 0740, LG 143 (Gambut No 3), one of 12 Blenheims, eight from 45 Sqn and eight from GB Lorraine, detailed to bomb motor transport. They were attacked by 20 Bf 109 fighters S of Barce, and two from each unit were shot down. **Op: Ghemines**

45 Sqn   **Blenheim IV**   **V6132 R**   **Op: Ghemines**
F/Sgt J Burns +   Took off 0740, LG 143 (Gambut No 3), detailed as above,
Sgt R E J Reeves +   and likewise lost. All the crew are commemorated on the
Sgt J E Wilcock +   Alamein Memorial.

84 Sqn   **Blenheim IV**   **T2394**   **Op: Gazala**
F/Sgt C S H Bayford +   Took off LG 139 (Gambut No 1/Main), detailed to bomb
Sgt C S Mort +   Axis motor transport but flew into an escarpment in a
Sgt T W Sherratt +   sandstorm near Gambut and exploded on impact. All are
Passenger: buried in Tobruk War Cemetery.
W/O 2 C H Bumstead RCAF +

GB Lorraine   **Blenheim IV**   **V6505**   **Op: Ghemines**
Lt/Col C Pijeaud FAFL +   Took off 0740, LG 143 (Gambut No 3), detailed as for the
P/O G Guigonis FAFL   45 Sqn aircraft above, and likewise lost. With the aircraft
Sgt L Delcros FAFL +   badly damaged and an engine on fire, the pilot gave the
order to bail out. The observer did so, but when about to
jump Lt Colonel Pijeaud noticed that Sgt Delcros was still
in his turret and, unaware that the WOp/AG was dead
returned to the controls and crash-landed the aircraft.
Captured by the Italians in a seriously burnt condition he
was handed over to the Allies who took him to
Alexandria Hospital, where he died on 20 January 1942.
Sgt Delcros is buried in Barce War Cemetery and Lt
Colonel Pijeaud in Alexandria War Cemetery.

GB1 Lorraine   **Blenheim IV**   **L8832**   **Op: Ghemines**
F/Sgt J Redor FAFL +   Took off 0740, LG 143, detailed as above and likewise shot
F/O M Jacquelot du Boisrouvray FAFL+   down. NFD. The crew were buried locally but re-interred
F/Sgt J Perbost FAFL +   in France after the War.

---

21 Dec
1941   **OADU**   **Blenheim IV**   **Z9825**   **Delivery Flight**
Sgt G W Williams   Took off Gibraltar for Luqa, but the undercarriage
Crew   jammed after take-off and the aircraft crash-landed at
Gibraltar on return, 0950. DBR.

---

22 Dec
1941   **14 Sqn**   **Blenheim IV**   **T2127 K**   **Transit Flight**
P/O P Goode   Took off LG 139 (Gambut No 1/Main), one of six
P/O C Hargreaves   Blenheims being sent forward for a briefing at Mechili.
F/O E Burdon   An engine cut on take-off, causing the aircraft to swing
and the pilot throttled back but before any further action
could be taken the Blenheim hit the ground. DBR.

107 Sqn   **Blenheim IV**   **Z7915**   **Op: Army Co-operation**
Sgt R F J Henley +   Took off Luqa, one of six Blenheims despatched in pairs
Sgt H F D Parsons +   to attack targets of opportunity along the road W of Sirte.
Sgt D P Darcy +   60km W of Sirte a convoy of motor transport consisting of
a petrol tanker, trucks and an armoured car was located
and attacked. Probably hit by return fire from the
armoured car, the Blenheim crashed into the sea. Sgt
Henley is commemorated on the Alamein Memorial, the
others buried in Tripoli War Cemetery.

15 Sqn SAAF   **Maryland II**   **1673 J**   **Training**
2/Lt R Edwards SAAF +   Took off Germiston on circuits and landings. The ORB
states that 2/Lt Edwards 'Crashed when he became
unstuck' (that is, at lift-off). He is buried in Durban
(Stellawood) Cemetery. He was serving with 71 Flt SAAF.

OADU Sgt F V Clayton Crew	**Wellington IC**	**Z9021**	**Delivery Flight** Took off Gibraltar for Luqa, but the port engine failed to go into coarse pitch. On return to Gibraltar the aircraft landed heavily on one wheel and the undercarriage collapsed. DBR.

23 Dec **1941**	**12 Sqn SAAF** Lt C J Morgan SAAF 2/Lt H MacFarlane SAAF Air Sgt H L Hyde SAAF Air Sgt J A Hill SAAF	**Maryland II** inj inj inj inj	**1618 J** **Op: Marble Arch** Took off 0920, LG147 (Bu Amud), one of five Marylands from 12 and 21 Sqns SAAF detailed to make a high-level bombing attack on the Axis airfield at Marble Arch. On the return journey attacked at 1225 hrs by two Bf 109s of I/JG27 (ObLt Ludwig Franziket and Lt Hans Remmer) each claiming a Maryland. Shot down over Msus, Lt Morgan and his crew crash-landed, to be picked up by tank crews of the 7th Armoured Division. After an eventful time with the tanks, Lt Morgan and Air Sgt Hill returned to the squadron while 2/Lt MacFarlane and Air Sgt Hyde were admitted to hospital in Tobruk.
	12 Sqn SAAF Lt H C Lotz SAAF 2/Lt C Jefferies DFM MiD SAAF Air Sgt B J Reed SAAF Air Sgt N J M Roodt SAAF	**Maryland II** + + + +	**AH382** **Op: Marble Arch** Took off 0920, LG 147 (Bu Amud), detailed as above and likewise lost. All of the crew are commemorated on the Alamein Memorial.

24 Dec **1941**	**107 Sqn** Sgt E Crossley Sgt K T Hewson Sgt H G Luke	**Blenheim IV** + + +	**Z7848** **Op: Zuara** Took off Luqa, one of three Blenheims detailed to attack shipping in Zuara harbour. When the aircraft's wingtip hit a stay on a small schooner, it turned onto its back and crashed. Sgts Crossley and Luke are buried in Tripoli War Cemetery and Sgt Hewson commemorated on the Malta Memorial.
	OADU Sgt K H Owens RCAF Crew	**Wellington II**	**Z8377** **Delivery Flight** Took off Gibraltar for Luqa. After landing the aircraft was taxying to dispersal with the sun in the pilot's eyes. It swung off the taxying strip into soft ground and hit a pile of stones. Damaged but repairable, it was destroyed in an air raid, Luqa, 23.2.42.

26 Dec **1941**	**18 Sqn** Sgt O C Summers Sgt J F Billett Sgt W C Marshall	**Blenheim IV** + + +	**Z7796 J** **Op: Anti-shipping** Took off 0815, Luqa, on an S.F.2b patrol. Probably shot down by Uffz Kitzenmaier of 5/JG 53. All are commemorated on the Malta Memorial.
	Middle East	**Blenheim IV**	**Z7959** **Ground** DBF in an air raid, presumably at Luqa.
	Middle East	**Blenheim IV**	**Z7978** **Ground** DBF in an air raid, presumably at Luqa.
	OADU Sgt R C Grant Crew	**Blenheim IV**	**Z7301** **Delivery Flight** Took off Portreath, on delivery to the Middle East. Overshot on landing at Gibraltar, 1520, and ran off the end of the runway. DBR.
	OADU Sgt G F Wallace RCAF P/O J G Heatherington Sgt G T Weston	**Blenheim IV** inj + inj	**Z7972** **Delivery Flight** After take-off from Gibraltar for Malta, an engine cut and the aircraft ditched 7.5km E of Gibraltar. P/O Heatherington is commemorated on the Runnymede Memorial.

27 Dec 1941	**11 Sqn**	**Blenheim IV**	**L9308**	**Unknown**

An engine cut; the aircraft crashed in a forced landing, Sidi Suarod. NFD.

28 Dec 1941	**OADU**	**Blenheim IV**	**Z7294**	**Delivery Flight**
	P/O A T Lawson-Tancred	inj		
	Sgt D R McKinnon RCAF	inj		
	Sgt R Sangster	+		
	Passenger:			
	Cpl W H Wallett	+		

Took off Portreath on delivery to the Middle East. An engine cut on approach to Gibraltar, the flaps were raised instead of the undercarriage, and the aircraft stalled, crashing into the sea 400m E of the airfield. Sgt Sangster and Cpl Wallett are commemorated on the Runnymede Memorial.

	OADU	**Wellington IC**	**DV416**	**Delivery Flight**
	P/O S Beckett	pow		
	Sgt S M Cross	pow		
	Sgt R P Holmes	pow		
	Sgt E R Ashton	pow		
	Sgt R Veitch	pow		
	Sgt R C Davis	pow		

Took off Gibraltar for Luqa. Crash-landed at Ragusa, out of fuel, probably because of a navigational error.

29 Dec 1941	**40 Sqn**	**Wellington IC**	**X9889 D**	**Ground**

Destroyed in an air raid, Luqa.

	40 Sqn	**Wellington IC**	**X9907**	**Ground**
	Sgt F J Sunley	+		
	Sgt A J Brogan	inj		
	Sgt J A Tipton	inj		
	Sgt J D Martin	inj		
	Sgt D T Taylor RCAF	inj		
	Sgt S Shepherdson	inj		

Destroyed in an air raid, Luqa. The crew were waiting to board the aircraft when it was bombed. Sgt Sunley is buried in the Malta (Capuccini) Naval Cemetery.

	40 Sqn	**Wellington IC**	**X9919**	**Ground**

Destroyed in an air raid, Luqa.

	40 Sqn	**Wellington IC**	**Z8991**	**Ground**

Destroyed in an air raid, Luqa.

	40 Sqn	**Wellington IC**	**Z9018**	**Ground**

Destroyed in an air raid, Luqa.

	40 Sqn	**Wellington IC**	**Z9020**	**Ground**

Destroyed in an air raid, Luqa.

	104 Sqn	**Wellington II**	**W5429 N**	**Ground**

DBF in an air raid, Luqa.

	OADU	**Wellington IC**	**Z9041**	**Ground**

Destroyed in an air raid, Luqa.

	OADU	**Wellington IC**	**Z9024**	**Ground**

Destroyed in an air raid, Luqa.

30 Dec 1941	**18 Sqn**	**Blenheim IV**	**Z9816 A**	**Op: Anti-submarine patrol**
	P/O K W Wyatt	int		
	Sgt J Y Burke	int		
	Sgt J Giles	int		

Took off 0702, Luqa, on patrol. Landed on the Kirkenna Banks in bad visibility. The crew were interned in Tunisia, but freed in November 1942.

Chapter 6

Rommel's Second Offensive
January to May 1942

Like 1941, 1942 began promisingly, with Rommel on the defensive at El Agheila, and General Ritchie, Field Marshal Auchinleck's choice as replacement for General Cunningham, confident that the Axis forces were so weakened after their recent retreat that they would constitute no immediate threat, even though Ritchie's forces were exhausted, with their tanks, transport and artillery in urgent need of repair. In this he was wrong. During January Rommel had received a fresh shipment of 55 tanks, 20 armoured cars and good supplies of fuel. With these, he was ready to attack once more, which he did on 21st January. For several days his offensive was felt, despite early successes, to be no more than local, but Rommel, emboldened by the ease with which his forces were driving the Eighth Army units back, pressed forward, took Benghazi on 28th January, and then, taking advantage of captured British supplies, took Derna, before being halted at Gazala, as much by his own lack of resources as by the resistance of the Eighth Army.

Between 4th February, when the front stabilised, and mid-May, no major engagements took place, with the Eighth Army developing a strong but not continuous defence line, consisting of a series of strong points, or 'boxes' protected by deep minefields. Behind this defence line preparations were made for a fresh offensive. By 10th May, however, it had become apparent that Rommel had been able to complete his preparations for an offensive more quickly than General Ritchie, and on 26th May a new Axis offensive began.

The bomber contribution to the war in North Africa during this period continued as before, with the day squadrons involved in close support of the army, bombing targets such as roads, motor transport, troop concentrations and landing grounds, while the night bombers of 205 Group concentrated on the ports of Benghazi and (using the few remaining Liberators of 108 Squadron) Tripoli, as well as landing grounds. In addition both day and night bomber units made a steady series of raids on airfields and harbours on Crete, which had become a major supply base for the Axis forces in North Africa, and one less vulnerable than the much shorter one from Sicily and Southern Italy to Tripoli, vulnerable as the latter was to attacks by aircraft based on Malta.

As noted earlier, six 109 Squadron Wellingtons had been detached to Egypt in November 1941 to carry out radio intelligence and countermeasures. In January 1942 the surviving aircraft and crews were absorbed into the newly formed 'Special Signals Squadron', which in March became 162 Squadron, equipped with Wellingtons and Blenheims.

During this period, several units re-equipped, with the ageing Blenheims and Marylands giving place, gradually, to new American aircraft, the Douglas Boston and the younger sibling of the Maryland, the Baltimore. 223 Squadron, operating Baltimores for the first time on 23rd May, suffered a fate similar to that of the Bostons of 24 Squadron SAAF the previous December. Of the four Baltimores operating three were shot down and the fourth crash-landing short of its base.

While the day bomber squadrons continued to re-equip, however, the size of the force was further weakened, with two of the remaining Blenheim squadrons, 84 and 211, despatched to the Far East in January.

On Malta, crucial to the stemming of the flow of supplies to North Africa, attempts were made to sustain a night bomber force, but 40 and 104 Squadrons suffered crippling losses on the ground, and the remnants of 104 Squadron were withdrawn to Egypt in January, followed by the few remaining Wellingtons of 40 Squadron in mid-February. A 37 Squadron detachment of six aircraft, flown in on 21st February, was virtually wiped out in a fortnight, but nonetheless managed, on the night of 2nd/3rd March, to inflict massive damage on shipping in Palermo harbour, where three ships were sunk, six heavily damaged, and a further 33 slightly damaged when an ammunition carrier exploded. In late April, a further attempt was made to base Wellingtons at Luqa, but this fared even worse, with six of 148 Squadron's aircraft destroyed on the ground the day after their arrival, and two more on operations that night. The last two returned to Africa the next day.

Also withdrawn in early January, and likewise decimated, were the last two of the Blenheim squadrons which had been rotating to Malta on detachment from the United Kingdom, 18 and 107 Squadrons. They were evacuated to Egypt. Henceforth the anti-shipping offensive would be carried out by Beauforts and Beaufighters.

1 Jan 1942	**11 Sqn** F/O A J W Froggatt Sgt J D M Prentice F/Sgt D A Young	**Blenheim IV**	**T2226** + + +	**Op: Army Co-operation** Took off 1155, LG 147 (Bu Amud), to bomb motor transport at Belandah, SE of Ajdabiya. Hit by flak just after leaving the target and shot down in flames, exploding on hitting the ground. All of the crew are buried in Benghazi War Cemetery.
	OADU	**Wellington IC**	**DV415**	**Ground** Destroyed in an air raid, Luqa.
2-3 Jan 1942	**70 Sqn** Sgt A V Parker Sgt G T I Salmon Sgt Reynolds Sgt Winterflood Sgt Bryan Sgt Francis	**Wellington IC**	**X9987 P**	**Op: Ras Lanuf - Marble Arch Rd** Took off c.2030, LG 60. On return, short of fuel, the aircraft force landed on a beach 48km W of Sidi Barrani, sank into soft sand and swung into the sea, the undercarriage collapsing.
3 Jan 1942	**37 Sqn**	**Wellington IC**	**X9688**	**Ground** Destroyed in an air raid, Luqa. (Since 37 Sqn was not on Malta at this time, this aircraft was presumably left behind for repair after earlier damage.)
	40 Sqn	**Wellington IC**	**X9990**	**Ground** Destroyed in an air raid, Luqa.
	40 Sqn	**Wellington IC**	**Z1079 F**	**Ground** Destroyed by a strafing Bf 109, Luqa.
	138 Sqn	**Whitley V**	**Z9140**	**Ground** Destroyed in an air raid, Luqa.
	138 Sqn	**Whitley V**	**Z9295**	**Ground** Destroyed in an air raid, Luqa.
	OADU	**Wellington IC**	**Z9042**	**Ground** Destroyed in an air raid, Luqa.
	OADU	**Wellington IC**	**Z9045**	**Ground** Damaged in an air raid, Luqa; later destroyed.
	Malta	**Wellington II**	**W5396**	**Ground** DBR, presumably in an air raid, Luqa.
	Malta	**Blenheim IV**	**Z9818**	**Ground** SOC. Probably DBR during an air raid on 29 December 1941.
4 Jan 1942	**45 Sqn** F/O C W Head RAAF	**Blenheim IV**	**Z7588 H** +	**Ferry Flight** Took off Heliopolis, one of four Blenheims on a ferry flight from Helwan to Gambut, but stalled and crashed, 1045. DBF. The pilot is thought to have been the only person on board. He is buried in Heliopolis War Cemetery.
	82 Sqn Sgt D W Beirnes DFM Sgt P Chaning-Pearce Sgt J J H Robbins	**Blenheim IV**	**Z7689** + + +	**Ferry Flight** Took off Egypt for Malta, but failed to arrive and believed shot down by an enemy fighter. All of the crew are commemorated on the Alamein Memorial.

82 Sqn Sgt A L Guy F/Sgt W C McNally RCAF Sgt R M Mander	**Blenheim IV** + + +	**Z9676**	**Ferry Flight** Took off Egypt for Malta, but failed to arrive and believed shot down by an enemy fighter. All of the crew are commemorated on the Alamein Memorial.

4-5 Jan 1942

40 Sqn F/Sgt J F Lewthwaite RNZAF Sgt P F Lill F/Sgt W R Pick RCAF Sgt W Chalmers Sgt M Bryan Sgt S H James	**Wellington IC** + + + + + +	**Z9036**	**Op: Castelvetrano** Took off Luqa, one of a second wave of four Wellingtons attacking enemy transport aircraft on Castelvetrano aerodrome. Brought down by flak during a low-level attack. All are buried in Catania War Cemetery.

6-7 Jan 1942

148 Sqn F/Lt D A Cracknell Sgt A C Fisk Sgt J J Hunter Sgt C B Cox Sgt W H Rothemel RCAF Sgt F J Cunnliffe RCAF	**Wellington II**	**Z8363 F**	**Op: Tripoli** Took off 2300, El Adem ALG, and on return landed at LG 60, but as the detachment was leaving, decided to fly on to LG 09. Became lost and after unsuccessfully attempting to obtain QDMs ran out of fuel and crashed 6.5km S of El Shaba. All save F/Lt Cracknell were treated for shock.

7 Jan 1942

18 Sqn Sgt S R Baker Sgt R Hillman Sgt D H Phillips	**Blenheim IV** + + +	**Z7652 A**	**Op: Anti-shipping** Took off Luqa on SF14 patrol between Malta and the Cape Bon - Kerkennah Island area. FTR. All of the crew are commemorated on the Malta Memorial.

37 Sqn S/Ldr Alexander P/O C F Butler P/O Spencler Sgt Lepp Sgt Dowd Sgt A T Hawkins Passenger: Merritt, L G USMC Five others	**Wellington IC** inj inj	**Z8763**	**Op: Capuzzo** Took off Kabrit, and while making a reconnaissance of Capuzzo aerodrome the aircraft was hit by flak and crash-landed S of Halfaya Pass, behind enemy lines. The crew and passengers (6) were picked up by the army. Lewis G Merritt subsequently became a Brigadier General in the USMC.

OADU Sgt Lockhart Sgt L Jennings Sgt H W Tindley RAAF Sgt M D Gould Sgt A J Griffiths Sgt A T R Renshaw	**Wellington IC** + + + + +	**Z9040**	**Delivery Flight** Took off St Eval for Gibraltar, but crashed into the sea 6.5km from Portreath. Sgt Jennings is buried in Shaw Cemetery, Newbury, and Sgt Tindley in Illogan (St Illogan) Churchyard. The others are commemorated on the Runnymede Memorial.

8 Jan 1942

24 Sqn SAAF Lt J J Daniels SAAF Sgt R E Colbert RAAF Sgt K A Mooney RAAF Sgt A B Davies	**Boston III**	**Z2161 W**	**Transit Flight** Took off 1000, LG 153 (Sidi Rezegh), in transit to LG 21 (Qotafiyah III). All of 24 Squadron's Bostons were being withdrawn from the front line because of serious problems with the engines. En route this aircraft and the following crashed in bad weather 8km W of Fort Maddelena.

24 Sqn SAAF Lt W M Lindsay SAAF Sgt A A J Hanson RAAF Sgt G C Geerdts SAAF Sgt J T Bonnes RAAF Lt J H O Dellow SAAF	**Boston III**	**Z2168 A**	**Transit Flight** Took off 1000, LG 153 (Sidi Rezegh), in transit to LG 21 (Qotafiyah III), and lost as above.

9 Jan **1942**	**OADU** F/O T G Moloney RAAF F/O J McG M Patterson RAAF Sgt W S C Atherton RAAF Sgt E G T Hall Sgt A Morris Sgt K H J Harrison RAAF	**Wellington IC** + + + + + inj	**Z9101**	**Delivery Flight**

Took off Gibraltar, 2326, for Malta, but crashed into the sea 1km S of Europa Point after take-off. All but the rear gunner were killed instantly, he being rescued by ASR launch. F/O Moloney and Sgt Hall are remembered on the Runnymede Memorial and Sgt Atherton (whose body was recovered but buried at sea) on the Gibraltar Memorial, while F/O Patterson is buried in Màlaga British Cemetery, and Sgt Morris in Le Petit Lac Cemetery, Oran.

	OADU P/O A H C Corser RAAF F/O T M Clark RAAF P/O J M Marchington Sgt W L Taylerson Sgt J Baylis Sgt R J Ledlie	**Wellington IC** + + + + + +	**DV417**	**Delivery Flight**

Took off Gibraltar for Malta, but failed to arrive. All six are commemorated on the Runnymede Memorial.

9-10 Jan **1942**	**37 Sqn** Sgt J F R Morrison P/O R Salmon P/O La Brish Sgt Clay Sgt D Giffin Sgt James	**Wellington IC**	**L7864 D**	**Op: Buerat El Hsun - Sirte Rd**

Took off 2315, El Adem, but an engine cut en route to the target, and the aircraft lost height and belly landed in the desert 12km NE of El Adem. DBR.

10 Jan **1942**	**220 Sqn** F/O F W Sturmey F/O T Franks F/Sgt H Mennie Sgt D E Tuson Passenger: F/O A J Barwood	**Fortress I** inj + + inj	**AN521 K**	**Air Test**

Abandoned after an engine caught fire 10km NNW of Shallufa. The two who died, one after hitting the tailplane on bailing out, are buried in Suez War Memorial Cemetery. The crew were part of a 90 Sqn detachment to the Middle East. F/O Barwood was the 90 Squadron Medical Officer.

11-12 Jan **1942**	**148 Sqn**	**Wellington IC**	**T2892**	**Unknown**

Ditched 12.1.42 (A-B Serials). Other source, SOC Malta 3.2.41. Not mentioned in the 148 Sqn ORB.

12 Jan **1942**	**148 Sqn** P/O T F B Geary P/O T L Bennett RCAF P/O A L Fraser RCAF F/Sgt W I Fairley RCAF Sgt J Cardwell Sgt E Hudspith	**Wellington II** + + + + + +	**Z8347 L**	**Op: Buerat El Hsun**

Took off LG 09. Hit by a flak ship and blew up 48km E of Buerat El Hsun. All are commemorated on the Alamein Memorial.

13 Jan **1942**	**113 Sqn** P/O R Huggins P/O J A Hilton Sgt J F Lait	**Blenheim IV** + + +	**Z7790**	**Op: Patrol**

Took off Takali. Shot down by return fire from Ju 52s 66km off Lampedusa. All are commemorated on the Malta Memorial.

14 Jan **1942**	**21 Sqn** F/Lt H F Dukes-Smith Sgt A J Wratten F/Sgt A Hussey	**Blenheim IV** + + +	**Z7342 H**	**Op: Anti-Shipping Patrol**

Took off 1145, Luqa, one of four Blenheims detailed to carry out an anti-shipping patrol off the Kerkennah Islands. They located and attacked the 5,000 ton German motor vessel *Brook* and its escort, the Italian destroyer *Zuri* at position 34° 50' N, 12° 00' E. Z7342 hit the mast of the *Brook* during the attack and plunged into the sea. F/Sgt Hussey is commemorated on the Alamein Memorial, and the others on the Malta Memorial.

	21 Sqn P/O K J Coakley RNZAF Sgt D B McLaren Sgt D I Groves	Blenheim IV + + +	Z7431 F	Op: Anti-Shipping Patrol	

Took off 1145, Luqa, detailed as above, and lost when it was hit by flak from the *Zuri* during the attack, at 1320. All are commemorated on the Malta Memorial.

15 Jan 1942	40 Sqn	Wellington IC	X9909	Ground

SOC in Malta, presumably DBR in an air raid, Luqa.

40 Sqn	Wellington IC	X9921	Ground

SOC. NFD, but presumably destroyed in an air raid, Luqa.

40 Sqn	Wellington IC	Z8859	Ground

DBR in an air raid, Luqa. SOC.

55 Sqn F/O A D Walker Sgt Grant Sgt Lewis	Blenheim IV	Z7584	Unknown

An engine cut; hit a ridge during a belly landing 6km E of Giovanni Berta.

104 Sqn	Wellington II	W5415	Unknown

SOC in Malta. Probably DBR in an air raid, Luqa.

104 Sqn	Wellington II	Z8408	Unknown

SOC in Malta. Probably DBR in an air raid, Luqa.

104 Sqn	Wellington II	Z8413	Unknown

SOC in Malta. Probably DBR in an air raid, Luqa.

107 Sqn	Blenheim IV	Z7760	Ground

DBF in an air raid on Luqa.

12 Sqn SAAF	Maryland II	1633	Unknown

SOC. NFD.

Malta	Wellington IC	Z8710	Ground

SOC. NFD. Probably DBR in an air raid, Luqa.

Malta	Wellington IC	Z8717	Ground

SOC. NFD. Probably DBR in an air raid, Luqa.

16-17 Jan 1942	OADU F/Sgt E M F Bearcroft Sgt G D Evenett Sgt C R Collinson Sgt E J Barrett Sgt A J N Fry Sgt D W Bellamy	Wellington IC + + + + + int	Z9030	Delivery Flight

Took off Gibraltar for Luqa. Hit a hillside in a storm, 850km W of Bône. The dead are buried in Bône War Cemetery. Sgt Bellamy, in the rear turret, survived, and was interned until November 1942.

17 Jan 1942	55 Sqn Sgt G A Corbett Sgt I A Stark Sgt G Souter	Blenheim IV	Z7512	Unknown

Overshot on landing at Berka I, 1415 hrs. DBR.

OADU Sgt J M Brady RAAF Sgt J H Hehir RAAF Sgt R Brown RAAF Sgt M W Scott Sgt J E Browne	Wellington IC + + + + +	Z9043	Delivery Flight

Took off Gibraltar for Luqa. Crashed into the sea off Bône. All are commemorated on the Runnymede Memorial.

20 Jan 1942	**OADU** Sgt L George RAAF Sgt J D Shanahan RCAF P/O J Bergson P/O J Gardiner Sgt L J Rymal RCAF Sgt T H Webb	**Wellington II** + + +	**Z8504**	**Delivery Flight** Took off Portreath for Gibraltar, but ditched after an engine failed. After eight days in a dinghy, the survivors were washed ashore about 45km E of Mostagnem, French Morocco. The dead are commemorated on the Runnymede Memorial. The others were released from internment in November 1942, both Sgt Shanahan and Sgt Webb later killed on active service.
	OADU Sgt R W Ticknor RCAF Sgt J W McPhee RCAF Sgt J T Park Sgt A J Nuttall Sgt E Connelly Sgt N C Slee	**Wellington IC** + + + +	**AD602**	**Delivery Flight** Crashed into the sea on take-off, Gibraltar, for Malta. All the dead are buried in Gibraltar North Front Cemetery.
20-21 Jan 1942	**148 Sqn** S/Ldr M E Abbott F/O W J Carroll RAAF P/O J B Scard Sgt J A Sellars Sgt H T McGrath RCAF Sgt I T James	**Wellington II** + + + + + +	**W5584 W**	**Op: Salamis** Took off 0000-0055, LG 09. FTR. All are commemorated on the Alamein Memorial. P/O Scard was serving under the name of P/O H R Merry.
21 Jan 1942	**40 Sqn**	**Wellington IC**	**Z8959**	**Ground** Destroyed in an air raid, Luqa.
22 Jan 1942	**11 Sqn** Sgt P L Payne RAAF Sgt M K Burnside RAAF Sgt E Cameron RAAF	**Blenheim IV**	**V5506**	**Op: Army Co-operation** Took off Msus No 1, to attack 100 to 150 Axis motor vehicles at 45km E of El Agheila. On return to Msus, at the point of break away, this Blenheim collided with Z7434 and crashed.
	11 Sqn S/Ldr K Ault Sgt J S Thompson Sgt J C A Bell	**Blenheim IV**	**Z7434**	**Op: Army Co-operation** Took off Msus No 1, detailed as above, and lost in collision with V5506.
	38 Sqn F/Sgt W G Brodie Crew	**Wellington IC**	**N2740 Y**	**Formation flying exercise** Engine cut in circuit and the undercarriage, not fully locked down, collapsed on landing, Shallufa. DBF.
23 Jan 1942	**38 Sqn** Sgt R W Dibb Crew	**Wellington IC**	**Z8790 B**	**Formation flying exercise** On landing at Shallufa, the port undercarriage collapsed, the aircraft swung, and the starboard undercarriage also collapsed. DBR.
	104 Sqn P/O D J Haydon RNZAF S/Ldr H M Young Crew	**Wellington II**	**Z8414 A**	**Night Flying Test** Took off, Kabrit, but on landing undershot and hit telegraph wires. DBR.
	12 Sqn SAAF	**Maryland II**	**AH385**	**Ground** Destroyed in an air raid, Luqa.
24 Jan 1942	**40 Sqn**	**Wellington IC**	**Z8855**	**Ground** SOC Malta. Presumably DBR in an air raid, Luqa.

25 Jan 1942	11 Sqn	Blenheim IV	V5899	Op: Army Co-operation

25 Jan 1942 — **11 Sqn** — **Blenheim IV** — **V5899** — **Op: Army Co-operation**
Sgt F B Borrett RAAF — inj
F/Sgt J Richmond DFM — +
Sgt H L Mackey RAAF — inj
Took off 1518, LG 147 (Bu Amud), to bomb motor transport along the Antalat-Agedabia road. Flak caused engine failure on the return flight and the pilot force-landed. The observer is commemorated on the Alamein Memorial.

1 OADU — **Wellington IC** — **AD608** — **Delivery Flight**
Sgt P F Monk
Crew
Took off Portreath for Gibraltar.Undershot on approach and hit a seawall. The undercarriage collapsed, the aircraft swung and hit Z9021. DBR.

1 OADU — **Wellington IC** — **Z9021** — **Ground**
Hit by AD608 while parked, Gibraltar. DBR.

1 OADU — **Wellington IC** — **Z9098** — **Delivery Flight**
P/O K D Adams — +
Sgt N A Graystone — +
Sgt J K Evans — inj
Sgt T P McBride — +
Sgt H Berry — +
Sgt L F J Harris — inj
Took off Portreath 0630 for Gibraltar, fired on by HM Trawler *Loch Oskaig* after failing to answer a challenge, and crash-landed on the beach at Sisimbra, Portugal.

27-28 Jan 1942 — **108 Sqn** — **Wellington IC** — **X9885 B** — **Ferry Flight**
Sgt W E Moffat
Crew
Took off 2020, LG 09, for Agedabia. The port engine cut and the aircraft crash-landed 3km N of El Adem when a promised flare-path was not laid out.

28 Jan 1942 — **11 Sqn** — **Blenheim IV** — **Z7359** — **Ferry Flight**
Engine cut on a ferry flight. Crash-landed near Mechili.

14 Sqn — **Blenheim IV** — **V5947** — **Op: Army Co-operation**
Sgt R G S Linley
Sgt A J B Humphreys RAAF
Sgt T G Smail RAAF
Took off 0800, Mechili No 1, to search for and bomb an enemy troop concentration E of Msus, but lost a propeller on take-off and crash-landed. Destroyed on evacuation.

29 Jan 1942 — **21 Sqn** — **Blenheim IV** — **Z7271 J** — **Op: El Zauir**
F/Lt E Fox — +
P/O R E Taylor — +
Sgt A L Pepper — pow
Took off 1145, Luqa, detailed to bomb El Zauir. An error of 20° in the leading aircraft's compass meant that instead buildings were bombed on the coastal road E of Tripoli. Z7271 was hit by debris from exploding bombs from the leader's Blenheim, crashed and exploded. The dead are buried in Tripoli War Cemetery.

55 Sqn — **Blenheim IV** — **V6244 P** — **Unknown**
Sgt R C Payne RAAF
Sgt L C Wheeler
Sgt G Sparrow
Took off LG 145 (El Gubbi West). The port engine seized, the aircraft lost its port propeller and crash-landed near Apollonia. The crew destroyed it to prevent it falling into enemy hands.

30 Jan 1942 — **45 Sqn** — **Blenheim IV** — **N3581 J** — **Unknown**
P/O E G Christensen RAAF
Sgt B F Pearce RAAF
Sgt R D Hilditch RAAF
Crash-landed in sandstorm, LG 147 (Bu Amud) and DBR. This aircraft had previously been SOC on 4.6.41, but then repaired!

1-2 Feb 1942 — **38 Sqn** — **Wellington IC** — **X9735 H** — **Practice attacks**
P/O E W Knowles
F/Sgt B J Tyson
Sgt R J Winstanley — +
P/O G D Dodd — +
Passengers:
Took off 2105, Shallufa for torpedo-dropping exercises. Flying low in Suz Bay it hit the sea and sank almost immediately. Knowles and Iles escaped and made for the dinghy, then picked up Tyson and Webb, all being picked up 25 min later by HMS *Sagitta*. P/O Dodd is

	Lt Iles RN Lt Webb RN			buried in Suez War Memorial Cemetery, and Sgt Winstanley commemorated on the Alamein Memorial.

2 Feb 1942	55 Sqn Sgt G A Corbett Sgt I A Stark Sgt G Souter	Blenheim IV	Z6076	**Unknown** Took off LG 17 (Fuka Main). An engine cut in a severe sandstorm and the pilot belly-landed the aircraft 12km S of LG 121. DBR.

4 Feb 1942	21 Sqn Sgt M Houston P/O J O'Grady Sgt L J Frost	Blenheim IV	Z7341 + + +	**Op: Palermo** Took off Luqa, detailed to bomb shipping in Palermo harbour; crashed into cloud-covered hills. The crew are buried in Catania War Cemetery.
	21 Sqn W/Cdr W R Selkirk MiD P/O F C Ashley Sgt S Phillips RCAF	Blenheim IV	Z9806 Z + + pow	**Op: Palermo** Took off Luqa, detailed as above. The pilot banked sharply to avoid high ground, a wing clipped the sea, and the aircraft cartwheeled and sank. The dead are commemorated on the Malta Memorial.
	21 Sqn F/O F J Workman RAAF P/O K J E Smethurst Sgt V T Lewis	Blenheim IV	Z9812 D + + +	**Op: Palermo** Took off Luqa, detailed as above. Hit by flak and crash- landed near Palermo. F/O Workman (badly injured) was captured while trying to destroy his aircraft; he died on 6 February and is buried along with his crew in Catania War Cemetery.
	21 Sqn F/Sgt J K Ibbotson RNZAF P/O D J Clement Sgt H E Graham	Blenheim IV	Z9824 K + + pow	**Op: Palermo** Took off Luqa, detailed as above. Crashed into cloud- covered hills. The dead are buried in Catania War Cemetery.

6 Feb 1942	21 Sqn S/Ldr R R Stewart RNZAF P/O D J Morris P/O R E Smaridge	Blenheim IV	Z7308 + + +	**Op: Anti-shipping** Took off 1415, Luqa, on an anti-shipping strike off Bu'ayrat al Hasun, Libya, the leader of the operation, in which three aircraft were shot down. Failing to find ships in the target area they returned to base, but on nearing Malta they were intercepted by Bf 109 fighters and shot down into the sea near the island of Filfla. All are commemorated on the Malta Memorial.
	21 Sqn F/Sgt G R Cameron RNZAF Sgt R D Fletcher Sgt G Hancock	Blenheim IV	Z9725 + + +	**Op: Anti-shipping** Took off 1415, Luqa, detailed as above, and also shot down off Filfla. F/Sgt Cameron is commemorated on the Malta Memorial; the others are buried in the Malta (Capuccini) War Cemetery.
	21 Sqn P/O J G C Grieve P/O C J Rowley Sgt R R Hall	Blenheim IV	Z9822 + + +	**Op: Anti-shipping** Took off 1415, Luqa, detailed as above and also shot down. Sgt Hall is buried in the Malta (Capuccini) War Cemetery; the others are commemorated on the Malta Memorial.
	37 Sqn P/O H C E Downer	Wellington IC	AD650	**Ground** Taxied into a bomb crater filled with loose soil when under direction by ground crew, Luqa.
	38 Sqn Sgt Buckingham Sgt R W Dibb Crew	Wellington IC	P9250 D	**Ferry Flight** A tyre burst on take-off for a ferry flight, and on landing at Heliopolis the aircraft swung and the undercarriage collapsed. DBF.

7 Feb 1942	37 Sqn Sgt B R Steward Sgt K M Cochrane RAAF Sgt R E Lloyd RNZAF Sgt E Bailey Sgt Killarin Sgt Williams	Wellington IC	Z8734 S	Op: Benghazi

Took off 2200, LG 09. On return hydraulic problems forced Sgt Steward to belly-land his aircraft. DBR.

	1 OADU	Wellington IC	Z9037	Ground

DBR in an air raid, Luqa.

	1 OADU	Wellington IC	DV453	Ground

Destroyed in an air raid, Safi Strip, Luqa.

	Malta Sgt M S Taylor	Blenheim IV	Z9712	Air Test

Took off Safi on an air test but overshot on a downwind landing; believed later DBR in an air raid, Safi, while under repair.

8 Feb 1942	14 Sqn Sgt W S McLellan RAAF F/Sgt J R Vernon RAAF Sgt J Nankervis RAAF	Blenheim IV	V6231 L	Unknown

An engine cut; unable to maintain height with a heavy bomb load, the aircraft crash-landed on rough ground near Sollum; believed not repaired and SOC 18 September.

	55 Sqn P/O A W Archer RAAF	Blenheim IV	Z7595	Unknown

An engine cut, and the aircraft overshot landing at LG 17 (Fuka). DBR.

	148 Sqn F/Lt A R Hayter Crew	Wellington II	Z8430	Unknown

Took off LG 09. The port engine was shut down after a radiator leak, and the aircraft belly-landed near Wadi Natrun. DBR.

9 Feb 1942	38 Sqn Sgt R W Manuel Crew	Wellington IC	X9947 U	Ferry Flight

Took off Shallufa for LG 09, but the port engine cut, and the aircraft landed at Abu Zabel quarries, the undercarriage collapsing. DBR.

	55 Sqn Sgt T W Howard Sgt F Elliott Sgt Wilkins	Blenheim IV	V6364	Unknown

The aircraft lost a propeller and crash-landed 9km E of Halfaya. DBR.

	1 OADU Sgt L J Hogan RCAF Crew	Wellington IC	DV496	Delivery Flight

Took off Portreath for Gibraltar, but undershot on approach to land, hitting a seawall; the undercarriage collapsed. DBR.

9-10 Feb 1942	70 Sqn S/Ldr R D Davis Sgt F W Sortwell F/Lt W H Norledge F/Sgt F McGregor Sgt K J Powell Sgt G S Smith	Wellington IC	Z1166 O + + + + + +	Op: Martuba West

Took off 2230-0005, LG 104, detailed to bomb Martuba West LG. FTR. All are commemorated on the Alamein Memorial.

	70 Sqn Sgt A V Parker Sgt Allison Sgt Reynolds Sgt Carter Sgt Bryan Sgt Francis	Wellington IC	Z8769 Z	Op: Martuba West

Took off 2335, LG 104, detailed as above. Undershot landing in heavy ground mist on return, LG 104.

11 Feb 1942	**21 Sqn** Sgt J H Stubbs RAAF Sgt J S Grabham Sgt P Tyas	**Blenheim IV** + + +	**Z9823**	**Op: Anti-shipping** Took off Luqa on a shipping sweep. Shot down by a Bf 109 fighter (Oblt H J Heinecke 8/JG 53) near the island of Filfla. All the crew are commemorated on the Malta Memorial.
14 Feb 1942	**1 OADU** P/O E Griffiths Sgt C Hall P/O H S Wilson Sgt J Stuart Sgt J Howard Sgt G Kennington	**Wellington IC** int int int int int int	**Z9026**	**Delivery Flight** Took off Portreath for Gibraltar, but force-landed in Portugal after the port engine failed. The crew was briefly interned.
15 Feb 1942	**162 Sqn** P/O D W Fenton Sgt R Moore P/O Boyle Sgt J W Neu Sgt Nott	**Wellington IC**	**AD589 A**	**RDF Calibration** Took off Shallufa. On return the port engine ran out of oil and cut on approach, the aircraft crash-landing at Wadi Natrun. Three were injured. The crew had failed to replenish the oil tanks from the overload tank using the Zwicky pump.
	1 OADU	**Wellington IC**	**DV413**	**Ground** One of four Wellingtons destroyed in an air raid, Luqa. Corporal J A Webb, 40 Squadron, was killed when taxying one of these four machines. He is buried in the Malta (Capuccini) Naval Cemetery.
	1 OADU	**Wellington IC**	**DV414**	**Ground** Destroyed in an air raid, Luqa.
	1 OADU	**Wellington IC**	**DV482**	**Ground** Destroyed in an air raid, Luqa.
	1 OADU	**Wellington IC**	**DV454**	**Ground** Destroyed in an air raid, Luqa.
16 Feb 1942	**458 Sqn RAAF** W/Cdr N G Mulholland Sgt A R Wills RAAF F/Lt L A Brain Sgt E Anstee Sgt J E Andrews F/O J Willis-Richards	**Wellington IC** + + + + + pow	**DV539**	**Relocation Flight** Took off Stanton Harcourt for Luqa, but shot down 45km from Malta by Ju 88s. F/O Willis-Richards, the Squadron Gunnery Officer, was rescued by an Italian destroyer. W/Cdr Mulholland and Sgt Anstee are buried in Catania War Cemetery. The others are commemorated on the Runnymede Memorial.
16-17 Feb 1942	**1 OADU** P/O R W King RNZAF Sgt R Bowling RNZAF F/Lt T A Pavely Sgt G T Elliott Sgt E Ackroyd RNZAF Sgt M Molyneux Passenger: Lt Catlow RN	**Wellington IC** pow pow pow pow pow + pow	**AD591**	**Delivery Flight** Took off Gibraltar for Malta. Off course, they were hit by flak and force-landed near Castelvetrano airfield. Sgt Molyneux is buried in Syracuse War Cemetery.
	1 OADU P/O A O'Brien RNZAF Sgt W B Stehr RNZAF Sgt J D Sandilands RAAF Sgt W R Wren RAAF Sgt A L Strang RAAF Sgt C J Foote	**Wellington IC** + + + + + +	**AD635**	**Delivery Flight** Took off Gibraltar for Malta but flew off course and crashed into the mountains about 8m E of La Calle, Algeria. The six crew were buried at the crash site but later re-interred at Bône.

17 Feb 1942	**1 OADU** P/O J C Hardy RCAF P/O F H Phillips P/O R A Green RCAF P/O R T Bromwich Sgt G McIntyre Sgt W W Morton	**Wellington IC** int int int int + +	**DV458**	**Delivery Flight** Took off Gibraltar for Malta, damaged by enemy fighters, and crash-landed in a lake 12km S of Bizerte. The survivors were interned by the Vichy French. Sgt McIntyre is buried in Massicault War Cemetery, while Sgt Morton is commemorated on the Runnymede Memorial.
	1 OADU Sgt C Dancer Sgt R Clark Sgt R O R Morgan Sgt C A Pacey Sgt J Sackfield Sgt F W Sergent DFM RNZAF	**Wellington IC** pow pow pow pow pow pow	**DV497**	**Delivery Flight** Took off Gibraltar for Luqa but shot down by a German fighter (Lt R von Keudall). The crew were rescued from the sea near Delle Correnti Is, Syracuse.
	1 OADU P/O I C Beckwith RCAF Crew	**Wellington IC**	**AD649**	**Delivery Flight** Took off Gibraltar for Malta, but overshot landing at Luqa and crashed into the quarry.
19 Feb 1942	**11 Sqn** Sgt J T Small RAAF Sgt H A Clements RAAF Sgt W R Wheeler RAAF	**Blenheim IV** + + +	**R3872**	**Communication Flight** Took off LG 116 to deliver airmen's kits to LG 121. In circumstances which are obscure, the aircraft was involved in a flying accident at 1130 hrs and crashed 90km W of Mersa Matruh. The crew are all commemorated on the Alamein Memorial.
	40 Sqn F/Sgt C A Armstrong RNZAF Sgt P Street F/Sgt C Ruggles RCAF Sgt M K Johnson Sgt B Holloway Sgt R D Kirkwood	**Wellington IC**	**Z9113**	**Ferry Flight** Took off Luqa for Shallufa, but the port engine failed, the reduction gear sheared and the propeller fell off. The aircraft crash-landed near El Khankar. DBR.
20 Feb 1942	**148 Sqn** S/Ldr R A G Baird Crew	**Wellington II**	**Z8346**	**Night Flying Practice** Took off 1800, Luqa. The port tyre burst on landing and the undercarriage collapsed when the aircraft swung in soft ground, Luqa. DBR.
21 Feb 1942	**21 Sqn SAAF**	**Maryland II**	**AH369 O**	**Unknown** SOC Luqa. Almost certainly written off because it was worn out, like other Marylands flown to Malta and rejected by 69 Sqn.
	1 OADU Sgt P F Monk Sgt E M C Fahmy Sgt J R Worwood RAAF Sgt R Rowley Sgt H C Hadley Sgt E G Oakley	**Wellington IC** + + + + + +	**Z8952**	**Delivery Flight** Took off Gibraltar for Malta, and perhaps shot down by a Bf 110 (Oblt P Habicht). The crew sent out an SOS at 0103 hrs, and was still in contact with Malta at 0235, but nothing further was heard. Sgt Worwood, whose body was recovered from the sea on 4 April, is buried in Salerno War Cemetery. The others are commemorated on the Runnymede Memorial.
22 Feb 1942	**14 Sqn** F/Sgt L W Jones Sgt E V Hopkinson Sgt R Burgess	**Blenheim IV** + + +	**Z9657 C**	**Op: Italian warships** Took off 1205, LG 147 (Bu Amud), one of six Blenheims (three each from 55 and 18 Sqns) detailed to attack the Italian Battle Fleet escorting a convoy reported in position approx 35° 00' N, 20° 20' E. At 1503 hrs one engine caught fire and the aircraft ditched 200km NW of Benghazi. The crew were seen to get into the dinghy, but were never found. They are commemorated on the Alamein Memorial.

	108 Sqn P/O F H McDonald Crew	**Liberator II**	**AL574 O** Op: Reconnaissance On take-off, 0230, Fayid, detailed to carry out a daylight reconnaissance of the Mediterranean, the engines were throttled back and the undercarriage retracted too soon. The aircraft crashed and was DBF.
22-23 Feb **1942**	**70 Sqn** Sgt J A McArdle Sgt Hegarty Sgt Clarke Sgt A Bolton Sgt Cooper Sgt Simmons	**Wellington IC**	**X9736 U** Op: Martuba Took off 1830, LG 104. The port throttle jammed on landing, and though the engine was switched off the aircraft swung, hit a bump, and the undercarriage collapsed, LG 104.
	148 Sqn Sgt R Hamilton Sgt B W Spence RNZAF Sgt B J L Lilly Sgt R W Girdham Sgt J M Hudson P/O R Turner	**Wellington II** pow pow pow pow pow pow	**Z8360** Op: Convoy attack Took off 1935-2035, LG 09, to attack a convoy between Sicily and Tripoli. The port engine seized and the aircraft crash-landed 108km behind enemy lines; the crew were captured after several days.
23 Feb **1942**	**14 Sqn** Sgt J Bosworth Sgt R K Swann RAAF Sgt A W Hoyle Passenger: Sgt E J Curtis RAAF	**Blenheim IV** + inj	**Z9729 A** Relocation Flight Took off Bir el Baheira on relocation to LG 116. Attacked four times by four Bf 109s and crash-landed with both engines on fire and the elevator and rudder control cables shot away. Sgt Swann received head injuries and died the following day; he is buried in Halfaya Sollum War Cemetery. Sgt Hoyle was wounded in the chest and arms.
	105 Sqn	**Blenheim IV**	**Z7420 M** Ground DBR in an air raid, Luqa.
	1 OADU	**Wellington II**	**Z8367** Ground Destroyed in an air raid, Luqa.
	1 OADU	**Wellington II**	**Z8377** Ground Destroyed in an air raid, Luqa, while awaiting repair after having been damaged while taxying, 24.12.41.
	Malta	**Blenheim IV**	**Z9607** Unknown SOC. Malta. NFD.
23-24 Feb **1942**	**108 Sqn** F/O B A Willis RAAF F/Sgt J Bradbury W/O2 N S Hall RCAF Sgt F Coulsen Sgt P R Cooper F/Sgt C M Gray RNZAF	**Wellington IC** + + + + + +	**AD599 E** Op: Martuba Took off 1845-1910, LG 09, detailed to attack the airfield at Martuba. Believed to be the aircraft seen to catch fire and explode on hitting the ground. All are buried in Knightsbridge War Cemetery, Acroma.
	108 Sqn Sgt W B Moffat Sgt H Brown Sgt R C Hook F/Sgt A Stirrup F/Sgt L R Sinclair RCAF Sgt J A Acaster	**Wellington IC** + + + + + +	**AD606 K** Op: Martuba Took off 1845-1910, LG 09, detailed as above. All buried in Knightsbridge War Cemetery, Acroma.
24-25 Feb **1942**	**38 Sqn** P/O E W Knowles Sgt E E Hammett	**Wellington IC** +	**Z9108 R** Op: Benghazi Took off 2050, LG 09, detailed to lay mines outside Benghazi Harbour. Hit by flak while minelaying, leaving

	Sgt K W Bevan		+	most of the instruments unserviceable and the pilot
	Sgt T O Docherty			wounded. Deteriorating weather made it impossible to
	Sgt R A White			control the aircraft, and P/O Knowles gave the order to
	Sgt A R B Durie		+	bail out. Sgts Hammett, White and Docherty were picked
				up by Eighth Army motor transport. The dead are
				commemorated on the Alamein Memorial.

	104 Sqn	**Wellington II**	**W5422 E**	**Op: Berka**
	Sgt R H Richardson		+	Took off ALG, detailed to attack the landing grounds at
	F/Sgt K E J Evans		+	Berka. FTR. All are commemorated on the Alamein
	Sgt D Barkway		+	Memorial.
	Sgt J McKenna		+	
	Sgt C N Bower		+	
	Sgt G W Franks		+	

25 Feb 1942	**14 Sqn**	**Blenheim IV**	**V5657 O**	**Op: Martuba**
	F/Sgt J T Willis			Took off 1640, LG 116, detailed to make an independent
	Sgt E W Barr RNZAF		inj	attack on Martuba airfields. The aircraft was severely
	Sgt H P Tew		+	damaged by flak before reaching the target and the
				pilot jettisoned the bombs and turned for home. When
				the aircraft caught fire the pilot and observer bailed out
				over Allied territory near Bir Hacheim. Sgt Tew, unable
				to bail out, was killed when the aircraft crashed at
				approximately 2030. He is buried in Knightsbridge War
				Cemetery, Acroma.

	14 Sqn	**Blenheim IV**	**Z6443 C**	**Op: Martuba**
	P/O F R Brown RAAF			Took off 1630, LG 116, detailed as above. Ran out of fuel
	Sgt H Young			on return and ditched in the Mediterranean 1km off
	Sgt R W Danks RAAF		inj	Ras-al-Kanayis at approximately 2230 hrs.

	55 Sqn	**Blenheim IV**	**V6074 Q**	**Relocation Flight**
	Sgt H Anderson			Took off LG 17 (Fuka Main), to fly to an ALG, but the
	Crew			starboard engine cut and the aircraft belly landed 12km
				SW of LG 11 (Qasaba).

25-26 Feb 1942	**70 Sqn**	**Wellington IC**	**Z8803 K**	**Op: Benghazi**
	Sgt J A McArdle			Took off 2130-2150, LG 104. Engine cut. Force-landed in
	Sgt Hegarty			sea near Isheila Rocks (off Sidi Barrani). The crew took to
	Sgt Clarke			the dinghy and drifted out to sea before reaching land
	Sgt A Bolton		+	13 hours later. The dinghy overturned and Sgt Bolton
	Sgt Cooper			drowned (commemorated on Alamein Memorial).
	Sgt Simmons			

26 Feb 1942	**1 OADU**	**Wellington II**	**Z8569**	**Delivery Flight**
	F/Lt J L Moore			Took off Portreath for Gibraltar, but on landing used
	Crew			insufficient flap, overshot the runway and crashed in the
				sea just off the North Front.

	1 OADU	**Wellington IC**	**Z9025**	**Ground**
			DBR in air raid, Luqa.	

27 Feb 1942	**70 Sqn**	**Wellington IC**	**Z9023 X**	**Ground**
	F/Sgt G Malpass		+	A bomb exploded during bombing-up, LG 104; DBF.
	Sgt A Stringfellow		+	Five ground crew were killed and four injured.
	LAC R R McClean		+	
	LAC W A Hopewell		+	
	LAC S Jarvis		+	
	LAC J F Callow RAAF		inj	
	Unknown		inj	
	Unknown		inj	
	Unknown		inj	

	24 Sqn SAAF	**Boston III**	**Z2175** **Relocation Flight**
	Lt T J P Botha SAAF	+	Took off 0730, LG 140 (Bir el Baheira No 1), to return to
	2/Lt J D P Bester SAAF		LG 21 (Qotafiyah III), but shot down on take-off by two
	Air Sgt W K F Collender SAAF		Bf 109s. The mortally wounded pilot made a perfect belly-
	Sgt J D Matthews	inj	landing, thereby saving the lives of his crew. 2/Lt Bester
			tried to rescue him but was forced back by the flames. Sgt
			Matthews had been wounded in the attack and Air Sgt
			Collender helped him from the Boston before it was DBF.
			Lt Botha is buried in Tobruk War Cemetery.

	1 OADU	**Blenheim IV**	**V5535** **Delivery Flight**
	Sgt W Teale RCAF	inj	Took off Portreath for Gibraltar. One engine cut on radio
	Sgt J P Barnett	inj	test, and on approach to Gibraltar, at 15 metres the
	Sgt M V Cole	inj	starboard wing dropped and the aircraft dived into the
			sea 900m E of North Front aerodrome.

	1 OADU	**Wellington IC**	**DV510** **Delivery Flight**
	P/O G A Kennedy RNZAF	pow	Took off Gibraltar for Luqa but encountered violent
	Sgt T Bell	pow	electrical storms which forced the aircraft down to 200m.
	Sgt R H Watton	pow	The radio was for a time unserviceable but when a
	Sgt M H C Berrie RAAF	pow	bearing was finally obtained it turned out to be a false
	Sgt J L Turner RCAF	pow	one from an Italian station. Out of fuel, the aircraft crash-
	Sgt R Jefferson	pow	landed at Pachino, near Syracuse, after the port engine
			cut out. This was a 99 Sqn Wellington and crew en route
			to the Far East.

	1 OADU	**Wellington IC**	**BB475** **Delivery Flight**
	F/Sgt A Moran RCAF	pow	Took off Gibraltar for Luqa, but ditched in the Straits of
	Sgt G Foster RCAF	pow	Messina, out of fuel. The crew, from 99 Squadron, was
	Sgt T L Kenner	pow	rescued from the sea. Like DV510 this aircraft was en
	Sgt R S Daniel RCAF	pow	route to the Far East.
	Sgt C Grimwood RCAF	pow	
	Sgt W Oxendale RCAF	pow	

27-28 Feb **1942**	**148 Sqn**	**Wellington II**	**Z8423 V** **Op: Benghazi**
	P/O D Wisdom	pow	Took off c.2000, LG 09. FTR, and reported as shot down
	Sgt R J Beck	pow	in flames over Benghazi. The crew were believed to have
	P/O D H Yeoman RNZAF	pow	been captured at Sidi Chalifa (about 19km NE of
	Sgt R E Bale	pow	Benghazi). Sgt Beck was later reported as a POW in
	Sgt P W Lowe	pow	hospital.
	Sgt A G E Tidd	pow	

	1 OADU	**Wellington IC**	**Z9097** **Delivery Flight**
	P/O S W Reid RNZAF	+	Took off Gibraltar for Luqa, but flew off course and
	Sgt J N Vincent RNZAF	+	crashed in Tunisia. The crew are buried at Enfidaville.
	Sgt R H Clark	+	
	P/O H Cookson	+	
	Sgt E Thorpe	+	
	Sgt T Peirpoint	+	

28 Feb **1942**	**15 Sqn SAAF**	**Blenheim IV**	**V5870** **Conversion Training**
	Maj J L V de Wet SAAF		Took off LG 29 (Amiriya), on conversion training.
	Capt B L Hutchinson SAAF		Crashed at 1010 hrs 4km from Amiriya when the engine
			cut.

1 Mar **1942**	**104 Sqn**	**Wellington II**	**Z8415** **Night Flying Test**
			SOC. NFD.

	104 Sqn	**Wellington II**	**Z8506** **Unknown**
	P/O R H Palmer		The undercarriage was retracted too soon on take-off,
	Crew		Kabrit. The shock was not felt, but the undercarriage
			collapsed on landing. DBR and SOC.

2 Mar 1942	12 Sqn SAAF Lt R H van Breda SAAF Lt G Aaronson SAAF Air Sgt A R Kool SAAF Air Sgt P J Morgan SAAF	Boston III inj inj	AL805 **Training** Took off LG 21 (Qotafiyah III), on conversion training. While low flying the aircraft hit the ground at over 200 mph near LG 99. The crew had remarkable escapes, all save the pilot escaping with nothing more than a bad shaking. The observer was hurled out of the broken nose of the aircraft, while the pilot and gunners managed to scramble clear before the aircraft was DBF.
	15 Sqn SAAF 2/Lt J Reid SAAF	Blenheim IV	Z5864 **Training** Took off LG 29 (Amiriya), on conversion training. The port propeller flew off when the reduction gear seized and sheered. The aircraft crash-landed at 1220 hrs, 1.5km W of LG 29 with the undercarriage up. DBR. This was a solo flight by the pilot.
2-3 Mar 1942	37 Sqn S/Ldr E E C Tomkins W/Cdr R R Nash P/O James F/Sgt Lawson Sgt Adams F/Sgt Friend	Wellington IC	Z9111 D **Op: Palermo** Took off Luqa to attack shipping in Palermo harbour, and overshot landing on return. Not repaired. (Note: 37 Sqn ORB records 2 aircraft being burnt out on the 3rd, during raids on Luqa.)
	148 Sqn P/O D M Crossley Crew	Wellington II	W5555 D **Op: Supply Drop** Took off 2117, LG 09, to drop supplies to partisan groups on Crete. The aircraft developed engine trouble and lost height as it approached the drop zone. The second engine caught fire 7km N of Daba Point and aircraft was ditched. The crew took to the dinghy, were spotted by an ASR aircraft 4 hours later, and were rescued by ship.
3 Mar 1942	14 Sqn S/Ldr L E Leon F/Sgt J A Hibbert F/Sgt G P Rylands	Blenheim IV inj	Z7908 L **Training** Took off LG 116, to practice formation flying. Collided with Blenheim V6184, both aircraft crash-landing 20km from LG 116; DBR.
	38 Sqn	Wellington IC	T2580 **Ground** Destroyed in an air raid, Kabrit.
	38 Sqn P/O M Foulis	Wellington IC	T2989 **Non-operational Flight** Took off Kabrit. The throttle to the port engine disconnected and the aircraft force-landed successfully with the undercarriage retracted. Seemingly not repaired, it was SOC by inventory return, 31.10.43.
	148 Sqn	Wellington II	Z8371 A **Ground** One of two aircraft destroyed during an air raid at LG 09. SOC 26 March.
4 Mar 1942	14 Sqn F/O J A Harvie RAAF	Blenheim IV +	Z7893 U **Delivery Flight** Took off Qasaba on a ferry flight to 14 Squadron. The pilot misjudged his approach and the port wing struck the Officers Mess, the aircraft crashing and bursting into flames. The pilot is buried in the El Alamein War Cemetery.
	37 Sqn	Wellington IC	X9886 **Ground** Destroyed in an air raid, Luqa.
	55 Sqn F/Sgt J C Campbell Crew	Blenheim IV	Z6437 N **Delivery Flight** Took off LG 17 (Fuka Main). An engine cut, the aircraft lost height and belly-landed near LG 121.

GB1 Lorraine	**Blenheim IV**	**T1817** SOC. NFD.	**Unknown**

RAF Takoradi   **Boston III**   **AL787**   **Night Flying Test**
S/Ldr Rayski PAF   Took off Lagos, in preparation for a delivery flight to the Middle East, but the aircraft swung on landing, one wing hit the ground, and the undercarriage collapsed. DBR.

4-5 Mar   **70 Sqn**   **Wellington IC**   **Z1042 S**   **Op: Benghazi**
1942   F/Lt P J Fisher   +   Took off 2245-2250, LG 104. Last heard of at 0249. The
     P/O G P Chambers RNZAF   +   aircraft was later found by army personnel, crashed in
     F/O R Maggs   +   the forward army area 70-80km S of Bomba, DBF. Two
     F/Sgt R C V Rogers   +   bodies were found, but their graves could not be located
     Sgt K M Tuck   +   post-war. All are thus commemorated on the Alamein
     Sgt T G Middlebrook   +   Memorial.

---

6 Mar   **38 Sqn**   **Wellington IC**   **Z8797 A**   **Unknown**
1942   F/Lt Gilliard   Took off 1100, LG 86. One engine cut on approach to
     Crew   Shallufa, and the aircraft crashed. SOC 1.3.44, by
          inventory entry.

6-7 Mar   **162 Sqn**   **Wellington IC**   **Z8905 O**   **Op: Rhodes**
1942   Sgt M H Knowles   pow   Took off 2020, LG 09, on a radio intelligence mission to
     Lt Baker RN   Rhodes. FTR. NFD. It is presumed that Lt Baker was also
     Sgt A F Murrel   pow   taken prisoner, though this has not been confirmed.
     Sgt R G Tregenza RAAF   pow
     Sgt K Westbrook RCAF   pow
     Sgt A Levy   pow
     Sgt J A Drever   pow
     Sgt R C Rawlins   pow

---

7 Mar   **14 Sqn**   **Blenheim IV**   **V5954**   **Op: Tmimi**
1942   F/Sgt K W Stevenson   +   Took off 2300, LG 116, to bomb Tmimi satellite LG, but
     F/Sgt W V Howey RCAF   +   flew into the ground in haze 2km NW of LG 116 and
     Sgt L Johnson   +   blew up. The pilot and WOp/AG were killed in the crash
          and the observer died the following day. All are buried in
          the El Alamein War Cemetery.

     24 Sqn SAAF   **Boston III**   **Z2278**   **Ground**
     Lt L H Murrow   DBR taxying at Bir-el-Baheira. (Two Bostons were
     Crew   involved in accidents at Bir-el-Baheira when the
          nosewheels collapsed on landing.)

     1 OADU   **Wellington IC**   **AD644**   **Ground**
          Destroyed in an air raid, Luqa.

7-8 Mar   **148 Sqn**   **Wellington II**   **W5388 N**   **Op: Benghazi**
1942   P/O J W Pelletier RAAF   Took off LG 106. Ditched off Sollum on return, after the
     Crew   failure first of the starboard engine and then of the port
          engine also. The crew was spotted in their dinghy by
          FAA Walrus and rescued by launch, 8m E of Sollum.

---

8 Mar   **108 Sqn**   **Wellington IC**   **W5675**   **Unknown**
1942   Took off Fayid and on landing at Berka 3 swung, the
          undercarriage collapsed, and the aircraft was DBF.

8-9 Mar   **37 Sqn**   **Wellington IC**   **Z9038 H**   **Op: Sicily**
1942   W/O1 S J Kozlowski RCAF   +   Detailed to lay mines off Sicilian ports, the pilot taxied
     F/Sgt J H A Marcotte RCAF   inj   onto the flarepath, Luqa, and the aircraft was struck by

Sgt E Goodfellow		+	DV483, taking off. Both aircraft caught fire and their
Sgt H N Walker RAAF		+	mines exploded, The dead are buried in Malta
Sgt V F O'Hagan		inj	(Capuccini) Naval Cemetery.
Sgt A T Thomas		inj	

37 Sqn	**Wellington IC**		**DV483 Y** **Op: Sicily**
F/O C J L Boyd		inj	Hit Z9038, Luqa. Both aircraft caught fire and the mines
Sgt A G Thomas		inj	exploded. F/O Kirkman was blown out of his turret when
Sgt N J Knight RAAF		+	the mines exploded and escaped unhurt. Sgt Herman is
Sgt R McG Herman RAAF		+	commemorated on the Malta Memorial, and Sgt Knight is
Sgt H Williams		inj	buried in Pembroke Military Cemetery, Malta.
F/O Kirkman			

9 Mar **1942**	**37 Sqn**	**Wellington IC**	**Z8731** **Ground**
			Destroyed in an air raid, Luqa.

37 Sqn	**Wellington IC**	**DV421** **Ground**
		Destroyed in an air raid, Luqa. A-B Serials lists this as an
		OADU aircraft, but the 37 Sqn ORB gives it as 37 Sqn, so
		it was presumably taken on strength at Luqa to replace
		earlier losses in air raids.

38 Sqn	**Wellington IC**	**W5646 V** **Ground**
		Destroyed in an air raid, LG 09.

40 Sqn	**Wellington II**	**Z8417** **Ground**
		Destroyed in an air raid, Luqa. This aircraft was one of
		two with 4,000 lb bomb capacity transferred to 40 Sqn
		when 104 Sqn left for Egypt. 40 Squadron had transferred
		to Shallufa by this date, so this aircraft was presumably
		awaiting repair.

12 Sqn SAAF	**Boston III**	**AL671 F** **Ground**
		Strafed by an enemy aircraft during a raid on a
		Wellington airfield adjacent to LG 21 (Qotafiyah III). DBF.

9-10 Mar **1942**	**38 Sqn**	**Wellington IC**	**Z9099 C** **Op: anti-shipping**
W/Cdr J H Chaplin DFC			Took off 2140-2240, LG 05. Shot down by 2 Bf 109s near
P/O J D N Lister		+	Fort Maddelena on a positioning flight (the aircraft had 2
F/O B O Fryer		+	torpedoes fitted). P/O Lister and F/O Fryer both died in
Sgt W E Pring			the crash-landing, P/O Lister when thrown from the
F/Sgt A E Rainer			aircraft. The survivors walked back to Allied lines. W/Cdr
			Chaplin had minor injuries. The dead are
			commemorated on the Alamein Memorial.

10 Mar **1942**	**14 Sqn**	**Blenheim IV**	**T2387 Y** **Unknown**
Crew			Returning from Bir el Baheira as one of a formation of
Passenger			three; an engine cut and the aircraft crashed in a forced-
			landing in the western desert. The crew and passenger
			were uninjured, and picked up the following day.

104 Sqn	**Wellington II**	**W5431** **Unknown**
		SOC. NFD.

11 Mar **1942**	**108 Sqn**	**Wellington IC**	**X9948 G** **Ground**
Sgt W J Spencer			At LG 09 taxied before take-off into X9887, which was not
Crew			marked by obstruction lights. The aircraft was SOC
			27.7.44, still on charge to 108 Sqn, by inventory entry.

108 Sqn	**Wellington IC**	**X9887 A** **Ground**
Sgt J Metcalf		See above. SOC 31.10.43, still on charge to 108 Sqn, by
Crew		inventory entry.

12 Mar 1942	**37 Sqn**	**Wellington IC**	Z1043 Destroyed in an air raid, Luqa.	**Ground**
	37 Sqn	**Wellington IC**	Z8731 Destroyed in an air raid, Luqa.	**Ground**

13 Mar 1942	**12 Sqn SAAF** Maj J I Nash SAAF Crew	**Boston III**	AL810 Y **Training** Had engine trouble on take-off LG 21 (Qotafiyah III) and severely damaged in a belly-landing. Assessed as Cat B, the aircraft was nonetheless reduced to salvage to keep the squadron's other aircraft flying.

15-16 Mar 1942	**108 Sqn** Sgt L R Williams RAAF W/Cdr R J Wells DFC P/O J P Tolson F/Sgt P H Morey Sgt C J Ingram Sgt H J Gibbons F/Lt F C Barrett Passengers: Sgt C R Amos F/O J R Anderson DFC Sgt W P Brooks Cpl A M S Brownlie F/Sgt G Buchanan F/Sgt C V S Goodenough RCAF Sgt S F Hayden F/Sgt L G Jordan P/O G F King RCAF Sgt H W T Sloman RAAF P/O W B Stephens	**Liberator II** + + + + + + + inj inj + + + + inj + + + inj	AL577 **Ferry Flight** Took off from Gibraltar for the United Kingdom, but at 0730, in bad weather, crashed into high ground at Jenkinstown, near Dundalk, Eire. All of those who survived the crash were seriously injured, and P/O Stephens subsequently died of his injuries. The aircraft was carrying air and ground crews to collect further Liberators for ferrying to Egypt to convert 108 Squadron entirely to Liberators. This plan was now abandoned. Wg/Cdr Wells is buried in Diss Cemetery, P/O Tolson in Harpenden (Westfield) Cemetery, F/Sgt Morey in Shirley (St John) Cemetery, Sgt Ingram in West Ham Cemetery, Sgt Gibbons in Newport (Christchurch) Cemetery, Sgt Brooks in Wandsworth (Putney Vale) Cemetery, Cpl Brownlie in Glasgow (Eastwood) Cemetery, F/Sgt Buchanan in Abbey Cemetery, Thorn, F/Sgt Jordan in Brighton (Downs) Cemetery, and P/O Stephens in the City of Westminster (Paddington) Mill Hill Cemetery. The others are interred in Belfast City Cemetery.

16 Mar 1942	**14 Sqn** S/Ldr A C Mills Sgt R N Ey RAAF Sgt J A R Hunt RAAF	**Blenheim IV** evd evd evd	V5446 M **Op: Army Co-operation** Took off 0815 LG 116, to bomb the Agedabia-El Agheila road, but for reasons unknown force-landed at 1250 approximately 113km SW of El Agheila. The crew walked for nine days behind enemy lines covering some 200km and living on aircraft rations until they were picked up by a British armoured patrol.

17 Mar 1942	**14 Sqn** F/Sgt R G S Linley Sgt A J B Humphries RAAF Sgt T G Smail RAAF	**Blenheim IV** + + +	Z7991 **Op: Anti-shipping** Took off 1130, LG 140 (Bir el Baheira No 1), detailed to carry out an anti-shipping strike. Collided in mid-air with T2124 while forming up and crashed. All are buried in Tobruk War Cemetery.
	14 Sqn Sgt R J Good RAAF Sgt J S Windmill Sgt W B T Godly RAAF	**Blenheim IV** + + +	T2124 B **Op: Anti-shipping** Took off 1130, LG 140 (Bir el Baheira No 1), detailed as above, and lost in collision with Z7991. All are buried in Tobruk War Cemetery.
	37 Sqn	**Wellington IC**	W5646 **Ground** Destroyed in an air raid, Luqa. (A-B Serials: 38 Sqn, destroyed in air raid, 9.3.42; 37 Sqn ORB: 37 Sqn).
	37 Sqn	**Wellington IC**	DV493 **Ground** Destroyed in an air raid, Luqa. (A-B Serials: OADU, 37 Sqn ORB: received by 37 Sqn in Malta).
	40 Sqn	**Wellington IC**	Z9039 **Ground** Destroyed in an air raid, Luqa. Since 40 Sqn left Malta in late February, this was presumably a damaged aircraft left behind for repair.

	1 OADU	Wellington IC	Z1164	Ground

Destroyed in an air raid, Luqa.

18 Mar 1942	14 Sqn	Blenheim IV	Z5886 S	Delivery Flight

On take-off, Maaten Baggush, struck a barrel, damaging its undercarriage. DBR after landing at LG 116 with one leg down, but not locked.

	40 Sqn	Wellington IC	Z9104	Air Test
	Sgt H W Garvin RCAF		+	
	W/O F E Johnson		+	
	Sgt J C Joss		+	
	Sgt R J J Robb		+	

Took off Shallufa for a fuel consumption test, but dived into the ground. The cause was not established, but pilot illness was suspected. All are buried in Suez War Memorial Cemetery. There is an account of this accident in David Gunby's *Sweeping the Skies*, p196.

19 Mar 1942	14 Sqn	Blenheim IV	Z5893 W	Op: Candia
	Sgt E Bowling RAAF		inj	
	Sgt W J MacMichael RAAF		+	
	Sgt P Munyard RAAF		+	

Took off 2345, LG 116, detailed to bomb Candia, but climbed too steeply, stalled and crashed. The dead are buried in the El Alamein War Cemetery.

	70 Sqn	Wellington IC	DV485 O	Unknown
	Sgt D J Kerr			
	P/O Smith			
	F/Sgt McLachlan			
	P/O King			
	F/ Sgt Bidlake			
	Sgt Morgan			

An engine cut in circuit during a sandstorm and the air craft crash-landed at LG 104, hitting a telegraph pole and cables. DBR.

	1 OADU	Wellington IC	Z9035	Ground

DBR in an air raid; Luqa. (The 37 Sqn ORB also notes that a damaged Sqn aircraft was destroyed in an air raid this day.)

	1 OADU	Blenheim IV	V6394	Delivery Flight
	F/Sgt A J Smith		+	
	Sgt J W Robinson		+	
	F/Sgt F MacI Wood		+	

Took off Gibraltar for Malta. Crashed, apparently after engine failure, in the sea 40km off Cape Bon, Tunisia. The pilot is commemorated on the Alamein Memorial and the others on the Runnymede Memorial.

	Middle East	Blenheim IV	Z7773	Unknown

DBR. NFD.

20 Mar 1942	14 Sqn	Blenheim IV	L9418	Op: Candia
	Sgt K M Dee RAAF		inj	
	Sgt H G Marshall RAAF		inj	
	Sgt J L H Du Boulay RAAF		inj	

Took off LG 116, detailed to bomb Candia airfield, but failed to gain height and struck a petrol drum on the LG boundary, damaging the tailplane and crashing a few seconds later. Sgt Marshall had severe leg injuries, and the others suffered concussion of the lungs when one of the bombs exploded.

20-21 Mar 1942	70 Sqn	Wellington IC	BB502 F	Op: Berka
	Sgt Parker			
	Crew			

Took off LG 104, detailed to attack landing grounds at Berka and Berka Satellite. On return, crashed on landing. SOC 5 June.

	108 Sqn	Wellington IC	R1098 U	Op: Heraklion
	F/O V G Owen-Jones			
	Crew			

Swung on take-off and the undercarriage collapsed, LG 09; DBR.

	104 Sqn	Wellington II	Z8510 R	Op: Eleusis
	P/O F N Pope		+	

Took off c.1455, Kabrit. FTR. All are commemorated on

	Sgt W B Cattrall		+	the Alamein Memorial. P/O Boyers was attached from
	P/O J C Boyers		+	226 Sqn.
	Sgt E F Welfare		+	
	Sgt A D Walker		+	
	Sgt O H Leggett		+	

21 Mar **1945**	**104 Sqn** W/Cdr P R Beare	**Wellington II**		**Z8415 T** **Ground** Destroyed on the ground at an ALG by an exploding flare, which set the aircraft on fire.
	24 Sqn SAAF Capt J P Verster SAAF 2/Lt J D P Bester SAAF Sgt J M Lefroy RAAF Air Sgt F H J Bender SAAF	**Boston III**	+	**Z2225** **Op: Barce** Took off 0615, LG 140 (Bir el Baheira No 1), one of three Bostons detailed to attack Barce. Attacked on the return flight by two Bf 109F fighters (Lt Friedrich Korner and Lt Karl von Lieres u Wilkau of 2/JG 27, each claiming one Boston) and after a long low-level chase shot down 46km SW of Bir Hacheim. The crew, after walking for two days without water, were picked up by a Free French patrol and returned to base. This was 2/Lt Bester's first fully operational sortie, but he had also been in Boston Z2175 on 27th February. He thus had the dubious honour of being shot down twice in two operational trips. Air Sgt Bender is commemorated on the Alamein Memorial.
	24 Sqn SAAF Lt Col A J M Mossop SAAF P/O B A Coleborne RAAF F/Sgt R C van Eyssen SAAF Air Sgt R E M Hague SAAF	**Boston III**	inj inj inj inj	**AL733** **Op: Barce** Took off 0615, LG 140 (Bir el Baheira No 1), detailed as above and shot down at 0830 SW of Bir Hacheim, either by Lt Friedrich Korner or Lt Karl von Lieres u Wilkau. All four crew were badly injured, the pilot when the aircraft was strafed after crashing, a cannon shell penetrating the armour plating of his seat and badly injuring his back. Although badly burnt, P/O Coleborne undertook an arduous journey to get help, for which he was subsequently awarded an MBE.
	1 OADU	**Wellington IC**		**Z9035** **Ground** DBR in an air raid, Luqa.
22 Mar **1942**	**38 Sqn** F/Sgt J R H Main Sgt J E Durrant Sgt E C Johnson Sgt W E Smith Sgt J H Broadhead Sgt A S Ratcliffe	**Wellington IC**	+ + + + + +	**Z9110 Q** **Sea Search** Took off LG 09 to search for an aircraft dinghy. Ditched off Qotafiya in rough seas, and sank immediately. The dinghy surfaced but no crew were seen. All are commemorated on the Alamein Memorial.
	Malta Sgt M L Cecil RAAF Crew	**Blenheim IV**		**Z7315** **Transit Flight** On take-off, Luqa, failed to become airborne, swung into an obstruction, and was DBF. (A-B Serials lists this as a 21 Sqn aircraft, but 21 Sqn had been disbanded in Malta and reformed in the UK on 14 March. Z7315 was thus presumably moving to Egypt to serve with another unit.)
23 Mar **1942**	**24 Sqn SAAF** Lt J J B Steyn SAAF Lt J H O Dellow SAAF Air Sgt S F Oosthuizen SAAF Air Sgt V D Spuy SAAF	**Boston III**	pow	**Z2206** **Op: Martuba West** Took off LG 140 (Bir el Baheira No 1), one of twelve Bostons detailed to attack Martuba West airfield. Approaching from the sea, the Bostons encountered intense flak over Bomba and Martuba East airfield. The pilot briefly lost control and instructed the crew to bail out, but intercom damage meant that only the observer received the instruction and bailed out. Lt Steyn then regained control and after evading attacks by a lone Bf 109 fighter crash-landed the aircraft near Tobruk.

	24 Sqn SAAF	**Boston III**	Z2287	**Op: Martuba West**

24 Sqn SAAF — **Boston III** — **Z2287** — **Op: Martuba West**
Lt G P O'Donovan SAAF
Sgt R H Kelly RAAF
Sgt G Catchlove RAAF — inj
Sgt S B Harvey SAAF

Took off LG 140 (Bir el Baheira No 1), detailed as above, and likewise hit by flak over Bomba and Martuba East. With the aircraft on fire, and despite an attack by a Bf 109 (Feldwebel W Hillgruber, 7/JG 27) which injured Sgt Catchlove, the pilot managed to crash-land on the Trig Capuzzo road, 4km W of Sidi Rezegh.

24 Sqn SAAF — **Boston III** — **AL800** — **Op: Martuba West**
Maj R Tennant SAAF +
Lt G Bennett SAAF +
Sgt D N Johnston SAAF +
Sgt C J Kincaid SAAF +

Took off LG 140 (Bir el Baheira No 1), detailed as above. Brought down in flames by flak over Martuba East. Lt Bennett is commemorated on the Alamein Memorial and the others are buried in Benghazi War Cemetery.

25 Mar 1942 — **1 OADU** — **Wellington IC** — **AD640** — **Delivery Flight**
Sgt H J McNeill RNZAF +
Sgt J E Clarke RNZAF inj
Sgt R J Wood +
Sgt W J Lambie +
Sgt R O'Donnell +
Sgt R R Pole +

Suffered starboard engine failure just after take-off for Malta, and ditched 1km E of North Front, Gibraltar. Sgt Clarke was rescued after two hours in the water. Sgts McNeill, Pole and O'Donnell are buried at Gibraltar. The others are commemorated on the Runnymede Memorial.

27 Mar 1942 — **55 Sqn** — **Blenheim IV** — **Z5905** — **Unknown**
Lost. NFD.

162 Sqn — **Wellington IC** — **DV489 A** — **Relocation Flight**
S/Ldr Willis
P/O D W Fenton
P/O Clifford
Sgt Matten
A/C Kinkhead
A/C Davies
A/C McDonald
A/C Hanton
A/C Beveridge
A/C Turner
A/C Tapp

Took off Aqir, 0840, for Shallufa, as relief aircraft for calibration duties, but crashed on landing at Shallufa.

27-28 Mar 1942 — **38 Sqn** — **Wellington IC** — **AD596 M** — **Op: Patras Shipping**
Sgt H Buckingham pow
Sgt W E Lucan +
Sgt V A Munnings pow
Sgt S J Padgham pow
Sgt J F Offen RCAF pow

Took off 1952-2124, LG 05. Hit by flak and crashed into the sea after a torpedo attack. Sgt Lucan is commemorated on the Alamein Memorial.

148 Sqn — **Wellington II** — **Z8571 V** — **Op: Benghazi**
F/Sgt E M Papworth +
Sgt Moon
Sgt G S Mills inj
Sgt Buckley
Sgt Robinson
Sgt Cooper

Took off 2223, ALG 106, detailed to attack shipping in Benghazi harbour. On return the controls were handed to Sgt Moon, who attempted to synchronise the engines, which were surging. Height was lost but proximity to ground was not realised until the aircraft touched down on rock near Tolmeta. SOC 30 March. F/Sgt Papworth is buried at El Alamein War Cemetery.

148 Sqn — **Wellington II** — **Z8337 P** — **Op: Benghazi**
Sgt C Wild evd
Sgt D C Egles evd
Sgt G A Barton evd
Sgt H G Morris evd
Sgt E J Chippett evd
F/Sgt A E Farrant evd

Took off 2215-2305, ALG 106, detailed as above but FTR. The crew were rescued on 6 April by a Long Range Desert Group patrol and returned to base on 13 April.

28-29 Mar 1942 — **148 Sqn** — **Wellington II** — **Z8516 L** — **Unknown**
Took off 2223, LG 106. Crashed 59km WNW of Mersa Matruh.

	1 OADU Sgt M J Smithson Sgt H Smith — inj W/O J D McLaren Sgt R E Dixon + Sgt E H Giersch RAAF Sgt W Cansick +	Wellington IC	DV503 **Delivery Flight** Took off Portreath for Gibraltar, but after engine failure ditched off Cape Espichel, Portugal. Sgts Cansick and Dixon drowned. The others were rescued by a Portuguese fishing boat.
30 Mar 1942	14 Sqn F/Lt H K Keck RAAF + F/Sgt J H Hibbert + F/Sgt G P Rylands +	Blenheim IV	Z7627 **Unknown** Took off LG 116. Shot down in error by Hurricanes, and at 1320 crashed into the Mediterranean near Ras Alam El Rumb. All are commemorated on the Alamein Memorial.
	1 OADU Sgt H Janney RAAF + Sgt J M Shiner RAAF + Sgt C E Johnson RAAF +	Blenheim IV	Z9832 **Delivery Flight** Took off 0110, Luqa, for Egypt, but failed to arrive. All of the crew are commemorated on the Malta Memorial.
	1 OADU P/O G Featherstone + Sgt R Grisdale + P/O R Dargavel + P/O C Newell-Jones + Sgt K R Clark + Sgt C F Bryant +	Wellington IC	BB511 **Delivery Flight** Took off Gibraltar for Malta but failed to arrive. All are commemorated on the Runnymede Memorial.
	104 Sqn	Wellington II	Z8433 **Op: Eleusis** Missing (A-B Serials). The 104 Sqn ORB shows no such operation or target. The aircraft serial is not found in Nov-Mar ops records, but many serials are missing.
31 Mar 1942	70 Sqn	Wellington IC	Z1041 **Ground** DBF in an air raid LG104 (Qotafiyah II).
	1 OADU	Blenheim IV	V6434 **Ground** Destroyed in an air raid, Luqa.
	1 OADU P/O N W Knight RCAF Crew	Wellington IC	DV517 **Delivery Flight** Took off Portreath for Gibraltar; landed heavily, swung to starboard, ran off the runway and struck Spitfires AB304 and BP892. DBR.
1 Apr 1942	104 Sqn	Wellington II	Z8341 **Ground** Lost due to enemy action; NFD.
2 Apr 1942	14 Sqn Sgt G W Clarke-Hall RAAF Sgt W A Bethune RAAF Sgt E G Clarke RAAF	Blenheim IV	V5950 V **Transit Flight** Took off LG 116, for the forward landing ground at Bir el Baheira. The starboard engine cut on take-off; the undercarriage was then raised to stop the aircraft. DBR.
	1 OADU	Wellington IC	DV412 **Ground** DBR in an air raid, Luqa.
3-4 Apr 1942	37 Sqn F/Sgt A E Lomas Sgt W Gordon Sgt D O Neill-Shaw Sgt McOmish Sgt J Strachan Sgt E Miller	Wellington IC	Z9031 K **Op: Benghazi** Took off 2225, LG 09. Just prior to landing at Heliopolis the port engine lost its propeller and burst into flames. The aircraft was landed with undercarriage retracted, 8km S of Burg el Arab. It was declared Category B, but probably not repaired, being SOC by inventory entry on 1.1.47.

4 Apr 1942	**1 OADU** F/Sgt G Wylie Sgt F Collins Sgt W Bodger	**Blenheim IV**	**V6310**	**Delivery Flight** Took off Portreath for Gibraltar, and landed there with the undercarriage retracted because of hydraulic failure. SOC 19.1.44 by inventory entry.
	1 OADU Sgt A Orr Crew	**Wellington II**	**Z8575**	**Ground** Hit by BB512 while taxying Luqa (see below). DBR.
	1 OADU Sgt J M Pearce Crew	**Wellington IC**	**BB512**	**Delivery Flight** Took off Gibraltar for Malta. On landing at Luqa the pilot saw another aircraft taxying in front of him, and attempted to take off again, colliding with Z8575. DBR.
	1 OADU F/O N E Waugh Sgt Dash Crew	**Wellington IC**	**DV519**	**Delivery Flight** On take-off, Luqa, the wing struck an aircraft parked on the flare-path; the aircraft crash-landed and was DBR. One crew member, unidentified, was injured.
4-5 Apr 1942	**38 Sqn** P/O R Langley + Sgt R G Giddings + Sgt P A Foster + Sgt G Jackson + Sgt H F Pocock +	**Wellington IC**	**DV419 J**	**Op: Shipping Sweep** Took off c.2106, LG 09, for a shipping sweep off Salamis. FTR. All are commemorated on Alamein Memorial.
	70 Sqn Sgt G T L Salmon pow P/O R E Brain RNZAF pow Sgt R T Marquet RNZAF pow Sgt L L Clark RAAF pow Sgt K G Fausett RNZAF pow Sgt G J W Galland RNZAF pow	**Wellington IC**	**AD632 Z**	**Op: Benghazi** Took off 2305-2350, LG 104, detailed to attack shipping at Benghazi. FTR.
5-6 Apr 1942	**148 Sqn** Sgt B Nethercote evd Crew	**Wellington II**	**Z8359 H**	**Op: Benghazi** Took off c.2305, ALG 106, to bomb the harbour facilities at Benghazi, creating a diversion for mine-laying aircraft. The engine cut, and the aircraft crash-landed in the desert, 208km E of Benghazi, on return. The crew walked toward British lines and were picked up by a Desert Patrol.
6-7 Apr 1942	**37 Sqn** F/Sgt R Hinton Crew	**Wellington IC**	**Z9107**	**Unknown** On take-off from Shallufa dropped back onto wheels as undercarriage partly retracted after take-off. On landing undercarriage collapsed. SOC 31.7.44 by inventory entry.
7 Apr 1942	**162 Sqn** P/O D W Fenton P/O King Sgt Reid Sgt Matten Sgt Bird Sgt Hammerston Sgt Middlemiss Sgt Blinman	**Wellington IC**	**BB463 O**	**Transit Flight** Took off 1400, Shallufa, to fly to LG 09, preparatory to operations; the undercarriage collapsed on landing. DBR.
7-8 Apr 1942	**37 Sqn** W/O 1 C H Tourville RCAF + Sgt S Walker + Sgt G C Pearson + Sgt J L Stuart +	**Wellington IC**	**DV411**	**Op: Benghazi** Took off LG 09, but crashed shortly after becoming airborne and blew up. All six crew are buried in El Alamein War Cemetery.

Sgt J V Magrane		+	
Sgt J McLean		+	

38 Sqn	**Wellington IC**	**AD604 U**	**Op: Benghazi**
F/Sgt T A Holdsworth		+	Took off 2230-2300, LG 09, to attack shipping in Benghazi
Sgt J C Webb		inj	harbour. On return descended below cloud to determine
F/Sgt J R P Mann		+	its position, the starboard engine cut and caught fire and
Sgt E C Fiorini		+	aircraft crashed near Mersa Matruh. The dead are buried
Sgt S R Allaway		inj	in Halfaya Sollum War Cemetery.
Sgt A Rothwell		inj	

10 Apr **1942**	**14 Sqn**	**Blenheim IV**	**V6453**	**Op: Maleme**
	P/O B S Slade RAAF		Took off 2240, LG 116, to attack Maleme Airfield, but	
	P/O G W McD Allingame RAAF		failed to gain height and hit telephone wires. Believed	
	Sgt G A Lindschau RAAF		not repaired. SOC 3 June.	

14 Sqn	**Blenheim IV**	**Z9722**	**Op: Maleme**
Sgt P D Clauson RAAF		+	Took off 2240, LG 116, detailed as above, but side-slipped
Sgt C O Thorne RAAF		inj	into the ground and burst into flames. Sgt Clauson is
Sgt C R Grandfield		inj	buried in the El Alamein War Cemetery.

15 Sqn SAAF	**Blenheim IV**	**Z9717**	**Unknown**
Lt C R Bruton-Simmonds SAAF		inj	Took off LG 98 in bad visibility. One wing hit the ground
2/Lt A M Jones SAAF		inj	and the aircraft crashed 1km W of LG 98.
Crew member			

11 Apr **1942**	**1 OADU**	**Wellington IC**	**DV656** **Delivery Flight**
			DBR (Cat E). SOC. NFD.

11-12 Apr **1942**	**37 Sqn**	**Wellington IC**	**DV420** **Op: Benghazi**
	P/O R A V Salmon		Took off 1945, LG 09, to attack shipping at Benghazi. The
	P/O P Ward	inj	hydraulics were damaged by flak, and the undercarriage
	F/O I Spencler		could not be locked down, collapsing on landing at
	Sgt A Hawkins		Mersa Matruh. DBR.
	Sgt D Giffin		
	F/Sgt A Dowd		

13 Apr **1942**	**148 Sqn**	**Wellington IC**	**T2817** **Ground**
			SOC. NFD.

148 Sqn	**Wellington IC**	**DV502** **Ground**
		DBR in an air raid, Luqa. The aircraft was formerly with
		458 Sqn.

1 OADU	**Wellington IC**	**Z1178** **Ground**
		DBR in an air raid, Luqa; SOC.

1 OADU	**Wellington IC**	**DV537** **Ground**
		DBR in an air raid, Luqa.

Malta	**Wellington IC**	**BB505** **Ground**
		DBR in an air raid, Luqa.

14 Apr **1942**	**211 Sqn**	**Blenheim I**	**L8537** **Unknown**
			Crashed 48km from Wadi Halfa sometime prior to 14
			April, when a party from 52 RSU salvaged and
			subsequently dismantled the aircraft. The aircraft is
			recorded as on charge with 211 Sqn, which went to the
			Far East in December 1941. Since it and its aircraft was the
			forming unit for 72 OTU, however, it is possible that this
			aircraft was lost while with that unit.

16 Apr 1942	24 Sqn SAAF Lt A Jordan SAAF Lt H L Bosman SAAF	Boston III	AL757	Unknown

Took off LG 21 (Qotafiyah III), presumably on a flight test, and got into an inverted spin when the pilot attempted a loop. Lt Bosman bailed out, but the pilot recovered control sufficiently to make a forced landing 4km NE of Gasr-el-Arid. Fouled by the open escape hatch, the nosewheel collapsed. DBR.

18 Apr 1942	14 Sqn 2/Lt P J Chapman SAAF + Sgt D W McConville RAAF + Sgt R R Richardson RAAF +	Blenheim IV	Z7963	Communications Flight

Took off LG 116 to fly to LG 05, but crashed in a forced landing 1.5km E of Sidi Barrani. All of the crew are buried in Halfaya Sollum War Cemetery.

	108 Sqn F/Sgt W D Burd RCAF + LAC W B Macfarlane + LAC J Norman + AC2 E Hopkins + AC1 C V John +	Wellington IC	Z8955 F	Air test

Took off 1000, Fayid, and crashed at 1015 while low flying near Geneifa. Cause not known. All are buried in Fayid War Cemetery.

	15 Sqn SAAF Lt J S Whittle SAAF inj Lt A D Swart SAAF inj Air Sgt A P Turnbull SAAF inj	Blenheim IV	T2243	Training

Took off 0740, LG 98 and undershot and crashed while landing at LG 99.

18-19 Apr 1942	37 Sqn Sgt B R Steward + Sgt K M Cochrane RAAF + F/Sgt R E Lloyd RNZAF + Sgt C K Nurse + Sgt E Bailey + Sgt M G C Scanlon +	Wellington IC	AD642 N	Op: Benghazi

Took off 2236, probably from LG 09, to attack shipping at Benghazi. Bad weather forced the abandonment of the mission, and on return the aircraft flew into the ground 5km SE of LG 09, probably while the crew were trying to ascertain their position. All are buried in El Alamein War Cemetery

19 Apr 1942	1 OADU Sgt E A Sanders Crew	Wellington IC	ES995	Delivery Flight

Took off Gibraltar for Malta, but on landing at Luqa, overshot because of brake failure and the undercarriage collapsed. DBR.

19-20 Apr 1942	70 Sqn P/O R A Sharp RCAF Sgt Dawson P/O Carr Sgt Todd Sgt Taylor Sgt E D Allen +	Wellington IC	T2842 P	Op: Benghazi

Took off 2055, LG 104, to attack shipping at Benghazi. Abandoned near LG 21, because of instrument failure. Sgt Allen later died of head injuries, and is buried in El Alamein War Cemetery.

20-21 Apr 1942	104 Sqn P/O White Crew	Wellington IC	Z8331 U	Op: Benghazi

Took off LG 106 to attack shipping in Benghazi harbour. On return crashed in a forced landing 208km S of Cairo. DBR.

21 Apr 1942	148 Sqn	Wellington IC	AD652 D	Ground

Destroyed in an air raid, Luqa.

	1 OADU	Wellington II	Z8584	Ground

DBR in an air raid, Luqa.

	1 OADU	Wellington IC	Z9032	Ground

DBR in an air raid, Luqa.

22-23 Apr 1942	**1 OADU** P/O J H Reid Sgt R S Oliver F/Sgt E H Martin RCAF Sgt E F Bramley RCAF F/Sgt A W C E King RCAF Sgt J Smith	**Wellington IC** + + + + + +	**DV548**	**Delivery Flight**

Took off Luqa for Egypt, but never arrived. All are commemorated on the Runnymede Memorial.

| | **1 OADU**
Sgt A P Westle
Sgt C J Beatty RAAF
Sgt E P Bradley
Sgt R Easton
P/O A S Dryden
Sgt L P D Fordham
Passengers:
F/Sgt R L Vince
Sgt R L Miller
S/Ldr S O'R Surridge MC | **Wellington IC**
+
+
+
+
+
+

+
+
+ | **HF849** | **Delivery Flight** |

Took off Luqa for Egypt but never arrived. S/Ldr Surridge is commemorated on the Malta Memorial, the others on the Runnymede Memorial.

| **23 Apr**
1942 | **148 Sqn** | **Wellington IC** | **ES984   C** | **Ground** |

Destroyed in an air raid, Luqa.

| | **1 OADU** | **Wellington IC** | **DV412** | **Ground** |

DBF in an air raid, Luqa.

| **23-24 Apr**
1942 | **148 Sqn**
F/Lt A R H Hayter
Sgt D C King
Sgt M W Buckley
Sgt G W Tull
Sgt E H March
Sgt J B Kehoe | **Wellington IC**
pow
+
+
+
+
+ | **BB483   Q** | **Op: Comiso** |

Took off 2045, Luqa, to bomb Comiso, but shot down over Acate. F/Lt Hayter participated in the Great Escape and was murdered by the Gestapo on 6.4.44. He is buried in Poznan Old Garrison Cemetery. The others are buried in Catania War Cemetery.

| | **148 Sqn**
F/O R McM Harper RAAF
Sgt G H King
Sgt E F Wear
Sgt R T Perrin
Sgt T P Hosking
F/Sgt H G Powell | **Wellington IC**
+
+
+
+
+
+ | **DV573   O** | **Op: Comiso** |

Took off Luqa, 2040-0355, to attack Comiso, and shot down over the target. All are buried in Catania War Cemetery.

| **25 Apr**
1942 | **104 Sqn** | **Wellington II** | **Z8497** | **Ground** |

Destroyed in an air raid, Kabrit.

| **25-26 Apr**
1942 | **70 Sqn**
Sgt P R Darby
Sgt G L Taylor RNZAF
Sgt J K Cleeves RAAF
Sgt B W Linklater RAAF
Sgt W J D Powell
Sgt E L Morris | **Wellington IC**
pow
+
pow
pow
pow
pow | **Z8984   D** | **Op: Benghazi** |

Took off 1955-2050, LG 104, to attack harbour facilities and shipping at Benghazi. The aircraft was crippled by flak over the target, and the second pilot killed. The others bailed out, and the aircraft crashed and exploded 24km S of Benghazi near Berka. Sgt Taylor is commemorated on the Alamein Memorial.

| **26 Apr**
1942 | **38 Sqn** | **Wellington IC** | **DV555** | **Ground** |

Destroyed in an air raid, probably at Luqa.

| | **70 Sqn**
W/Cdr J H T Simpson
Sgt E A C Barfoot
Sgt Donald
Sgt Ackerman
Sgt Elliott
Sgt Navin
P/O Mansell | **Wellington IC**

inj | **Z1045** | **Unknown** |

Lost as a result of enemy action. NFD.

	223 Sqn	**Baltimore I**	**AG729**	**Training**
	Sgt S E Hunt	+	Took off LG 116, on the second operational exercise of the	
	Sgt A M Hunter	+	day but FTR. Last seen 27km out to sea off Alexandria.	
	Sgt S K Annesley RAAF	+	All are commemorated on the Alamein Memorial.	
	Sgt J A Nelson	+		

27-28 Apr 1942	**70 Sqn**	**Wellington IC**	**Z8787 J**	**Op: Benghazi**
	Sgt L Holliday		Took off 2030, LG 104, to bomb shipping at Benghazi.	
	Sgt Battersby		On return the port airscrew fell off, the wireless was	
	Sgt Riley		unserviceable, and in foggy conditions made a belly-	
	Sgt Lord		landing in the desert. DBR.	
	Sgt Howarth			
	Sgt G W B Robinson	inj		

28 Apr 1942	**1 OADU**	**Blenheim IV**	**V5733**	**Delivery Flight**
	Sgt R S Parker	+	Took off Portreath for Gibraltar, but failed to arrive. Sgt	
	Sgt E B Downs	+	Parker's body was recovered and buried at sea, and he is	
	Sgt I W Chance	+	commemorated on the Gibraltar Memorial. The others	
			are commemorated on the Runnymede Memorial. The	
			crew was from 21 Sqn.	

28-29 Apr 1942	**70 Sqn**	**Wellington IC**	**Z8766 Y**	**Op: Benghazi**
	P/O A C White RCAF	+	Took off 2000, LG 104. Shot down by an intruder over the	
	Sgt J F Bunting	+	base. Sgts Douglas and Croft were injured, the former	
	F/Sgt J Paton RCAF	+	fatally. The dead are buried in El Alamein War Cemetery.	
	F/Sgt M L Doyle RCAF	+		
	Sgt G Douglas	+		
	Sgt C W Croft	inj		

	104 Sqn	**Wellington II**	**Z8500 B**	**Op: Martuba**
	Sgt H J Bennett	+	Took off LG 106, to attack LGs at Martuba. An aircraft	
	Sgt W J Brandon RNZAF	+	was seen caught by flak in searchlights, going down into	
	F/Sgt D Gilligan	+	the sea and bursting into flames. Two crew were reported	
	Sgt G Scully	+	buried by the Germans but their graves were never	
	Sgt J R Martin	+	found. All are accordingly commemorated on the	
	Sgt H M McHarg	+	Alamein Memorial.	

29 Apr 1942	**38 Sqn**	**Wellington IC**	**T2825 Y**	**Air Test**
	P/O A L Wiggins RAAF		Took off LG 251 (Shallufa Satellite), but bounced on an	
	Passengers:		attempted landing and P/O Wiggins decided to go	
	AC1 Johnson		around again. He raised the flaps completely, rather than	
	LAC C R N Holloway	inj	to 15 degrees, and the aircraft sank, hit the ground and	
			caught fire. All aboard escaped before the aircraft blew up.	

	162 Sqn	**Blenheim IV**	**V5508**	**Unknown**
	Sgt F Walton	+	Stalled and dived into Lake Idku, Egypt, on approach at	
	F/Sgt W H Weller MiD	+	1030, and DBF. All are buried in Alexandria (Hadra) War	
	Sgt J W Jessett	+	Cemetery. Sgt Walton is recorded by the CWGC as with	
	Passenger:		213 Squadron, and F/Sgt Weller with 55 Squadron.	
	AC2 B A Hannan	+		

	1 OADU	**Wellington IC**	**HF861**	**Delivery Flight**
	Sgt W H Mitchell		During the take-off run, Luqa, the starboard tyre burst,	
	Crew		the aircraft swung, and despite attempts to correct the	
			swing with the port engine, hit a parked Beaufighter.	
			DBR.	

1 May 1942	**40 Sqn**	**Wellington IC**	**DV512**	**Ground**
			Hit by Beaufighter X7752, Shallufa. SOC.	

2 May 1942	223 Sqn S/Ldr L J Joel Sgt M Bailey F/Sgt W G Daynes P/O F H Taylor	Baltimore I	AG716	Relocation Flight

Took off from the ALG to return to base, but belly-landed at LG116 when the aircraft's hydraulic system failed completely, all attempts at lowering the undercarriage, including pouring beer into the hydraulic tank, having failed. DBR.

	1 OADU Sgt S Parker Crew	Wellington IC	HF861	Delivery Flight

Took off Luqa for Egypt, but suffered wireless failure after take-off, and progressive engine problems as it returned to Luqa. It landed heavily and the undercarriage collapsed.

3-4 May 1942	108 Sqn F/Lt D H McArthur DFC + P/O I R J Perkins + F/Lt P J Camp pow P/O L A D Speller pow P/O D Hudson + F/Sgt D F Clifford RNZAF + G/Capt F M V May pow	Liberator II	AL511 A	Op: Tripoli

Took off 1830, Fayid, to attack harbour facilities/shipping at Tripoli. Shot down over Libya by a night fighter and crashed near Soluch. G/Capt May, serving at 242 Wing HQ, died in hospital on 22 May and was buried at Barce (later re-interred at Benghazi). The others' graves could not be located post-war, hence they are commemorated on the Alamein Memorial. P/O Speller was aboard for navigational experience, G/Capt May for operational experience.

	1 OADU F/Sgt W B Fulcher RCAF Crew	Wellington IC	HF903	Delivery Flight

Took off Gibraltar for Malta. Drifted off course on landing at Luqa, overshot and in beginning a circuit crashed while turning. DBR.

4 May 1942	15 Sqn SAAF Maj J L V de Wet SAAF + 2/Lt J S du Toit SAAF + Air Sgt A P Vos SAAF + Air Mech N St M Juul SAAF	Blenheim IV	Z7513 R	Training

Took off 0545, Kufra Oasis, one of three (the others being T2252 and Z7610) on a familiarising training flight. They became hopelessly lost and force-landed. On 5 May, after other attempts to locate Kufra had failed, Maj de Wet had the remaining fuel transferred from the other aircraft to Z7513, which took off captained by 2/Lt J H Pienaar, with 2/Lt F J Reed and Air Sgt W W Oliver as crew, to attempt to locate Kufra. Z7513 eventually landed some 32km away. All aboard died of thirst, as did all, save Air Mech Juul, of those who stayed with the other two aircraft. Z7613 was located by a 162 Sqn Wellington on 9 May 200km E of Kufra, but abandoned. The others were located on 11 May and recovered. In February 1959 Z7513 was rediscovered in the Central Cyrenaican Desert by an oil exploration team.

	1 OADU	Wellington IC	HF903	Delivery Flight

Hit the ground in a turn after an overshoot, Luqa. DBR.

5 May 1942	148 Sqn	Wellington IC	DV605 U	Ground

Destroyed in an air raid, Luqa.

8 May 1942	12 Sqn SAAF Lt F Beamish SAAF Sgt G H Martin F/Sgt M O'Reilly SAAF F/Sgt E C V Thomas SAAF	Boston III	AL780	Training

Took off LG 21 (Qotafiyah III) on night-flying training, but crashed on landing at LG 99. DBR.

8-9 May 1942	104 Sqn Sgt R C Brady F/Sgt B P Kopp RCAF + Sgt W R Cook Sgt D G Symons Sgt R Slimings	Wellington II	Z8651	Op: Benghazi

Took off, LG 106, detailed to attack shipping and harbour facilities at Benghazi, but flew into the ground 60km SE of Sollum because of altimeter malfunction. F/Sgt Kopp is commemorated on Alamein Memorial.

9-10 May 1942	37 Sqn	Wellington IC	Z8987 B	Op: Benghazi
	P/O H E A Scard	+	Took off c.2000, LG 09, detailed to attack harbour facilities	
	P/O E S Taylor	+	and shipping. FTR. All are commemorated on the	
	F/O L H Smith RCAF	+	Alamein Memorial.	
	Sgt D A Douthwaite	+		
	Sgt S S F Scott	+		
	Sgt A S Woodbridge	+		

10 May 1942	70 Sqn	Wellington IC	T2543	Unknown
			SOC. NFD.	
	1 OADU	Wellington IC	HF829	Delivery Flight
	Sgt S A Elcock		Took off Portreath for Gibraltar, but turned back with low	
	Sgt A L Robinson RNZAF		boost, lost height rapidly and hit a hedge on approach.	
	Sgt Hill		DBR. No serious injuries were suffered.	
	Sgt Fyle			
	Sgt Pratt			
	Sgt Peacock			

13 May 1942	104 Sqn	Wellington II	Z8572 N	Op: Benghazi
			Took off LG 106. Missing. (A-B Serials; not mentioned 104 Sqn ORB: Z8572 listed as on ops to 30 May, but not after.)	

13-14 May 1942	104 Sqn	Wellington II	Z8574 L	Op: Benghazi
	P/O A F O'Donnell	+	Took off LG 106, detailed to attack the harbour and	
	Sgt S H Mortimore RNZAF	+	shipping. FTR. The crew is commemorated on the	
	Sgt R A Coward	+	Alamein Memorial. (A-B Serials dates this loss 17 May.)	
	Sgt A Scott	+		
	Sgt R J C Hazelton	+		
	Sgt S Lang	+		

16 May 1942	37 Sqn	Wellington IC	Z9022	Ground
			Caught fire on the ground, LG 09, when an oxygen hose burst while the instrument section was charging the oxygen system.	

16-17 May 1942	104 Sqn	Wellington II	Z8498 M	Op: Benghazi
	Sgt R A Baker		Took off, LG 106, detailed to attack the harbour and	
	Crew		shipping. The starboard engine cut on return; the aircraft lost height and crash-landed in the western desert. DBR.	

17 May 1942	1 OADU	Blenheim IV	BA376 V	Air Test
	Sgt E J Singleton	inj	Took off Gibraltar, but stalled from 10m, a tyre burst, and	
	Crew		the undercarriage collapsed on landing. DBR.	
	1 OADU	Wellington IC	BB498	Delivery Flight
	Sgt G G Organ RNZAF		On take-off from Luqa for Egypt swung and collided	
	Crew		with a dispersal point. The aircraft, awaiting repair, was destroyed in an air raid on 24 June.	

18-19 Mar 1942	162 Sqn	Wellington IC	Z8944	Op: Derna
	Sgt H W Percival		Took off LG 09, 2000. Crashed on landing on return, 0230.	
	F/Sgt Boucher		DBR.	
	Sgt Lee			
	Sgt Owens			
	Sgt Middlemiss			
	Sgt Seidel			
	Sgt Barnes			
	Sgt Bealey			

19-20 May 1942	**37 Sqn** P/O A D J Salt RCAF P/O R D Flitton RCAF P/O W A Hayworth RCAF F/Sgt A H Winters RCAF F/Sgt R W Hood RCAF Sgt E A Samuel	**Wellington IC** + + + + + +	**AD626** Took off 2310, LG 09, to attack the aerodrome at Heraklion. FTR. All are commemorated on the Alamein Memorial.	**Op: Heraklion**

20 May 1942	**211 Sqn**	**Blenheim I**	**L8454** SOC. NFD. But presumably an inventory entry.	**Unknown**
	1 OADU P/O H G Bancroft Sgt A A Robinson Sgt S H Irving F/Sgt F S MacNeil Sgt R C Hanley Sgt E S Bell	**Wellington II** pow pow pow pow + pow	**Z8589** Took off Gibraltar for Malta, but became lost and was attacked and damaged by a Ju 88, ditching out of fuel off Filiscudi Is, just N of Sicily. In the ditching the front gunner was lost and Sgt Robinson badly injured. The crew drifted for 6 days and nights in their dinghy, then Bancroft and Bell swam for shore, Bancroft reaching Filiscudi Is. The others were then rescued.	**Delivery Flight**

21 May 1942	**104 Sqn** P/O G G Retallack RAAF Crew	**Wellington II**	**Z8512** Lost height after engine failure during an navigational exercise and crash-landed, Machefa.	**Training**
	148 Sqn	**Wellington II**	**Z8494** DBF presumably at Kabrit; NFD.	**Ground**
	1 OADU Sgt R N Leverett P/O A E Wigner Sgt W J Dale	**Blenheim IV** inj Inj inj	**BA365** Took off normally from Gibraltar, but could not maintain height and ditched. Cause put down to the inexperience of the pilot in a heavily laden aircraft.	**Delivery Flight**

22 May 1942	**148 Sqn**	**Wellington II**	**Z8350 C** Caught fire, Kabrit, and destroyed.	**Ground**

22-23 May 1942	**38 Sqn** F/Sgt D R Ward F/Sgt G W Rossen W/O G A Armstrong RCAF Sgt J G Smith Sgt S R Mason Sgt G F Ostram RCAF	**Wellington IC** evd evd evd evd + evd	**BB484 X** Took off 2024, LG 117, detailed to lay mines outside Benghazi Harbour. The crew bombed below safety height and the aircraft was so badly damaged that the pilot ordered the crew to bale out, which they did SE of Benghazi. Ward kept control for another three hours before bailing out himself, being picked up near Wadi Natrun on 29 May in a weak condition. Sgt Mason died in the desert, and is commemorated on the Alamein Memorial, but with Senussi help the others reached Siwa Oasis.	**Op: Benghazi**

23 May 1942	**223 Sqn** P/O D G W Leake RAAF P/O D C Cummins RAAF Sgt R Roberts Sgt B G May	**Baltimore I** inj inj	**AG703** Took off 1032, LG 167 (Bir el Baheira No 2), detailed to attack Derna Main Landing Ground. At 1200 hrs the formation was attacked, near Ras el Tin, by three Bf 109F fighters. Badly damaged, the Baltimore was crash-landed at 1225 at LG 170 (Bir el Gubi). Two Baltimores were claimed by Oblt Hans-Joachim Marseille and one by Ofw Karl Mentnich of 3/JG 27.	**Op: Derna**
	223 Sqn F/O L W Bangley F/Sgt R E R Cotton P/O L J R Back P/O D L Muir	**Baltimore I** + + + +	**AG708** Took off 1032, LG 167 (Bir el Baheira No 2), detailed as above, and shot down by the Bf 109F fighters. P/O Back is buried in Tobruk War Cemetery, where the others are remembered on Special Memorial C.	**Op: Derna**

	223 Sqn	**Baltimore I**	AG717	**Op: Derna**
	Sgt H C Horsfield	+	Took off 1032, LG 167 (Bir el Baheira No 2), detailed as	
	F/Sgt W J Taylor RAAF	+	above and lost to Bf 109F fighters. All of the crew are	
	F/Sgt K E Stewart RAAF	+	buried in Tobruk War Cemetery.	
	Sgt C A Downing	+		

	223 Sqn	**Baltimore II**	AG762	**Op: Derna**
	W/O A G Maclure RAAF		Took off 1032, LG 167 (Bir el Baheira No 2), detailed as	
	F/Sgt L S Middleton RAAF		above, and attacked by Bf 109F fighters. The aircraft made	
	F/Sgt R Richards RAAF		it back to base but was so badly damaged that it was SOC	
	Sgt G E Murray		on 25 May.	

23-24 May 1942	**104 Sqn**	**Wellington II**	W5554 Q	**Relocation Flight**
	P/O J C Morton	inj	Took off LG 106 for Malta, but undershot landing at Luqa	
	Sgt A R Merritt	+	and hit a wall. The front end of the aircraft plunged into a	
	Sgt J R Wilshire	inj	crater and the nose turret broke off. Sgt Merritt is buried	
	Sgt J Williams	inj	in Malta (Capuccini) Naval Cemetery.	
	Sgt Martin			
	Sgt Tood			
	Sgt Hills			
	Sgt McCall			
	LAC R Martin			
	LAC Whitehorne			
	AC1 Rogerson			

24 May 1942	**1 OADU**	**Blenheim V**	BA371	**Delivery Flight**
	Sgt P A Taverner	inj	Took off from for Malta, but failed to climb, and excessive	
	Sgt B J C Halley	inj	vibration forced the pilot to ditch, having reached only	
	Sgt J J Caner RAAF	inj	16m. The cause was found to be overloading.	

26 May 1942	**1 OADU**	**Wellington IC**	HX368	**Delivery Flight**
	P/O G L Donne RNZAF		Burst a tyre on take-off, Luqa, for Egypt, swung, and	
	Crew		undercarriage collapsed. DBR.	

Chapter 7

The Summer Crisis
May to September 1942

Rommel's second great offensive of 1942 opened on 26th May, with a feint attack in the Gazala area masking his main thrust, including all his armour, round the southernmost of the defensive boxes comprising the Gazala line, that held by the Free French, under General Koenig, at Bir Hakeim. This he failed to take, but driving northward, reached the Trig Capuzzo, along a line from Knightsbridge to El Adem. The next day his units swept forward again, overwhelming several units, and capturing the headquarters of the 7th Armoured Division. Around Knightsbridge, at the western end of the Trig Capuzzo, a major armoured battle developed, and the Axis advance halted, holding the salient established on the opening two days, but only resuming the advance on 31st May, after the Italian Ariete Division had cleared a gap in the British minefields, enabling the German panzer units to be resupplied. The renewed advance was as successful as the first, with attempts to counter-attack from the north twice failing, and after the French had finally been forced to evacuate Bir Hakeim, on the night of 10/11th June, Rommel was able to move to encircle the Eighth Army. A fierce tank battle on 13th and 14th June resulted in yet another defeat for the British, and retreat was in consequence ordered.

The original intention was to hold Tobruk, both as a forward defensive outpost and as a source of supplies when an Eighth Army advance could be resumed. This time, however, there was to be no lengthy and unsuccessful German siege. Two days after the isolation of Tobruk was completed, Rommel attacked, and by evening that day, 20th June, Tobruk had fallen. 30,000 men were taken prisoner, and though petrol and water installations had been destroyed, a large amount of stores, and of transport, fell into German hands.

It had been thought that the attempt to take Tobruk would delay Rommel for some time, but its loss in a single day meant that Eighth Army attempts to fashion a defence line along the Egyptian frontier had to be abandoned. It was General Ritchie's intention to fashion a defensive line at Mersa Matruh, but General Auchinleck, who had come to Ritchie's Headquarters to assess for himself the chances of such a move succeeding, first relieved Ritchie of his command, and then (convinced that any attempt to hold a line at Matruh would result in the Eighth Army being surrounded) ordered a further retreat to a much more defensible position at El Alamein. Here, where the impassable Qattara Depression extended to within 40 miles of the coast, Rommel's advance was at last halted. Urging his exhausted units forward, Rommel made a final attempt to break the British defensive line, beginning on 1st July, but failed, his panzer units meeting for the first time a defence organised along German lines, with close co-ordination of tank, anti-tank and artillery units. Attempts by General Auchinleck to drive Rommel back were also unsuccessful, though significant local gains were made during July, with several Italian divisions virtually annihilated. A stalemate followed as both armies consolidated their positions, Rommel with a view to a further offensive, which was intended to destroy the Eighth Army, and Auchinleck with a view to a renewed counter-offensive.

The series of defeats, followed by headlong retreat, which had ensued since the end of May led to rising alarm in Cairo, culminating in the panic of 1st July, or 'Ash Wednesday' as it was sardonically called, on account of the ash from Headquarters files being burnt to prevent them falling into enemy hands. By the next day, however, the level of anxiety was dropping, and with Auchinleck's success in halting and then defeating (though not driving back) Rommel, confidence returned. There was no longer at the highest level the same confidence in the command structure in the Middle East, however, and on 15th August there were major changes, with General Auchinleck giving place to General Sir Harold Alexander, and command of the Eighth Army passing to General Montgomery.

Under the latter, the second half of August was spent restoring confidence, strengthening the positions at El Alamein, and building a powerful strategic reserve strong in armour. When on 31st August, Rommel at last launched what he intended should be his final offensive, he met with failure. The plan had an air of familiarity, two feint assaults near the coast, with the main thrust to the south with the intention of turning the left flank of the Eighth Army. Montgomery's defensive dispositions, however, meant the bulk of his armour was waiting on the Alam el Halfa Ridge, where Rommel's assault was halted, Allied air supremacy enabling heavy air attacks to support the tanks and guns. By 3rd September it was clear to Rommel that the attack had failed, and a withdrawal began, ending on 7th September with the Axis forces back more to less to where they had started, having clearly suffered a defeat. It was to be followed, two months later, by a far greater one, which determined the course of the war in North Africa.

During this period of crisis, the role of the bomber force was two-fold. During the series of battles which marked these summer months, the night bombers undertook sorties (often two a night) over the 'battle area', in search of targets of opportunity, illuminated by Fleet Air Arm Albacores, but during the lulls in fighting the Wellington squadrons, reduced to six with the conversion of 38 Squadron to a torpedo-bomber unit, attacked ports and airfields: the 'milk run', in 1941 to Benghazi, now being to Tobruk. They were joined during the summer crisis by the Wellington flight of 162 Squadron, which devoted most of its activity during this period to regular bombing missions. A long-range force also came into being, with Halifaxes of 10 and 76 Squadrons, detached from Bomber Command and in early September formed into 462 Squadron, supporting the Liberators of 159 and 160 Squadrons, destined for the Far East, but in the crisis weeks of July retained for operations in North Africa, not continuing their journey east until September. These longer-range bombers, supported by the B-24s and a handful of B-17s of the USAAF's Halversen Detachment, operating under RAF control, undertook a series of daylight formation raids on airfields and ports on Crete, as well as on Benghazi.

The USAAF also placed its few available day bomber units, equipped with the B-25 Mitchell, under RAF command, these operating alongside RAF and SAAF squadrons, the latter having relinquished their worn-out Marylands, and operating the Maryland's younger sibling, the Baltimore, alongside their Bostons and, in two squadrons, the Blenheim V.

On Malta the attack on Rommel's lines of supply continued to be sustained by Beauforts and Beaufighters, but for a brief period, from 23rd May to 11th June, 10 aircraft of 104 Squadron were detached to Luqa to attack airfields and ports in Sicily, Sardinia and mainland Italy, the aim being to assist the passage to Malta of a convoy from Gibraltar and Alexandria. At great cost in warships and aircraft, two of the convoy's merchant ships were got through to Malta. 104 Squadron's stint had cost it three of the ten aircraft detached.

27-28 May 1942	37 Sqn P/O J Burrough Sgt B Martin P/O I Duxbury F/Sgt M Davis Sgt J Bell Sgt W Collins	Wellington IC	Z9033		Op: Tmimi Detailed to attack the Landing Ground at Tmimi, but a tyre burst during take-off, LG 09, the aircraft swung and the undercarriage collapsed. The starboard engine then burst into flames.
28 May 1942	12 Sqn SAAF	Boston III	AL773		Unknown Damaged. NFD.
28-29 May 1942	104 Sqn Sgt R J Hills Sgt E Martin F/Sgt G R C Davis RCAF Sgt A McColl Sgt E K Roberts F/Sgt K J Ross	Wellington II	Z8366		T	inj + + + inj	Op: Catania Took off Luqa, detailed to attack the aerodrome at Catania. One engine failed over enemy territory, and the crew jettisoned all armament and bombs to maintain height. On approach the aircraft crashed at Il Hotob, near Attard, and burst into flames. The second pilot died of his injuries eight days later. The dead are buried at Malta (Capuccini) Naval Cemetery.
29 May 1942	15 Sqn SAAF Lt C J Harrison SAAF Crew	Blenheim IV	T2252		B	Unknown Took off Kufra, but crash-landed 4km from the landing ground when an engine cut. Note: this was one of the aircraft involved in the Kufra tragedy (see 4 May above).
	24 Sqn SAAF Lt L H Murrow SAAF Lt E F Wakeling SAAF Sgt J M Lefroy SAAF Air Sgt E D King SAAF	Boston III	Z2176		+ + + +	Op: Derna Took off 2100, LG 140 (Bir el Baheira No 1) detailed as above, but FTR. Possibly brought down by heavy flak over the target. All the crew are commemorated on the Alamein Memorial.
	24 Sqn SAAF Lt L H Butler SAAF Lt C J Visage SAAF Air Sgt B Katz SAAF Air Sgt O Berkowitz SAAF	Boston III	AL673		W	inj inj	Op: Derna Took off 2100, LG 140 (Bir el Baheira No 1), one of eight Bostons detailed to attack shipping in Derna harbour. The port engine was disabled by flak, but the pilot nonetheless managed to fly the aircraft back to within 5km of base before crash-landing when the other engine cut.

29-30 May 1942	**148 Sqn** F/Lt J A Watts Crew	**Wellington IC** evd	**Z8974**	**Op: Tmimi**

Took off 0005, ALG 106, to attack the landing ground at Tmimi. On return one engine vibrated badly, then failed. The aircraft lost height and belly-landed behind enemy lines 5km. N of Bir Hacheim. After walking for 2 days the crew was found by a Free French Patrol which was cut off from the main force. The patrol broke through lines the next night, and the crew returned to base.

	148 Sqn F/O J G Brown Sgt M A Bennetto RCAF P/O J A Mahood Sgt R C Drake Sgt C J Griffiths Sgt C S Parker	**Wellington IC**	**DV654**	**Op: Tmimi**

Took off 00028, ALG 106, to attack the landing ground at Tmimi. Belly-landed after engine fire 28km SSW of Sidi Barrani, and destroyed by the crew. They then walked to the frontier wire at El Beida, and signalled a Bombay, which later returned and circled, dropping a message and water bottles, the crew being later rescued by lorry.

30 May 1942	**1 OADU** F/Lt G H Lonnberg Sgt F A Rawlings Sgt A J P Palmer Sgt W J McCullough Sgt R Blythe Sgt E H Engledow	**Wellington IC** pow pow pow pow pow pow	**HX369**	**Delivery Flight**

Took off Gibraltar for Malta, but hit by flak over Pantelleria. Sought, but did not receive, QDMs from Malta, and eventually force-landed at Licata. The crew was captured after several days.

	1 OADU Sgt J G Daniels P/O J P Anstey Sgt I Wallace-Cox Sgt J W Gould Sgt H Jackson Sgt M H Thompson	**Wellington IC** + inj +	**HX390**	**Delivery Flight**

Took off Portreath for Gibraltar but ditched 1.5km off Lisbon. Sgts Daniels and Thompson are buried in St James British Churchyard, Oporto.

30-31 May 1942	**104 Sqn** Sgt K F Ward Crew	**Wellington II**	**Z8357 O**	**Op: Messina**

Took off Luqa to bomb Messina harbour. Engine failure on approach to Luqa, and distress signals on landing lights were not seen. The pilot attempted to go round again, but lost height and landed across the flarepath, colliding with two parked delivery Wellingtons; DBR.

	104 Sqn Sgt Curtis Sgt Dowse Sgt Patterson Sgt Fugar Sgt Marshall Sgt Moore	**Wellington II**	**Z8513**	**Op: Messina**

Took off Luqa detailed as above. The aircraft had engine trouble and ditched 5km off Malta on return, the crew being rescued by HSL128 from Kalafrana. An account of this rescue is given in Frederick Galea's *Call-Out*, p159.

	1 OADU Sgt J V Evans RNZAF Crew	**Wellington IC**	**HF845**	**Delivery Flight**

Swung on take-off, Luqa, for Egypt, and the undercarriage collapsed. DBR.

31 May - **1 Jun** 1942	**148 Sqn** F/O W Astell Sgt F Mackintosh P/O A W Dodds Sgt B J Filby F/Sgt F Hooper Sgt I E Robinson	**Wellington II** evd evd pow pow pow pow	**AD653 R**	**Op: Derna**

Took off 2100-2125, ALG 106, to bomb the LG at Biret el Cheiba. Attacked and crippled by a night fighter near the target, the Wellington caught fire, and was crash-landed by F/O Astell and P/O Dodds after the others had bailed out. The two made their way to the front line, which Astell successfully crossed on the night of 5 June, meeting a South African unit, but Dodds was taken prisoner. Sgt Mackintosh had also evaded, travelling separately.

1 Jun 1942	223 Sqn	Maryland II	AH337	Unknown

SOC. NFD.

	1 OADU	Wellington IC	HF843	Delivery Flight

Collided with another aircraft on the ground, Luqa. NFD.

1-2 Jun 1942	70 Sqn	Wellington IC	DV521 R	Op: Derna

Sgt E N Wheal
Sgt Mann
F/Sgt Close
Sgt Prudhoe
Sgt Learwood
Sgt Regan

Took off 2050, LG 104, to attack the landing ground at Derna. On return the aircraft crash-landed cross wind when both engines cut owing to petrol shortage. DBR.

3-4 Jun 1942	104 Sqn	Wellington II	Z8345 S	Op: Tmimi

P/O R S White
Crew

Took off 2245, ALG 106, detailed to attack the landing grounds at Tmimi. On return the starboard engine failed; unable to land at LG 05 because of an air raid, the crew diverted to LG 121 and the port engine cut in circuit; the undercarriage, not locked down, collapsed on landing.

4 Jun 1942	12 Sqn SAAF	Boston III	AL720 Q	Op: Derna

Lt C T Dawson SAAF +
Lt C F Drake SAAF +
Air Sgt W Sagar SAAF +
Air Sgt J Zylstra SAAF inj

Took off 0310, LG 140 (Bir el Baheira No 1), to attack the Derna Airfields, but swung, hit the tail of AL783 180m to the right of the flare-path, burst into flames and two of the bombs on board exploded. The dead are buried in Halfaya Sollum War Cemetery.

6 Jun 1942	70 Sqn	Wellington IC	Z9096 M	Op: Martuba

Sgt F B Leach pow
P/O D H McAllan RCAF pow
Sgt J C Taylor pow
Sgt E R Bristowe pow
Sgt A V W Rymer RAAF pow
Sgt R Marlow pow

Took off c.0025, LG 104, detailed to attack the landing ground at Martuba. After flak damage force-landed in the desert 160km SW of Tobruk on return.

7 Jun 1942	148 Sqn	Wellington IC	BB508 Z	Ground

The aircraft caught fire whilst being started up at LG 106, and the bomb load exploded. No casualties.

7-8 Jun 1942	148 Sqn	Wellington IC	DV618 A	Op: Benghazi

F/Lt V G Gane
Crew

Took off 2010, ALG 106, detailed to attack the harbour and shipping. An engine cut due to a high oil temperature and the aircraft was unable to maintain height – eventually force-landing. The crew took rations from the dinghy and headed E, walking for two days before attracting the attention of a Baltimore. They were picked up in a weak condition by two other 148 Sqn aircraft.

8 Jun 1942	14 Sqn	Blenheim IV	Z7419	Night Flying Test

Sgt J R Burt

Took off LG 116 on a night-flying test, but hit a sandhill low flying and crashed 3km NE of Maaten Bagush.

	223 Sqn	Baltimore II	AG777	Op: Barce

Sgt F J A Saunders RAAF +
Sgt T A Auld RAAF +
F/Sgt R C A Ash RAAF +
Sgt S M Moore +

Took off 1152, LG 140 (Bir el Baheira No 1), to bomb Barce LG. The aircraft exploded over the target, cause unknown. All are buried in Benghazi War Cemetery.

223 Sqn	**Baltimore II**	AG825	**Op: Barce**
F/Lt N A Gidney		Took off 1152, LG 140 (Bir el Baheira No 1), to bomb Barce	
F/Lt F G Buckle	inj	LG. DBR when AG777 exploded over the target.	
F/Sgt R S C Goddard			
Sgt I T Lucas			

8-9 Jun 1942	**14 Sqn**	**Blenheim IV**	Z9656 J	**Op: Heraklion**
	F/O D W R Brooks	inj	Took off 2200, LG 116, on a night intruder operation. On	
	F/O C R Cowan RAAF	+	returning the pilot was unable to identify the flare path	
	P/O W E Hickman RAAF	inj	because of heavy mist, and crashed at 0330, half a	
			kilometre S of the airfield. The observer is buried in the El	
			Alamein War Cemetery.	

9-10 Jun 1942	**148 Sqn**	**Wellington IC**	DV566	**Unknown**
	P/O Loos		Took off LG 106 and on return crashed at LG 14 Maaten	
	Crew		Bagush. NFD.	

10 Jun 1942	**148 Sqn**	**Wellington IC**	BB508 Z	**Ground**
			DBF at LG 106. NFD.	

10-11 Jun 1942	**108 Sqn**	**Wellington IC**	BB482 K	**Op: Kastelli Pediada**
	F/Sgt R H McRae RCAF	+	Took off 2005, LG 105. Attracted much flak from Maleme	
	F/Sgt J W Brown RCAF	+	and hit. Signals received up to 50 mins later reported	
	Sgt H G Baden	+	engine failure. Believed ditched in sea off the coast of Crete.	
	Sgt J R Irwin	+	Lt Strang, flying as front gunner, was attached from 85	
	Lt R B Strang RA	+	Battery Royal Artillery as an anti-aircraft interpreter.	
	Sgt J Oliphant	+	All are commemorated on the Alamein Memorial.	

12 Jun 1942	**14 Sqn**	**Blenheim IV**	V5582	**Training**
	Sgt T C Bullock		Took off LG 116 on a night landing training flight, but	
			stalled at 7m on landing and the undercarriage collapsed.	
			DBR. Loss put down to inexperience of the pilot making	
			a night landing without the aid of the Chance light.	

12-13 Jun 1942	**104 Sqn**	**Wellington II**	Z8592 Z	**Op: Benghazi**
	P/O F H Shackleton	+	Took off c.2150, ALG 106, part of a force detailed to bomb	
	Sgt A W Corby RNZAF	+	Benghazi while mines were laid offshore. The aircraft	
	F/Sgt W R Cook	+	was coned, hit by flak and and crashed into the sea 2km	
	F/Sgt R E Fuller RCAF	+	SW of Benghazi harbour. All are commemorated on the	
	Sgt D G Symons	+	Alamein Memorial.	
	Sgt R Slimings	+		

13 Jun 1942	**14 Sqn**	**Blenheim IV**	Z6044 X	**Training**
	Sgt C M Leaver	+	Took off LG 116 on a night-flying practice for less	
	F/Sgt H M J Powell	+	experienced crews, but the presence of enemy aircraft	
	Sgt R J Hehir RAAF	+	necessitated two of the aircraft flying to a pre-arranged	
			position over the Mersah Matruh beacon until the all	
			clear was given. Despite efforts by all local radio stations	
			to recall these aircraft when the warning period had	
			ended, it was impossible to contact them. All the crew are	
			commemorated on the Alamein Memorial.	

	14 Sqn	**Blenheim IV**	Z7517	**Training**
	Sgt G F Highman RAAF	+	Took off LG 116 detailed as above, and likewise lost.	
	Sgt W D Lynch RAAF	+	Wreckage of the aircraft, and the dead crew, were	
	Sgt W L Carnie	+	discovered on 15 June 10km S of LG 10. It was thought	
			that the aircraft crashed when the pilot was distracted by	
			searchlights and flares. All the crew are commemorated	
			on the Alamein Memorial.	

14 Jun 1942	**38 Sqn** Sgt P Le Brocq Sgt G Fothergill F/Lt Hancock Sgt R Smith Sgt C Geens	**Wellington IC**	**DV418 W**	**Op: Mine-laying**

Took off 0200, Luqa, detailed to lay mines off Benghazi, but failed to become airborne and was deliberately swung off the runway. DBF.

	1 OADU P/O D St C Brown RNZAF F/Sgt J Smith P/O G W Ely Sgt J B Hopkinson RAAF Sgt J J Curr RAAF P/O Beaton	**Wellington IC** inj inj inj inj inj	**DV547**	**Delivery Flight**

On take-off from Sharjah, en route to India, the aircraft failed to become airborne. It and its crew were 99 Sqn, en route to the Far East.

14-15 Jun 1942	**108 Sqn** Sgt G Watkins Sgt J A Varnham Sgt F A R May Sgt N D McAlary RAAF Sgt T Gilmour Sgt G W Benge	**Wellington IC** pow pow pow pow pow pow	**AD624 T**	**Op: Benghazi**

Took off 2020-2045, LG 105, detailed to attack Benghazi. The crew sent messages indicating the aircraft was force-landing, which it did 64km SE of Bir Hacheim.

15 Jun 1942	**14 Sqn** Sgt J H Elliott RAAF Sgt C R Davies RAAF Sgt C H Simmonds RAAF Passengers: P/O H C Ridley Sgt A F Payne	**Blenheim IV**	**Z6425**	**Search and Rescue**

A tyre burst on take-off LG 116 to search for Z9795 (see below). The aircraft and crew were located and rescued, but Z6425 burst a tyre on take-off on rough ground, and when the aircraft landed at LG 116 the undercarriage collapsed. DBR.

	14 Sqn S/Ldr A N Pirie P/O H C Ridley Sgt A F Payne	**Blenheim IV**	**Z9795**	**Op: Crete**

Took off 2100, LG 116, to attack targets on Crete. On return became lost and belly-landed in the desert 46km S of El Daba. See previous entry.

	159 Sqn Sgt W J Wilson RAAF Crew	**Liberator II**		**Op: Convoy Escort**

Took off, Fayid, and on return from escorting a convoy from Alexandria to Malta, crash-landed short of Fayid, one gunner, not yet identified, being reported killed. No verification of this loss has been found by AHB, but the aircraft may be AL553, SOC on 31 July.

15-16 Jun 1942	**148 Sqn** Sgt W D F Ross Sgt R G Gravell Sgt Iliffe F/Sgt Douglas Sgt Rolph Sgt Ross	**Wellington IC**	**DV615 J**	**Op: Biret el Cheiba**

Took off LG 106, and on return crashed on landing in foggy conditions. The aircraft caught fire and later blew up.

16 Jun 1942	**223 Sqn** F/Sgt G E Cornes Sgt F B Menzies Sgt M G Waters Sgt J Temple	**Baltimore II**	**AG756**	**Unknown**

Crashed on landing in poor visibility, LG 167 (Baheira Satellite), the pilot misjudging his height.

16-17 Jun 1942	**108 Sqn** Sgt Carson Crew	**Wellington IC**	**W5614 N**	**Op: Tmimi**

Took off 2035, LG 105, to attack LGs at Tmimi. On return, in low cloud, struck high ground at 160mph, continued flying with the port engine on fire, and crash-landed at LG 76. The crew had cuts and bruises.

17 Jun 1942	12 Sqn SAAF	Boston III	W8382 G	**Transit Flight**

Took off LG 140 (Bir el Baheira No 1) to fly to LG 148 (Sidi Azeiz) to escape advancing enemy troops. The aircraft hit wires on approach to Sidi Azeiz and damaged its landing gear. In an effort to save it from falling into enemy hands or destruction by Allied troops it was towed down the Trigh Capuzzo by tractor, but finally had to be abandoned. Believed later DBF.

18 Jun 1942	12 Sqn SAAF	Boston III	AL669 M	**Ground**

Several unserviceable Bostons had to be left behind by 12 and 24 Sqns SAAF at LG 140 (Bir el Baheira No 1), when the airfield was hastily evacuated with enemy troops only a short distance away. Col Willmott, CO of 3 (SA) Wing sent Capt Pope, the Armament Officer, back to LG 140, with instructions to disable them to prevent them falling into enemy hands. Designated Cat E on 28 June.

	12 Sqn SAAF	Boston III	W8376 N	**Ground**

As above.

	1 OADU	Blenheim IV	BA445	**Delivery Flight**
	Sgt W J Bratt	+		
	Sgt W B Smith	+		
	Sgt J E Cook	+		

Took off Portreath for Gibraltar, but failed to arrive. All of the crew are commemorated on the Runnymede Memorial.

19 Jun 1942	14 Sqn	Blenheim IV	Z7516	**Op: Crete**
	P/O B S Slade RAAF			
	P/O G W McD Allingame RAAF			
	Sgt G A Lindschau RAAF			

On take-off, LG 116, detailed to make a night intruder raid on Cretan aerodromes, an engine cut, and on landing again the undercarriage collapsed. DBR.

	223 Sqn	Baltimore II	AG772	**Op: Tmimi**
	P/O M L Bowley	+		
	P/O J N Bignold	inj		
	Sgt I A H Laughton RAAF	+		
	Sgt J D Paulich	+		

Took off 2110, LG 116, to bomb Tmimi LG. With oil and fuel problems the pilot was given permission to land at LG 116, despite nil visibility because of ground mist. The pilot attempted a belly-landing but his wingtip struck the ground and the aircraft crashed. A bomb which had hung up then exploded. The three dead are buried in the El Alamein War Cemetery.

19-20 Jun 1942	37 Sqn	Wellington IC	DV669 W	**Op: Benghazi**
	F/O W L Kauter RNZAF	+		
	P/O W G D Thurston RNZAF	+		
	P/O I P Duxbury	+		
	F/Sgt L R Feasey RNZAF	+		
	Sgt F V Bretherton	+		
	Sgt V G F Walklin	+		

Took off LG 09 (Bir Koralyim) c.2000, detailed to attack the harbour and shipping. A stricken aircraft (thought to be DV669) was seen going down steadily near the target. All are buried in Benghazi War Cemetery.

20 Jun 1942	223 Sqn	Baltimore II	AG758	**Op: Tmimi**
	P/O H B Nickolls RAAF			
	F/Sgt J S Thomson	inj		
	Sgt D W McNeil RAAF			
	Sgt Lindsay			

Took off 2120, LG 116, to bomb Tmimi LG. Force-landed 15km SE of Mersa Matruh. DBR.

21 Jun 1942	38 Sqn	Wellington IC	Z9095 D	**Relocation Flight**
	W/Cdr C J V Pratt			
	Crew			

Crashed on take-off for Malta, LG 05. DBR.

	1 OADU	Blenheim V	BA288	**Delivery Flight**
	Sgt G Ashplant	int		
	Sgt W B H Smalley	int		

Took off 0800, Portreath, for Gibraltar, but ran out of fuel because of a cracked tank and forced-land at Ealala

Sgt H W R Bakewell RAAF		int	Aerodrome, Portela, Portugal. After destroying all their secret documents and equipment the crew were arrested by the Military and taken to Lisbon where they were questioned and then turned over to the civil police. They returned to the UK via Gibraltar, arriving back on 12 July.	

1 OADU	**Blenheim V**	**BA377** **Delivery Flight**
Sgt L Martin	int	Took off Gibraltar for Malta and presumably crash- or
Sgt A Cockin	int	force-landed in French North Africa, since the crew were
Sgt A Saunders	int	interned at Algiers.

1 OADU	**Blenheim V**	**BA446** **Delivery Flight**
W/O2 H C Langton RCAF	pow	Took off Luqa for Egypt, but crashed into the sea off
Sgt D H Leather	pow	Derna. All were picked up by an Italian hospital ship, but
Sgt G W Wicks	+	Sgt Wicks, severely injured, died shortly after rescue, and was buried at sea. He is commemorated on the Alamein Memorial.

21-22 Jun 1942	**148 Sqn**	**Wellington IC**	**ES990 S** **Op: Gazala**
	W/Cdr D A Kerr DSO	+	Took off c.2030, ALG 106, detailed to attack the LG at
	F/Lt F W A Westcott	pow	Gazala. Hit by flak, the aircraft exploded. F/Lt Westcott
	F/Sgt D W Cross RNZAF	+	woke on the ground with his open parachute beside him
	F/Sgt G R Ferguson RAAF	+	about 8km E of Benghazi. The dead are commemorated
	F/Sgt G Booth RNZAF	+	on the Alamein Memorial.
	Sgt L M Washer	+	

---

22 Jun 1942	**55 Sqn**	**Baltimore II**	**AG813** **Training**
	Sgt W H R Anniss		Took off LG 99, on a solo training flight. On landing the aircraft bounced, the port wing dropped, the wingtip struck the ground, and the aircraft cartwheeled. DBR.
	70 Sqn	**Wellington IC**	**T2704** **Ground**
			An engine caught fire starting up, LG 104; DBR. SOC 12 August.

---

24 Jun 1942	**1 OADU**	**Blenheim IV**	**V5681** **Delivery Flight**
			Crashed in Iraq on a delivery flight to India. SOC.
	Middle East	**Blenheim IV**	**Z7907** **Unknown**
			SOC in Iraq. NFD.
	Middle East	**Wellington IC**	**BB498** **Unknown**
			Undershot landing at Luqa and hit a wall. NFD.

24-25 Jun 1942	**37 Sqn**	**Wellington IC**	**DV643** **Op: Benghazi**
	F/Lt C P T Halliwell	+	Took off 2050-2120, LG 09. FTR. F/O Jones is buried in
	P/O M C De Clifford RNZAF	+	Benghazi War Cemetery, and the others commemorated
	F/O P C Jones RCAF	+	on the Alamein Memorial.
	F/Sgt R D Stevenson	+	
	F/Sgt G R Harlock RAAF	+	
	Sgt H E Noble	+	
	40 Sqn	**Wellington IC**	**DV652 E** **Op: Benghazi**
	Sgt R E White	inj	Took off Shallufa to attack the harbour and shipping at
	Sgt L W H Chappell	inj	Benghazi. Excessive fuel consumption led to fuel
	P/O E H Laithwaite	inj	exhaustion. Both engines cut and the aircraft crashed
	Sgt Price		19km S of LG 115 and caught fire. Sgt Rees is
	Sgt P D Rees	+	commemorated on the Alamein Memorial.
	Sgt Wheetley		

25 Jun 1942	12 Sqn SAAF	Boston III	AL691 W	Op: Army Co-operation
	Lt E Jones SAAF	+		
	Lt A McR Donnelly SAAF	+		
	Air Sgt J A Hill SAAF	pow		
	F/Sgt J A T Colverd SAAF	+		

Took off 1239, LG 21 (Qotafiyah III), to attack German armour advancing along the railway line to the old desert railhead at Hisheifa. Hit by flak in the starboard engine over the target, the aircraft burst into flames and spun into the ground near Sidi Barrani; only Air Sgt Hill bailed out. The dead are commemorated on the Alamein Memorial.

25-26 Jun 1942	37 Sqn	Wellington IC	DV522	Op: Battle Area
	Sgt I G Medwin RNZAF	inj		
	F/Sgt K Andrews	inj		
	Sgt T A Dixon			
	F/Sgt D W Mogg			
	Sgt J L Abson	+		
	Sgt T A Richardson			

Took off 0001-0045, LG 09. 40km SW of Mersa Matruh they were attacked by a fighter which fired one long burst and started a fire. The crew were ordered to prepare to bail out, but Sgt Abson misheard and jumped. The others stayed with the aircraft, which was belly-landed in the desert, both pilots receiving head injuries. The crew walked to British lines and was picked up after 3 hours by a forward army patrol. Sgt Abson is commemorated on the Alamein Memorial.

	70 Sqn	Wellington IC	DV564 L	Op: Enemy concentrations
	F/Sgt Stewart RNZAF			
	Sgt W J Brown	inj		
	P/O T E W Howes RAAF			
	Sgt K E Calvert	inj		
	Sgt Payne			
	F/Sgt G J Wagner RCAF	+		

Took off 2140, LG 104, to attack enemy forces around Mersa Matruh and Sidi Barrani. After a successful attack on an enemy convoy, the aircraft was attacked by a Ju 88 night fighter, the rear gunner being fatally wounded. Small fires were started, which the observer, P/O Howes, managed to extinguish. The aircraft was badly damaged and made a belly-landing off the flare-path.

	104 Sqn	Wellington II	Z8572 N	Ground
	Sgt P M Sharplin	inj		
	P/O R G Tait RNZAF	inj		
	P/O G Smith-Windsor RCAF	+		
	F/Sgt G H Kirby RAAF	+		
	Sgt J B Yule	inj		
	Sgt J T Jones	inj		

At 2031, just prior to take off from ALG 106 for a second sortie, the aircraft was hit by a bomb. The dead were buried at ALG 106, but their graves were lost, and they are commemorated on the Alamein Memorial.

	148 Sqn	Wellington IC	DV646 A	Op: Enemy concentrations
	F/Lt Hankin			
	Crew			

Took off 2215, ALG 106. A presumed burst oil pipe led to engine failure, the aircraft crashing in a forced landing 1km SE of Fuka railway station.

26 Jun 1942	104 Sqn	Wellington II	Z8508 Y	Ground
	F/O A C Chaldecott			
	P/O B R W Blogg			
	F/O C Stotesbury			
	Sgt J A Anscombe			
	Crew			

Collided with Z8580 on take-off in crosswind, LG 106. DBR.

	104 Sqn	Wellington II	Z8580 Z	Ground
	Sgt Luscombe			
	Crew			

Hit by Z8508 at LG 106 while taxying in a dust cloud; DBR.

	223 Sqn	Baltimore II	AG748	Op: Army Co-operation
	Sgt H Hewitt			
	Sgt E T Cosby			
	Sgt D P Wayn RAAF			
	Sgt D N Edgcumbe			

Took off 1315, LG 116, to attack enemy motor transport at Pin Point 630.330. At 1345 the formation was attacked 10.5km NW of Bir el Gallas by fighters. Badly damaged, the aircraft lost its port propeller and crash-landed 33km W of LG 116. SOC.

223 Sqn	**Baltimore II**	**AG797**	**Op: Army Co-operation**

P/O D G W Leake RAAF
F/Sgt J H Campbell
F/Sgt C N Chenoweth RAAF
Sgt B G May

Took off 1315, LG 116, detailed as above, and also damaged by fighters. It crash-landed on return to LG 116. SOC.

15 Sqn SAAF   **Blenheim V**   **BA373**   **Unknown**

Lt J W Bowman SAAF
Crew

The undercarriage collapsed on landing, LG 116.

1 OADU   **Wellington IC**   **HX447**   **Delivery Flight**

Sgt S Blackburn
Sgt C L Lamb   inj
Sgt McDonnell
Sgt Calder
Sgt Fleckney
Sgt Westcott

Took off Portreath for Gibraltar. Stalled and crashed on landing, Gibraltar; DBF.

26-27 Jun 1942

40 Sqn   **Wellington IC**   **Z9028**   **V**   **Op: Battle Area**

Sgt S H Gunn RNZAF   +
Sgt P T Halstead   +
F/Sgt H F Thompson RCAF   +
F/Sgt O M Kileen RCAF   +
F/Sgt S Gregory RCAF   +
Sgt H J Morgan   +

Took off Shallufa, detailed to search for targets in the El Alamein area. Shot down by a night fighter and crashed near Halfaya railway station. All were buried at the time in a common grave by the wreckage of the aircraft but later re-interred in the Halfaya Sollum War Cemetery.

70 Sqn   **Wellington IC**   **Z9102**   **A**   **Op: Battle Area**

Sgt F V Clayton   +
Sgt G Jackson
Sgt A J Hickox
P/O W J McPherson
F/Sgt M L Berg RNZAF   +
Sgt T L Brown

Took off 2120-2315, LG 224, to search for targets of opportunity around Daba, but attacked by a fighter. An engine was set on fire, and the crew abandoned the aircraft, which dived into the ground. The bombs exploded, scattering wreckage over a wide area. The 4 survivors walked NE, sighted a truck on an escarpment, and were taken to Fuka. Both dead are commemorated on the Alamein Memorial.

108 Sqn   **Wellington IC**   **ES981**   **A**   **Op: Sidi Barrani**

Sgt P K J Street   +
Sgt L A Lister   +
Sgt M E Warburton   +
Sgt O Ackerman
Sgt J E Brooks   inj
F/Sgt G A K Hunter   +

Took off 2100, Kabrit, to attack enemy targets at Sidi Barrani. Attacked by a Ju 88, which started a fire in the aircraft. Sgts Ackerman and Brooks met units of the 7th Armoured Division. The dead are commemorated on the Alamein Memorial.

---

27 Jun 1942

223 Sqn   **Baltimore II**   **AG771**   **Relocation Flight**

F/Lt N A Gidney   +
P/O R A Swann   +
F/Sgt R S C Goddard   +
Sgt I T Lucas   +

Took off LG 116, on relocation to LG 24, one of three Baltimores shot down just after take-off, crashing 6.5km E of LG 116. All are buried in El Alamein War Cemetery.

223 Sqn   **Baltimore II**   **AG774**   **Relocation Flight**

Sgt P W Carruthers
W/O J Sands
Sgt E W Hargreaves
Sgt D G Tupper   inj
Passenger:
LAC J Parker   inj

Took off LG 116, on relocation and shot down by fighters, crashing 32km SE of LG 100 (Wadi Natrun) at 1055 hrs. SOC. 1.1.47 by inventory entry.

223 Sqn   **Baltimore II**   **AG782**   **Relocation Flight**

P/O I H G Davis RAAF   +
Sgt F G Mantle RAAF   +
Sgt R P Griffiths   +
Sgt F A Rhoden   +

Took off LG 116, on relocation and shot down by fighters, crashing 8.5km E of LG 116 at 1030 hrs. P/O Davis and Sgt Mantle are buried in El Alamein War Cemetery, while Sgt Rhoden and Griffiths are commemorated on the Alamein Memorial. SOC 3 August.

	24 Sqn SAAF	Boston III	Z2302 — **Ground**

Abandoned by the SAAF RSU at LG 11 (Qasaba) as Axis forces approached, Z2302 was the subject of an attempted recovery when on 27 June a Boston with a spare pilot and ground crew flew to LG 11. Shells were falling within a few hundred yards as efforts to get the derelict Boston serviceable failed. It was destroyed by the army on 5 July.

28 Jun 1942 — 40 Sqn — Wellington IC — DV652 — **Unknown**

Damaged by flak, not repaired. NFD.

Middle East — Wellington IC — DV621 — **Ground**

DBR in an accident. NFD.

1 OADU — Wellington IC — HX478 — **Delivery Flight**
Sgt L E Snaar RCAF
Crew

Took off Portreath for Gibraltar, and on landing overshot, and ran over the end of the runway onto the beach. DBR.

28-29 Jun 1942 — 104 Sqn — Wellington II — Z8646 B — **Op: Enemy concentrations**
F/Lt D J Haydon RNZAF +
Sgt R F Lander RNZAF +
P/O R Stringfellow +
Sgt G E Scales +
Sgt P H Benson +
Sgt Price

Took off 2320, Kabrit. The starboard engine cut shortly after take-off; the bombs (fused, contrary to instructions) were jettisoned at 200-250m, and their explosion caused the aircraft to dive into the Great Bitter Lake. The dead are buried in Fayid War Cemetery.

108 Sqn — Wellington IC — R1029 S — **Op: Mersa Matruh**
S/Ldr Jacklin DFC
Crew

Took off 2150, Kabrit, to attack enemy positions at Mersa Matruh. Attacked by a Ju 88 and badly damaged, the aircraft crashed in a forced landing at Amriya. The front gunner returned fire, setting the fighter on fire.

29 Jun 1942 — 14 Sqn — Blenheim IV — V5960 — **Unknown**

SOC. NFD.

14 Sqn — Blenheim IV — Z9746 — **Ground**

SOC as destroyed by enemy action, perhaps as a result of a strafing attack on LG 116 by a Bf 110 at 0100 on 27 June.

29-30 Jun 1942 — 70 Sqn — Wellington IC — Z1170 O — **Op: Sidi Barrani**
F/Sgt J H Gunyon RCAF +
F/Sgt H B Stevens RNZAF +
F/Sgt W H Rowles RNZAF +
F/O W M Pugh RAAF +
Sgt L H Harrison RNZAF +
Sgt N C Harrop RNZAF

Detailed to attack LG 121 and motor transport near Sidi Barrani, but crashed on take-off, LG 05, perhaps because the flaps were prematurely raised, and blew up. The dead are buried in Ismailia War Memorial Cemetery.

HALPRO — B-24D — **Op: Tobruk**
Capt F E Nestor USAAF
1/Lt C A Shaw USAAF
1/Lt M L Phillips USAAF +
Sgt C W Hunter USAAF +
S/Sgt A M Umstead USAAF +
Sgt S B Rosanski USAAF
Cpl H W Kramer USAAF +

Took off El Fayid, detailed to attack the harbour and shipping, and brought down by flak over Tobruk. Lt Phillips, Sgts Hunter and Umstead, and Cpl Kramer, are commemorated on the Tablets of the Missing at the North Africa American Cemetery, Carthage, Tunisia. The others were presumably re-interred in the US post-war.

30 Jun 1942 — 14 Sqn — Blenheim IV — Z7485 — **Ground**
Cpl H Gibbons +

Destroyed, when parked at LG 97, by a Curtiss Kittyhawk fighter, AK753, attempting to land in bad visibility. The Kittyhawk pilot, 2/Lt J S Warden (2 Squadron SAAF) was killed, and Cpl Gibbons, a mechanic working on the Blenheim, was mortally injured, dying 30 minutes later.

	162 Sqn	Blenheim IV	V5508 B	Air Test
	Sgt A I Thompson	inj	On take-off, Bilbeis, hit trees and crashed. DBF.	
	Sgt W N B Bower	inj		
	Cpl A Beard	inj		
	AC1 L A Ross	inj		

	15 Sqn SAAF	Blenheim IV	BA367	Relocation Flight
	Lt J F Kinnery SAAF		Took off LG 98 on relocation to El Ballah. A tyre burst on	
	Crew		landing, the Blenheim swung and the undercarriage collapsed. DBR.	

	15 Sqn SAAF	Blenheim IV	BA440	Relocation Flight
			Took off LG 98 on relocation to El Ballah. The hydraulics failed and the aircraft landed on one wheel and without flaps. DBR.	

	Middle East	Wellington IC	BB471	Unknown
			Lost. NFD.	

30 Jun - 1 Jul 1942	37 Sqn	Wellington IC	DV675	Op: Fuka Main
	P/O G W Allan	+	Took off 2005, Abu Sueir, to attack aircraft on LG 17 (Fuka	
	Sgt K Hargreaves		Main). On return an engine caught fire and the propeller	
	P/O T Matthews		fell off, the aircraft lost height, and the crew bailed out.	
	P/O W Noyes	inj	Three landed safely in the Delta area, but P/O Noyes	
	Sgt J Gilmore		received severe injuries in a heavy landing, while the	
	Sgt H L Watkins	+	pilot and rear gunner drowned in the River Nile. Both are buried in Ismailia War Memorial Cemetery.	

1-2 Jul 1942	104 Sqn	Wellington II	Z8655 B	Op: Enemy concentrations
	F/O G G Retallack RCAF	+	Took off 0030-0110, Kabrit, to attack transport in the	
	Sgt M A Brett	+	Western Desert, and FTR. A very large explosion,	
	Sgt E W Bond	+	followed by falling burning debris, was seen in the sky,	
	Sgt J S Kennedy	+	and it is thought Z8655 collided with X9986 (see below).	
	Sgt N Todd	+	All are buried in El Alamein War Cemetery.	

	162 Sqn	Wellington IC	X9986	Op: Battle Area
	F/O A P Ouellette RCAF	+	Took off c.2300, Shallufa. Crashed after collision at night	
	Sgt R L Hill	+	near El Daba, presumably with Z8655. All are	
	F/Sgt A W Doughty	+	commemorated on the Alamein Memorial.	
	Sgt J W Neu	+		
	P/O J H Moss RAAF	+		
	F/Sgt T G Wood	+		

2 Jul 1942	159 Sqn	Liberator II	AL552	Training
	P/O N B Pattie RAAF		Took off, Fayid on night-landing training, but crashed on	
	F/Sgt H E Birk RAAF		landing. The pilot was inexperienced on the type, and the aircraft 2,000lb over maximum landing weight. DBR.	

	24 Sqn SAAF	Boston III	Z2298 D	Op: Army Co-operation
	Lt J J B Steyn SAAF		Took off LG 99 on the third raid of the day to bomb	
	Lt P W Bosman SAAF		enemy armour and motor transport west of El Alamein,	
	Air Sgt C C van der Spuy SAAF		but on return flew into the ground in a dust storm near	
	Air Sgt A McN Harvey SAAF		LG 99 at 1600 hrs.	

2-3 Jul 1942	37 Sqn	Wellington IC	Z1179	Op: Enemy concentrations
	P/O F A Scott	+	Took off 0001-0010, Abu Sueir, to attack enemy forces in	
	P/O G L Donne RNZAF	+	the El Daba area. Shot down by a night fighter c.24km	
	Sgt W W Hughes	+	W of El Daba. All are commemorated on the Alamein	
	Sgt E J Simmons	+	Memorial.	
	W/O E Berry	pow		
	Sgt K C Swaby	+		

	37 Sqn	Wellington IC	Z8990	**Op: Naqb Abu Dweis - Alamein**

37 Sqn — Wellington IC — Z8990 — **Op: Naqb Abu Dweis - Alamein**

F/O S J Thorne +
F/Sgt B H Martin RCAF +
Sgt P Murphy
Sgt A Bethell
Sgt F Easterling
Sgt L Hare

Took off 0025, Abu Sueir to attack enemy motor transport. The aircraft was badly shaken by the explosion of its target, the starboard propeller fell off and an engine caught fire. Near LG 100 the crew were ordered to bail out. F/O Thorne left the controls to open the bulkhead door for the front gunner and fell through the escape hatch on his return. He and F/Sgt Martin both died when their parachutes either failed or were not clipped on correctly.

104 Sqn — Wellington II — Z8647 W — **Op: Enemy concentrations**

F/Lt D Ellis pow
Sgt G Wilson RNZAF pow
Sgt K I Austin pow
W/O R O L Humphrey pow
P/O R G Bennett pow
Sgt J G Laurence pow

Took off 0030-0100, Abu Sueir, to attack enemy motor transport. An engine was lost to flak and eventually the aircraft crash-landed in the desert. The crew, uninjured, walked E for three days, being captured just short of the Allied front line.

3 Jul 1942

70 Sqn — Wellington IC — N2739 — **Unknown**

Sgt E A C Barfoot
Crew

Took off, Abu Sueir, but lack of power in one or both engines meant that when the flaps were raised the aircraft sank back and crashed. DBF.

159 Sqn — Liberator II — AL542 — **Unknown**

F/Sgt F P Russell
P/O E P Mahoney RCAF
Crew

The nosewheel collapsed in a heavy landing, Heliopolis; apparently not repaired.

3-4 Jul 1942

40 Sqn — Wellington IC — HF914 G — **Op: Mersa Matruh**

Sgt W E Dwyer +
Sgt S R Burford +
Sgt W F Lefevre +
Sgt A L Potts +
Sgt W T Balchin +
Sgt J A P Goss +

Took off Shallufa, detailed to bomb a tank repair shop at Mersa Matruh. Hit by flak on the bombing run, the aircraft went down in flames. All are commemorated on the Alamein Memorial.

4 Jul 1942

14 Sqn — Blenheim IV — T2389 E — **Unknown**

Sgt T G N Russell RAAF
Sgt F V Dyson RAAF
Sgt W J Nicholas RAAF

Took off LG 21. An engine failed and the aircraft crash-landed in the Western Desert 133km W of Wadi Natrun. The crew walked back, rejoining their unit three days later.

5 Jul 1942

70 Sqn — Wellington IC — Z1175 L — **Op: Battle Area**

Sgt J R Milligan RCAF
Sgt P F Smith
P/O R F Watson RNZAF
Sgt R J Smart RNZAF
Sgt F O H Harrison RNZAF
Sgt C A Clack inj

Took off 0200, Abu Sueir, to seek out targets of opportunity in the Alamein area. The starboard engine cut during the raid, the aircraft lost height and crash-landed near Qassassin, 48km W of base. All the crew were slightly injured, Sgt Clack being admitted to hospital.

70 Sqn — Wellington IC — Z8972 B — **Op: Battle Area**

Sgt E A C Barfoot
Sgt K E McKay
Sgt M T Fitton inj
Sgt J C Mitchell
P/O P Manning
P/O P F Smith

Took off 0200, Abu Sueir, to seek out targets of opportunity in the Alamein area. Forced to jettison remaining bomb load when attacked by a Ju 88 night fighter over the battle area, the pilot overshot on landing and hit an obstruction.

108 Sqn — Wellington IC — DV662 L — **Op: Daba**

F/Sgt Metcalf
Sgt Treherne
Sgt Cohen
Sgt G A Arnold RAAF +

Took off 0035, Kabrit, to seek out enemy concentrations around Daba. Attacked and badly damaged by a Ju 88, the aircraft was put into a violent dive. As the pilot pulled out at about 50m, a yellow flash was seen behind,

	Sgt Anderson		possibly the Ju 88 crashing. The aircraft swung on landing because of a punctured tyre and the undercarriage sheared off. Sgt Arnold, fatally wounded in the attack, died soon after being taken from the aircraft and is buried in Fayid War Cemetery.
	Sgt Cross		

5-6 Jul 1942	**37 Sqn**	**Wellington IC**	**DV508 G** **Op: Daba**
	P/O G D B Raffil	+	Took off 0100-0150, Abu Sueir, to seek out targets of
	Sgt S Myers	+	opportunity in the Daba area. Several crews reported an
	Sgt K J Smith	+	aircraft attacked by a night fighter about 24km SE of
	Sgt G Tomkins	+	Daba. All 6 are commemorated on the Alamein Memorial.
	Sgt G Cutter	+	
	P/O P E Stumbles	+	

6 Jul 1942	**14 Sqn**	**Blenheim IV**	**Z7712** **Op: Army Co-operation**
	S/Ldr A N Pirie		Took off 0310, LG 97, detailed to attack Axis motor
	Sgt J E Beckett RCAF		transport and LGs between Fuka and Mersa Matruh, and
	Sgt W J Bartholomew	+	shot down near Fuka after bombing. The WOp/AG is buried in the El Alamein War Cemetery.

6-7 Jul 1942	**148 Sqn**	**Wellington IC**	**DV603 H** **Op: Enemy motor transport**
	Sgt C Handley	+	Took off, Kabrit, to attack enemy motor transport, but
	Sgt H W Brayshaw	+	crashed on the edge of the Great Bitter Lake and blew up.
	Sgt J G Fry	+	Sgt Robinson, whose turret was blown clear when the
	Sgt A Rae	+	aircraft exploded on hitting the water, was trapped up to
	Sgt M W Stanley RAAF	+	his neck in water, suffering minor cuts, exposure and
	Sgt J E Robinson		shock. The dead are buried in Fayid War Cemetery.

7 Jul 1942	**70 Sqn**	**Wellington IC**	**N2739** **Unknown**
			Took off Abu Sueir, but crashlanded 3km from the aerodrome, cause unknown.
	15 Sqn SAAF	**Blenheim V**	**BA314** **Unknown**
	Capt B L Hutchinson SAAF		Belly-landed after take-off, LG 99. NFD.
	15 Sqn SAAF	**Blenheim V**	**BA 325** **Unknown**
	Lt O C Venn SAAF		Belly-landed at LG 97. NFD.

7-8 Jul 1942	**70 Sqn**	**Wellington IC**	**Z8986 T** **Op: Battle Area**
	Sgt J R Milligan RCAF		Took off Abu Sueir to seek out targets of opportunity in
	Sgt L T B Phillips	+	the Alamein area but at about 30m suddenly lost
	P/O R F Watson RNZAF	+	momentum, sank, struck the ground and DBF. The dead
	Sgt R J Smart RNZAF	+	are buried in Ismailia War Memorial Cemetery.
	Sgt F O H Harrison RNZAF	+	
	Sgt C A Clack		
	148 Sqn	**Wellington IC**	**T2985** **Op: Tobruk**
	F/O F Tribe	+	Took off 2055-2125, Kabrit, to attack the harbour and
	Sgt S G Rimmer	+	shipping at Tobruk, but FTR, and found crashed 18km
	Sgt L G I Owen	+	SW of Shallufa. All are buried in Fayid War Cemetery.
	P/O J P Michael RCAF	+	
	Sgt N A Burr	+	
	Sgt B J Worsfold	+	

8 Jul 1942	**1 OADU**	**Halifax II**	**W1178 T** **Relocation Flight**
	P/O Hillier		Took off Gibraltar for Aqir, but forced to turn back and
	Crew		on landing bounced, an undercarriage leg collapsing. The
	Passengers		crew were unhurt; the aircraft DBR. The aircraft was a part of the Middle East Detachment of 10 Sqn.

8-9 Jul 1942	104 Sqn	Wellington II	Z8520 N	Op: Tobruk

8-9 Jul 1942

104 Sqn   **Wellington II**   **Z8520 N**   **Op: Tobruk**

Sgt C S Maxfield — evd
F/Sgt Evans — evd
Sgt Morgan — evd
Sgt F A J Jobson — evd
Sgt Booth — evd
Sgt Hepworth — evd

Took off 2145, Kabrit, to attack the harbour and shipping at Tobruk. Failure of the port engine and then partial failure of the starboard engine necessitated a belly landing 64km S of Sidi Barrani. The crew travelled 200 miles through enemy lines before being rescued by a Baltimore which landed in the desert. See Appendix 3 for Sgt Maxfield's account of this event.

148 Sqn   **Wellington IC**   **DV540 G**   **Op: Tobruk**

W/O W D F Ross RCAF
Crew

Took off 2102, Kabrit, to attack the harbour and shipping at Tobruk. Difficulties with navigation were experienced and a QDM request was not answered. Low on fuel, the pilot attempted to land at Kabrit in ground mist, but lost sight of the aerodrome, and both engines cut, the aircraft force-landing in shallow water.

9 Jul 1942

14 Sqn   **Blenheim IV**   **V6021**   **Unknown**

P/O B K Armstrong RAAF — +
F/O J Maurin-Bonnemain RAAF — +
P/O R M McCawley RAAF — inj

Crashed on take-off 2200, Abu Sueir, and DBF. P/O Maurin-Bonnemain died of burns the next day in No 6 General Hospital. He and the pilot are buried in Tel-El-Kebir War Cemetery.

9-10 Jul 1942

1 OADU   **Halifax II**   **W7695 D**   **Relocation Flight**

W/O D J O'Driscoll RCAF
Sgt Spaven
Sgt Wiles
Sgt Garrett-Ree
Sgt Oakford
F/Sgt McLaughlan
F/Sgt Dew
Passengers:
LAC R H Saunders — inj
Two others

Took off Gibraltar for Aqir, but unable to locate a landing ground, crashed into the sea 32km E of Alexandria. All on board made their way to shore by dinghy. Two were injured, but only LAC Saunders identified. This aircraft, like W1178 above, was part of the 10 Squadron Middle East detachment.

HALPRO   **B-24D**   **Op: Anti-shipping**

1/Lt K W Butler USAAF — +
1/Lt H A Kysar USAAF — +
1/Lt W H Hiatt USAAF — +
Cpl J M Thompson Jr USAAF — +
S/Sgt M Cwikiel USAAF — +
S/Sgt T A Blair Jr USAAF — +
Cpl P Bedrosian USAAF — +

Took off Lydda, detailed to attack a convoy sailing from Crete to Tobruk. Shot down by Bf 109s off Sidi Barrani, crashing into the sea with the starboard wing ablaze. All are commemorated on the Tablets of the Missing at the North Africa American Cemetery, Carthage, Tunisia. The serial number was either 41-11618 or 41-11600 (see 13-14 July).

10 Jul 1942

40 Sqn   **Wellington IC**   **HX374 F**   **Op: Tobruk**

P/O K Liversidge
Sgt C Mortimer
F/Sgt J I Reddell RNZAF
Sgt H G Horton RNZAF
Sgt J Hammond
Sgt R Beatson RNZAF

Took off Shallufa to attack the harbour and shipping at Tobruk, but engine trouble shortly after take-off forced the crew to return. The aircraft caught fire on landing and burnt out, the bombs exploding.

55 Sqn   **Baltimore II**   **AG795**   **Op: Army Co-operation**

Sgt E C Hyde
Sgt N W Orr
F/Sgt J L Granda RCAF
Sgt F M Taylor

Took off 0941, LG 98, detailed to bomb Axis motor transport around El Alamein. Stalled from about 3m, the port wing dropping and striking the ground; the undercarriage collapsed. DBR.

10-11 Jul 1942

70 Sqn   **Wellington IC**   **DV616 A**   **Op: Tobruk**

Sgt R A C Billen
Sgt C J Fraser RNZAF
Sgt W A Rylance

Took off 2035, Abu Sueir, to attack the harbour and shipping at Tobruk. Running low on fuel, and unable to see the flarepath because of low cloud, the crew,

	F/Sgt A T Kinne			descending through cloud, crashed 8-10km from Abu
	F/Sgt H C Cameron			Sueir. DBR.
	Sgt C R Holley			

11-12 Jul	**108 Sqn**	**Wellington IC**	**DV674 E**	**Op: Tobruk**
1942	W/O2 R A A Chalmers RCAF	+	Took off 2020, Kabrit, to attack the harbour and shipping
	Sgt T L Roberts	+	at Tobruk. Unable on return to find LG 224, the crew
	Sgt R W Luck		continued toward Cairo. The pilot tried landing at
	Sgt H J Wigley RAAF		Heliopolis but collided with AD601 on overshoot. Sgt
	Sgt M D Richards		Thomas was seriously injured. The two pilots are buried
	Sgt I M Thomas	inj	in Heliopolis War Cemetery.

148 Sqn	**Wellington IC**	**T2749**	**Op: Tobruk**
P/O P W Hoad	pow	Took off 2056-2115, Kabrit, to attack the harbour and
P/O D A Newman RCAF	pow	shipping at Tobruk. An engine caught fire after flak
F/O R W McNichol RCAF	pow	damage, and the aircraft crash-landed on the beach. P/O
Sgt T Greggs	pow	Hoad stayed with the injured Sgt Hall. The others walked
Sgt L L Horsman	pow	for four days but were captured near Sidi Barrani when
Sgt A L Hall	pow	trying to commandeer a German truck.

148 Sqn	**Wellington IC**	**DV505 K**	**Op: Tobruk**
F/Sgt H E Kemball	+	Took off 2056-2115, Kabrit, to attack the harbour and
Sgt L P Plum	+	shipping at Tobruk. FTR. All are commemorated on the
F/Sgt K G Baugh	+	Alamein Memorial.
Sgt P F Porter	+	
Sgt G S Mills	+	

12 Jul	**107 Sqn**	**Blenheim IV**	**Z7643**	**Unknown**
1942			Crashed on landing, Luqa. NFD.	

108 Sqn	**Wellington IC**	**Z8944**	**Ground**
		Hit by DV674 while parked, Heliopolis. The aircraft was	
		lying on its belly in a dismantled condition after an earlier	
		accident, date uncertain.	

108 Sqn	**Wellington IC**	**DV438 M**	**Unknown**
P/O I C Beckwith		Crash-landed LG 224. Apparently not repaired, and SOC	
Crew		by inventory entry, 31.10.43.	

12-13 Jul	**40 Sqn**	**Wellington IC**	**HX373 N**	**Op: Tobruk**
1942	S/Ldr F J Steel RNZAF		Took off Shallufa to attack the harbour and shipping at
	F/O K R Holmes RNZAF		Tobruk. The target was not located because the compass
	P/O D A Adams RNZAF		was unserviceable, and the aircraft was off course on the
	P/O R Sharp		return journey for the same reason. Out of fuel, the
	Sgt A Aldersey		aircraft crash-landed in the Qattara Depression. S/Ldr
	Sgt G Herford		Steel and P/O Adams went for help, while the latter
	P/O E Proctor		remained with the aircraft. The latter were seen by a
			reconnaissance aircraft and quickly rescued, while Steel
			and Adams, assisted by Arabs, walked for three days
			before spotted at an Arab encampment at El Magra, S of
			the Alamein line, being rescued by a 40 Sqn crew who
			landed in the desert. There is an account of this, together
			with a photo of the rescue of S/Ldr Steel and P/O Adams
			in David Gunby's *Sweeping the Skies*, pp204-205.

104 Sqn	**Wellington II**	**Z8588 V**	**Op: Tobruk**
P/O J E Harlton RCAF	pow	Took off 2120-2155, Kabrit, to attack the harbour and
W/O2 J O Waltenbury RCAF	+	shipping at Tobruk. On return crash-landed 48km SW of
P/O R S Spear RAAF	pow	Sidi Barrani. W/O2 Waltenbury died in the crash and is
Sgt E Burford RAAF	pow	buried in Halfaya Sollum War Cemetery. The others were
F/Sgt R C Andrews	pow	captured on 19 July.
Sgt K Graley	pow	

	108 Sqn P/O E R Wardley Sgt L S Cowell	Wellington IC	DV571 Q	Op: Tobruk

Took off 1945, Kabrit, to attack the harbour and shipping at Tobruk. On return, aerial trouble prevented the crew locating LG 224 and a wheels-up landing was made just NW of Wadi Natrun. The ORB reported only slight damage to the aircraft, but it was not repaired.

13 Jul 1942	108 Sqn P/O F O'Donnell F/O D A Pascoe Sgt P S Burrow F/Sgt J H Bell RAAF Passenger: LAC S Schlaichter	Wellington IC + + inj inj inj	DV553 P	Ferry Flight

Took off 1515, Kabrit, to ferry the aircraft to Aqir for an engine change. Wing damage caused by unauthorised low flying meant the aircraft flew port wing low. The pilot made an error of judgement on landing and collided with HF830. DBF. The pilot and observer are buried in Ramleh War Cemetery.

	108 Sqn	Wellington IC	HF830	Ground

Hit by DV553 while parked, Aqir.

	148 Sqn	Wellington IC	T2749	Unknown

Lost. NFD.

	GB1 Lorraine	Blenheim IV	V6293	Unknown

Crashed on take-off, Wadi Seidna, when a tyre burst. DBR.

13-14 Jul 1942	10/227 Sqn P/O H C Drake F/Sgt Jones Sgt Plummer Sgt J F H Steer Sgt Burney Sgt Bussey	Halifax II inj inj	W1171 X	Op: Tobruk

Took off, Aqir, to attack the harbour and shipping at Tobruk. Damaged by flak over target, the aircraft crashed on landing at Almaza and blew up. Several Egyptian firemen were killed when a bomb exploded in the wreckage.

	104 Sqn Sgt G T Cairns Sgt W D M Embree RCAF Sgt J F Crozier RAAF Sgt S J Berry Sgt J C Dickenson Sgt T A Clarke	Wellington II +	Z8650 Q	Op: Tobruk

Took off 2200-2228, Kabrit, to attack the harbour and shipping at Tobruk. Descending to pin-point the Delta, they flew into high ground in haze 48km SW of Wadi Natrun, hitting the ground at 170mph.

	HALPRO 1/Lt C O Brown Jr USAAF 1/Lt J R Taylor USAAF 1/Lt M H Anderson USAAF S/Sgt M A Cannon USAAF S/Sgt I Cutler USAAF Cpl H L Osgood USAAF Cpl D J Perry Jr USAAF	B-24D + + +		Op: Benghazi

Took off Lydda, detailed to attack the harbour and shipping at Benghazi. Brought down by flak over the target. Lt Taylor, Sgt Cutler and Cpl Perry are commemorated on the North Africa American Cemetery, Carthage. The fate of the others is unclear, though presumably they were taken prisoner. The serial number was either 41-11618 or 41-11600 (see 9-10 July).

14-15 Jul 1942	37 Sqn Sgt R Gordon Sgt A Payne Sgt Baxter Sgt W D Drew Sgt R Austin Sgt Teasdale	Wellington IC	DV495 U	Op: Tobruk

Took off 2200-2230, Abu Sueir, to attack the harbour and shipping at Tobruk. The aircraft developed engine trouble, and the fuel gauges showed nil, so the pilot force-landed 8-16km S of Fuka. Some fuel was still found to be in the tanks, so Sgt Gordon attempted a solo take-off but the aircraft crashed as a result of the tailwheel being damaged. The crew walked toward Allied lines and reached El Maghra on the 22nd, where they contacted the 7th Armoured Division and were returned to base.

104 Sqn	Wellington II		Z8649 C	Op: Tobruk

P/O G Richards — pow
F/O D P Williams — pow
Sgt E W B Howard RNZAF — pow
Sgt J A Kilner — pow
F/Sgt G M Frostick RNZAF — +
F/Sgt J M Squire RAAF — +

Took off c.2150, Kabrit, to attack the harbour and shipping at Tobruk. Hit by flak and set on fire, the aircraft became uncontrollable. The crew bailed out into the sea but no trace of F/Sgt Frostick was found. He is commemorated on the Alamein Memorial. Sgt Squire died on the 19th of pneumonia and is buried in Tobruk War Cemetery.

104 Sqn	Wellington II		Z8657 J	Op: Tobruk

Sgt D C Davies — inj
Sgt J W R Atkinson — +
Sgt A J M Leete — +
Sgt J Greenshields RCAF — inj
Sgt R Sissons — inj
Sgt I Reid — +

Took off c.2150, Kabrit, to attack the harbour and shipping at Tobruk. On return flew into the ground in mist near Wadi Natrun. The dead are buried in Alexandria (Chatby) Military and War Memorial Cemetery; the others were slightly injured.

104 Sqn	Wellington II		Z8658 H	Op: Tobruk

P/O R C Horton — +
Sgt K S Smith — +
F/O R P Lutz RAAF — +
Sgt F J Pitcher — +
Sgt W C Hutchinson RNZAF — +
Sgt E P Smith — inj

Took off 2146, Kabrit, to attack the harbour and shipping at Tobruk. One engine failed on return, the aircraft was unable to maintain height and struck the ground violently on landing 64km S of El Daba, bursting into flames. The rear gunner managed to struggle clear, but was unable to help the remaining crew, who are commemorated on the Alamein Memorial. Sgt Smith was helped by Arabs to reach an advanced unit of the 7th Armoured Division.

15 Jul 1942

104 Sqn	Wellington II		W5481 W	Op: Tobruk

Sgt J A C Anscomb
Crew

Took off 2150, Kabrit, to attack the harbour and shipping at Tobruk, but engine problems led to an early return, and an engine cut on approach, 2220; the aircraft swung and hit a Chance light, Kabrit; DBF.

104 Sqn	Wellington IC		HF851	Unknown

Missing, according to AM Form 78. But the 104 Sqn ORB records no loss, and 104 did not operate the Wellington IC.

159 Sqn	Liberator II		AL566	Op: Benghazi

P/O J C Pottie RAAF — +
W/O W S Miller — +
P/O H Leisk RAAF — +
P/O G G Mallaby RAAF — +
F/Sgt M C Fell MiD RNZAF — +
F/Sgt J S A Hodge — +
F/Sgt H E Birk RAAF — +

Took off St Jean to attack the harbour and shipping at Benghazi. Another crew saw the aircraft under attack by fighters and spiralling into the sea. Sgt Birk's body was washed ashore at Guiliana and is buried in Benghazi War Cemetery; the others are commemorated on the Alamein Memorial.

1 OADU	Blenheim V		BA383	Delivery Flight

Crashed on take-off, Maidaguru. NFD.

15-16 Jul 1942

37 Sqn	Wellington IC		AD645 H	Op: Tobruk

P/O J R Dudley
F/Lt T R Nelson
Sgt D P L O'Neill Shaw
Sgt P H Attfield
W/Cdr De Salas
Sgt E H Miller

Took off 2006, Abu Sueir, to attack the harbour and shipping at Tobruk. The aircraft was low on fuel, and obliged to land at Helwan, but the flare path was not laid out, and the aircraft landed heavily, the undercarriage collapsing. DBR.

104 Sqn	Wellington II		Z8653 E	Op: Tobruk

Sgt R A Newman
P/O Richards
Crew

Took off 2145, Kabrit, detailed to attack the harbour and shipping at Tobruk. On return an altimeter error resulted in the aircraft flying into the ground 18km NE of El Khanka; DBF.

16 Jul 1942	1 OADU	Blenheim V	BA542	Delivery Flight
	F/Sgt P P Adams RAAF	+		
	Sgt G E Price RCAF	+		
	Sgt G A Russell	+		

Took off 0425, Luqa, on the final leg of a delivery flight to Egypt, but failed to arrive. The body of Sgt Price was washed ashore at Port Said on 12 August, and he is buried in Port Said War Cemetery; the other two crew members are commemorated on the Runnymede Memorial.

16-17 Jul 1942	37 Sqn	Wellington IC	AD645	Op: Tobruk
	Sgt J V Glansfield			
	Sgt W Cameron			
	P/O L S E Watkinson			
	Sgt T Roberts			
	Sgt L Dennis			
	Sgt H Crutchley			

Took off 2112, Abu Sueir, detailed to attack the harbour and shipping at Tobruk. The undercarriage collapsed on landing at LG 05.
(The 37 Sqn ORB and AM 1180 give this loss as DV645, which was SOC with 215 Sqn in India in July 1944.)

	148 Sqn	Wellington IC	HX400	Op: Tobruk
	F/Lt J G Brown	+		
	P/O M A Bennetto RCAF	+		
	F/Sgt H J Ford	+		
	Sgt R C Drake	+		
	Sgt C J Griffiths	+		
	Sgt C S Parker	+		

Took off 2100-2120, Kabrit, detailed to attack the harbour and shipping at Tobruk. FTR. All but F/Lt Brown and Sgt Parker (both commemorated on the Alamein Memorial) are buried in Tobruk War Cemetery.

18-19 Jul 1942	14 Sqn	Blenheim IV	Z6428	Op: Mersa Matruh
	S/Ldr R H Moore DFC			
	F/Sgt L Bradford			
	Sgt A J Tucker			

Took off 1945, LG 88, to attack Axis tank workshops. Crashed 1.5km SE of LG 88 on return when an engine failed.

	160 Sqn	Liberator II	AL554	Op: Tobruk
	F/Lt N E Sharp	+		
	F/Sgt W C Stanbury	+		
	F/Sgt G S Anderson	+		
	F/Sgt R L Somerville	+		
	F/Sgt Cullen	inj		
	F/Sgt D Flockhart	+		
	Sgt D J Godfrey	+		
	P/O H C S Cotton RNZAF	+		

Took off St Jean, detailed to attack the harbour and shipping at Tobruk. On return ran out of fuel and force-landed 1.5km S of Caesure (sic), Palestine. F/Sgt Stanbury died of injuries the following day, and F/Sgt Cullen was seriously injured. The dead are buried in Khayat Beach War Cemetery, Haifa.

19-20 Jul 1942	40 Sqn	Wellington IC	HX399 S	Op: Tobruk
	F/Sgt P R Kingsford RNZAF	+		
	Sgt J A Tovey RNZAF			
	Sgt J Clark			
	Sgt R J Laing RAAF	+		
	Sgt L McTaggart			
	Sgt I Goss RAAF			

Took off 2210, Shallufa, detailed to attack the harbour and shipping at Tobruk. On return the starboard engine caught fire. All but the pilot and W/Op bailed out, they stayed with the aircraft, which crashed near Wadi Natrun. F/Sgt Kingsford and Sgt Laing were trapped in the ensuing fire. Both are commemorated on the Alamein Memorial.

20-21 Jul 1942	1 OADU	Wellington IC	HX518	Delivery Flight
	P/O A R Houstoun	+		
	Sgt W E Konigkramer	+		
	P/O J H Kinsey	+		
	Sgt G R Halliwell	+		
	Sgt E Lister	+		

Took off Portreath for Gibraltar, but failed to arrived. NFD. All are commemorated on the Runnymede Memorial.

21 Jul 1942	148 Sqn	Wellington II	Z8494 M	Unknown

Lost. NFD. (All 148 Sqn Wellington IIs were transferred to 104 Sqn in March and April 1942, hence this must either be an error, or an inventory entry.)

	12 Sqn SAAF	**Boston III**	**AL745 Q**	**Op: Army Co-operation**
	Lt D W Luke SAAF	inj	Took off 0735, LG 99, to bomb attacking German armour.	
	Lt A A Green SAAF	+	On return at approximately 0910 hrs, the starboard	
	Air Sgt D H Costigan SAAF	inj	engine failed on approach and the aircraft swerved into	
	Air Sgt J D Ellis SAAF	inj	the slipstream of another Boston, stalled, crashed into the	
			ground nose first and caught fire. Lt Green died of his	
			injuries shortly after and is buried in Alexandria (Hadra)	
			War Memorial Cemetery.	
	15 Sqn SAAF	**Blenheim V**	**BA442**	**Cross Country Training Flight**
	Lt M J Bernitz SAAF		Took off Helwan, but on return at 0820 the starboard	
			undercarriage failed to lower, and the aircraft belly-landed.	
22 Jul 1942	**40 Sqn**	**Wellington IC**	**HX440 U**	**Op: El Alamein**
	Sgt R A King	inj	Took off Shallufa to attack motor transport near El	
	Sgt N Housden	inj	Alamein. Surviving three attacks by night fighters, the	
	Sgt L Greenwood	inj	aircraft crashed on overshoot at Shallufa. Sgt Mackaskill	
	Sgt T R A Merry	inj	is buried in the Suez War Memorial Cemetery.	
	Sgt J Smart	inj		
	Sgt A Macaskill	+		
	55 Sqn	**Baltimore II**	**AG824**	**Training**
	P/O C G Russell RNZAF	+	Took off LG 98, on low flying and formation practice.	
	Sgt P A Webber	+	Over LG 207/LG Y Qassassin, at 0730 hrs, struck the	
	Sgt G F Studley	+	ground, burst into flames and then blew up. All are	
	Sgt R Collier	+	buried in Tel-el-Kebir War Memorial Cemetery.	
22-23 Jul 1942	**14 Sqn**	**Blenheim IV**	**Z9655**	**Op: Mersa Matruh**
	P/O R W Lapthorne RAAF	inj	Took off 2000, LG 116, on a night attack on Mersa Matruh	
	P/O D L Jones	+	Harbour. The aircraft was hit by flak and holed in the	
	P/O G M King RAAF	+	mainplane. The pilot sustained head injuries but	
			managed to fly the aircraft safely back to base. DBR.	
23 Jul 1942	**37 Sqn**	**Wellington IC**	**DV642**	**Unknown**
			Suffered flying battle damage. NFD. SOC 25 July.	
	40 Sqn	**Wellington IC**		**Ferry Flight**
	F/Lt H Grant		Took off Shallufa and on landing at Lydda swung to	
	Crew		avoid a Fortress parked near the runway, and the	
			undercarriage collapsed when the aircraft ran into a	
			ditch. The serial number is given as CT2832, which is	
			clearly wrong.	
	159 Sqn	**Liberator II**	**AL534**	**Op: Benghazi**
	F/O R A Malcolm	pow	Took off St Jean, detailed to attack the harbour and	
	W/O R J Male	pow	shipping at Benghazi. FTR. F/Sgt Peterson is buried in	
	F/Sgt J S Peterson RCAF	+	Benghazi War Cemetery, while F/Sgt Hogg is	
	F/Sgt J H Hogg	+	commemorated on the Alamein Memorial.	
	Sgt W Bell	pow		
	Sgt A Charlton	pow		
	Sgt J A Westwood RCAF	pow		
	24 Sqn SAAF	**Boston III**	**Z2223**	**Op: Qotafiyah**
	Lt L A Nichol SAAF	+	Took off 2055, LG 99, Egypt to attack LG 20 (Qotafyiah I)	
	Lt C W D Grey SAAF	+	and LG 104 (Qotafyiah II). Heavy and accurate anti-aircraft fire was encountered and the aircraft damaged.	
	Air Sgt H J P Bayley SAAF	+	It crashed at approximately 2310 hours at Kilo 120 near	
	Air Sgt A C Essery SAAF	+	LG 99 and was DBF. The crew are buried in El Alamein	
			War Cemetery.	

23-24 Jul 1942	1st Prov Bomb Gp Capt C Fountain USAAF Lt H L Mengal Jr USAAF Lt A G Rodriguez USAAF T/Sgt G F Wrigley USAAF Sgt Lalonde USAAF Sgt D E Sane USAAF Sgt J B Wells USAAF T/Sgt J G Lesich USAAF	B-24D + inj	41-11615 N Op: Benghazi Took off Fayid, 1530, to bomb harbour facilities, and on return was unable to lower the port undercarriage, and ran out of fuel circling its base, Lydda. The crew bailed out, but Sgt Wrigley's parachute fouled the tail of the aircraft and he was killed when it crashed.
24 Jul 1942	108 Sqn	Wellington IC	Z9031 Ground DBF by debris when DV655 blew up, Kabrit.
	108 Sqn AC1 R J Bonds AC1 R T Hooper LAC G W Lacey AC1 J Lindsay LAC R L F Tong	Wellington IC + inj + + inj	DV655 C Ground Caught fire at Kabrit after a 40lb incendiary bomb exploded, probably because the bombing-up party attempted, contrary to orders, to remove or insert a detonator.
	108 Sqn	Wellington IC	DV659 S Ground Set on fire by debris when DV655 blew up, Kabrit. DBF.
	12 Sqn SAAF Lt W P Colman SAAF Lt G S T Warren SAAF Air Sgt A L Robinson SAAF Air Sgt S Hughes SAAF	Boston III + + + +	Z2215 C Op: El Daba Took off 0927, LG 99, to attack Axis airfields in the El Daba area. Damaged by flak over LG 104 (Qotafiyah II) and last seen heading E, under control, at 300m S of El Daba. One of the crew was seen to bail out and the Boston crash-landed near El Daba at 1033 hrs. All are commemorated on the Alamein Memorial.
24-25 Jul 1942	37 Sqn P/O F J Pearce Sgt R Thompson Sgt A Morris Sgt D Cowie Sgt W A W Sutcliffe RNZAF Sgt D Croston	Wellington IC inj inj inj + inj	AD648 T Op: Heraklion Detailed to bomb the aerodrome at Heraklion, but hit a sandbank on take-off, Abu Sueir, when the engines failed to deliver sufficient power, caught fire and blew up. Sgt Sutcliffe died shortly after, and is buried at Tel-el-Kebir War Memorial Cemetery.
	104 Sqn Sgt A J Wills Sgt J L Joyce RNZAF P/O J King Sgt R Hartley Sgt J C Weston Sgt J C Barr	Wellington II evd evd evd pow evd evd	Z8509 R Op: Tobruk Took off 2215-2230, Kabrit, detailed as above. Hit by flak en route, and forced down S of Sollum, near Halfaya Pass. The crew spent 12 days in the desert, escaping from captivity twice, the second time after 36 hours, during which they travelled 230 miles in a commandeered German car before capture. All but Sgt Hartley later escaped from Italians by overpowering their guards and driving their truck E until meeting up with a LRDG patrol.
	104 Sqn Sgt R A Milner Sgt G L Eke Sgt D C Porter F/Sgt T L Vinnicombe RAAF Sgt M R Morey RAAF Sgt H McL Stokes	Wellington II + + + + + pow	Z8568 P Op: Tobruk Took off 2215-2230, Kabrit, detailed to bomb the harbour and shipping at Tobruk. On return crash-landed with engine trouble in the Burg El Arab area. Sgts Milner and Morey, and F/Sgt Vinnicombe were killed in the crash, while Sgts Porter and Eke died of injuries at the crash site. The dead are commemorated on the Alamein Memorial.
	104 Sqn Sgt L W Rowley Crew	Wellington II	Z8654 Op: Tobruk Took off 2215-2230, Kabrit, detailed to attack the harbour and shipping at Tobruk. The starboard engine failed and caught fire, but went out after feathering. Unable to maintain height, the pilot crash-landed the aircraft 16km SW of LG 237. SOC 31.10.43 by inventory entry.

25 Jul 1942	**14 Sqn**	**Blenheim IV**	**Z7989 R**	**Unknown**

Undercarriage collapsed on landing, LG Y. DBR.

	1 OADU	**Blenheim V**	**AZ929**	**Ground**

Hit by BA388 while parked, Takoradi. DBR.

	1 OADU Sgt A R Fitton Crew	**Blenheim V**	**BA388**	**Ground**

Hit AZ929 on take-off, Takoradi. DBR.

25-26 Jul 1942	**108 Sqn** P/O O H Clement Sgt D Smith P/O H M Russell Sgt J L Wilson RAAF Sgt C C McPherson RAAF Sgt H Condron	**Wellington IC**	**HF844 O** + + + + + +	**Op: Heraklion**

Took off 2150, LG 86, to bomb Heraklion aerodrome. FTR.
All are commemorated on the Alamein Memorial.

---

26 Jul 1942	**1 OADU** Sgt Reeder Crew	**Wellington IC**	**HX533**	**Delivery Flight**

Crashed in a forced-landing, LG 224, presumably
en route from Luqa to Egypt. NFD.

27-28 Jul 1942	**40 Sqn** Sgt W H Mitchell Sgt H G Graham RCAF Sgt R H Lowe Sgt G McK Duff Sgt C E Tipper F/Sgt J J Thompson RCAF	**Wellington IC**	**HX370 Y** + + + + + +	**Op: LG 20**

Took off Shallufa, detailed to attack LG 20, and believed
crashed in flames near the target. All are commemorated
on the Alamein Memorial.

	70 Sqn Sgt H R Osborne Sgt R H Hearn RAAF Sgt R E S Osborn RAAF Sgt K S McDonald RAAF Sgt B K Hatch Sgt E A Jones RAAF	**Wellington IC**	**HX364 K** pow pow pow pow pow pow	**Op: Tobruk**

Took off 1946-2231, Abu Sueir, detailed to bomb Tobruk
harbour and shipping. Crashed in a forced landing 48km
SE of Tobruk. Sgts Hatch, Jones and McDonald drowned
when the Italian ship *Lino Bixo* was torpedoed by an RN
submarine S of Greece on 17 August. They are
commemorated on the Alamein Memorial. Sgts Osborne
and Hatch were attached from 37 Sqn, the others from
458 Sqn.

---

28 Jul 1942	**37 Sqn**	**Wellington IC**	**W5617**	**Unknown**

Undercarriage collapsed in landing at Shallufa. DBR.
NFD.

29-30 Jul 1942	**37 Sqn** P/O N H Moran RAAF Sgt J S Whitworth Sgt C T McLoughlin RAAF Sgt D E Bottomley Sgt J G Barlow F/Sgt W R Darling RNZAF	**Wellington IC**	**DV673 C**	**Op: Tobruk**

Took off 2138, Abu Sueir, detailed to bomb Tobruk
harbour and shipping. The port engine failed and later
caught fire, and the propeller broke away. The aircraft
lost height and eventually crash-landed 64km W of Wadi
Natrun. The crew were unhurt and walked 13km E,
contacting a 57 RSU party in the area. The aircraft was
DBR.

---

30 Jul 1942	**1 OADU** Sgt L W Mears P/O H S W Fordyce Sgt A McCluer Sgt C Maxwell Sgt G W S Crompton	**Wellington IC**	**HX580** pow pow pow pow +	**Relocation Flight**

Took off Gibraltar for Luqa but failed to arrive. This was
was a 458 Sqn aircraft and crew, en route to the Middle
East.

30-31 Jul 1942	37 Sqn	Wellington IC	HF833	Op: Tobruk

F/O C E L Hare RCAF — pow
Sgt A E O Barras RAAF — evd
F/Lt C D R Chappell RCAF — pow
Sgt J Shirra — evd
Sgt A I Jones — evd
F/Sgt C R Warwick RAAF — evd

Took off 2116-2215, Kabrit, detailed to bomb Tobruk harbour and shipping. The starboard engine failed over Tobruk, so they bombed the aerodrome. When the other engine seized they crash-landed 48km from Tobruk. The crew walked for 9 days, then split into parties of two, Hare and Chappell being captured on the 18th day. The others were picked up after 22 days by an 8th Army unit. The crew was attached from 458 Squadron.

	148 Sqn	Wellington IC	ES991 V	Op: Tobruk

Sgt T B Henry RNZAF
Sgt B S J Monkhouse
Sgt Bendle
Sgt N H Attwood
Sgt J H Chandler — +
Sgt A L F Fish

Took off 2129, Kabrit, detailed to bomb Tobruk harbour and shipping, but failed to maintain height and crashed into Little Bitter Lake. Sgt Chandler (buried in Fayid War Cemetery) was concussed and drowned. The others escaped with minor cuts and bruises.

	24 Sqn SAAF	Boston III	Z2163 D	Op: Sidi Haneish

Lt A E Corby SAAF — +
Sgt R H Kelly RAAF — +
Air Sgt J Forsyth SAAF — +
Air Sgt A N Hutchinson SAAF — +

Took off 2343, LG 99, to attack LG 13 (Sidi Haneish South), where heavy and accurate flak was encountered. The aircraft crashed and burst into flames 18.5km SE of LG 99 at approximately 0042 hours and burnt out. The cause was probably flak damage. All of the crew are buried in El Alamein War Cemetery.

31 Jul 1942	37 Sqn	Wellington IC	DV673	Unknown

F/O Moran RAAF
Crew

Took off Abu Sueir. An engine failed and the propeller flew off. The aircraft forcelanded with wheels up 64km W of Wadi Natrun. SOC.

	148 Sqn	Wellington IC	HX527	Op: Tobruk

F/O W D Bohl RAAF — +
P/O R E Vaupel RCAF — +
Sgt J W Southgate — +
Sgt R G L Holton RAAF — +
Sgt R Vernon — +

Took off 2125-2235, Kabrit, detailed to bomb Tobruk harbour and shipping. Missing. All are commemorated on the Alamein Memorial.

	159 Sqn	Liberator II	AL553	Unknown

SOC. NFD. See entry for 15 June.

31 Jul - 1 Aug 1942	76/454 Sqn	Halifax II	W7765 D	Op: Tobruk

P/O H Wickham
W/O D Boyd
Sgt R E Chambler
Sgt E E Maltwood
Sgt D Fitzgerald
F/Sgt W A Gillies

Took off Fayid, detailed to bomb Tobruk harbour and shipping The port inner engine was disabled by flak over the target and the starboard outer failed some 256km from Alexandria on the return flight. All removable fittings were thrown overboard, but eventually, 16km from Alexandria, Wickham bailed out his two gunners and, after a last unsuccessful search for their base, crash-landed at LG 09. SOC 6 October.
There is mystery concerning Halifax W7762 'D', which P/O Wickham and crew are recorded as flying out to the Middle East, landing at Aqir on 10 July, but which never appears in the 76 Sqn ORB thereafter, and W7765, which is not listed as flown out to the Middle East, but then appears on operations. It seems likely that W7762 was in fact W7765, particularly since the Aircraft Movement Card (AM78) gives the loss details as identical to those of W7765, but has W7762 SOC by inventory entry, obviously, on 30 September 1943.

1 Aug 1942	14 Sqn	Blenheim IV	Z9614	Op: Fuka

Sgt A E Ellis RAAF — pow

Took off 0320, LG 88, one of three Blenheims despatched

Sgt H B A Langmaid		pow	at 10-minute intervals to bomb LG 18, Fuka South. Hit by
Sgt M German		pow	flak, the aircraft was crash-landed, the crew escaping

unhurt, but Sgt German lost his right foot when he stood on a mine near the crash site. The others left him to get help and 14 hours later he was rescued by a hospital plane and taken to an Axis hospital at Fuka. The date and circumstances of Sgt German's death are uncertain. Sgt Ellis believed that he was on a hospital ship which was torpedoed en route to Italy. If so, he died considerably later than 1 August, the date given in Commonwealth War Grave Commission records. Sgt German is commemorated on the Alamein Memorial.

211 Sqn — **Blenheim I** — **L4825** — **Unknown**
SOC as Cat E, NFD. Presumably an inventory entry.

223 Sqn — **Maryland II** — **AH338** — **Unknown**
SOC. NFD.

1 OADU — **Wellington IC** — **HX577** — **Delivery Flight**
F/L P Bray
F/Sgt V A Rutherford
Crew

Took off, Gibraltar, for Bathhurst, Gambia, and crashed into sea off Bathhurst after running short of fuel, the crew uncertain of their position in bad weather. All were rescued.

1 Prov Bomb Gp — **B-24D** — **41-11601** — **Op: Anti-shipping**

2/Lt H N Sturkie USAAF	inj	Took off Lydda, 1420, to attack an enemy convoy 90 miles
2/Lt G B Swope USAAF	+	N of Benghazi, and on return undershot, crashed into a
2/Lt L C Moore USAAF	+	building housing Palestinian police and burst into flames.
2/Lt M B Strait USAAF	+	Lt Sturkie, thrown from the aircraft, survived badly
Pfc R C Jenkins USAAF	+	burned. Lts Swope and Moore are buried in the North
Cpl M A Trumbel USAAF	+	Africa American Cemetery, Carthage. The others were
Pvt H L Burdette USAAF	+	presumably repatriated post-war. The crew was flying its
S/Sgt G H Pearce USAAF	+	first operational sortie.

2 Aug 1942

37 Sqn — **Wellington IC** — **DV641** — **Ground**
DBF when DV644 blew up, Abu Sueir.

37 Sqn — **Wellington IC** — **DV644** — **Ground**

Sgt J S Whitworth	Preparing to take off from Abu Sueir, DV644 was hit by
Sgt C T McLoughlin RAAF +	Boston AL696 (24 Sqn SAAF), which was landing, set on
Sgt D E Bottomley +	fire and blew up. The dead, attached from 458 Sqn, are
Sgt J G Barlow +	buried in Tel-el-Kebir War Memorial Cemetery.
F/Sgt W R Darling	

37 Sqn — **Wellington IC** — **HX480** — **Ground**
DBF when DV644 blew up, Abu Sueir.

37 Sqn — **Wellington IC** — **HF832** — **Ground**
DBF when DV644 blew up, Abu Sueir.

24 Sqn SAAF — **Boston III** — **AL696** — **Ferry Flight**

Lt W H Martin SAAF	+	Took off 1915, OLG LG 99, ferrying the aircraft to Bilbeis.
Lt D Geddes SAAF	+	Disorientated, the pilot landed down wind at Abu-Sueir,
Sgt A L Hopkins RNZAF	+	overshot on the landing run and crashed into Wellington

IC (DV644) of 37 Sqn waiting to take off (see above). A commentator later said that this accident did more damage than any enemy air raid had achieved up to that time. All the crew are buried in Tel-el-Kebir War Memorial Cemetery.

RAF Takoradi — **Blenheim IV** — **Z7788** — **Delivery Flight**

Sgt J M McCann		Took off, Takoradi, but crashed after engine failure
Sgt R G Norton		10km W of Damat. Sgt Mayhew died of his injuries on
Sgt J F Mayhew	inj	4 August, and is buried in Maiduguri War Cemetery.

| 2-3 Aug 1942 | 148 Sqn | Wellington IC | DV568 L | Op: Tobruk |

	Sgt H Tricks		
	Sgt R J Reynolds	inj	
	Sgt W Maskell		
	Sgt J Vincent		
	Sgt R A Whitefield		
	Sgt B Edwards	inj	

148 Sqn — Wellington IC — DV568 L — **Op: Tobruk**
Sgt H Tricks
Sgt R J Reynolds — inj
Sgt W Maskell
Sgt J Vincent
Sgt R A Whitefield
Sgt B Edwards — inj

Took off 2222, Kabrit, detailed to bomb shipping at Tobruk. An engine cut over the battle area, and despite jettisoning everything moveable the aircraft still lost height. It eventually hit the ground and was wrecked. The crew signalled other aircraft using Verey cartridges and an Aldis lamp. The injured were picked up by a Lysander, the rest by a lorry.

---

3 Aug 1942 — 70 Sqn — Wellington IC — Z8778 — **Search and Rescue**
F/O J T Dick DFC — +
P/O H G Locke RCAF — +
P/O R C Prince RCAF — +
Sgt J C Daley RAAF — +
F/Sgt H S Impett — +
Sgt R S Hughes — +
Sgt I A Baines RAAF — +

Took off Abu Sueir, but failed to return from a search for a missing aircraft. All are commemorated on the Alamein Memorial.

1 OADU — Wellington IC — HX515 — **Delivery Flight**
F/Sgt G Nelson — +
F/Sgt G Glasgow — +
Sgt N J Durkan — +
Sgt D Smith — +
Sgt H Rossbottom — +
Sgt J Urwin — +

Took off Gibraltar for Luqa, but crashed into the sea S of Malta. All are commemorated on the Runnymede Memorial. An account of the unsuccessful search for this crew is found in Frederick Galea's *Call-Out*, p174.

---

5 Aug 1942 — 1 OADU — Wellington II — W5498 — **Air Test**
P/O H S Wilson
Sgt C Hall
Crew

Took off Gibraltar for an air test and overshot landing, running onto the beach. DBR.

5-6 Aug 1942 — 40 Sqn — Wellington Ic — HF898 B — **Op: Tobruk**
Sgt V Murray — pow
P/O W H Young — pow
Sgt J S Cameron RAAF — pow
Sgt A R Tonkin RAAF — pow
Sgt W R Thompson RAAF — pow
Sgt P W Northway RAAF — pow

Took off, Shallufa, detailed to bomb Tobruk harbour and shipping. After shedding the port propeller the aircraft lost height and the crew bailed out.

10/227 Sqn — Halifax II — W7757 W — **Op: Tobruk**
Sgt De Clerk
Crew

Took off Fayid, detailed to bomb Tobruk harbour and shipping. One engine was put out of action and another had to be feathered. The remaining two engines later overheated and the aircraft was ditched, the crew making its way to shore in a dinghy.

---

6 Aug 1942 — 55 Sqn — Baltimore II — AG773 — **Unknown**
P/O A M Cameron — inj
P/O C B Carter RCAF — inj
P/O M J G Harvey — inj
Sgt J M Marvin — inj

Took off LG 98. While coming into land at Abu Sueir at 1930 hours the pilot overshot and when he applied brakes the aircraft overturned. DBR.

12 Sqn SAAF — Boston III — AL712 X — **Op: Mersa Matruh**
Lt W T Dalling SAAF
Lt C F Marais SAAF
Sgt A V Pearson SAAF
Sgt V V Offer SAAF

Took off c.0445, LG 99, one of six Bostons sent to bomb Mersa Matruh. Belly-landed on returned to LG 99 at 0500 hrs with engine failure. A-B Serials indicates it was destroyed.

6-7 Aug 1942 — 159 Sqn — Liberator II — AL580 — **Op: Tobruk**
F/Sgt Corney
Sgt Corless

Took off St Jean, 1520, one of six aircraft detailed to attack the harbour and shipping at Tobruk. On return

	P/O Budden Crew		the undercarriage was found to be damaged, and after circling to allow the other crews to land, F/Sgt Corney landed, the undercarriage collapsing. DBR.

7 Aug 1942	**RAF Takoradi** Sgt R Yates Sgt Martin Sgt J Jury Passengers: Sgt Dean Sgt Murzynowski PAF	**Blenheim V**	**BA530** **Delivery Flight** Took off Lagos on Delivery Flight 453 for Kano, but swung on landing, crashed, and DBR.

7-8 Aug 1942	**40 Sqn** F/Sgt L P Kerr RNZAF F/Sgt E K Hainey Sgt J I Thomson RNZAF Sgt F R Smith RAAF Sgt R StC Gowdie RAAF Sgt D Wolstenholme RCAF	**Wellington IC** + + + + + +	**DV663** **U** **Op: Tobruk** Took off, Shallufa, detailed to attack the harbour at Tobruk. Collided with HX431. All are commemorated on the Alamein Memorial.
	40 Sqn F/Lt H Grant Sgt G Whyte P/O A E Hull F/Sgt C E Dauphin RCAF F/Sgt A W Dunn F/Sgt J Ware DFM	**Wellington IC** pow pow + pow pow pow	**HX431** **O** **Op: Tobruk** Took off, Shallufa, detailed as above. Crash-landed after a mid-air collision with DV663. P/O Hull and F/Sgt Dauphin bailed out, Hull too low for his parachute to open. He is commemorated on the Alamein Memorial. F/Sgt Dauphin and F/Sgt Ware were seriously injured, the latter having a leg amputated in a German Field Hospital.
	104 Sqn S/Ldr J A H Sargeaunt P/O S D Parnell RNZAF Sgt L B Thick Sgt W Hutton Sgt J Holliday RAAF F/Sgt J J Plunkett BEM RAAF	**Wellington II** pow pow pow pow pow pow	**Z8436** **D** **Op: Tobruk** Took off 2240, Kabrit, to bomb port facilities and shipping, Tobruk. Crash-landed 40km SW of Tobruk after engine failure. The crew, on detachment from 458 Sqn, walked for 16 days before they were captured.

8 Aug 1942	**70 Sqn**	**Wellington IC**	**HX486** **Ground** Caught fire on ground and destroyed when the bomb load blew up, Abu Sueir.
	162 Sqn Sgt F Trovillo RCAF Sgt B Watts Gower Sgt J K Pridmore	**Blenheim V**	**BA5445** **Calibration Flight** Took off 1515, Bilbeis, on a calibration flight of Tel-El-Kebir. On return belly-landed when the aircraft sank back after overshoot, 1005.

9-10 Aug 1942	**40 Sqn** F/Sgt G P A Yates RCAF Sgt G A Westthorp F/O F Waterman Sgt J Dickenson Sgt R Gardiner Sgt J Egan	**Wellington IC**	**HX560** **S** **Op: Tobruk** Took off, Shallufa, to bomb port facilities and shipping, Tobruk. The port engine failed on the return journey and the aircrew and reduction gear sheared off. Eventually the starboard engine overheated, seized and caught fire. The crew bailed out after reaching the Allied lines at El Alamein.

10-11 Aug 1942	**108 Sqn** P/O A Armstrong Sgt J C E Leaning RNZAF Sgt D C Willis Sgt E A Martin RAAF Sgt R Gemmell-Smith	**Wellington IC** pow pow pow pow pow	**DV667** **L** **Op: Tobruk** Took off 2225, Kabrit, to bomb port facilities and shipping, Tobruk. The aircraft developed engine trouble over the target, and became uncontrollable. The crew bailed out and were captured immediately.

11-12 Aug 1942	**40 Sqn** Sgt C E Hickman Sgt G S Ferrero RAAF Sgt P C Lloyd Sgt G Martin Sgt L R A Beasley Sgt G T Holt	**Wellington IC** pow pow pow pow pow pow	**HX377 A** Took off, Shallufa, to bomb port facilities and shipping, Tobruk. An engine failed, and eventually the crew bailed out, covering 144km in seven days before capture.	**Op: Tobruk**
	108 Sqn Sgt A S Graeme-Cook W/O2 J L Roach RCAF Sgt T C Clucas Sgt F Butler Sgt R M Hutchinson RAAF	**Wellington IC** pow pow pow pow pow	**HX484 P** Took off 2235, Kabrit, to bomb port facilities and shipping, Tobruk but reported turning back with engine failure, and later sent an SOS. All were captured when the aircraft crashed in the desert, but Sgt Graeme-Cook and W/O Roach lost their lives on 23 August when the Luftwaffe aircraft in which they were being flown to Greece crashed into the sea off the island of Hydra. They are commemorated on the Alamein Memorial.	**Op: Tobruk**
12 Aug 1942	**1 OADU** P/O A B Kidson P/O W R Simpson P/O E O Hampshire Sgt T S Woodley Sgt E W Draper Sgt L C Neave	**Wellington II** int + int int + int	**W5565** Took off, Gibraltar, for Bathhurst, but ditched off French West Africa after an attack by French fighters. The two dead went down with the aircraft. The others were interned until December 1942.	**Delivery Flight**
	1 OADU	**Wellington IC**	**HF882** Took off from Gibraltar for Bathhurst but failed to arrive. NFD. Air Historical Branch can supply no information about this loss.	**Delivery Flight**
12-13 Aug 1942	**70 Sqn** P/O H E Turner Sgt A D Bebbington P/o H E Norton Sgt J Holmes Sgt H B Goldberg Sgt A F Abbott	**Wellington IC**	**Z8960 O** Took off 2116, LG 86. Force-landed on a beach lost and out of fuel, with the wireless and sextant unserviceable. The aircraft nosed over in soft sand at the end of its landing run. SOC 1.42.	**Op: Tobruk**
	108 Sqn Sgt E D Sherman RCAF Sgt R J Monk RNZAF Sgt Kennedy Sgt R L McCue RAAF Sgt A J F Sim	**Wellington IC** inj inj inj +	**T2735 W** Took off 2220, Kabrit, detailed to attack the harbour at Tobruk, but the starboard engine cut and the pilot force-landed in the Great Bitter Lake. DBF. Sgt Sim is buried in Fayid War Cemetery.	**Op: Tobruk**
	108 Sqn F/Sgt D M Watts RAAF F/O W Gengos RAAF P/O R B Harris Sgt M D Hart RAAF Sgt A L Opas RAAF Sgt J H Taylor	**Wellington IC** + + + + + +	**AD629 J** Took off 1945, Kabrit, detailed to attack the harbour at Tobruk. FTR. All are commemorated on the Alamein Memorial. All save Sgt Taylor were attached from 458 Sqn.	**Op: Tobruk**
	162 Sqn Sgt W A Fergie RNZAF F/Sgt N D Fairclough LAC R Garmory Sgt T W Hirst LAC M Bray	**Blenheim V** + + + + +	**BA317** Took off 0515, Habbaniya, to deliver spares for Prime Minister Winston Churchill's Liberator, which had been delayed with engine trouble. The aircraft became airborne but gradually swung to starboard and struck the top of a bund, crashing and catching fire just beyond the airfield perimeter. All are buried in Habbaniya War Cemetery.	**Communication Flight**

13 Aug 1942	1 OADU	Wellington IC	HX583	Delivery Flight
	P/O R McIlraith RNZAF	int	Took off Gibraltar for Bathhurst, but attacked by French	
	Sgt G A Waugh	int	fighters (one of which was shot down), off Senegal. The	
	P/O R Isherwood	int	fuel tanks were holed and the aircraft force-landed near	
	P/O C Todd RNZAF	int	Tiaroye, Senegal, being deliberately DBF. Sgts Waugh	
	Sgt R S Moncreiff	int	and Isherwood were injured, and the crew interned until	
	Sgt J Holmwood	int	December 1942.	

14 Aug 1942	162 Sqn	Blenheim V	BA585	Unknown
			Hit an obstruction on take-off, Habbaniya/Dhibban. NFD.	

	1 OADU	Wellington IC	HX585	Delivery Flight
	P/O A E Beer	int	Took off RAF Hastings, Sierra Leone. The port engine	
	Sgt P L Palmer	int	seized and the propeller fell off, the aircraft force-landing	
	P/O J McG Johnstone	int	on a beach, 64km W of Bingerville, Ivory Coast. The	
	P/O A E Bransgrove	int	crew was interned at Jackville until December.	
	Sgt C E Lawrence	int		
	Sgt A R Brace	int		

14-15 Aug 1942	40 Sqn	Wellington IC	HX506 N	Op: Tobruk
	P/O K R Holmes RNZAF		Took off Shallufa, 1910, detailed to attack the harbour at	
	P/O D A Adams RNZAF	inj	Tobruk. On return overshot, crashed, and DBF.	
	P/O R Sharp			
	Sgt J Vickers			
	Sgt G Herford			
	Sgt E Procter			

15 Aug 1942	Ferry Command	Wellington IC	HX603	Delivery Flight
	F/Sgt G B Simpson RCAF	+	The undercarriage was retracted prematurely on take-off	
	Sgt G H Lawrence	+	from RAF Hastings, Sierra Leone, for Lagos. The aircraft	
	Sgt J W Cullen RCAF	+	sank back, skidded on its belly into trees and caught fire.	
	Sgt J D M Nelson	+	F/Sgt Simpson was killed outright and three others died	
	Sgt F Browning		of their injuries on 16 August. All are buried in King Tom	
			Cemetery, Sierra Leone.	

15-16 Aug 1942	70 Sqn	Wellington IC	HX451 B	Op: Tobruk
	F/Sgt D R Stewart RNZAF		Took off 1930, Abu Sueir, detailed to attack the harbour at	
	P/O R P Muirhead		Tobruk. Navigation problems meant the aircraft ran out	
	Sgt D Welch		of fuel and crash-landed in the desert.	
	Sgt T A Oldale			
	Sgt E J Payne			
	Sgt C C Owens			

	108 Sqn	Wellington IC	DV676 X	Op: Tobruk
	Sgt J G Bond RAAF	inj	Took off 1950, Kabrit, detailed as above. An engine failed	
	Sgt A R Beaven	inj	before reaching the target, and the aircraft crash-landed	
	P/O F H Smith	inj	in the Qattara Depression. Sgt Shapir (commemorated	
	Sgt D Rodden	inj	on the Alamein Memorial) was fatally injured, and was	
	Sgt M W Shapir	+	buried beside the aircraft, but his grave could not later be	
	Sgt A A Taylor	inj	located. The others were picked up by patrolling tanks	
			and taken to hospital, where Sgt Beaven died on 18	
			August. He is buried in El Alamein War Cemetery.	

	148 Sqn	Wellington IC	DV606 P	Op: Tobruk
	F/Sgt J C Williams		Took off 1910, Kabrit, detailed to operate as a flare	
	Sgt N S Ayres		dropper. The port engine cut, then the other, and the	
	Sgt A H Threlfall		aircraft quickly lost height. The crew bailed out and	
	Sgt J Weir		returned safely to base.	
	Sgt C H Clark			
	Sgt J M S Moir			

16-17 Aug 1942	40 Sqn Sgt J Mason Sgt D Syddall Sgt L W H Stevens Sgt C A Boyer RNZAF Sgt D A Carmichael RNZAF Sgt D White	Wellington IC pow pow pow pow pow pow	HX425 H **Op: Tobruk** Took off, Shallufa, detailed to attack the harbour and shipping at Tobruk. Engine failure on return, perhaps because of flak damage, forced the crew to bail out near Fuka.
17 Aug 1942	40 Sqn	Wellington IC	BB473 **Night Flying Test** DBR. NFD.
	55 Sqn Sgt J I Henderson Sgt P T Fletcher Sgt K Burns Sgt J W Shaw	Baltimore II	AG790 **Unknown** Crashed on take-off from LG 98 when the port engine cut as the aircraft became airborne. DBR.
	24 Sqn SAAF Maj J P Verster SAAF Lt C E Nicholls SAAF Air Sgt P Swanepoel SAAF Sgt R A F Greene SAAF	Boston III	Z2294 N **Op: Mersa Matruh** Took off 1730, OLG LG 99 to attack MTB and 'F' boats in Mersa Matruh Harbour. Hit by intense and accurate anti-aircraft fire over the target, the aircraft caught fire, the pilot effecting a belly-landing in the middle of the German camp 6.5km E of Mersa Matruh. The aircraft exploded thirty seconds later, but all the crew had escaped safely.
18 Aug 1942	148 Sqn	Wellington IC	X9684 F **Ground** DBF at Kabrit; the cause was not determined, but the fire was believed to have started in the rear turret.
18-19 Aug 1942	70 Sqn Sgt J R Milligan RCAF Sgt E Benning Sgt H P Dyson Sgt T A Hughes Sgt A H Page Sgt R Evans	Wellington IC	DV513 J **Op: Tobruk** Took off 1900, Abu Sueir, detailed to bomb Tobruk. On return the aircraft ran out of fuel and force-landed on what appeared to be a stretch of sand but turned out to be the SW corner of Lake Qarun near Fayoum. The aircraft came to rest in water almost up to the wingtips. The crew swam ashore and walked to a nearby village.
	104 Sqn P/O B R W Blogg Sgt F Rowell P/O C E Stotesbury Sgt A Broomhead Sgt J H R Ledoux RCAF	Wellington II inj + inj inj	Z8492 O **Op: Tobruk** Took off 1950, Kabrit, detailed to bomb Tobruk, but an engine cut, the aircraft lost height and crash-landed near Deversoir. P/O Stotesbury is buried in Fayid War Cemetery.
19 Aug 1942	108 Sqn	Wellington IC	**Unknown** Took off from Gaza and suffered engine failure. NFD. The serial given, MO887, is clearly wrong.
	159 Sqn F/O Rostance Crew	Liberator II	AL509 **Ground** While taxying at Aqir after landing, the nosewheel ran into a gully, and when the pilot tried to move the aircraft by opening up both starboard engines, the nosewheel collapsed. DBR.
	RAF Takoradi Sgt F B Borrett RAAF F/Sgt A J Bowditch RAAF Sgt R F Henderson RAAF	Blenheim V + + +	BA597 **Delivery Flight** Took off, Lagos, on Delivery Flight 474 to the Middle East, but failed to respond when the convoy leader ordered a return to base because of an impending storm. Spun into the ground 9km N of Oshogbo, after entering the storm. All of the crew are buried in Oshogbo War Cemetery.

19-20 Aug 1942	70 Sqn	Wellington IC	AD634 N	Op: Tobruk

Sgt P J King RNZAF — pow
Sgt R G Harding — pow
P/O S E Thomson RAAF — pow
Sgt A Waterworth — pow
Sgt F Rawson — pow

Took off 1915-1950, Kabrit, detailed to attack Tobruk. Force-landed 48km S of Sollum, after engine trouble. The crew were captured on the tenth day. There is a detailed account of this loss in Robert Harding's self-published *Copper Wire*, pp23-32.

---

20 Aug 1942 14 Sqn Marauder I FK157 Unknown

Col Garrison USAAF
Crew

Took off LG 224, probably on a familiarisation flight, and crashed on landing, hitting a lorry which attempted to cross the runway. Three Egyptian labourers were killed and a fourth was injured.

20-21 Aug 1942 37 Sqn Wellington IC Z8761 Op: Tobruk

Sgt I F L Arthur — pow
Sgt D J Bristow — pow
Sgt E H Farrow RCAF — pow
Sgt G Bonnar — pow
Sgt F C Easterling — pow
Sgt N Crutchley — pow

Took off 1910-1925, Abu Sueir, detailed to attack Tobruk. FTR. Sgt Easterling died when the Luftwaffe aircraft carrying him to Greece crashed on 23 August. He is buried in Phaleron British Military Cemetery.

---

22 Aug 1942 82nd Bomb Sqn B-25C 41-12862 Op: Mersa Matruh

1/Lt S L Powell Jr USAAF
2/Lt M J Stolk USAAF
2/Lt M P Swartz USAAF
2/Lt A W Hatten USAAF
S/Sgt J L Reed USAAF +
T/Sgt W P Shannon USAAF +

Took off Deversoir, detailed to attack a tank depot. On the return flight the IFF failed and the aircraft was shot down in error by an RAF Beaufighter. The two crew who died were buried near the scene of the crash, but later re-interred in the United States.

22-23 Aug 1942 40 Sqn Wellington IC HX488   Y Op: Mersa Matruh

Sgt R H Ceha
Sgt G Dawson
Sgt D MacMichael
Sgt T Vickers
Sgt F Mason
Sgt K Davidson

Took off, Shallufa, detailed to act as flare dropper for an attack on a tank depot. The loss of the port propeller and a failing starboard engine forced the crew to bail out over Allied territory near Wadi Natrun.

---

23 Aug 1942 81st Bomb Sqn B-25C 41-12853 Op: Tobruk

Capt R W Carlisle USAAF +
1/Lt R E Wynkoop Jr USAAF +
2/Lt W H Davis USAAF +
Sgt W A Kirkman USAAF +
Sgt J J Schneit USAAF +

Took off LG 86, one of nine Mitchells detailed to attack an enemy convoy in the harbour. The aircraft was hit by flak over the target and blew up. All are commemorated on the Tablets of the Missing in the North Africa American Cemetery, Carthage.

---

24 Aug 1942 159 Sqn Liberator II AL537   S Op: Tobruk

F/Sgt F D Hamilton-Wilkes +
F/Sgt L N Owen +
F/Sgt L M Petersen +
Sgt R McCulloch +
Sgt D B Crabb +
Sgt D T B Williams +
Sgt D T Jones +
Sgt A M Temple +

Took off St Jean, detailed to bomb the harbour and shipping at Tobruk. Hit by flak, the aircraft was seen losing height with smoke and debris coming from the aircraft. All save Sgt Jones (buried at Knightsbridge War Cemetery, Acroma) are commemorated on the Alamein Memorial.

---

25 Aug 1942 1 OADU Wellington IC HX631 Delivery Flight

P/O J T Hutton
Crew

Took off Gibraltar for Bathhurst, but force landed on the coast of Rio de Oro after both engines ran roughly, and ripped wing fabric meant higher fuel consumption. The crew were presumably interned.

25-26 Aug 1942	**70 Sqn** S/Ldr E B Panter P/O L D Cox Sgt B A Brooke RAAF Sgt C V N Shawyer LAC L F R Halford Sgt I J Morgan	**Wellington IC** pow pow pow pow pow pow	**DV514 U**	**Op: Battle Area**

Took off 2210-2240, LG 86, to seek out targets of opportunity over the battle area. The aircraft was shot down by a night fighter, crashing in flames, but all bailed out successfully. S/Ldr Panter was wounded.

26 Aug 1942	**1 OADU** F/Sgt McWilliams Crew	**Wellington IC**	**HX579**	**Delivery Flight**

The accident card says six killed, but the pilot is not on the CWGC Register. AHB cannot help.

27 Aug 1942	**21 Sqn SAAF**	**Baltimore II**	**AH122**	**Training**

Took off Zwartkop, South Africa, on a training flight, but crash-landed on return and reduced to spares. SOC 1.1.47 by inventory entry.

	1 OADU P/O A M Leigh RCAF P/O K A W Morris P/O L R Smith P/O E J Scott Sgt T R W Smith P/O E E Wright	**Wellington IC** int int int int int int	**HD967**	**Delivery Flight**

Took off Portreath for Gibraltar, but bad weather prevented a landing there. The aircraft force-landed on a beach on the island of Santa Lucia, off Tavira, Portugal. The crew were briefly interned.

28 Aug 1942	**15 Sqn SAAF**	**Blenheim V**	**BA149**	**Unknown**

Crashed on landing, Alexandria/Maryut. NFD.

	15 Sqn SAAF Lt N B Boyd SAAF Lt L A Carnovski SAAF Air Sgt F G Olivier SAAF	**Blenheim V** + + +	**BA309 L**	**Op: Supply Train**

Took off 1410, Gianaclis, detailed to carry out a low-level attack on a supply train 73km W of Mersa Matruh. Badly damaged by return fire from two flat-bed trucks attached to the train, the aircraft crashed with an engine on fire 4km from the scene of the attack. All are commemorated on the Alamein Memorial.

	15 Sqn SAAF Maj G K Jones SAAF Lt B Slome SAAF Air Sgt A G Hipkin SAAF	**Blenheim V**	**BA407 O**	**Op: Supply Train**

Took off 1410, Gianaclis, detailed as above, and badly damaged by fire from the flat-bed trucks. With the undercarriage shot away the aircraft crash-landed at Gianaclis on return at 1822. DBR.

	1 OADU F/L G H M Riddell F/Lt J D Willis P/O G S Bishop P/O R C Spooner Sgt D M Leitch LAC W J Killick	**Wellington IC** inj + + +	**T2545**	**Ferry Flight**

Took off Bathhurst for Gibraltar, but shot down in international waters off Rabat, Morocco, by French fighters. F/Lt Willis was a member of 42 Sqn and LAC Killick an armourer.

	1 OADU Sgt M H Riddell Sgt L Sutherland P/O E Whittaker Sgt G A Taylor Sgt R Webber Sgt C W Buchner RCAF	**Wellington IC** + + + + int +	**HX566**	**Delivery Flight**

Took off Portreath 0700 for Gibraltar. Off course, the aircraft hit a hill in mist between Tarifa and Algeciras. Sgt Webber was rescued by soldiers from a Spanish coastal battery and spent six weeks in hospital. He was released from internment on 25 December. The dead are buried in Gibraltar (North Front) Cemetery.

	RAF Takoradi P/O R J Purser Sgt P W Hearne RAAF F/Sgt J W Mortimer	**Blenheim V** + + +	**BA531**	**Delivery Flight**

Took off 1430 Takoradi, but at 1515 spun into the ground out of cloud 4km W of Saltpond, 3km N of Brazzi, Gold Coast. All are buried in Takoradi European Cemetery.

29 Aug 1942 — **45 Sqn** — **Blenheim IV** — **Z6156** — **Communication flight**
F/Lt L F Penny
Sgt J A H Kirkpatrick RCAF — inj
Sgt G George — inj

Took off Habbaniyahh/Dhibban, detailed to transport a British delegation from Mosul to meet Soviet officials at Tiflis, Georgia. One of the engines caught fire on the return flight, the Blenheim lost height and belly-landed on rough ground near Nakhuda (near Lake Urmia), Iran.

29-30 Aug 1942 — **108 Sqn** — **Wellington IC** — **ES988 F** — **Op: Battle Area**
Sgt R G Evans RNZAF
Sgt W Chambers
Sgt K P Smith — +
Sgt Pinning
Crew

On take-off, LG 237, the aircraft swung slightly to port, the port wheel struck a glim lamp and burst. The aircraft went out of control, crashed and caught fire. The front gunner is buried in Heliopolis War Cemetery. One other crew member was injured.

30 Aug 1942 — **15 Sqn SAAF** — **Blenheim V** — **BA407 O** — **Op: Supply Train**
Maj G K Jones SAAF
Lt B Slome SAAF
Air Sgt A G Hipkin SAAF

Took off 1410, Gianaclis, detailed to carry out a low-level attack on a supply train 73km W of Mersa Matruh. The undercarriage was shot away by return fire from the flat-bed trucks, and the aircraft crash-landed on return to Alexandria/Maryut at 1822. DBR.

24 Sqn SAAF — **Boston III** — **AL78?** — **Op: Army Co-operation**
Capt J P Furstenburg SAAF — +
Lt R Cameron SAAF — +
Air Sgt P L Mathieu SAAF — +
Air Sgt V E M England SAAF — +

Took off LG 99, detailed to bomb and strafe Axis units along the Fuka-El Rahman road in the early hours of the morning. Shot down while strafing, probably by flak. All four of the crew are commemorated on the Alamein Memorial.

1 OADU — **Wellington IC** — **HD970** — **Ground**
While parked, hit by Hudson FH445, which was taking off, Bathhurst. DBR.

30-31 Aug 1942 — **76/454 Sqn** — **Halifax II** — **W7754 F** — **Op: Tobruk**
P/O G W Raymond
F/O D Earle
P/O R M Craine
Sgt H Coates
Sgt L Gill
Sgt W J Paine

Took off Fayid, detailed to bomb the harbour and shipping at Tobruk. Returning, the aircraft lost first the port outer engine and then, successively, the port and starboard inner engines. The aircraft crash-landed near Bilbeis and was DBF. The mid-upper gunner bailed out 5 mins before the aircraft crashed, and landed safely. The crew suffered minor injuries.

31 Aug 1942 — **55 Sqn** — **Baltimore II** — **AG694** — **Unknown**
Sgt J I Henderson
Sgt P T Fletcher
Sgt K Burns
Sgt J W Shaw

One engine cut on take-off from LG 86 and the aircraft was belly-landed. DBR.

55 Sqn — **Baltimore II** — **AG794** — **Ground**
Bombed-up but parked, AG794 received a direct hit in an air attack on LG 86 at 0430, and was completely destroyed.

70 Sqn — **Wellington IC** — **ES992 H** — **Op: Battle Area**
F/Lt R E Fawcett
Sgt F C McCrae
F/O W G Luty
Sgt F E Whitby
Sgt J F Matthews
Sgt A Colvin

Took off 0010, Abu Sueir, to seek out targets of opportunity in the battle area. The aircraft was twice attacked by a night fighter, the hydraulics being damaged and the port engine set on fire. The pilot belly-landed the aircraft within Allied lines, and the crew were picked up by the Household Cavalry and returned to base.

223 Sqn	**Baltimore III**	**AG881**	**Unknown**

Sgt J T Collyer
Sgt C A Sollas
Sgt K L Nattrass RAAF
Sgt J R Bertram

Took off LG 86. A dust storm blew up, and in attempting to land at the wrong airfield (LG 88), the aircraft crashed in the dispersal area.

223 Sqn	**Baltimore III**	**AG887**	**Op: Army Co-operation**

F/Sgt W E Wilson   +
Sgt F Fowler   +
Sgt G Cunningham   +
Sgt J Bryce   +

Took off 0653, LG 86, detailed to attack a concentration of some 3,000 motor vehicles at pin point 870.258. Hit by heavy flak over the target, the aircraft was last seen heading for the coast. Sgt Cunningham is commemorated on the Alamein Memorial; the others are buried in El Alamein War Cemetery.

31 Aug - 1 Sep 1942

108 Sqn	**Wellington IC**	**DV887 Y**	**Op: Tobruk**

Sgt N W Culblaith   pow
Sgt J C Darnley   pow
Sgt S A Lewis   pow
Sgt A Taylor   pow
Sgt J T Worrall   pow
Sgt W J Bennetts   pow

Took off 2240, LG 237, detailed to bomb the harbour and shipping at Tobruk. The starboard engine failed on leaving the target, and the aircraft eventually crash-landed 96km SW of Mersa Matruh. The crew was captured on 5 September, just S of Mersa Matruh.

1 Sep 1942

55 Sqn	**Baltimore II**	**AG828 H**	**Op: Army Co-operation**

F/Sgt R C Payne RAAF
Sgt L C Wheeler
Sgt G Sparrow
Sgt S F Howe

Took off 0707, LG 86, detailed to bomb the main German armoured force W of Deir el Ragil. Badly damaged by flak over El Daba the Baltimore crash-landed at LG 86 on return. DBR.

107 Sqn	**Blenheim V**	**BA541**	**Unknown**

Sgt R S Murdock RAAF   inj
Sgt W D Crawford
Sgt T Newman   inj

On take-off, Lydda, a tyre burst and the undercarriage collapsed. DBR.

223 Sqn	**Baltimore III**	**AG843**	**Op: Battle Area**

Sgt P W Carruthers   pow
F/Sgt C H Pierson RAAF   +
Sgt E W Hargreaves   +
Sgt R A Cherrington   +

Took off 1756, LG 86, to bomb Axis motor transport at El Alamein. Shot down by flak over the target c.1850 hrs, which blew the port engine off the aircraft. The three dead are commemorated on the Alamein Memorial.

24 Sqn SAAF	**Boston III**	**AL674**	**Op: Battle Area**

Lt J A Pocock SAAF   +
Lt A B Shuter SAAF   pow
Air Sgt B Katz SAAF   +
Air Sgt O Berkowitz SAAF   +

Took off 1725, LG 99, detailed to attack Axis motor transport at El Alamein. The aircraft's tail was blown off by flak 26km S of El Alamein, only the observer managing to bail out. The dead are commemorated on the Alamein Memorial.

1 OADU	**Wellington IC**	**DV733**	**Instrument Test**

Sgt D N Parkes   +
Sgt Wicks   inj
Sgt L D J Holmes   +
LAC J E Moor   +
LAC F Chaston   +
LAC W B Jones   +

Took off Kano and on approach to land lost height when the wheels were lowered, struck high-tension cables and trees, crashed, and caught fire. The pitot head cover was still on, and this may have contributed to the crash. The five dead are buried in Kano Township Christian Cemetery.

83rd Bomb Sqn	**B-25**	**Op: Battle Area**

Capt H P Croteau USAAF   +
2/Lt T F Archer USAAF   +
2/Lt I Biers USAAF   +
2/Lt R J McPartlin USAAF   +
S/Sgt R V Rakow USAAF   +
Sgt L G Anderson USAAF   +

Took off Deversoir, part of a mixed USAAF and SAAF force detailed to attack enemy forces in the Battle Area. Hit by flak and went down in flames with the tail assembly shot away. Lts Archer and McPartlin and Sgt Anderson are commemorated on the Tablets of the Missing at the North Africa American Cemetery, Carthage. The others were re-interred in the United States post-war. The crew were flying an 82nd Bombardment Squadron aircraft.

1-2 Sep 1942	**104 Sqn** Sgt H C Hunt RAAF Crew	**Wellington II**	**Z8369**	**Op: Battle Area** Took off 2255-2305, Kabrit, to seek out targets of opportunity in the battle area, but returned with the starboard engine feathered. The port engine also cut on approach to LG 237, and the aircraft stalled and crashed.

2 Sep 1942 — 1 OADU — Wellington IC — HD962 — Delivery Flight

Sgt A L Mayers — int
Sgt P D Sykes — int
Sgt E Carlton — int
Sgt G P Crockett — int
Sgt W Bruce — int
Sgt W P Heyworth — int

Took off Gibraltar for Bathurst, but the crew signalled that it was experiencing engine trouble. The port engine failed and the aircraft landed on the beach at Safi, French Morocco. The crew, having destroyed the aircraft, was interned.

2-3 Sep 1942 — 40 Sqn — Wellington IC — X9938 T — Op: Battle Area

Sgt V Baker — inj
P/O G J Nicholson — inj
F/Sgt R D Walker RAAF — +
Sgt A R Duncanson RAAF — +
Sgt R J Evans RAAF — +
Sgt J Roach — +

Took off Kabrit, detailed to attack targets of opportunity in the Alam Halfa area. Two 250lb bombs hung up and could not be dislodged, but on landing at LG 237 they fell and exploded under the aircraft. The dead are buried in Heliopolis War Cemetery.

3 Sep 1942 — 148 Sqn — Wellington IC — DV893 — Op: Battle Area

F/O J Clark RAAF
F/Sgt J Souden — inj
Sgt P Hall — inj
Sgt F Makin — inj
Sgt A R Downe RAAF — +
Sgt J M Scott

Took off 0035 LG 237. On return visibility was poor at base and aircraft crashed into high ground 2.5km from LG 224. Sgt Downe is buried in Heliopolis War Cemetery.

15 Sqn SAAF — Blenheim V — BA239 U — Op: Anti-submarine patrol

Lt J S Whittle SAAF
Lt A D Swart SAAF
Air Sgt A P Turnbull SAAF — inj

Took off Alexandria/Maryut, 0620, one of three Blenheims detailed to carry out an anti-submarine escort patrol over the Mediterranean convoy 'Roman' located at map reference 32° 10' N, 33° 20' E. The port engine of the aircraft cut and the pilot ditched at 0920 hrs, 40km N of Port Said. The crew were located and rescued at 0820 hrs the following day by HM Destroyer *Kelvin*.

24 Sqn SAAF — Boston III — Z2156 V — Op: Battle Area

Maj D U Nel SAAF
P/O B A Coleborne RAAF
Sgt W R Anderson SAAF
Sgt M A Smit SAAF

Took off 1410, LG 99, to attack Axis motor transport at El Alamein. A collision occurred when the No 2 aircraft in the formation (AL723) was blown by a flak burst into this, the lead aircraft. Z2156 had a big piece of the wing chewed off by a propeller; the wing of the second aircraft also impaled the fuselage just aft of the mid-gunner's position, leaving the tail almost chopped off. DBR.

24 Sqn SAAF — Boston III — AL723 Z — Op: Battle Area

Lt F A L de Marrillac SAAF
Lt D van der Byl SAAF — inj
Air Sgt R S Hoelson SAAF
Air Sgt A Brown SAAF

Took off 1410, LG 99, detailed as above, and collided with Z2156 as described above. Both aircraft, as one observer said, returned 'On a wing and a prayer'. DBR.

4 Sep 1942 — 1 OADU — Wellington IC — AD647 — Delivery Flight

Sgt B Palmer — +
Sgt F E Watkins — +
P/O W R Foxlee — +
Sgt L G Rees — +
P/O W G Storrier — +
Sgt E Barr — +

Took off Gibraltar for Bathurst, but failed to arrive. All are commemorated on the Runnymede Memorial.

5 Sep 1942	21 Sqn SAAF	Baltimore III	AH138	Relocation Flight

5 Sep 1942 — **21 Sqn SAAF** — **Baltimore III** — **AH138** — **Relocation Flight**

Capt D J Jacobs DFC SAAF +
Lt S D Davis SAAF +
F/Sgt R B Jennings SAAF +
Air Mech W Weekes SAAF +
F/Sgt P Metcalfe SAAF inj

In transit to the Middle East theatre of war, the aircraft spun into the ground near Lake Naivasha. The dead are buried in Gil Gil War Cemetery, Kenya.

5-6 Sep 1942 — **10/227 Sqn** — **Halifax II** — **W7679 C** — **Op: Heraklion**

S/Ldr A H Hacking +
F/O N H Turner RCAF +
Sgt J Bradley +
Sgt J W McFarlane +
F/Sgt W J Porritt RCAF +
F/Sgt A E Carson RAAF +

Took off Fayid, detailed to bomb Heraklion airfield. Seen going down with an outer engine on fire, and crashed S of Castelli Padiada on return. S/Ldr Hacking and F/Sgt Porritt are buried in Suda Bay War Cemetery; the others are commemorated on the Malta Memorial.

70 Sqn — **Wellington IC** — **Z8976 T** — **Op: Tobruk**

Sgt R S Carter
Sgt A D Bebbington
Sgt I Davies
P/O B E Johnston
Sgt J C Haldon
F/Sgt G Croisiau RCAF pow

Took off 1900-2105, Abu Sueir, detailed to bomb the harbour and shipping at Tobruk. The aircraft force-landed in Quattara Depression on return. The crew returned after one month, having walked back.

70 Sqn — **Wellington IC** — **BB477 W** — **Op: Tobruk**

F/Sgt J D Gordon RNZAF +
F/Sgt E D B Rae +
P/O R H McLelland +
Sgt D E Harrison +
Sgt S I Gallagher RNZAF +
Sgt J D Love +

Took off 1855-1940, Abu Sueir, detailed to attack the harbour and shipping at Tobruk, and brought down by flak near the target. The bodies of F/Sgt Rae and Sgt Gallagher were recovered and buried in Tobruk War Cemetery. The others are commemorated on the Alamein Memorial.

76/454 Sqn — **Halifax II** — **W1144 Q** — **Op: Heraklion**

F/Lt J Bryan +
Sgt E Robinson pow
Sgt A Potts +
Sgt C R Jones pow
Sgt W R Young pow
Sgt T P Blatch pow

Took off Fayid, to bomb Heraklion aerodrome. Attacked by a Bf 109 (Fedwebel Liebhold, III/JG27) and perhaps also hit by flak over target, and caught fire. Sgts Robinson and Blatch were injured. The dead are buried in Suda Bay War Cemetery. Sgt Blatch twice escaped from captivity, joining Polish partisans, but was recaptured.

---

6 Sep 1942 — **162 Sqn** — **Wellington IC** — **AD643** — **Ferry Flight**

S/Ldr D G Warren
P/O N R King
P/O R L McDonnell
Sgt R R P Rate
F/Lt R H C Burwell

Crashed on take-off, Bilbeis, for Wadi el Sham. DBR.

7-8 Sep 1942 — **37 Sqn** — **Wellington IC** — **DV457 W** — **Op: Tobruk**

Sgt H S Shepherd RNZAF
Sgt G W Brewster +
Sgt J H Stuffins
Sgt E C Hare
F/Sgt W T Crabb RCAF +
P/O R K Simmonds

Took off 1915-1936, Abu Sueir, detailed to bomb the harbour and shipping at Tobruk. On return flew into a hill, Gebel Abu Shama. The dead are commemorated on the Alamein Memorial.

37 Sqn — **Wellington IC** — **ES989 A** — **Op: Tobruk**

W/O 1 S A G Turner RCAF +
W/O 2 A B Cameron RCAF +
W/O 2 R B Clements RCAF +
F/Sgt R D MacDonald RAAF +
Sgt G D Rawbone +
Sgt P McIntyre +

Took off 1915-1936, Abu Sueir, detailed as above. FTR. All are commemorated on the Alamein Memorial.

70 Sqn F/O R C Elliott F/Sgt R F Smith P/O T C Prothero P/O F Grenfell Sgt W Wastney RNZAF Sgt T Bower	**Wellington IC**	**BB462 O**	**Op: Tobruk**

Took off 2040, Abu Sueir, detailed as above. Force-landed in the Qattara Depression, 45km W of Allied lines. The crew returned two days later, having been picked up by an advanced patrol.

8-9 Sep 1942

104 Sqn W/O C S Maxfield P/O J A G Anscomb F/Sgt J A Rowley Sgt J Williams Sgt S J Berry Sgt F Wood	**Wellington II**	**Z8374 Z** + + + + + +	**Op: Tobruk**

Took off 2110, Kabrit, to attack the harbour and shipping at Tobruk and shot down in flames. All but Sgt Wood (buried in Tobruk War Cemetery) are commemorated on the Alamein Memorial.

---

10 Sep 1942

15 Sqn SAAF Lt A D Donaldson SAAF 2/Lt M B Hall SAAF Air Sgt G M A van Rensburg SAAF	**Blenheim V** inj	**BA321 BC**	**Op: Anti-submarine patrol**

Took off 0615, Alexandria/Maryut, on an anti-submarine patrol for Fleet exercises off Port Said. At 0707 the port engine seized and the propeller flew off. The aircraft crash-landed on an island in the Nile Delta, 13km S of Damietta Mouth.

24 Sqn SAAF Lt R T E Morrison SAAF Air Sgt D W Reynolds SAAF	**Boston III**	**AL289** + +	**Training**

Took off LG Y/LG 207 (Qassassin), on night-flying training, but flew into the ground on approach to land at 2030 hrs, crashing 16km W of Ismailia. DBF. The crew are buried at Tel-el-Kebir War Cemetery.

---

11 Sep 1942

12 Sqn SAAF	**Boston III**	**AL797**	**Ground**

Nosewheel collapsed on landing, Hurghada. DBR in an air raid while under repair at 113 MU.

---

12 Sep 1942

1 OADU P/O J G Wynne P/O J A Thompson Crew	**Wellington IC**	**HD968**	**Delivery Flight**

Took off Portreath for Gibraltar, but after landing selected undercarriage up while taxiing. DBR.

1 OADU Sgt J R Morris Crew	**Wellington II**	**W5396**	**Delivery Flight**

On take-off, Luqa, for Egypt, the starboard tyre burst. On landing in Egypt the undercarriage collapsed.

---

13 Sep 1942

12 Sqn SAAF Capt A L Thackwray SAAF Lt L G Artus SAAF F/Sgt D C Henricksen SAAF Air Sgt N H H Osselton SAAF	**Boston III**	**41-19236 S**	**Op: Sidi Haneish**

Took off 0118, LG 99, one of eleven Bostons detailed to attack LGs 12 and 13 (Sidi Haneish North and South). Force-landed 3km from LG 99 when an engine failed on take-off.

13-14 Sep 1942

70 Sqn F/Lt E F W McCartan-Mooney Sgt C G Gaddes F/O N Spence RNZAF Sgt B J Landen Sgt B Prole F/Sgt C C Piper RNZAF	**Wellington IC**	**Z8787 R** pow pow pow pow pow pow	**Op: Tobruk**

Took off 1855-2130, Abu Sueir, to attack the harbour and shipping at Tobruk as part of a diversion to assist a combined forces operation. All were captured, but several attempted to escape. F/Lt McCartan-Mooney, F/O Spence and F/Sgt Piper were killed during a skirmish with an evening patrol on 18.9.42. They were buried 3km S of the 62km stone on the Sidi Barrani- Sollum road. F/O Spence's body was later recovered (now at Halfaya Sollum); the other two are commemorated on the Alamein Memorial.

70 Sqn	Wellington IC	Z9044 B	Op: Tobruk

P/O R B Muirhead	+
F/O P D Short	+
W/O M W Gilding	+
Sgt T A Oldale	evd
Sgt P G Burrell	+
Sgt C Owens	+

Took off 1855-2130, Abu Sueir, detailed to attack the harbour and shipping at Tobruk. On return the aircraft made a forced-landing and the crew started walking back. On 20 September they met with Sgt Frampton of 148 sqn (see 19-20 Sept). Exhausted, W/O Gilding and Sgts Burrell and Owens had to drop out, as later did P/O Muirhead and F/O Short, leaving Sgts Oldale and Frampton to make their way to Allied lines. The dead are commemorated on the Alamein Memorial.

70 Sqn	Wellington IC	BB462 G	Op: Tobruk

P/O M V Hodge	pow
G/Capt R Kellett DFC AFC	pow
P/O W R Duncan RNZAF	pow
P/O D F Bratchell	pow
Sgt D P Nilsson RNZAF	pow
Sgt R G Baker RNZAF	pow

Took off 1855-2130, Abu Sueir, detailed as above. One engine failed over the target and eventually the aircraft force-landed in the desert behind enemy lines. The crew evaded capture until 20 September. G/Capt Kellett, flying as second pilot, was Senior Air Staff Officer, 205 Group.

108 Sqn	Wellington IC	HF864 S	Op: Tobruk

P/O E R Wardley	pow
Sgt L S Cowell	pow
P/O F P N Dyer	pow
W/O C T Ord	pow
Sgt F Buckley	pow
Sgt H Hellewell	pow

Took off 2000, LG 237, detailed as above. FTR. A message was received stating the aircraft was returning with engine trouble. W/O Ord died when the Italian ship *Scillin* was torpedoed by a RN submarine on 14 November, and is commemorated on the Alamein Memorial.

81st Bomb Sqn	B-25C	41-12855	Op: Sidi Haneish

Capt J G Freeland USAAF	+
1/Lt H B Eanes USAAF	+
1/Lt A E Malmstrom USAAF	+
Sgt C E Meinhardt USAAF	
Sgt W S Durfee USAAF	

Took off Deversoir to attack LG101, Sidi Haneish. Shot down over Tobruk. Sgts Meinhardt and Durfee were presumably taken prisoner.

81st Bomb Sqn	B-25C	41-13849	Op: Sidi Haneish

1/Lt H F Belobraidich USAAF	+
1/Lt L B Hicks USAAF	pow
2/Lt E F Jobb USAAF	pow
2/Lt O B Reeves USAAF	+
Sgt C H Fry RCAF	+
Sgt L J Shore USAAF	+

Took off Deversoir, detailed as above. Shot down over Tobruk. Lts Belobraidich and Reeves, and Sgt Shore are commemorated on the Tablets of the Missing at the North Africa American Cemetery, Carthage. Sgt Fry is comemorated on the Alamein Memorial.

81st Bomb Sqn	B-25D	41-29681	Op: Sidi Haneish

Col C G Goodrich USAAF	pow
2/Lt R G Ries USAAF	pow
1/Lt K H Young USAAF	+
Sgt H Reid RCAF	pow
Sgt J E Venink USAAF	
Maj H B Houston USAAF	pow

Took off Deversoir, detailed as above, and also shot down over Tobruk. Major Houston, the Group Intelligence Officer, was flying as an observer. Sgt Venink's fate is not known. (Note: prior to the operation Col Goodrich had protested against the use of B-25s at night because of the flames given off by their exhausts. He was overruled, but following this night's losses a ban was imposed.)

82nd Bomb Sqn	B-25C	41-12858	Op: Sidi Haneish

1/Lt L P Redburn USAAF	pow
2/Lt W J Thomas II USAAF	+
2/Lt C A Horr USAAF	+
Sgt K W Haglund RCAF	+
Sgt E L Delaney USAAF	+

Took off Deversoir, 0200, detailed as above, and shot down by flak during the bombing run. 2/Lt Thomas bailed out, but died of burns and was buried by the Germans in the British cemetery at Mersa Matruh. He and the others, including Sgt Haglund, an American citizen serving in the RCAF, were re-interred in the United States post-war, Sgt Haglund in Keokuk National Cemetery, Iowa.

14-15 Sep 1942	70 Sqn	Wellington IC	HX525	Op: Tobruk

Force-landed in the desert on return. NFD.

15 Sep 1942	**223 Sqn** F/Sgt R G Hampson P/O N R Calcutt RAAF Sgt Sandery Sgt W Price	**Baltimore II**	**AG810**	**Training**

Took off LG 86, but on landing at LG 207/LG Y (Qassassin) the aircraft turned nose over tail when the brakes were applied too heavily.

16 Sep 1942 · **55 Sqn** · **Baltimore III** · **AG787** · **Training**
Took off LG 86, on a training flight, but crashed in a forced landing, 31'08N:33'15E.

1 OADU · P/O T G Leggett · Sgt Hatfield · **Wellington IC** · **DV661** · **Delivery Flight**
Took off Portreath for Gibraltar, but an engine cut, and the aircraft ditched 24km W of the Scillies. AM 1180 gives the date as 19 September – and the serial as BM661.

345th Bomb Sqn · **B-24D** · **41-11883** · **Ground**
Reduced to salvage after non-battle damage. NFD.

17 Sep 1942 · **Middle East** · **Wellington II** · **W5571** · **Unknown**
Form AM78 says lost this day, FB. NFD. If in squadron service, the aircraft would have been with 104 Squadron.

17-18 Sep 1942 · **104 Sqn** · F/O B G Johnston RCAF · Crew · **Wellington II** · **Z8582 F** · **Op: Tobruk**
Took off Kabrit. An engine cut out on return and force-landed at Kom Hamada, approximately 3km S of El Hadeen. DBR.

18 Sep 1942 · **14 Sqn** · **Blenheim IV** · **Z5767** · **Unknown**
SOC. NFD.

223 Sqn · F/Sgt W D J H Ball + · Sgt J A Bradshaw + · Sgt T Crankshaw + · Sgt A Smith + · Sgt C A Sollas + · **Baltimore III** · **AG893** · **Flying Display**
Took off LG 86, one of 16 aircraft of 223 Sqn taking part in a large light bomber demonstration over Cairo, but collided in formation with another squadron aircraft and lost its tail. All are buried in El Alamein War Cemetery.

18-19 Sep 1942 · **37 Sqn** · Sgt A B Greenwood · Sgt L B Franich RNZAF · Crew · **Wellington IC** · **AD636** · **Op: Tobruk**
Took off 1850, Abu Sueir. Landed heavily, tyre burst, aircraft swung, and the undercarriage collapsed.

37 Sqn · F/Lt T R Nelson pow · Sgt Brown pow · Sgt Goldsworthy pow · Sgt A V Rimes pow · Sgt Barber pow · F/Sgt Gordon RCAF pow · **Wellington IC** · **HD963 Q** · **Op: Tobruk**
Took off c.1845, Abu Sueir. The port engine failed en route to Tobruk and caught fire. All bailed out save the pilot, who crash-landed the aircraft, which was DBF. F/Lt Nelson walked E and was captured trying to cross battle lines near El Alamein on 7 October.

19-20 Sep 1942 · **108 Sqn** · W/Cdr R H Maw DFC pow · Sgt N R Milsom pow · Sgt P Greenstein pow · Sgt G Bennett pow · Sgt R L Berry pow · Sgt B E Doublard pow · **Wellington IC** · **DV872 W** · **Op: Tobruk**
Took off 2010, LG 237, detailed to attack Tobruk. FTR. An SOS was picked up by another aircraft. Sgt Bennett was captured on 23 September, but the date of capture of the others is not known.

	148 Sqn	**Wellington IC**	**HF840 B**	**Op: Tobruk**

148 Sqn   **Wellington IC**   **HF840 B**   **Op: Tobruk**
Sgt H L Curtois — pow
Sgt T B Prosser — pow
Sgt A K Newnes de Souza — pow
Sgt A T Coles — pow
Sgt A E Frampton — evd
Sgt J H T Bullock RAAF — pow

Took off 2031, LG 237, detailed to attack Tobruk. On return the aircraft crashed in the desert 124km S of Mersa Matruh. On 28th, Sgt Frampton was reported safe after having walked back with a member of a 70 Sqn crew (see Z9044 on 13-14 Sept for details).

20 Sep 1942   **24 Sqn SAAF**   **Boston III**   **AL778**   **Unknown**
SOC. NFD.

20-21 Sep 1942   **70 Sqn**   **Wellington IC**   **DV546 U**   **Op: Tobruk**
F/Sgt W M Marvin — +
Sgt E Benning — +
Sgt J H W Livesey — +
Sgt R G Thomlinson — +
Sgt J E Thomas — +
Sgt A F Thomas — +

Took off 2105-2130, Abu Sueir, detailed to attack Tobruk, but FTR. Several crews reported a possible aircraft burning on the ground in the target area. All are commemorated on Alamein Memorial.

22 Sep 1942   **15 Sqn SAAF**   **Blenheim IV**   **T2349**   **Op: Escort**
Lt B E G MacLeod SAAF
Lt M W S Priday SAAF — inj
Air Sgt H H Lewis SAAF

Took off 0645, Kufra, as fighter escort to two Bombays evacuating casualties to LG 207/LG Y Qassassin, but crashed through engine failure at 0820 hrs, approximate position Base 300°/53km, Kufra. It was reported that the abandoned Blenheim was destroyed on the 27th by an enemy reconnaissance aircraft that appeared over the oasis at 1525 hrs.

24 Sep 1942   **24 Sqn SAAF**   **Boston III**   **Z2248**   **Training**
Capt S K Blake SAAF

Took off LG Z/LG 208 (Mahsma), on a solo night training flight doing circuits and landings. The Boston's port engine caught fire immediately after take-off and since the pilot was at too low an altitude to bail out he did a quick circuit to attempt a landing on the flare path. On final approach the port wing burnt off, but having jettisoned his hood for a rapid escape, Capt Blake stuck his back into the slipstream and pulled the ripcord. His parachute barely opened before he hit the ground, and he almost fell into the burning aircraft, but survived.

1 OADU   **Wellington II**   **Z8534**   **Delivery Flight**
Swung and crashed on take-off, Waterloo, Sierra Leone.

1 OADU   **Wellington IC**   **HX643**   **Delivery Flight**
Sgt T J Large
Crew

As the aircraft was taking off at Takoradi, Nigeria, the pilot noticed the airspeed indicator was not registering. He tried to abort the take-off, but on reaching the aerodrome boundary had to swing the aircraft and the undercarriage collapsed.

25 Sep 1942   **223 Sqn**   **Baltimore II**   **AG814**   **Training**
Sgt A M Kettle RAAF — +
Sgt J R Bannister RAAF — +
Sgt N R Buchanan RAAF — +
Sgt G H Patterson — +

Crashed on take-off, 1520, LG 86 and DBF. All of the crew are buried in El Alamein War Cemetery. The cause was thought to be fuel starvation of the engines, perhaps because of pilot error.

25-26 Sep 1942   **40 Sqn**   **Wellington IC**   **HF846 P**   **Op: Tobruk**
F/Sgt G F Langham RNZAF — +
F/O D A Adams, MiD RNZAF — +
Sgt J M Welsh RNZAF — +

Took off 2001, Shallufa, detailed to bomb Tobruk. Seen to crash 1.5km SW of LG 146, El Gubbi. All are commemorated on the Alamein Memorial.

Sgt R H Cook RNZAF +
Sgt M G Smart RAAF +
Sgt W G J Price +

27-28 Sep 1942	**148 Sqn**	**Wellington IC**	**DV520 O**	**Op: Tobruk**

Sgt N G Beadle +
F/Sgt T N Thomas RAAF +
W/O2 R J Williams RCAF +
Sgt J Weir +
Sgt J Noble +
Sgt J M S Moir +

Took off 2010, LG 237, detailed to attack Tobruk. FTR.
All are commemorated on the Alamein Memorial.

24 Sqn SAAF   **Boston III**   **Z2288**   **Op: Sidi Haneish**

Took off between 2140 and 2215, LG 99, one of nine Bostons
detailed to make a night attack on LGs 101 and 13 (Sidi
Haneish South). One of three which attacked LG 101,
Z2288 was badly damaged by flak and SOC on return.

24 Sqn SAAF   **Boston III**   **AL785 S**   **Op: Sidi Haneish**

Lt G Cohen SAAF +
Lt J H Arangies SAAF pow
Air Sgt J C van Eck SAAF +
Air Sgt I I Kreel SAAF pow

Took off and detailed as above. One of four which
attacked LG 13 (Sidi Haneish South), AL785 was hit by
flak over the target and went down in flames at 2309. The
pilot is buried in El Alamein War Cemetery, and Air Sgt
van Eck commemorated on the Alamein Memorial.

28 Sep 1942	**24 Sqn SAAF**	**Boston III**	**AL791**	**Op: Sid Haneish**

Took off, detailed to attack LG 13 (Sidi Haneish South) FTR,
and presumed shot down by flak, LG 13. No records seem
to survive concerning this day's operations, and AHB
cannot help. It is assumed the crew survived, since no
SAAF deaths with this date appear in the CWGC Registers.

1 OADU   **Wellington IC**   **HX676**   **Delivery Flight**

Sgt F A McClellan RCAF inj
Sgt J Huggler
Sgt C Baynton
Sgt S Jerram RNZAF
Sgt W R Burton RCAF
Sgt M Beneteau RCAF

Took off Maidugiri for El Ghanya, but ran out of fuel and
crash-landed between Fort Lamy and Geneina. The crew
made their way, with local assistance, to the French base
at Fort Lamy.

28-29 Sep 1942	**70 Sqn**	**Wellington IC**	**Z1041 W**	**Op: Tobruk**

Sgt W Goody
Sgt B J Frew
F/O W A Hockney
P/O V R Burt
Sgt S Payne
Sgt L H Edinburgh

Took off 2230, Abu Sueir, detailed to attack Tobruk.
Crash-landed 48km S of Tobruk after sending out an
SOS. NFD, but the crew were presumably rescued,
uninjured.

148 Sqn   **Wellington IC**   **HD947**   **Op: Tobruk**

P/O S C Pearse +
F/Sgt R H Gresham +
F/Sgt A H Threlfall +
F/Sgt D A Mitchell +
W/O2 D D Miller RCAF +
F/Sgt R M G Banbury RAAF +

Took off 2235, LG 237, detailed to attack Tobruk. FTR.
All are commemorated on the Alamein Memorial.

29 Sep 1942	**434th Bomb Sqn**	**B-25**	**Training Flight**

Lt P D Bradshaw USAAF
2/Lt M L Dalton USAAF
1/Lt J P Wright USAAF
S/Sgt G H McCartney USAAF
Passenger: 1/Lt R L Flory USAAF

Took off Ismailia for a practice bombing flight, but on
return one of the main undercarriage wheels could not
be lowered and the crew was ordered to bail out.

| 29-30 Sep 1942 | 462 Sqn F/Lt J C Murray RNZAF F/Sgt R Jenkyn Sgt B Bevan Sgt R Walton Sgt S Oakford F/Sgt E M Cottrell | Halifax II | W1176 Z | Op: Tobruk |

Took off 2119, Fayid, detailed to bomb the harbour and shipping at Tobruk. The port engines failed successively and the aircraft crash-landed at 2123 about 8km NW of Fayid.

| | 462 Sqn W/O D W O'Driscoll RCAF Sgt J Ellyatt Passengers: 2/Lt Ferguson Cpl A Gardiner AC2 H Byrne | Halifax II inj | W7672 E | Air Test |

Took off 1215, Fayid, on an air test. The port outer engine had to be feathered, and this resulted in the wing dropping, and the aircraft crash-landed with the undercarriage retracted. DBF. The pilot broke his leg on jumping from the aircraft. Sgt Ellyatt, an engine fitter, was acting as Flight Engineer.

Chapter 8

El Alamein
October to November 1942

Following his loss at Alam el Halfa, it was apparent to Field Marshal Rommel that his goal of a drive to the Suez Canal was no longer practicable, and that with his growing inferiority in men and materiel, as well as his overstretched supply lines, the best he could hope for was to remain where he was. He therefore set about strengthening his defences, completing the laying down of a massive minefield, stretching the full distance from the coast to the Qattara Depression, and disposing of his forces, German and Italian, in such a way as to ensure that any attempted attack would meet an integrated defence, with infantry, artillery and tanks working in close coordination.

General Montgomery, however, fully informed by aerial reconnaissance of the disposition of the enemy forces, planned an offensive on lines different from any hitherto undertaken by either side in the Desert War so far. The grand sweep around the flank by armoured forces was not practical, given the Axis defences, so the general plan of the coming battle was to involve British infantry units forcing two corridors through the Axis minefields, and armoured units then passing through the Axis front lines to hold off the Axis tank units while the infantry eradicated the enemy infantry holding the forward positions. The main thrust was to be in the north, where two corridors through the minefields were to be cleared. Further south, a third corridor was to be created, but there the attack was not to be pressed too far, the 7th Armoured Division, which was to hold off the panzer units, being required to keep itself in readiness for the climactic breakthrough.

Where General Montgomery had ample evidence of what was going on on the Axis side, General Stumme, who had taken command of Axis forces while Rommel returned to Germany to recover his health, had little to go on. The Allied aerial superiority was so complete that no adequate picture of Allied movements was possible, in addition to which an elaborate plan of deception was put into operation, the result being that when the Eighth Army did attack, on the evening of 23rd October, the Axis high command had no clear sense of where the main thrust would come.

How valuable this was became clear on the first night of the offensive, which began with a massive artillery bombardment from about 1,000 guns – an awe-inspiring experience for anyone who heard and saw it, including the bomber crews overhead at the time. For while behind this barrage, intensified by air bombardment, 10th Corps, in the north, was painstakingly forcing two corridors through the enemy minefields, to the south 13th Corps, forcing a single corridor, was achieving just the success that General Montgomery wanted, holding a German panzer division in place until the night of the 26th.

The progress of the battle was slow, but sure. Gradually, salients were enlarged, and in the early hours of 2nd November, the final phase of the battle, which carried the codename *Supercharge*, began. In the face of fierce resistance, and strong anti-tank screens, progress was slow, but gradually, as General Montgomery had foreseen, Rommel's strength was crumbling, and on 3rd November there was evidence that the Axis forces were preparing a withdrawal. Early the next morning (4th November), the 5th Indian Brigade broke through, and the Axis forces began a wholesale retreat. The battle of El Alamein was won, and with it, ultimately, the war in North Africa.

The cost of the battle, in human as well as materiel terms, had been heavy, as General Montgomery had warned that it would be. The total Axis losses during the battle were some 59,000 killed, wounded and captured. The Eighth Army lost about 13,500. But at that cost the Axis resistance was broken, irremediably, so far as the war in the Western Desert was concerned. The Eighth Army began an advance which was to take it eventually to Tunisia, where with the American, British and French armies driving through from Algeria, the Afrika Corps, and its Italian equivalent, were finally to be destroyed.

In the lead-up to the Battle of El Alamein, the night bomber force, now consisting of six squadrons of Wellingtons, one of Liberators and one of Halifaxes, continued its nightly bombing of Tobruk, though facing constantly augmented anti-aircraft defences. Since the beginning of night bombing in North Africa, the method of attack had been that employed by Bomber Command early in the war, but abandoned in favour of concentration of force: namely, crews attacking individually over an extended period, in order to maximize disruption on the ground. With attacks on Tobruk proving increasingly costly, the decision was taken to introduce a 'blitz period' during which all crews would attack. First implemented on 5th October, the new technique proved highly successful, the 205 Group report on the raid noting that 'owing to the blitz tactics several aircraft (of the 39 operating) appear to have been entirely unmolested'. 205 Group was not only attacking Tobruk, however, but also devoting its attention increasingly to targets closer to the Axis front line, such as troop concentrations, the tank repair depot at Mersa Matruh, and landing grounds.

For the day bomber units, now comprising two squadrons of Bostons, and four of Baltimores, along with two recently re-equipped, 15 Squadron SAAF with Bisleys or Blenheim Vs and 14 Squadron with Marauders, the task remained that of close support of ground forces, attacking troop concentrations, transport, landing grounds and armoured vehicles. When the Battle of El Alamein began, however, the night bomber units were also allocated a close support role, roving over the battlefield looking for troop concentrations, transports, armoured vehicles and other targets of opportunity. Often flying two sorties a night, and again assisted by flare-dropping Albacores of the Fleet Air Arm, the Wellingtons played a significant part in disrupting the Axis defences, and keeping the German and Italian troops constantly wondering whether they were going to be illuminated by flares and then bombed. The task was rewarding, but not without risk, for in addition to the ever-present flak, German night fighters were active, and several crews were shot down by them.

30 Sep - 1 Oct 1942	37 Sqn Sgt M Spinley RNZAF Sgt E J Measures Sgt C M Zagerman Sgt E T Jordan Sgt C C Finch Sgt S Atkinson	Wellington IC		HD969 **Op: Tobruk** Took off 2108, Abu Sueir, detailed as above. On return flew into ground descending in cloud, 28km S of Wadi Natrun. DBF. Three of the crew were slightly injured.
	104 Sqn F/Sgt H C Hunt RAAF W/O2 R Sillis RCAF P/O W N Ramage Sgt J J Bowles Sgt J W Flint F/Sgt T L F Bailey RAAF	Wellington II	+ + + + + +	Z8514 **Op: Tobruk** Took off 2115, Kabrit, detailed to bomb Tobruk. On return an engine cut and the second engine failed on approach to LG 237. All are commemorated on the Alamein Memorial.
	148 Sqn F/Sgt T H Billingham F/Sgt S A Conibear Sgt P H Wood F/Sgt G J Matheson RAAF F/Sgt A MacLean RAAF F/Sgt L J LaBarge RCAF	Wellington IC	+ + + + + +	HF848 **Op: Tobruk** Took off 2130, LG 237, detailed as above. FTR. F/Sgt Billingham is buried in Halfaya Sollum War Cemetery, the others in Knightsbridge War Cemetery, Acroma.
2-3 Oct 1942	**Special Duties Flight** F/O E R Ridgeway P/O F A Wood P/O Mansfield Sgt Timlin F/Sgt N F T Goldsmith	Wellington IC	 +	X9734 **Op: Supply Dropping** Took off LG 237 (?) to drop supplies to partisans on Crete. On return the port engine failed, the aircraft lost height and eventually force-landed in the sea. The crew had difficulty pulling the unconscious or dead rear gunner through the escape hatch, and the aircraft sank. The survivors were in their dinghy for 43 hours in bad weather and with few rations before being rescued by MTB 268. F/Sgt Goldsmith, whom the CWGC describe as being of 159 Sqn, is commemorated on the Alamein Memorial.
3 Oct 1942	**21 Sqn SAAF** 2/Lt J P Zahn SAAF	Baltimore III	+	AH107 **Training** Took off LG 207/LG Y (Qassassin), on a solo night-flying training flight. Flew into the ground at 0400 hrs about 8km from LG Y. 2/Lt Zahn is buried at Tel-el-Kebir War Cemetery.
	1 OADU Sgt D H Struthers Sgt A S H Powell Sgt L Cooper Sgt R H MacIntyre Sgt W E Morton Sgt W S Shewell RCAF	Wellington II	int + int + int int	W5377 **Delivery Flight** Took off Gibraltar for Bathhurst, but ditched 3km off Cape Ghir, near Agadir, French Morocco. Sgts Powell and Macintyre died in the crash, and Sgt Shewell was injured. They were rescued by a Spanish fishing boat but intercepted by a French patrol boat and interned until mid-December. The dead are commemorated on the Runnymede Memorial.

	1 OADU	Wellington IC	HX597	Delivery Flight
	Sgt T P G Griffin	int		
	Sgt H Sansome	+		
	Sgt A O Evans	int		
	Sgt W D Pickin	int		
	Sgt A K Scarisbrick	int		
	Sgt S D Crick	int		

Took off Gibraltar for Bathurst, but ditched 16km off Fuenteventura, Canary Islands, and sank in 30 seconds. Sgt Sansome drowned and the rest of the crew spent two hours in their dinghy before rescue by a Spanish fishing boat. Sgt Scarisbrick was injured, and spent three months in a Spanish hospital. Sgt Sansome is commemorated on the Malta Memorial.

5-6 Oct 1942	**148 Sqn**	**Wellington IC**	**DV562 S**	**Op: Tobruk**
	Sgt W N Fethers RAAF	pow		
	Sgt J Murphy	pow		
	Sgt W Maskell	pow		
	Sgt J Vincent	pow		
	Sgt R A Whitfield RAAF	pow		
	Sgt J A Carpenter	pow		

Took off 1930, LG 237, detailed as above. FTR. A signal was received: 'Crashing near Sollum'.

	148 Sqn	**Wellington IC**	**DV649 Y**	**Op: Tobruk**
	F/Sgt H S Rodger RNZAF	+		
	Sgt I H Ridge	+		
	F/Sgt D G Chacksfield	+		
	Sgt R T Eria RNZAF	+		
	Sgt L Fitzgerald	+		
	Sgt T R Elliott	+		

Took off 1919, LG 237, detailed to attack Tobruk. FTR. The aircraft crashed in the Gambut area, where the remains of F/Sgt Chacksfield were later found and buried (grave since lost). All are commemorated on the Alamein Memorial.

6 Oct 1942	**55 Sqn**	**Baltimore II**	**AG769 B**	**Op: El Daba**
	P/O R D M Evers			
	W/O H R Callender RNZAF	pow		
	Sgt J Hall	pow		
	Sgt R J Wilson	pow		

Took off 1655, LG 86, one of twelve Baltimores detailed to bomb a petrol dump 4km E of El Daba railway station. Hit over the target by intense and accurate flak the aircraft shed its starboard propeller and lost revolutions from the port engine. Losing height, the pilot ordered the crew to bail out, but unable to do so himself because the cockpit hatch had jammed, the pilot belly-landed under fire between the front lines. He hid under the wing, to be eventually rescued by 2nd South African Army AFVs under cover of a smoke screen. An attempt was made at night to recover the aircraft by a tank transporter, but enemy fire proved too intense and the aircraft was finally destroyed.

	55 Sqn	**Baltimore II**	**AG807 P**	**Op: El Daba**
	F/Lt D H Hannah RAAF			
	Sgt J F Graham			
	Sgt J Slater			
	Sgt A J Coombes	+		

Took off 1655, LG 86, detailed as above, and also crippled by flak over the target. With the port engine stopped, the pilot managed to make the safety of the Allied lines and order the crew to bail out. Only Sgts Slater and Coombes heard the order, Sgt Graham remaining with the aircraft which the pilot safely belly-landed 1km E of El Alamein. Sgt Coombes landed in the Allied lines but was killed and is buried the El Alamein War Cemetery.

	55 Sqn	**Baltimore II**	**AG811 Z**	**Op: El Daba**
	F/Lt A Ward	+		
	F/O H W Tracy	+		
	Sgt D L Crowhurst	+		
	Sgt R Weymouth	+		

Took off 1655, LG 86, detailed as above, and likewise crippled by flak over the target. While attempting a recorded by forced landing the Baltimore crashed and blew up. All of the crew are buried in El Alamein War Cemetery. The pilot and observer are incorrectly recorded by the CWGC as being killed on the 5th.

	1 OADU	**Wellington IC**	**HE105**	**Delivery Flight**
	F/O J J Wright	+		
	Sgt S Henney	+		
	F/O J O B Wraith	+		
	Sgt G S A Thomson	+		
	Sgt R S Manktelow	+		

Took off Gibraltar for Bathhurst but the aircraft turned at 500ft and flew into a cliff face. All are commemorated on the Gibraltar Memorial.

7 Oct 1942	Middle East	Baltimore II	AG760 Missing. NFD.	Unknown
	223 Sqn	Baltimore II	AG761 Lost. NFD.	Unknown

7-8 Oct 1942 — **40 Sqn** — **Wellington IC** — **DV504 G** — **Op: Tobruk**

F/Sgt R L Spence RCAF	evd
Sgt K Bowhill	pow
Sgt C C Hill RCAF	pow
Sgt J K Wood RAAF	evd
Sgt E A Linforth	pow
Sgt A W Butteriss	pow

Took off Kabrit, 2240, detailed to bomb Tobruk. On the return flight an engine failed, and the crew bailed out. They set out E, although all but Spence and Wood, who reached Allied lines after 20 days in the desert, had to abandon the attempt through exhaustion or injury.

8 Oct 1942 — **1445 Transit FLt** — **Halifax II** — **DT493** — **Ferry Flight**

F/Lt Stagner	int
1st Off. C P Wilson	int
F/O H W McGill	int
P/O Ewart	int
Sgt A E Nicholls	int
F/Lt G W McPherson	int
Sgt H S Osborne	int

Took off, Lyneham, for Gibraltar, but force-landed at Azambuja, near Lisbon, and burnt by the crew. They were only briefly interned.

9 Oct 1942 — **223 Sqn** — **Baltimore II** — **AG975** — **Op: Qotafiyah**

Sgt B V Ekbery	pow
Sgt W E Bates	pow
Sgt E R Moss	pow
Sgt W R Johnstone	pow

Took off 1605, LG 86, to bomb Qotafiyah II (LG 104). Almost certainly hit by flak over the target, five minutes later this aircraft broke formation, and was last seen near the coast.

1 OADU — **Wellington IC** — **HX680** — **Delivery Flight**

P/O E H Whitehouse	int
F/O W Graham	int
F/O C C Maple RCAF	int
Sgt C G Phinney RCAF	int
Sgt F Dykes	int
Passengers:	
Cpl S A Wheeler	int
AC1 R Gardner	int

Took off Portreath, for Gibraltar. The radio was unserviceable, so no QDM could be obtained, while unforecast winds and haze made navigation difficult. The aircraft force-landed out of fuel on a beach at Zaven, near Archila, Spanish Morocco. The crew were released from internment on 7 February 1943. A Spanish Air Force pilot attempted to fly the Wellington off the beach but crashed, injuring himself. The passengers were serving with 24 Sqn.

9-10 Oct 1942 — **104 Sqn** — **Wellington II** — **Z8522 H** — **Op: Fuka**

F/Sgt E L Anderson RAAF	+
Sgt L J R Govett RAAF	+
Sgt A A C Peter RAAF	+
F/O A J Penman	+
Sgt M A Ball	+

Took off 2100, Kabrit, detailed to attack LGs 17 and 18 at Fuka. FTR. Nightfighters were active. All are commemorated on the Alamein Memorial.

10-11 Oct 1942 — **462 Sqn** — **Halifax II** — **W1183 M** — **Op: Maleme**

S/Ldr P G B Warner	
Sgt P A Gower	
F/Lt F T Collins	inj
Sgt A Watson	
Sgt G W Waddington	
Sgt R S Mortham	
Sgt R Wiltshire	

Took off 1912, Fayid, detailed to attack the aerodrome at Maleme. Struck in the nose by flak, seriously wounding the navigator, all electrical services in the forward fuselage were severed, and both outboard engines out of action. About to ditch, the pilot managed to restart the port outer engine and regain some height. When the engine failed again the aircraft force-landed 48km E of Mansura. For his courage in continuing to fulfil his duties despite severe injuries, F/Lt Collins was awarded an immediate DFC.

11 Oct 1942 — **223 Sqn** — **Baltimore III** — **AG964** — **Training**

Sgt F H Mason	

Took off LG 86, but on return stalled and crashed on landing, 1505.

11-12 Oct 1942	160 Sqn	Liberator II	AL603 T	Op: Convoy attack

160 Sqn — **Liberator II** — **AL603   T** — **Op: Convoy attack**

F/Sgt R E Brown
Sgt W W Dougan
Sgt E M Coe
Sgt F T S Powell
Sgt A Bain
Sgt S Crook
Sgt B J Moore
Sgt J Martin

Took off 1400, 'Field', to bomb a convoy in Suda Bay. The aircraft was attacked by a night fighter and the hydraulic tank was holed. No 1 engine cut on approach and No 2 began to splutter. The pilot was unable to go round again, so put the aircraft down, swung, and the undercarriage collapsed. DBR.

---

12 Oct 1942 — **15 Sqn SAAF** — **Blenheim V** — **BA497   H** — **Op: Rail traffic**

Lt C R Bruton-Simmonds SAAF   +
Lt W J du Plessis SAAF   +
F/Sgt R J Behrens SAAF   +

Took off 1340, Alexandria/Maryut, one of three aircraft, escorted by four Beaufighters, detailed to attack an east-bound train with 10 trucks, 93km W of Mersa Matruh. The formation encountered a Savoia-Marchetti SM.81 Pipistrello in the target area and near El Dwabis LG, where three more were seen. The SM.81 was forced down by machine gun fire but its upper gunner shot down BA497, which burst into flames on crashing. The Savoia was then bombed, receiving a direct hit from the leading Blenheim. All the crew are commemorated on the Alamein Memorial.

12-13 Oct 1942 — **70 Sqn** — **Wellington IC** — **DV570   M** — **Op: Tobruk**

Sgt S Fitton   pow
Sgt C W R MacFarquhar RNZAF   pow
Sgt H G Barnard   pow
Sgt S R Lowe   pow
Sgt G H Cross   pow
Sgt P F Cottle   pow

Took off 1825-1850, Abu Sueir, detailed to bomb Tobruk. FTR. The crew sent a signal that the aircraft was having engine trouble and might have to force-land.

148 Sqn — **Wellington IC** — **HX393   M** — **Op: Tobruk**

F/O J D MacKellar RAAF
Sgt K D Laird
F/O W M Sterns
Sgt W E Dight
Sgt J L Thomson
Sgt R O Fuller

Took off 1910, LG 237, detailed as above. The port engine failed at Lake Maghra on return, and the aircraft crashlanded at LG 237. A fire started in the bomb doors, and the aircraft was DBF.

---

13 Oct 1942 — **162 Sqn** — **Wellington IC** — **DV506** — **Personnel movement**

P/O A B Smith RNZAF
P/O R C Earl RNZAF
P/O K R Bingham
P/O K Liversidge
Sgt C R Harrison

Took off Rayak for Bilbeis, but a tyre burst, the aircraft swung, and the undercarriage collapsed. DBR.

14-15 Oct 1942 — **104 Sqn** — **Wellington II** — **Z8594   T** — **Op: Tobruk**

P/O E W Baldwin   +
W/O D M Keane RNZAF   +
P/O R J Elliot RCAF   +
Sgt H R Clark   +
Sgt J L Smith RAAF   +
Sgt R D Gannon RAAF   +

Took off 1815, Kabrit, detailed to bomb Tobruk. FTR, and believed to be the aircraft seen falling in flames over the target area. All are commemorated on Alamein Memorial.

---

17 Oct 1942 — **15 Sqn SAAF** — **Baltimore III** — **AH120** — **Delivery Flight**

Capt C S Margo SAAF
Crew

Took off on a delivery flight from 113 MU to 15 Sqn SAAF, RAF HQ Middle East. At Eastleigh, Nairobi, it landed on an extension of runway under construction and ran into the half-metre-higher edge of the existing runway. DBR.

19-20 Oct 1942	108 Sqn	Wellington IC	DV873 E	Op: Tobruk
	Sgt W N Simpson	pow	Took off 2110, LG 237, detailed to bomb Tobruk. On	
	P/O E R Patrick RCAF	pow	return the starboard engine failed and the aircraft crash-	
	F/Sgt J A Hutchinson RCAF	pow	landed near Sidi Barrani. The crew was captured by	
	Sgt A T Williamson	pow	Italian troops on 27 October.	
	Sgt H A Martin RAAF	pow		
	P/O J Mills	pow		

20 Oct 1942	21 Sqn SAAF	Baltimore III	AG912 O	Op: Fuka Main
	Capt J G Potgieter SAAF	pow	Took off 1518, LG 98, one of 15 Baltimores of 21 Sqn SAAF	
	Lt L E Bennett SAAF	pow	and three Bostons of 12 Sqn SAAF detailed to attack Axis	
	Air Sgt E S van der Merwe SAAF	+	aircraft at Fuka Main (LG 17). Shot down by heavy flak	
	F/Sgt J C C van Loggerenberg SAAF	+	while crossing the El Alamein front line, the aircraft spun	
			into the ground at 1612 hrs. The dead are buried in the El	
			Alamein War Cemetery.	

21-22 Oct 1942	70 Sqn	Wellington IC	R1029 S	Op: Tobruk
	F/Sgt G H Rapson	pow	Took off Abu Sueir, detailed to bomb the harbour and	
	Sgt D Jackson	+	shipping at Tobruk. FTR. Sgt Bryan died in captivity	
	F/Sgt M Hanna	+	on 30 October. He, Sgt Thorpe and F/Sgt Hanna are	
	Sgt J H Bryan	pow	commemorated on the Alamein Memorial, while Sgt	
	Sgt J R N Thorpe	+	Jackson is buried in El Alamein War Cemetery.	
	Sgt N S Forsythe	pow		

23 Oct 1942	104 Sqn	Wellington II	W5359	Air Test
	P/O L H Page		A tyre burst on take-off, Kabrit, and the undercarriage	
	Crew		collapsed. DBR. One crew member, unidentified, was	
			injured.	
	1 OADU	Wellington IC	HX775	Delivery Flight
	Sgt J W Chester RCAF	int	Took off, Gibraltar, 0300, en route to Bathhurst, but	
	Sgt W G Forsberg RCAF	int	force-landed at Las Palmas, on Gran Canarias, with	
	Sgt M N Walker RNZAF	int	engine trouble. The crew was interned until 7 March	
	Sgt H E M Howell RAAF	int	1943, save for Sgt Forsberg, who stowed away on an	
	Sgt D D Gardner RAAF	int	Italian tanker operating under Merchant Navy control,	
	Sgt J W Wilkinson RAAF	int	and reached Curacao.	

23-24 Oct 1942	462 Sqn	Halifax II	W7659 F	Op: Maleme
	F/Sgt A G De Clerck RAAF	+	Took off 2135, Fayid, to attack Maleme airfield, but	
	F/Sgt K H Whitmore	+	ditched with engine trouble and icing 20km N of Crete.	
	Sgt L W Giles	+	The dinghy failed to inflate, and only Sgt Simpson	
	Sgt G F Simpson	pow	survived, clinging to a petrol tank. He began to swim for	
	F/Sgt A H Pepper RCAF	+	shore, but was picked up by an Italian craft. The dead are	
	F/Sgt J W Tyson	+	commemorated on the Alamein Memorial.	

24 Oct 1942	223 Sqn	Baltimore III	AG854 Q	Op: Army Co-operation
	P/O D G W Leake RAAF	+	Took off LG 86, to attack vehicles and tanks W of the Sidi	
	F/Sgt J H Campbell	+	Abd el Rahman Road, El Alamein. Hit by heavy flak and	
	Sgt R Roberts RAAF	pow	crashed in flames S of the target. The dead are buried in	
	Sgt J R Bertram	+	the El Alamein War Cemetery.	
	12 Sqn SAAF	Boston III	W8383	Ferry Flight
	Lt N H P Dellow SAAF		One of the engines cut on approach to LG 99 and the	
	Crew		aircraft belly-landed. Form 1180 shows it as only Cat A	
			damage, but W8383 seems to have been used for spares.	
	12 Sqn SAAF	Boston III	Z2291 E	Op: Army Co-operation
	Lt A C E Glendinning SAAF	pow	Took off 0840, LG 99, one of 18 Bostons of 12 and 24 Sqns	
	2/Lt J R De la Harpe SAAF	pow	SAAF detailed to attack the 15th Panzer Division W of	
	Air Sgt W F Croston SAAF	pow	El Alamein. Badly damaged by flak over the target Z2291	
	Air Sgt S A Maritz SAAF	pow	crashed 20km W of El Alamein at approximately 0943 hrs.	

	12 Sqn SAAF	**Boston IIIA**	**41-19402**	**Op: Army Co-operation**
	Capt R H F Howarth SAAF			
	Lt W A Blount SAAF			
	F/Sgt H B Roodt SAAF	inj		
	F/Sgt F A Shultz SAAF			

Took off 1330, LG 99, detailed as above. Leading the formation, the aircraft was hit by flak over the target at 1440 hrs, and fell out of formation with the port engine on fire. The crew were ordered to bail out and the pilot was thrown clear of the aircraft when the port wing broke off. The Boston crashed 26km W of El Alamein.

	15 Sqn SAAF	**Blenheim V**	**BA335**	**Op: Patrol**
	Lt B E G MacLeod SAAF			
	Lt M W S Priday SAAF			
	Air Sgt H H Lewis SAAF			
	Air Mech D G Smart SAAF			

Took off 0715, Kufra, to patrol area - Base - Rebiana - Zighen - Base, but crashed in a forced landing near Kufra Oasis when the the starboard engine seized, because of a severed oil return pipe. DBR.

	24 Sqn SAAF	**Boston III**	**Z2237 Z**	**Op: Army Co-operation**
	Lt H H Roberts SAAF	+		
	Lt T C McD Browning SAAF	+		
	Air Sgt A H Geyser SAAF			
	Air Sgt H N B Bowker SAAF			

Took off 0849, OLG, LG 99, to attack the 15th Panzer Division at El Alamein. Damage to the tailplane in a collision over the target with another Boston forced Z2237 out of formation. It was then attacked and shot down by fighters at 0930 hrs. The dead are buried in the El Alamein War Cemetery.

	24 Sqn SAAF	**Boston III**	**AL727 S**	**Op: Army Co-operation**
	Lt B Nichols SAAF	+		
	Lt D R Carney SAAF			
	Air Sgt A H Hartley SAAF	inj		
	Air Sgt J P Woodliffe SAAF	inj		

Took off 0849, LG 99, detailed as above, but hit by heavy and accurate flak over the target and crashed near the beach, exploding on impact. Lt Nichols is buried in the El Alamein War Cemetery.

26 Oct	**15 Sqn SAAF**	**Blenheim V**	**BA234 P**	**Op: Anti-shipping**
1942	Lt A B Groch SAAF	pow		
	Lt A McL Johnston SAAF	+		
	F/Sgt R E Twigg SAAF	pow		

Took off 1235, LG 226 (Gianaclis), one of a mixed force of Blenheims, Beauforts and Beaufighters detailed to attack an Italian convoy 'TT', sighted at 1524 hrs 25km N of Tobruk. The convoy included three destroyers protecting the tankers *Proserpina* and *Tergestea*, carrying 1,000 tons of fuel and 1,000 tons of ammunition, and a smaller motor vessel. Shot down by flak. Lt Johnston is buried in the El Alamein War Cemetery.

	15 Sqn SAAF	**Blenheim V**	**BA368 K**	**Op: Anti-shipping**
	Lt E G Dustow SAAF	+		
	Lt A T D Farr SAAF	+		
	Air Sgt I E van Graan SAAF	+		

Took off 1235, LG 226 (Gianaclis), detailed as above. The aircraft hit the mast of a tanker during the attack and crashed into the sea, c.1530. All three crew are commemorated on the Alamein Memorial.

	15 Sqn SAAF	**Blenheim V**	**BA486 Y**	**Op: Anti-shipping**
	Lt S E Leisegang SAAF	+		
	Lt H C Francis SAAF	+		
	Air Sgt P J Swann SAAF	+		

Took off 1235, LG 226 (Gianaclis), detailed as above. After the attack and whilst altering course at a predetermined rendezvous point 66km out to sea, this aircraft collided at low level with Beaufort DE110 of 47 Sqn. Locked together, and on fire, they crashed into the sea, killing their crews. All are commemorated on the Alamein Memorial.

27 Oct	**21 Sqn SAAF**	**Baltimore III**	**AH141 M**	**Op: Army Co-operation**
1942	Capt T Rhodes SAAF	+		
	Lt E W Hudson SAAF	+		
	Sgt H G Hilton-Barber SAAF	+		
	F/Sgt R J Stringer SAAF	+		

Took off 1211, LG 98, one of twelve Baltimores of 21 Sqn SAAF and six Bostons of 12 Sqn SAAF detailed to attack Axis forces at El Alamein. Hit by flak over the Sidi Abd el Rahman area of the front line, AH141 crashed 20km W of El Alamein. All of the crew are buried in El Alamein War Cemetery.

27-28 Oct 1942	**160 Sqn** F/Lt E C Cox RNZAF F/Sgt P E Harwood F/Lt R S Lawrence F/Sgt H V Ellerker F/Sgt J A Gibbons P/O C R Durrant RNZAF P/O C C Reilly RNZAF F/Sgt D A Donaldson RAAF	**Liberator II** + + + + + + + +	**AL548 R** **Op: Maleme** Took off 1918, 'Field', to attack Maleme airfield. Captured German documents state that the aircraft was shot down near Maleme, the crew being killed in the crash. F/Sgt Gibbons was originally buried at Canea, the others in a single grave at Galatos. All are now buried in Suda Bay War Cemetery.
28 Oct 1942	**223 Sqn** F/O J Marriner P/O A Ainslie Sgt M V Grant Sgt F Hendron	**Baltimore III** + pow pow +	**AG959** **Op: Qotafiyah** Took off LG 86, to bomb Qotafiyah I (LG 20), but hit by flak just E of Qotafiyah II (LG 104), and went down with a plume of smoke, bursting into flames on impact. The dead are commemorated on the Alamein Memorial.
29-30 Oct 1942	**104 Sqn** F/O J S Martin W/O2 R D M Embree RCAF Sgt V R Spear Sgt B A Beeney Sgt A R G Hart RAAF Sgt D H Lee RAAF	**Wellington II** + + + + + +	**W5478 P** **Op: Battle Area** Took off 2255-1310, Kabrit, to attack targets of opportunity at El Alamein, but collided with Albacore T9136, which was flare dropping. All are commemorated on the Alamein Memorial.
1 Nov 1942	**162 Sqn**	**Wellington IC**	**AD630** **Night Flying Test** SOC. NFD.
	1 OADU Sgt J Ogden Sgt D H de Gruchy Sgt F J Davis F/Sgt C A Rowles RCAF Sgt G Arthur Sgt R Montgomery	**Wellington II** + +	**Z8418** **Delivery Flight** Took off, Gibraltar, for Bathhurst, but failed to arrive. Sgts Ogden and de Gruchy are commemorated on the Alamein Memorial. The fate of the others is uncertain, but they were presumably interned.
1-2 Nov 1942	**40 Sqn** Sgt M McKiggin Sgt W Sercombe Sgt G M Rea Sgt R A Brown Sgt G Armstrong Sgt A D Price	**Wellington IC** inj	**HX385 V** **Op: Battle Area** Took off, Kabrit, detailed to attack targets of opportunity at El Alamein. An engine failed, the aircraft lost height, and the crew bailed out over Allied territory. SOC 15 November.
2 Nov 1942	**55 Sqn** S/Ldr P D C Thomas DFC W/O L Smith Sgt K G Lambert Sgt L A Buckthorpe Lt J M Simpson SAAF	**Baltimore III** + + + + +	**AH109** **Op: Army Co-operation** Took off 0846, LG 86, one of twelve Baltimores of 55 Sqn and five B-25s of 434 Sqn USAAF detailed to attack enemy motor transport at PP 866.303 El Daba. Hit over the target by heavy and accurate flak, the aircraft crashed in flames at 0901, 16km SE of El Daba. Lt Simpson was the Senior Intelligence Officer of No 232 Group. All are commemorated on the Alamein Memorial.
	223 Sqn W/O A C Maclure RAAF F/Sgt L S Middleton RAAF F/Sgt C M Chenoweth RAAF F/Sgt T G Richard RAAF	**Baltimore III** + + + +	**AG852** **Op: Ghazal** Took off 0816, LG 86, to bomb Ghazal Station. Hit by light flak when bombing, the aircraft burst into flames and crashed near the target. All but F/Sgt Middleton (buried in the El Alamein War Cemetery) are commemorated on the Alamein Memorial.

	21 Sqn SAAF	Baltimore III	AG958	Op: Ghazal
	Lt B Metcalfe SAAF		Took off 0741, LG 98, one of 18 Baltimores detailed to	
	Sgt A R Kerr SAAF	inj	bomb ammunition dumps at Ghazal station. Shortly after	
	F/Sgt J B Forrest SAAF		take-off AG958 encountered problems with one of its	
	Sgt C D Herbst SAAF		engines and left the formation over Burg el Arab at 0821	

Took off 0741, LG 98, one of 18 Baltimores detailed to bomb ammunition dumps at Ghazal station. Shortly after take-off AG958 encountered problems with one of its engines and left the formation over Burg el Arab at 0821 hrs to jettison its bombs in the sea. Over the sea the other engine cut and the pilot force-landed in the surf on a beach near Alexandria.

2-3 Nov 1942

70 Sqn — **Wellington IC** — **Z8960 G** — **Op: Battle Area**

Sgt C J Fraser RNZAF
Sgt G E Banwell
P/O R O Lewis
Sgt E J Tyrell
Sgt E J Paterson
F/Sgt T W R Jones

Took off 0316, LG 224, detailed to attack targets of opportunity at El Alamein. Engine trouble developed and the pilot was forced to crash-land 64km N of Wadi Natrun. The crew walked for 10 hours before being spotted by an RAAF Wellington crew, which landed and picked them up. DBR and SOC.

---

3 Nov 1942

12 Sqn SAAF — **Boston III** — **AL270 U** — **Op: Army Co-operation**

Lt W B Dalglish SAAF — pow
Lt M H T Smuts SAAF — +
Air Sgt B S Clutterbuck SAAF — +
Air Sgt G E Nichols SAAF — +

Took off 0740, LG 99, one of 18 Bostons detailed to attack Axis ground forces at El Alamein. Hit by flak in the bomb bay over the target, the aircraft burst into flames, spun into the ground and exploded. The pilot bailed out, seriously wounded, but died on 7 November in a German hospital in Athens, being buried in Phaleron War Cemetery. The others are commemorated on the Alamein Memorial.

3-4 Nov 1942

108 Sqn — **Wellington IC** — **Z1180 T** — **Op: Battle Area**

Sgt A D Cooper RCAF
Crew

Took off 2315, LG 237, to attack targets of opportunity at El Alamein. An engine cut and the aircraft force-landed, wheels up, in the desert 8km S of El Alamein.

148 Sqn — **Wellington IC** — **HF842 D** — **Op: Battle Area**

W/O D L Iremonger — inj
Sgt T S Gregory — +
F/Sgt E A Howard — +
Sgt L G F Gravett — +
Sgt J Osborn — +

Took off 1901, LG 237, detailed to attack motor transport in the El Alamein area, but failed to gain sufficient speed to become fully airborne, crashed and exploded. The four dead are buried in Heliopolis War Cemetery, while W/O Iremonger, who was blown clear but sustained head injuries, recovered, but was killed in action on the last night of the year, operating with 104 Sqn.

162 Sqn — **Wellington IC** — **DV944 G** — **Op: Battle Area**

P/O J J Silcox RCAF — +
F/O P J Farren RNZAF — +
Sgt A M Nott — +
P/O W L Wallis RAAF — +
P/O N C Beck RAAF — +
Sgt H R Harrison — inj

On take-off, 2305, from LG 86, detailed to attack targets of opportunity at El Alamein, lost height as the undercarriage was retracted, and the propellers struck the ground. The port propeller flew off, the aircraft crashed, burst into flames, and 3 bombs exploded. The Capt and 2nd Pilot were killed and three others died of their injuries over the next two days. All are buried in El Alamein War Cemetery.

---

5 Nov 1942

223 Sqn — **Baltimore III** — **AG941** — **Op: Army Co-operation**

F/Sgt A J Newman RAAF — pow
Sgt H P S Annells RAAF — +
Sgt R H Stevens — +
W/O2 R C Mutch RCAF — +

Took off 1414, LG 86, to bomb retreating Axis forces at the road and rail crossing S of Maaten Baggush. Collided with AG 966 at the start of bombing, both going down out of control and exploding on hitting the ground. The dead are buried in the El Alamein War Cemetery.

223 Sqn — **Baltimore III** — **AG966** — **Op: Army Co-operation**

F/O B A Kirkham — +
F/O D F Rowe RAAF — +
Sgt E B Skuce RCAF — pow
Sgt J P Canavan — +

Took off 1414, LG 86, detailed (and lost) as above. The dead are buried in the El Alamein War Cemetery.

5-6 Nov 1942	**462 Sqn** F/Sgt M D Gribbin DFM P/O P P Siebert F/Sgt A J Jones F/Sgt W Stevens Sgt A E Hessel F/Sgt P Ellison	**Halifax II**	**DT499 D**	**Op: Battle Area** Took off 2046, Fayid, to attack targets of opportunity at El Alamein. A hung-up 40 lb bomb fell off on landing at 0140 and the aircraft was DBF.
6 Nov 1942	**55 Sqn** P/O R C Payne RCAF F/Sgt T Sanderson Sgt G Sparrow Sgt S F Howe	**Baltimore III** + + + +	**AG898 T**	**Op: Army Co-operation** Took off 1405, LG 86, one of three Baltimores detailed to attack enemy motor transport on the road W of Mersa Matruh. Not seen after the formation broke up to carry out attacks. All are commemorated on the Alamein Memorial.

Chapter 9

A Second Front
November to December 1942

With the Axis forces in full retreat, General Montgomery turned his attention to the pursuit, and if possible, entrapment of the retreating foe. Rommel was by now almost destitute of tanks; less than twenty remained, and equally few anti-tank guns, while petrol for the much diminished transport units was nearly exhausted. Even so, he conducted an effective withdrawal, aided by the skill of General Karl Buelowius, his Chief Engineer, in mining roads and setting booby traps. The Eighth Army's advance was steady, however, with Sidi Barrani taken on 9th November, Halfaya Pass on the 11th, Tobruk on the 13th, and Benghazi on the 20th, the capture of the latter greatly relieving the supply position. Rommel's first defensive position was, as before, at El Agheila, but by 16th December this line had been breached, and as the year ended, he was holding a defensive line at Buerat, some 250 miles further west, though with no great certainty that it could long be maintained.

Meanwhile, however, a new front had been opened in Rommel's rear, with landings, by British and American forces, in French Morocco and Algeria, on 8th November. Operation *Torch*, as the invasion was called, provided for American landings near Casablanca and Oran, and a joint British and American landing at Algiers. In the face of only moderate French resistance, all three landings succeeded, and after Axis forces occupied Vichy France, on 10th November, there was full co-operation by the French forces in Morocco and Algeria. In Tunisia, however, vacillation by the French Governor allowed a small German force to take control in Tunis, and to set up defensive lines which held the Anglo-American advance, just, some 30 miles west of Tunis, when a scratch German unit, with air support, forced a combined French, British and American force back across the strategic Medjerda River at Medjez-el-Bab. Further north, a coastal drive towards the port of Bizerte was also blocked, and the 'race to Tunis' stalled. Then, in the first week of December, the Germans counter-attacked. The attack made some progess, but then was halted, and despite attempts at a renewal of the Allied advance, the end of the year saw the front line stabilised along a line running north to south, halfway between the Algerian-Tunisian border and the coast. Behind that line, General Von Arnim's Fifth Panzer Army held off, from north to south, the British, French and Americans. Meanwhile on the coast, Rommel's Panzer Army Afrika held off General Montgomery's Eighth Army at Buerat. Having been begun with high hopes of a quick capture of Tunis, and the cutting off of Rommel's army, the invasion of North Africa had ended in disappointment and stalemate.

The role of the night bomber force during this period remained much as before, with 205 Group concentrating in the main on attacks on Rommel's retreating forces, but with forays also to Crete, attacking airfields there in an effort to disrupt the airborne supply route to North Africa and, after the capture of Benghazi, to hamper bomber attacks on the port. By mid-December, however, 205 Group was much depleted, with 40 and 104 Squadrons having been detached early in November to operate from Malta, and 108 Squadron disbanded in the same month, to reconstitute itself as a Special Duties squadron, operating its handful of Liberators. Finally, on the last day of the year, 148 Squadron was also disbanded, its remaining aircraft and crews, also detached to Malta, being absorbed into 40 and 104 squadrons.

All three squadrons had experienced earlier blitzes on Malta, and they returned to the island at a time when the island was experiencing its last great blitz, which began in October. Some losses to bombing were sustained, including four Wellingtons in a single attack on 18th December, but the strength of Malta's fighter defences meant that this was now an infrequent occurrence. The Wellingtons were detached to Malta to support the invasion of French North Africa by attacking ports and airfields both in Italy, Sicily and Sardinia, and in German occupied Tripolitania and (later) Tunisia.

In mid-December, with hopes of a quick victory in North Africa fading, the night bomber force was augmented by the detachment to Algeria of two Bomber Command Wellington squadrons, 142 and 150, whose task was to attack ports and airfields in German held Tunisia. A month earlier, a day bomber force, comprising 13, 18, 114 and 614 squadrons, all equipped with the Blenheim V, had flown in from Gibraltar to provide close support for the Allied armies. But two disastrous operations, on 17th November, when seven Blenheims out of 12 attacking Bizerta failed to return, and on 4th December, when ten out of eleven Blenheims were lost, made it clear that the Algeria-based squadrons could only operate under heavy fighter protection. It was a lesson which had been learnt much earlier in the Western Desert, where Baltimores and Bostons of the RAF and SAAF continued to provide close support for the Eighth Army.

7 Nov 1942	462 Sqn	Halifax II	W7671 H	**Op:**

The Air Movement Card (AM78) records Category E damage (BER) on this date, but there is a Flying Accident Card which records two nights earlier this aircraft and crew landing safely at Fayid after a fire in an engine. Damage was Cat B (and hence repairable). The 462 Sqn ORB corroborates this. W7671 is recorded once more on operations, to Heraklion from LG 237 on 23/24 November, returning safely, but then disappears from the record to be SOC in March 1945, by inventory entry.

7-8 Nov 1942	104 Sqn	Wellington II	Z8590 D	**Op: Decimomannu**
	F/Sgt L L A Craig RNZAF		+	
	F/O S C Morrison		+	
	F/Sgt H H Earney RNZAF		+	
	Sgt O L Holmes		+	
	Sgt K L Donald RNZAF		+	
	F/Sgt A S B Patterson RAAF		+	

Shortly after take-off, Luqa, at 1730, detailed to attack Decimomannu airfield, the aircraft hit a wall on high ground near Gebel Chantar, Malta. DBF. All are buried at Malta (Capuccini) Naval Cemetery.

9 Nov 1942	Middle East	Halifax II	W1152	**Unknown**

Cat E (M); NFD (A-B Serials). M = Missing, but there is no mention of this aircraft in the 462 Sqn ORB: the only unit operating Halifaxes in the Middle East at this time.

9-10 Nov 1942	70 Sqn	Wellington IC	BB499 N	**Op: Bardia**
	F/Sgt V C Ardis RCAF			
	F/Sgt L J Carter RNZAF			
	Sgt R Lees			
	Sgt R B Wynynard RNZAF			
	F/Sgt R T Hodgson			
	Sgt H Hansell			

Took off 2130, LG 224, detailed to attack Bardia. On return an engine failed, and the aircraft was abandoned 24km S of LG 75.

10 Nov 1942	40 Sqn	Wellington IC	HX468 Z	**Op: Tobruk**
	Sgt R G Workman		+	
	F/Sgt R A King		+	
	F/Sgt L Greenwood		+	
	Sgt C S McCormick		+	
	Sgt P P Armstrong		+	
	Sgt R T H Quinn		inj	

On take-off from LG 222a, detailed to bomb Tobruk, the aircraft failed to gain height, crashed and caught fire. The dead are buried in Heliopolis War Cemetery.

10-11 Nov 1942	18 Sqn	Blenheim V	BA738	**Relocation Flight**
	Sgt F Rounding		int	
	P/O P F Willis		int	
	Sgt E D Murphy		int	

Took off 2400, Portreath, on relocation to Blida, but force-landed with engine trouble in the Mediterranean at 0815 off Santa Pola, 18km S of Alicante. The crew was interned at Albacete, returning to the UK on 5 February 1943.

	37 Sqn	Wellington IC	DV619	**Op: Tobruk - Gazala Rd**
	Sgt R N Carter			
	Sgt C Robertson			
	Sgt R H Smith			
	Sgt F W Westoby			
	Sgt F Glover RNZAF			
	Sgt F J Cunliffe RCAF			

Took off 2037, Fayid, detailed to attack motor transport between Tobruk and Tmimi. The starboard engine overheated on the return flight, caught fire and was shut down. A crash-landing was effected at 0520. SOC by inventory entry on 31.10.43.

	40 Sqn	Wellington IC	R1182 D	**Op: Almas**
	Sgt W H Setterfield			
	Sgt R C Rainey RNZAF			
	Sgt W Heffernan			
	Sgt G Agnew			
	Sgt M Churchman			
	Sgt W Nicholson			

Took off, Luqa, detailed to bomb the aerodrome at Almas, but on return forced by engine failure to ditch 24km off Gozo. The crew were rescued by fishermen. There is an account of this ditching in David Gunby's history of 40 Squadron, *Sweeping the Skies*, p212.

	148 Sqn	**Wellington IC**	**HX483 K**	**Op: Tobruk-Tmimi**

Sgt J Coleman
Sgt E Shafto
Sgt B E J Heard
Sgt A J Sullivan
Sgt H L Horne

Took off 2230, LG 237, to bomb motor transport on the road between Tobruk and Tmimi. On return the port engine caught fire and was extinguished but then the starboard engine caught fire. The aircraft crashed in a forced landing 64km SW of Fuka, but the crew escaped unhurt and made their way back to base.

462 Sqn　　　　**Halifax II**　**DT498 C**　　　**Op: Tobruk - Derna Rd**

S/Ldr J R Goldston　　+
F/Lt J V Watts　　　　evd
F/Sgt W N Guertin RCAF　pow
F/Sgt W G Plummer　　pow
F/Sgt R Spencer　　　+
Sgt J F H Steer　　　+

Took off Fayid, detailed to attack motor transport on the Tobruk - Derna Road. Hit by flak, the aircraft caught fire, and was abandoned off Tobruk. F/Lt Watts swam ashore and hid for four days before being found by British troops. F/Sgt Spencer is buried in Knightsbridge War Cemetery, Acroma; the others are commemorated on the Alamein Memorial.

---

11 Nov 1942　　**18 Sqn**　　　**Blenheim V**　**BA811**　　　　**Relocation Flight**

S/Ldr R Eyton Williams
P/O I W N Speight
F/Sgt D K Franklyn

Took off Portreath, on relocation to Blida, but crashed in a forced landing when the aircraft ran out fuel, Sidi Moussa, 13km from Blida.

18 Sqn　　　**Blenheim V**　**BA870**　　　　**Ground**

DBR, probably in an attack on Blida airfield by German fighters. SOC.

11-12 Nov 1942　**70 Sqn**　　　**Wellington IC**　**DV639**　　　　**Unknown**

F/Sgt F B P Reynolds RCAF
Sgt J L Swift RCAF
Crew

Aircraft bounced in heavy landing at LG 224, and in attempting to go round again stalled and crashed. Apparently not repaired; SOC 27.7.44 by inventory entry.

---

12 Nov 1942　**55 Sqn**　　　**Baltimore III**　**AH144 C**　　　**Ground**

W/Cdr J F Roulston
F/Lt R Hornby
P/O J E Jenkins
P/O N W Skillicorn

Hit by another aircraft on take-off, LG 86. DBR.

12-13 Nov 1942　**40 Sqn**　　　**Wellington IC**　**DV489 A**　　**Op: Tobruk - Derna Rd**

P/O R G MacInnes
Sgt J F Turner
P/O Cottrell
Sgt A Venner
F/Sgt A Challand　　inj
Sgt A Liston

Took off LG 237 detailed to bomb Axis transport retreating along the Tobruk to Derna road. On return the aircraft crash-landed in the desert inside Allied lines. SOC 29 November.

70 Sqn　　　**Wellington IC**　**HD979 F**　　　**Op: Derna**

Sgt A L Robinson RNZAF
Sgt J D Rees
W/O M R Dreed
Sgt E W Presland
Sgt K Mayo
Sgt I G P Lewis

Took off 1955, LG 224, detailed to bomb Derna. The starboard engine failed and the aircraft, unable to maintain height, crash-landed. Presumably not repaired, it was not SOC until 31.10.43 by inventory entry.

148 Sqn　　　**Wellington IC**　**DV607 W**　　**Op: Gazala - Tobruk Rd**

F/O B S Beattie　　evd
W/O W B Fulcher　　evd
Sgt H McPherson　　evd
Sgt J T O Bell　　　evd
Sgt E Bates　　　　pow

Took off 1635, LG 237, to attack vehicles on the Gazala - Tobruk road. On return the aircraft had engine trouble, the crew bailing out, and the aircraft crashing SW of Derna: DBF. The crew bailed out. Sgt McPherson was captured by the Germans and interrogated but managed to escape by knocking out his guard.

	148 Sqn	Wellington IC	ES987 X	Op: Derna

Sgt P R Street
Sgt R J Reynolds
Sgt J Jones
Sgt J W G Reeves
F/Sgt P R Spurgeon
Sgt J Flux

Took off 1620, LG 237, detailed to attack motor transport around Derna. An engine failed over the target, and the second engine caught fire before reaching base and the undercarriage could not be pumped down. The aircraft crashed at LG 237 and was DBF.

13-14 Nov 1942

108 Sqn	Wellington IC	HX380	Op: Benghazi

Sgt M J S Kerby
P/O H A B Baker
Crew

Took off 1910, LG 106, detailed as above. On return, an engine cut over Sollum after flak damage, a propeller was lost and the aircraft belly-landed 48km S of Fuka. The crew found an Italian lorry while walking to base, repaired it and drove back, arriving on the 14th. SOC 16 December.

148 Sqn	Wellington IC	AD637 E	Op: Benghazi

P/O W G Sharpe RAAF   +
P/O I G E Davidson   +
Sgt J M Jones   +
W/O2 H M Lane RCAF   +
F/Sgt J L M Thomson RAAF   +
Sgt R E Swift   +

Took off 1933, ALG 106, detailed to bomb shipping and harbour facilities at Benghazi. FTR. All are commemorated on the Alamein Memorial.

---

14 Nov 1942

114 Sqn	Blenheim V	BA750	Relocation Flight

P/O W E Walker RCAF   int
P/O D K Young   int
Sgt N N Welch   int

Took off 0730, Portreath, on relocation to Blida, but ran out of fuel and force-landed at Tangier, Morocco.

114 Sqn	Blenheim V	BA826	Relocation Flight

Sgt A G G Johnson   int
Sgt R A Elliott   int
Sgt J S H Cox   int

Took off 0730, Portreath, on relocation to Blida, but force-landed with engine trouble at Lisbon Airport, where it and its crew were interned. The crew were released on 21 November and returned to the UK via Ireland on a BOAC flight.

---

15 Nov 1942

40 Sqn	Wellington IC	HX385	Unknown

SOC. NFD.

---

16 Nov 1942

18 Sqn	Blenheim V	BA736	Op: Bizerta

Sgt J Eccleston
F/Sgt H J Gates
Sgt J A Martin

Took off Blida, one of three Blenheims detailed to attack Bizerta/Sidi Ahmed aerodrome. The attack was abandoned when two of the aircraft were unable to locate the target and the third had technical problems. On return fuel shortage and navigational problems led to a crash while force-landing at Rouina 96km WSW of Blida. The crew returned to Blida by train.

---

17 Nov 1942

18 Sqn	Blenheim V	BA725 P	Op: Bizerta

F/Sgt R K Mead   +
Sgt R J Cheyne   +
Sgt G V Andrews   +

Took off 1113, Blida, one of 12 Blenheims detailed to attack Bizerta/Sidi Ahmed Aerodrome. Collided with BA815 while approaching the target and crashed at Cap Serrat. All are buried at Massicault War Cemetery.

18 Sqn	Blenheim V	BA780 B	Op: Bizerta

S/Ldr W J H Tucker
P/O W Docherty
F/Sgt J Bartley

Took off 1108, Blida, detailed as above. With the rudder shot away by light machine gun fire on the run in to the target the aircraft nonetheless bombed; pursued by Bf 109 fighters, it eventually crash-landed at Djidjelli.

18 Sqn	Blenheim V	**BA794 C**	**Op: Bizerta**
F/O C W Kaye	+	Took off 1108, Blida, detailed as above. Attacked and shot	
F/O E G Clegg	+	down by a Bf 109 off Cap Ben Sekka. All of the crew are	
Sgt J Walder	+	commemorated on the Malta Memorial.	

18 Sqn	Blenheim V	**BA815 O**	**Op: Bizerta**
F/O G H Berry	+	Took off 1113, Blida, detailed as above. Collided with	
Sgt V G Rowen	+	BA725 while approaching the target and crashed at Cap	
Sgt R E W Page	+	Serrat. All are buried at Massicault War Cemetery.	

18 Sqn	Blenheim V	**BA819 M**	**Op: Bizerta**
P/O G W Sims		Took off 1108, Blida, detailed as above. Attacked by	
Sgt S Litchfield		Bf 109s which destroyed the aircraft's hydraulic system;	
Sgt C Cosens		belly-landed on return at Blida.	

18 Sqn	Blenheim V	**BA828 H**	**Op: Bizerta**
F/Sgt W L Williams	pow	Took off 1108, Blida, detailed as above. Shot down by	
W/O J C McCombie	pow	Bf 109 fighters when leaving the target, and crashed near	
F/Sgt J Brown	pow	the airfield.	

114 Sqn	Blenheim V	**BA754**	**Op: Bizerta**
P/O D K Thornburn		Took off 0215, Blida, to bomb Bizerta/Sidi Ahmed	
P/O V S Swain		Aerodrome. Ran out of fuel when lost in bad weather on	
Sgt E E Newstead		return, and belly-landed in forced landing at Tizi Ouzon	
		at 0715 hrs.	

614 Sqn	Blenheim V	**BA829**	**Relocation Flight**
P/O C P C De Wesselow	int	Took off 0400, Portreath, on relocation to the Middle East	
F/Sgt I J Self	int	via Gibraltar, but force-landed at about 1000 hrs at Aldeia	
Sgt W D B Bunting RNZAF	int	Nova, Portugal. The crew was briefly interned.	

1 OADU	Blenheim V	**BA807**	**Relocation Flight**
F/O D G Fraser RCAF	int	Took off 0700, Portreath, for Gibraltar, but force-landed at	
Sgt W D Lloyd	int	1600 on a beach at Marzarron, near Cartagena. The crew,	
Sgt H S Machan	int	released from internment, arrived at Gibraltar on 15	
		January 1943. The crew was ex 13 Sqn.	

18 Nov	**161 Sqn**	Whitley V	**Z9160**	**Ferry Flight**
1942	P/O O A Cussen	int	Took off Gibraltar for the UK. Off Cape S Vincent	
	F/O J A Broadley	int	developed engine trouble and turned back to Gibraltar,	
	F/Sgt H Stephens	int	but force-landed at Armacao de Pera, Portugal.	
	Sgt R A Sharpe RCAF	int	F/O Broadley was injured.	

19-20 Nov	**104 Sqn**	Wellington II	**W5583 E**	**Op: Catania**
1942	F/Lt J H D Mercer	+	Took off c.1810, Luqa, to attack Catania, and shot down	
	W/O2 J Fearnside RCAF	+	over the target. W/O Fearnside is buried at Agira	
	F/Sgt C E Gray	+	Canadian War Cemetery, the remainder at Catania War	
	Sgt W E Hammond RNZAF	+	Cemetery.	
	Sgt J W Layton	+		
	Sgt B C D Holmes	+		

20 Nov	**614 Sqn**	Blenheim V	**BA726**	**Op: Bizerta**
1942	P/O N Marwood Tucker		Took off 0053, Blida, to bomb Bizerta Harbour. Hit by	
	F/Sgt E Yelland		flak, the undercarriage collapsing on landing, Blida. DBR.	
	Sgt A S Roberts RNZAF			

21 Nov	**15 Sqn SAAF**	Blenheim V	**BA233 A**	**Unknown**
1942	Lt O C Venn SAAF		A tyre burst on take-off LG 121, the aircraft swung and	
	Crew		the undercarriage collapsed. Salvaged by No 103 MU on	
			22 December, but DBR and SOC.	

22 Nov 1942	**40 Sqn**	**Wellington IC**	**HX438 R**		**Op: Trapani**
	P/O J L Dickinson		Took off, Luqa, to bomb the airfield at Trapani. On return		
	F/Sgt G T Dawson	+	the crew diverted to Bône with engine trouble. On take		
	Sgt L Hadley		off next day for Malta, the aircraft hit an embankment,		
	Sgt D A D Golby		lost height and crashed in a field.		
	Sgt A P Jones				
	Sgt W Jones				

23 Nov 1942	**14 Sqn**	**Marauder I**	**FK122 P**		**Training**
	F/O W R Bower RCAF	+	Took off, Fayid, for bombing practice at Shallufa bombing		
	W/O2 D L Rawson RCAF	+	range. The tailplane broke away, causing the aircraft to		
	F/O P McK Willis	+	crash. All are buried in Suez War Memorial Cemetery.		
	Sgt H G Williams	+			
	Sgt E Cookson	+			
	114 Sqn	**Blenheim V**	**BA799**		**Op: Bizerta**
	F/O J O Mathias		Took off Blida, to attack Bizerta/Sidi Ahmed aerodrome		
	F/O D Truscott		and FTR. All are commemorated on the Malta Memorial.		
	Sgt T W Catchpole				
	Middle East	**Blenheim IV**	**Z7905**		**Unknown**
			SOC. NFD.		

23-24 Nov 1942	**37 Sqn**	**Wellington IC**	**X9693 U**		**Op: Kastelli Pediada**
	F/O E D Fleishman RCAF	+	Took off 1935-2006, Abu Sueir, to attack the airfield at		
	W/O2 L E Mathews RCAF	+	Kastelli Pediada, and shot down over the target, crashing		
	Sgt G R Haugh	+	in the N part of the dispersals area. All are buried at Suda		
	Sgt R A Giles	+	Bay War Cemetery.		
	F/O E M W Bolton	+			
	Sgt T C Westwood	+			

24 Nov 1942	**614 Sqn**	**Blenheim V**	**BA821**		**Ground**
			Damaged, possibly in an air raid, Blida, and SOC.		

25 Nov 1942	**18 Sqn**	**Blenheim V**	**BA803 A**		**Op: Bizerta**
	Sgt A T Woodfield		Took off 1145, Blida, one of seven Blenheims detailed to		
	F/Sgt R W Duke RNZAF		attack Bizerta/Sidi Ahmed aerodrome. Crashed on		
	Sgt R I Parker		landing 2km from Picard. DBR.		
	223 Sqn	**Baltimore III**	**AG905**		**Training**
	F/Sgt W H J Hutt		Crashed on take-off, LG 86, on a training flight, when the		
	W/O R G Thompson		aircraft swung and corrective action was not taken.		
	F/Sgt P Smith RAAF				
	F/Sgt A J Deeble				

26-27 Nov 1942	**104 Sqn**	**Wellington II**	**W5550 Q**		**Op: Gerbini**
	P/O F M Benitz DFM RCAF	pow	Took off 0010, Luqa, to attack the airfield at Gerbini.		
	F/Sgt S W Thrower	pow	Ditched off Sicily on return. F/O Cope is commemorated		
	F/O K C W Cope	+	on the Malta Memorial.		
	Sgt F Parkinson	pow			
	Sgt B Jones	pow			
	Sgt A Haxton	pow			

27 Nov 1942	**223 Sqn**	**Baltimore III**	**AG886**		**Training**
	P/O S Cotter		Took off LG 86 on a training flight and crashed on		
	Sgt J A McLeod RCAF	inj	landing on return.		
	Sgt L H Wyatt				
	Sgt K S Fish				

	1 OADU	**Wellington IC**	**HE122**	**Delivery Flight**
	Sgt J C Webb	+	Took off Gibraltar for Egypt, but failed to arrive; found	
	Sgt A P Scott	+	crashed 10 miles NW of Guertrafa, Algeria. The dead are	
	Sgt K V Mayle	+	buried in the Dely Ibrahim War Cemetery.	
	Sgt W C Martin	+		
	Sgt Cooper RCAF			
	1 OADU	**Wellington IC**	**LA973**	**Delivery Flight**
	Sgt D J Rolfe	inj	Took off Gibraltar for Egypt, but, damaged by flak, stalled	
	Sgt A H Wallis	+	on approach and crashed, Mersa Matruh. DBF. Sgt	
	Sgt A B Standen	inj	Wallis is buried in the El Alamein War Cemetery.	
	Sgt J Wright	inj		
	Sgt K V Pike	inj		

28 Nov 1942	**18 Sqn**	**Blenheim V**	**BA797 T**	**Ground**
			Hit by a bomb during an air raid at Canrobert.	
	462 Sqn	**Halifax II**	**W7756 K**	**Ferry Flight**
	Sgt B J Gibbons RAAF		Took off, LG 237 for LG 09, but stalled while landing, the	
	Crew		port wing hit the ground, the undercarriage collapsed,	
			and the aircraft's back was broken. DBR.	

29 Nov 1942	**13 Sqn**	**Blenheim V**	**BA745 A**	**Op: Bizerta**
	F/Lt J H M Shaw	inj	On take-off 0200, Blida, to bomb Bizerta/Sidi Ahmed	
	P/O E A Martin	inj	Airfield, the aircraft hit a tree and crashed.	
	P/O R G Roberts			
	614 Sqn	**Blenheim V**	**BA748**	**Ground**
			Hit by another aircraft while parked, Blida, and DBR.	

30 Nov 1942	**13 Sqn**	**Blenheim V**	**BA755**	**Op: Bizerta**
	F/Lt D C Sandeman		Took off 0700, Blida, to bomb Sidi Ahmed aerodrome.	
	F/O W M Parsons		On the return journey the aircraft was attacked and	
	Sgt A B Murdoch RCAF		damaged by Fw 190s and crash-landed at 1030 hrs at Bone.	
	18 Sqn	**Blenheim V**	**BA730**	**Transit Flight**
	Sgt J Proud	+	Took off Blida, en route to 18 Sqn's new base at	
	Sgt D S Allen	+	Canrobert, but crashed at Jfa el Mizan. All are buried in	
	F/Sgt J W Evans	+	the Dely Ibrahim War Cemetery	
	Passenger: Cpl L Duncan	+		
	18 Sqn	**Blenheim V**	**BA739**	**Transit Flight**
	W/Cdr H G Malcolm MiD		The port tyre burst on take-off, Blida, for Canrobert. DBR.	
	F/O J Robb			
	P/O J Grant			
	1 OADU	**Wellington II**	**Z8405**	**Delivery Flight**
	P/O C W Price RNZAF		Swung on take-off, Gibraltar, for Egypt, and the port	
	Sgt J A Jones		wing struck HX746, taxiing outside the flarepath, then	
	Sgt W R Rich RCAF		ran into HE125. HX746 was badly damaged but not SOC.	
	Sgt J B Kennedy	inj		
	Sgt G A Clowes			
	1 OADU	**Wellington IC**	**HE125**	**Ground**
	F/Sgt D H Holland		Hit by Z8405 while parked, Gibraltar.	
	Sgt T L Knowles			
	Sgt B Newey			
	Sgt C Patterson			
	Sgt F W Hall	inj		

1 Dec 1942	**70 Sqn**	**Wellington IC**	**Z8960**	**Unknown**
			Cat E. FB damage. NFD. SOC.	

	104 Sqn	**Wellington II**	**Z8659** **Op: Bizerta**
	Sgt W W Newey		Took off 1740, Luqa, to bomb the docks at Bizerta.
	Crew		Crashed in a forced landing near Luqa. NFD.

	114 Sqn	**Blenheim V**	**BA690** **Op: Bizerta**
	F/Lt D S Fuller		Took off 0215, Blida, to bomb Bizerta/Sidi Ahmed
	Sgt J D S Weiss		Aerodrome. Returning early with engine trouble, the
	Sgt E E Newstead		aircraft crashed into the dispersal area on landing at Blida
			at 0351 hrs, hitting parked Beaufighter EL150.

	15 Sqn SAAF	**Blenheim IV**	**Z7610** **Unknown**
			Damaged in unknown circumstances, Kufra. Originally
			designated for repair, but in the event SOC 1 December.

2 Dec	**614 Sqn**	**Blenheim V**		**BA872** **Op: Tunis**
1942	F/O T A B Young		+	Took off 0215, Blida, to bomb Tunis Aerodrome, but on
	W/O1 G T Campbell RCAF		+	return crashed at Celle at 0625 hrs. The dead are buried
	Sgt A J Walsh RCAF		inj	at La Reunion War Cemetery, Bougie.

	1 OADU	**Wellington II**	**W5428** **Delivery Flight**
	Sgt T J McGreevey		Took off Gibraltar for Egypt but, short of fuel, attempted
	Sgt T T Murdoch		to land at the small Martuba 1 LG, overshot and hit
	Sgt E E Price		Hurricane BD926.
	Sgt H Meadowcroft		
	P/O A A Pierce		

2-3 Dec	**70 Sqn**	**Wellington IC**	**AD639** **H** **Op: Heraklion**
1942	Sgt G E Barwell		Swung on take-off 2115-30, LG 140, detailed to bomb the
	Sgt T C Mark		airfield at Heraklion and the undercarriage collapsed;
	P/O R O Lewis		DBF.
	Sgt H J Tyrrell		
	Sgt D S Robson		
	Sgt F Chaplin		

3 Dec	**18 Sqn**	**Blenheim V**	**BA824** **G** **Transit Flight**
1942	Sgt W G Stott		Took off Canrobert, forward to Souk el Arba, Tunisia, but
	P/O W Gent		crashed in a forced landing 5km E of Canrobert. The
	Sgt G A Booty		crew was from 13 Sqn.

3-4 Dec	**40 Sqn**	**Wellington IC**		**HX395** **Op: Ragusa**
1942	P/O V M Todd			Took off, Luqa, to bomb the airfield at Ragusa. On return,
	P/O N Simmonds			a hung-up bomb dropped off on landing and the aircraft
	Sgt E A Aspell		+	blew up. The dead are buried in Malta (Capuccini) Naval
	Sgt A W Ward			Cemetery.
	Sgt R Semley		+	

4 Dec	**18 Sqn**	**Blenheim V**		**BA790** **H** **Op: Robb**
1942	S/Ldr R Eyton Willams		+	Took off Canrobert, forward to Souk el Arba. Took off at
	F/Lt C Dent		+	1515 hrs to attack Robb Aerodrome 14km N of Chouigui,
	F/Sgt D K Franklyn		+	and crashed at Chouigui. All buried at Beja War Cemetery.

	18 Sqn	**Blenheim V**		**BA795** **N** **Op: Robb**
	P/O E J Holloway			Took off Souk el Arba, 1515 hrs, detailed as above.
	Sub-Lt H A Wallace RN		inj	Damaged by Bf 109s, crash-landed near BDJ Kochock, Beja.
	Sgt H G Parslow		inj	The aircraft caught fire and the bomb load exploded. Sub-
				Lt Wallace was the Naval Liaison Officer attached to 18 Sqn.

	18 Sqn	**Blenheim V**		**BA796** **D** **Op: Robb**
	Sgt W G Stott		+	Took off Souk el Arba, 1515 hrs, detailed as above. Shot
	F/O W Gent		+	down by Bf 109 fighters. The crew was from 13 Sqn.
	Sgt G A Booty		+	All are buried in Beja War Cemetery.

18 Sqn	Blenheim V	BA802 Y	Op: Robb

F/O R D Hill — +
F/Sgt S F B Bryant — +
F/Sgt C A Green — +

Took off Souk el Arba, 1515 hrs, detailed as above. FTR. All are buried at Beja War Cemetery.

18 Sqn	Blenheim V	BA820 Q	Op: Robb

F/Lt A W Eller
P/O A J W Harding — inj
P/O N C Eckersley — inj

Took off Souk el Arba, 1515 hrs, detailed as above. Damaged by Bf 109 fighters and crash-landed near BDJ Kochock, Beja. The aircraft was DBF.

18 Sqn	Blenheim V	BA875 W	Op: Robb

W/Cdr H G Malcolm MiD — +
F/O J Robb — +
P/O J Grant DFC — +

Took off Souk el Arba, 1515 hrs, detailed as above. Shot down in flames 20km W of Chouigui. W/Cdr Malcolm was awarded a posthumous VC for his exceptional bravery above and beyond the call of duty for this and operations flown on 17 and 28 November. All are buried at Beja War Cemetery.

70 Sqn	Wellington IC	BB464 Q	Op: Marble Arch

F/Sgt J E Albertson RNZAF — +
F/Sgt C T Eaton — +
F/Sgt R Evans — +
Sgt P L Bailey — +
Sgt J T Williams — +
Sgt F G Haw — inj

Engine cut on take-off, 0135-0200, LG 140, to bomb the landing ground at Marble Arch. The aircraft crashed and caught fire. The dead are buried at Tobruk War Cemetery. The engine problem was traced to reduction gear case failure.

114 Sqn	Blenheim V	BA804 Y	Op: Bizerta

F/Lt J B Coates
P/O J T Evans — inj
F/Sgt D V Symondson

Took off 0240, Blida, one of four Blenheims sent to bomb the docks and Robb LG at Bizerta. The pilot experienced trouble with the starboard engine and crash-landed 11km SE of Maison Blanche at 0255 hrs.

614 Sqn	Blenheim V	BA734 Y	Op: Robb

F/O W H Irving
F/O L A Quevatre
Sgt G A Limoges RCAF

Took off 1515, Canrobert, for Souk el Arba and from there to attack Robb Aerodrome 14km north of Chouigui. Damaged by Bf 109 fighters and crash-landed 5km east of Souk el Khemis.

614 Sqn	Blenheim V	BA800 D	Op: Robb

F/Lt A Breakey — +
F/Sgt A W Simpson — +
F/Sgt S H Greene — +

Took off Canrobert, 1515, then Souk el Arba, detailed as above. Almost certainly shot down by Bf 109 fighters in or near the target area. The crew, from 18 Sqn, is commemorated on the Malta Memorial.

614 Sqn	Blenheim V	BA869 N	Op: Robb

F/O C H Georges — +
F/Sgt J Taylor — +
Sgt W M Sorbie — +

Took off Canrobert, 1515, then Souk el Arba, detailed as above. Almost certainly shot down by Bf 109 fighters. The aircraft crashed near Beja and burnt out. All of the crew are buried at Beja War Cemetery.

5 Dec 1942	114 Sqn	Blenheim V	BA791	Op: Bizerta

F/Sgt R G Baikie RCAF — +
Sgt G R Acheson RCAF
Sgt J Cummings

Took off 0115, Blida, to bomb Bizerta Docks. Engine trouble led the pilot to jettison the bomb load and order the crew to bail out. They did so 14km S of Maison Blanche, but the pilot's parachute failed to open. He is buried at Dely Ibrahim War Cemetery.

1 OADU	Wellington IC	HD948	Delivery Flight

Sgt M F R Gardiner — inj
Sgt K Gleave — inj
Sgt C A Butt — inj
Sgt P C Shipman — +
Sgt R C Simmons — +

Took off Gibraltar for Egypt, but after climbing to 30m slowly lost height and hit the sea. Sgt Shipman is commemorated on the Runnymede Memorial, and Sgt Simmons, whose body was recovered, but buried at sea, on the Gibraltar Memorial.

5-6 Dec 1942	**104 Sqn** Sgt R D Harborow RNZAF Crew	**Wellington II**	**W5582 S**		**Op: Bizerta**

Took off 0040, Luqa, to bomb Bizerta, On return an engine lost power on approach; the aircraft swung on landing and hit X3528. DBR.

7 Dec 1942	**148 Sqn**	**Wellington IC**
	Sgt H Barrie	inj
	P/O G B Hunter	inj
	P/O R A Mackness	inj
	Sgt C R Grandfield	+
	Sgt G Bunnett	+
	Sgt G E Geeves RCAF	
	Passengers:	
	F/Sgt J I Kitchen	+
	Sgt Smith	inj
	LAC E Ford	+
	LAC Haywood	inj
	LAC Wilson	inj
	AC Brown	inj

HF887 **Relocation Flight**

Took off 1754, ALG 167, for Luqa. On approach to Luqa swung on approach, bounced, stalled, and hit a dispersal pen. DBF. All the survivors save Sgt Geeves were seriously injured. The dead are buried in Malta (Capuccini) Naval Cemetery. There is a vivid account of this accident in F R Chappell's *Wellington Wings*, p122.

7-8 Dec 1942	**40 Sqn**	**Wellington IC**
	F/O A D Bell	+
	Sgt A Marshall	+
	Sgt R Gill	+
	F/Sgt H J Wigley RAAF	+
	Sgt S Heywood	+
	Sgt L L McDonnell	pow

HF834   C **Op: Bizerta**

Took off, Luqa, detailed to bomb the docks at Bizerta. FTR. F/Sgt Wigley is buried in the Catania War Cemetery; the others are commemorated on the Malta Memorial.

8 Dec 1942	**47 Sqn**	**Wellesley I**
	F/Sgt R B Worthington	
	F/Sgt E D R Botten RCAF	
	Sgt C M Thompson	

K8531 **Op: Anti-submarine Patrol**

Took off 0540, LG 08 (Mersa Matruh), on anti-submarine escort to the convoy 'Siren'. At 0630 fabric tore off the starboard wing, forcing the pilot to keep close to the shore. The undercarriage collapsed when the aircraft crash-landed at LG 08. SOC by inventory entry,1.8.1943.

9 Dec 1842	**15 Sqn SAAF**	**Blenheim V**
	Capt Cromhout SAAF	
	Lt M B Hall SAAF	
	Col L A Wilmot SAAF	

BA378   P **Communication Flight**

Took off Alexandria/Maryut, on a communication flight. The starboard engine and hydraulics failed and the Blenheim crashed at approx 1320 hrs, 8km SW of the base.

10 Dec 1942	**138 Sqn**	**Halifax II**
	F/Lt J C K Sutton	
	Sgt F J Reardon RCAF	
	P/O G S Petrie	
	P/O L Fish	
	F/Sgt T A Meikle	
	Passengers:	
	Sgt R F Evans	
	LAC L Hilton	
	Cpl W V Lucas	
	LAC C E Elliott	
	F/O R T Fleming RNZAF (ex-40 Sqn)	
	F/O H Goddard RNZAF (ex-70 Sqn)	
	F/O Gray RNZAF (ex-70 Sqn)	
	Sgt F C McCrea RAAF (ex-70 Sqn)	
	Sgt G A Nunn (ex-70 Sqn)	
	F/O F O J Pearce (ex-37 Sqn)	
	Lt Col K Tantle	

L9618 **Ferry Flight**

Took off Luqa 0345 hrs for Gibraltar, but over Algeria suffered incremental engine failure, probably due to coolant loss. The pilot ordered a bail-out, and two passengers did so, but for unknown reasons the remainder stayed, and survived uninjured when, flying on only one engine, the Halifax crash-landed near Khebil.

138 Sqn	Halifax II	W1002	Ferry Flight

F/O L Anderle +
F/Lt V Krcha +
P/O M Rozprym +
P/O F Vanicek +
P/O J Tesir +
W/O V Pinek +
F/Sgt B Hajek +
Passengers:
P/O W T C Chambers (ex-70 Sqn) +
W/O 2 J R Milligan RCAF (ex-70 Sqn) +
F/Sgt C Bentley +
F/Sgt E B Davies +
Cpl R E Chandler +
AC1 H Hutchinson +
F/Sgt G G Organ RNZAF (ex-108 Sqn) +
Sgt J A Tovey RNZAF (ex-40 Sqn) +

Took off from LG.224 for Malta, but never arrived. The aircraft presumably came down in the Mediterranean, possibly as a result of a night fighter attack. The all-Czech crew and the passengers, including 5 tour-expired bomber crew, are commemorated on the Alamein Memorial.

---

12 Dec 1942

ADU	Blenheim V	AZ878	Delivery Flight

F/Lt R F Barnard inj
F/Sgt R M Birdsall +
Sgt A D Jenkins inj

Took off Takoradi on a delivery flight to the Middle East, but an engine cut and the aircraft crashed in a force landing near Takoradi. The observer is buried in Takoradi European Cemetery.

---

13 Dec 1942

37 Sqn	Wellington IC	DV614	Ground

Bombed by a Ju 88, LG 140.

37 Sqn	Wellington IC	HX571	Ground

Bombed by a Ju 88, LG 140. (A third Wellington, as yet unidentified, was also destroyed. But see below.)

108 Sqn	Wellington IC	AD633 H	Unknown

Last recorded on operations on 23 November, the last date on which 108 Sqn Wellingtons operated before the unit was reduced to cadre. Declared Cat E, due to enemy action, on 13 December, this may have been the third Wellington bombed at LG 140. SOC 18 December.

1 OADU	Wellington IC	LA965	Delivery Flight

Sgt D A Roberts
Sgt T A Thomas
Sgt G V Taylor
Sgt D Fairweather
Sgt D C Powell

Took off Gibraltar for Egypt, but shot down over the Gulf of Sirte. The crew was rescued uninjured.

---

14 Dec 1942

13 Sqn	Blenheim V	BA747	Op: Tunis

F/O J Kruytbosch +
Sgt J W Redman +
Sgt C F Day RNZAF +

Took off 0500, Canrobert, to bomb the docks at Tunis, but crashed on striking a hut some 530m. from the airfield perimeter. All are buried at Medjez-el-Bab War Cemetery.

---

15 Dec 1942

13 Sqn	Blenheim V	BA808 K	Op: Tunis

F/O R J Broughton inj
Sgt F H Westbrook inj
Sgt A A Smith inj

Took off Canrobert on a night raid on Tunis docks, but the starboard engine caught fire, and the aircraft crashed into the salt lake depression of Garaet Guellif.

114 Sqn	Blenheim V	BA742	Op: Tunis

P/O J L Steele
P/O R J Phillips
F/Sgt G Gregory

While taking-off 0430, Canrobert, to bomb Tunis docks, the aircraft experienced a heavy bang under the starboard undercarriage, which on retraction jammed partly closed. P/O Steele then tried to land but only one wheel would come down, so he decided to wait until daylight. After jettisoning 4 x 40 lb bombs he attempted unsuccessfully to shake the wheel down. When an engine seized he headed for Lake Gar et Tarf 13km S of Canrobert, but crash-landed 3km short, with 4 x 250 lb bombs still on board.

160 Sqn	Liberator II	AL513	Ferry Flight
F/Sgt J L O'Sullivan	int		
F/Sgt V E Whitehall	int		
F/Sgt W N Judd	int		
F/Sgt Clifton	int		
Sgt Macgregor	int		
Sgt Davey	int		
Sgt Webster	int		
Passengers:			
Cpl Agar	int		
Cpl Burton	int		
AC1 Walker	int		

Took off Lyneham 0120 hrs for Gibraltar, but ran short of fuel in bad weather, and force landed near Rota, N of Cadiz. DBF. The crew and passengers were interned until 14 January 1943. A-B Serials record this aircraft as on charge to 1446 Flight, which technically it may have been while in transit.

16 Dec 1942	14 Sqn	Marauder IA	FK367	Op: Offensive Patrol
	Sgt L A Einsaar RAAF			
	Sgt L R Dixon RAAF	inj		
	Sgt T E Exell RAAF	+		
	F/Sgt R I Ploskin	+		
	Sgt P Cockington RAAF	+		
	Sgt L B Willcocks	inj		
	Sgt A E Watts	+		

Took off c.0950, Berka III, on an offensive formation sweep along the Tripolitanian coast. Attacked by nine Malta-based Spitfires, the aircraft sustained multiple hits and was forced to ditch 20km off Benghazi, sinking almost immediately. The pilot, 2nd pilot, navigator and one of the air gunners survived, Sgt Dixon sustained a broken leg, and Sgt Willcocks burns. Sgt Einsaar rescued Sgt Exell, but he was badly burned and died shortly afterwards. The survivors were rescued two hours later by an ASR Launch. The dead are commemorated on the Alamein Memorial.

18 Sqn	Blenheim V	BA814	Unknown
F/Sgt B Yanover RCAF			

Took off Canrobert, but the port engine caught fire after two circuits were completed and F/Sgt Yanover crash-landed because of hydraulics failure.

24 Sqn SAAF	Boston III	Z2279 C	Op: Army Co-operation
Capt W C Caldwell SAAF			
Lt C F Thompson SAAF	+		
F/Sgt W H C Young SAAF			
F/Sgt B H Swart SAAF	+		

Took off Soluch, to attack and harry retreating Axis forces in the Ajdabiya area. Badly damaged by heavy flak, the aircraft belly-landed near Marble Arch at 1415 hrs. F/Sgt Swart was killed in the landing and is commemorated on the Alamein Memorial, while Lt Thompson died two days later and is buried in Benghazi War Cemetery.

40 Sqn	Wellington IC	HX382	Unknown

SOC. NFD.

17 Dec 1942	138 Sqn	Halifax II	DT542	Ferry Flight
	F/O K Dobromirski PAF	+		
	F/O S Pankiewicz PAF	+		
	F/O Z Idzikowski PAF	+		
	Sgt A Kleniewski PAF	+		
	Sgt R Wysocki PAF	+		
	Sgt A C Watt	+		
	F/Sgt O Zielinski PAF	+		
	Passengers:			
	Maj Lord A A B Apsley DSO MC TD	+		
	LAC C D Browne	+		
	LAC R Clegg	+		
	F/Lt F G T P Earle (ex-462 Sqn)	+		
	Cpl D S Hounslow	+		
	AC1 S E Kelly	+		
	Maj A D C Millar	+		
	Sgt D Spibey	+		
	S/Ldr J H Wedgewood DFC	+		
	F/Lt L A Vaughan DSO DFC	+		

Took off, Luqa, for the UK, but turned back with engine problems, and crashed E of Zetun at 0405, attempting a landing at Luqa. All are buried in Malta (Capuccini) Naval Cemetery.
F/Lt Vaughan, ex-40 Sqn, had completed 100 operational sorties.

614 Sqn S/Ldr P de L Le Cheminant F/O W Service P/O J W Ryder	**Blenheim V**	**BA732**	**Op: Tunis or Bizerta Docks** On take-off 1750, Canrobert, a tyre burst; the aircraft swung and the undercarriage collapsed. DBF. Of seven 614 Sqn Blenheims detailed, bad weather meant that only two managed to take off.

17-18 Dec 1942

104 Sqn F/O C W M Dallas F/O R L Coulter RCAF F/O G C Silver RCAF Sgt L Booth Sgt H G Lines Sgt C H Pooley	**Wellington II**	**Z8469 F** pow + + + + +	**Op: Tunis and La Goulette** Took off 1830, Luqa, to attack Tunis docks and La Goulette. Shot down by a Ju 88. All the dead save Sgt Pooley (buried at Enfidaville War Cemetery) are commemorated on the Malta Memorial.

18 Dec 1942

13 Sqn F/O A Jickling F/Sgt H McD Martin RCAF W/O2 J V Welsh RCAF	**Blenheim V**	**BA785** + + +	**Op: Bizerta** Took off Canrobert to bomb Bizerta Docks, but FTR. All of the crew are commemorated on the Malta Memorial.
40 Sqn	**Wellington IC**	**HD959**	**Ground** Destroyed in an air raid, Luqa.
40 Sqn	**Wellington IC**	**HE108**	**Ground** Destroyed in an air raid, Luqa.
40 Sqn	**Wellington IC**	**HX382**	**Ground** Cat E, possibly from damage in an air raid, Luqa, SOC.
108 Sqn	**Wellington IC**	**AD627**	**Ground** Destroyed by enemy action. Luqa. Though the Air Movement card lists the aircraft as 108 Squadron, it is probable that it had been taken on charge by 40 Sqn, 108 having relinquished its Wellingtons in late November, on becoming a Special Duties squadron.
142 Sqn P/O J Etchells Sgt L A Ding F/Sgt B E Shaver P/O G K Pickering Sgt J L MacDonald Passengers: Sgt Vickers LAC Weatherby	**Wellington III**	**DF708**	**Relocation Flight** Burst a tyre taking off from Gibraltar for Blida, and crashed on landing there. (The crew given is Etchells' crew on 9 December).
1 OADU	**Wellington II**	**Z8596**	**Ground** Destroyed by enemy action, presumably at Luqa; NFD.

19 Dec 1942

14 Sqn P/O J T Willis F/Sgt S H Porteous F/O E W Barr RNZAF F/O P B Martell Sgt H F Ford RAAF Sgt F Barratt	**Marauder IA**	**FK366** pow + + + + +	**Op: Minelaying** Took off Berka III, but crashed into the sea in the Bay of Tunis while minelaying. F/O Martell is commemorated on the Alamein Memorial, while the others are buried in Enfidaville War Cemetery.

20 Dec 1942

55 Sqn F/Lt R D Shepherd F/Lt D G Astington Sgt P G Simper Sgt H G Lloyd Passenger: P/O J D Kevill	**Baltimore III**	**AG980** +	**Training** Took off LG 86 on a training flight, but on landing the aircraft bounced and landed heavily; DBR. The observer is buried in Alexandria (Hadra) War Cemetery.

22 Dec 1942	18 Sqn W/O G F Wallace RCAF Sgt T V Parker Sgt W J Herring	Blenheim V	BA822	Unknown

inj after Sgt T V Parker

22 Dec 1942 — **18 Sqn** — **Blenheim V** — **BA822** — **Unknown**
W/O G F Wallace RCAF
Sgt T V Parker inj
Sgt W J Herring
Took off Souk el Arba, but an engine cut and the aircraft crash-landed. DBR.

25-26 Dec 1942 — **40 Sqn** — **Wellington IC** — **DV538 X** — **Op: Tripoli**
F/Lt L McLachlan RNZAF
P/O J D Kitchen
Sgt F Hughes
F/Sgt A Challand
Sgt G E Geeves RCAF
Took off Luqa, detailed to bomb Tunis docks. Unable to locate the target, the crew bombed Pantelleria. On return wireless problems led to difficulties locating Malta, and the crew ditched, being rescued by HSL107 from Kalafrana. There are photographs of the crew disembarking from HSL107 at St Paul's Bay in Frederick Galea's *Call-Out*, p206.

27 Dec 1942 — **114 Sqn** — **Blenheim V** — **BA817** — **Op: Tunis-Massicault**
P/O W R Berriman RAAF — inj
Sgt K E Smith RNZAF — +
Sgt T Barton — inj
Took off Canrobert to bomb a convoy on the Tunis-Massicault Road. On return, fog caused the pilot to circle for some time. At 0510, with fuel short, the port engine cut and five minutes later the Blenheim crashed while attempting to locate the LG for an emergency landing. Sgt Smith is buried at Medjez-el-Bab War Cemetery.

28-29 Dec 1942 — **104 Sqn** — **Wellington IC** — **Z8908 H** — **Op: Tunis**
Sgt R T Cottrell RNZAF — +
F/Sgt C N Stansbury — +
F/Sgt E C Turner RAAF — +
Sgt N Van Gelder — +
W/O2 S Jefferies RCAF — +
Sgt A M Coakey — +
Took off 1814, Luqa, detailed to bomb Tunis docks. FTR. All are commemorated on Malta Memorial. 104 Sqn was equipped exclusively with Merlin-engined Mk II Wellingtons, and it seems likely that Z8908, formerly with 37 Sqn and possibly taken on strength by 40 Sqn, also operating from Luqa, was being used because of a shortage of Wellingtons after severe Axis air raids.

29 Dec 1942 — **18 Sqn** — **Blenheim V** — **BA784** — **Op: Patrol**
P/O G W Sims
Sgt S Litchfield — inj
Sgt C Cosens — +
Took off 0428, Canrobert, Algeria, to patrol the Pont-du-Fahs-Tunis-Massicault roads. The aircraft developed engine trouble 5-10 minutes after take-off; this was corrected in flight but recurred when Souk El Arba was reached, and the pilot abandoned operations and jettisoned the bombs at 0513 hrs. In bad weather the base could not be located so he set course for the aerodrome at Souk El Arba, but the aircraft was hit by friendly fire 4km SE of Souk El Arba and crashed in a force-landing at Bangouch at 0715. P/O Sims was able pull F/Sgt Litchfield from the wreck but the fuel tanks exploded and the aircraft was DBF. Sgt Cosens was later found dead in the wreckage.

30 Dec 1942 — **160 Sqn** — **Liberator II** — **AL520** — **Relocation Flight**
F/Sgt A C Feisst RNZAF — +
F/Sgt R T C Dixon — +
P/O A I McFarlane RCAF — +
Sgt G V Brooks RNZAF — +
Sgt R H Fitchett RNZAF — +
F/Sgt J Henry RNZAF — +
Sgt R J Grimmitt — +
Sgt D K Dickson — +
Took off from Palestine and in cloud hit a hill near El Qutem, ENE of Amman, en route to India. All were buried at the crash site but in the 1950s re-interred in Damascus British War Cemetery.

31 Dec 1942 — **47 Sqn** — **Wellesley I** — **L2701** — **Unknown**
SOC, possibly as an inventory entry. NFD.

31 Dec	104 Sqn	Wellington IC	HD955	Op: Sfax
1942 -	W/O D L Iremonger	+		
1 Jan	Sgt T J Pritchard	+		
1943	Sgt E H Wright	+		
	Sgt J Bell	+		
	Sgt A Campbell	+		
	F/Sgt S Q Schrump RCAF	+		

Took off 1824, Luqa, to bomb Sfax. FTR. All are commemorated on the Malta Memorial. F/Sgt Schrump was attached from 37 Sqn. The aircraft movements card records this aircraft as lost with 99 Sqn, and it may have been detained for operations in Malta en route to the Far East, since 104 Squadron operated only Merlin-engined Wellington IIs. See Z8908 above.

Royal Air Force

BOMBER LOSSES

IN THE MIDDLE EAST AND MEDITERRANEAN

Appendices

Appendix 1

Maps of Bases

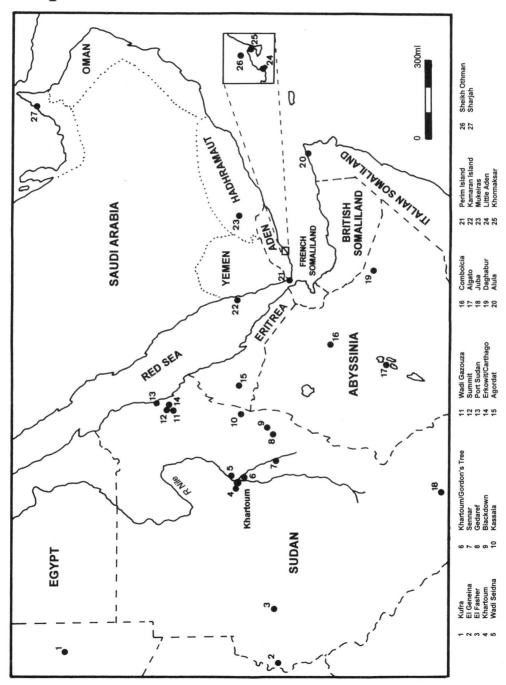

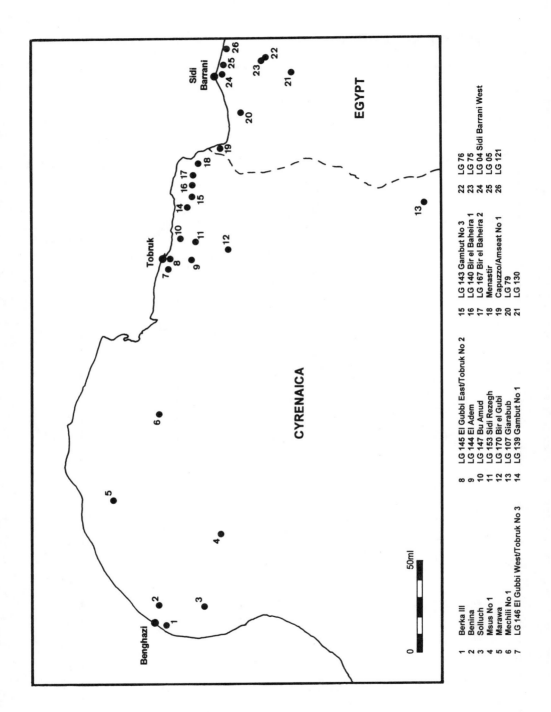

1 Berka III
2 Benina
3 Solluch
4 Msus No 1
5 Marawa
6 Mechili No 1
7 LG 146 El Gubbi West/Tobruk No 3

8   LG 145 El Gubbi East/Tobruk No 2
9   LG 144 El Adem
10 LG 147 Bu Amud
11 LG 153 Sidi Rezegh
12 LG 170 Bir el Gubi
13 LG 107 Giarabub
14 LG 139 Gambut No 1

15 LG 143 Gambut No 3
16 LG 140 Bir el Baheira 1
17 LG 167 Bir el Baheira 2
18 Menastir
19 Capuzzo/Amseat No 1
20 LG 79
21 LG 130

22 LG 76
23 LG 75
24 LG 04 Sidi Barrani West
25 LG 05
26 LG 121

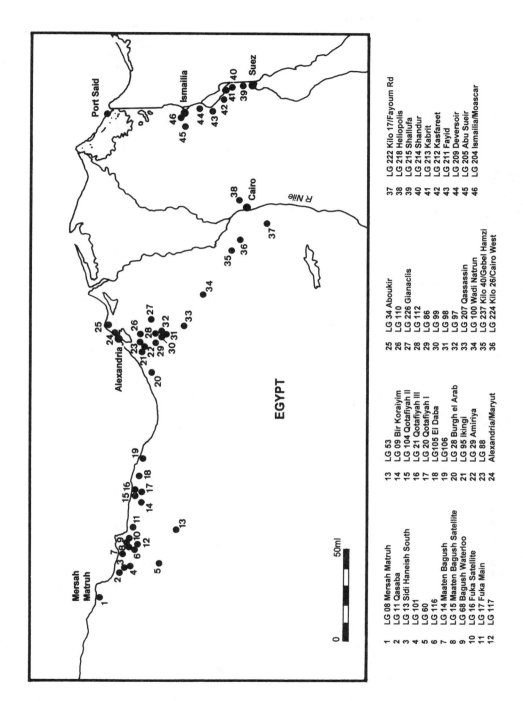

1 LG 08 Mersah Matruh
2 LG 11 Qasaba
3 LG 13 Sidi Haneish South
4 LG 101
5 LG 60
6 LG 116
7 LG 14 Maaten Bagush
8 LG 15 Maaten Bagush Satellite
9 LG 68 Bagush Waterloo
10 LG 16 Fuka Satellite
11 LG 17 Fuka Main
12 LG 117

13 LG 53
14 LG 09 Bir Koraiyim
15 LG 104 Qotafiyah II
16 LG 21 Qotafiyah III
17 LG 20 Qotafiyah I
18 LG105 El Daba
19 LG106
20 LG 28 Burgh el Arab
21 LG 95 Ikingi
22 LG 29 Amiriya
23 LG 88
24 Alexandria/Maryut

25 LG 34 Aboukir
26 LG 110
27 LG 226 Gianaclis
28 LG 112
29 LG 86
30 LG 99
31 LG 98
32 LG 97
33 LG 207 Qassassin
34 LG 100 Wadi Natrun
35 LG 237 Kilo 40/Gebel Hamzi
36 LG 224 Kilo 26/Cairo West

37 LG 222 Kilo 17/Fayoum Rd
38 LG 218 Heliopolis
39 LG 215 Shallufa
40 LG 214 Shandur
41 LG 213 Kabrit
42 LG 212 Kasfareet
43 LG 211 Fayid
44 LG 209 Deversoir
45 LG 205 Abu Sueir
46 LG 204 Ismailia/Moascar

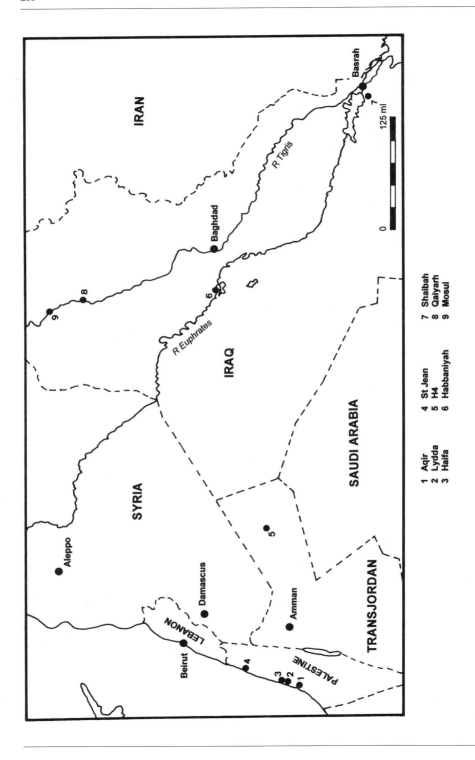

1 Aqir
2 Lydda
3 Haifa

4 St Jean
5 H4
6 Habbaniyah

7 Shaibah
8 Qaiyarh
9 Mosul

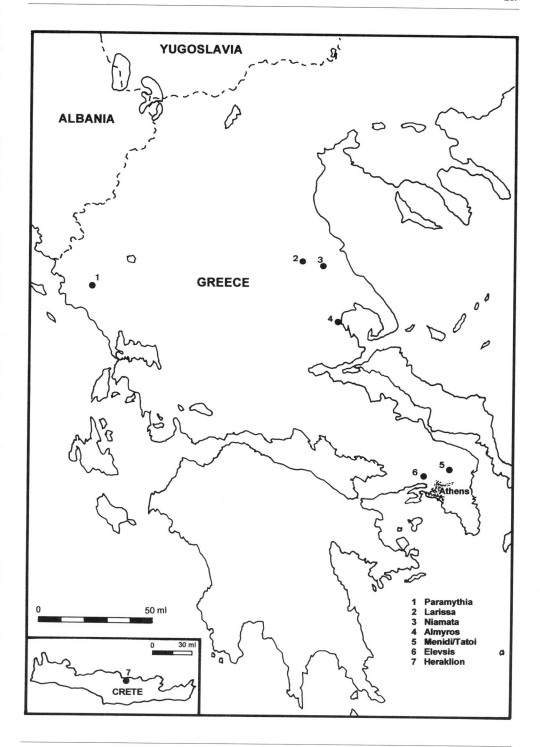

YUGOSLAVIA

ALBANIA

GREECE

2 3

1

4

Athens

5

6

0   50 ml

1 Paramythia
2 Larissa
3 Niamata
4 Almyros
5 Menidi/Tatoi
6 Elevsis
7 Heraklion

0   30 ml

7

CRETE

Appendix 2

Linked and Joint Squadrons

Some explanation is perhaps required for the occurrence in the losses lists during the summer of 1942 of 10/227 and 76/454 Squadrons. These linked units were formed as a temporary solution to an acute shortage of ground personnel to service the 16 Halifaxes each from 10 and 76 Squadrons, Bomber Command, detached to Egypt at the beginning of July 1942. Both 227 and 454 Squadrons were then in the converse position, with ground echelons awaiting aircraft and aircrews, so the decision was taken to link the 10 and 76 Squadron detachments with the ground echelons of 227 and 454 Squadrons.

The 10/227 Squadron linkage, a simple one, existed between 1st July and 7th September 1942, when the unit merged with 76/462 Squadron to become 462 Squadron. The parallel 76/454 Squadron linkage, however, was more complex, with 454 Squadron ground personnel assisting also in the servicing of the Liberators of 159 and 160 Squadrons. At an undetermined point, probably in late August, 76/454 Squadron was re-designated 76/462 Squadron, in anticipation, no doubt, of the formation of 462 Squadron as a separate entity, which it became on 7th September, on amalgamation with 10/227 Squadron.

Two other complex squadron arrangements also deserve explanation. One involves 458 Squadron, which in February 1942 was designated for transfer from Bomber Command to the Middle East. The aircraft were flown out via Malta beginning 23rd March, all save the CO (Wing Commander Mulholland) and crew arriving safely. There was a lengthy delay, however, before the ground crews could be brought by ship to the Middle East, and in the interim aircraft and their crews were attached to 37, 70, 108 and 148 Squadrons, while ground crews, on arrival in Egypt in May, were posted to service 159 Squadron Liberators, and also those of the USAAF Halversen Detachment. The ground crews and few remaining aircrews and aircraft were reunited when 458 Squadron was re-established at Shallufa on 1st September, to operate in an anti-shipping role.

The other complex squadron arrangement concerns 159 and 160 Squadrons. Newly-equipped with Liberators, both squadrons were posted to the Middle East, 159 Squadron arriving at Fayid on 7th June 1942, and 160 Squadron four days later. There 160 Squadron was effectively absorbed into 159 Squadron, the aircraft being serviced by ground crew from 147, 159, 160, 454 and 458 Squadrons (147 being designated for equipment with Liberators, though never in the event receiving them). On 16th September the joint squadron was renumbered 160, but 159 Squadron's Liberators transferred to the Far East, while those of 160 Squadron remained in Egypt, the squadron, much reduced in strength, being absorbed by 178 Squadron on its formation in January 1943.

Appendix 3

Walking Back

One of the peculiarities of the war in North African was that the geography made it possible, if always difficult physically, for a crew which force-landed in, or even bailed out over, the vast open spaces of the Western Desert behind enemy lines to evade successfully, and 'walk back'.

Many attempts to do this failed, most because the aircrew involved were captured, but some, sadly, because those attempting to walk back died of thirst and exhaustion. Others succeeded, however, and to recognise their achievement, a group of officers decided, in June 1941, to establish a 'Late Arrivals Club'. The Club is described thus on page 17 of *R.A.F Middle East – The Official Story of Air operations in the Middle East, from February 1942 to January 1943*, published by His Majesty's Stationery Office, 1945:

'Somewhere in the Western desert in June 1941, a few officers founded a club which they named the "Late Arrivals Club", for entry to which there was only one qualification. No man could become a member unless, in the words of the Club rules, "when obliged to abandon his aircraft on the ground or in the air, as a result of unfriendly action by the enemy, he succeeded in returning to his squadron, on foot or by other means, long after his Estimated Time of Arrival. It is never too late to come back." Members of the Late Arrivals Club wear a small emblem of a winged flying boot on the left breast of their flying suits.'

This volume records many cases where crews, or part-crews, attempted to walk back, and it seemed worthwhile appending here a report, to be found in File: AIR27/824, pp123-8, by the captain of one crew on their successful return three days after ETA as a salute to all those who attempted the difficult and dangerous feat:

From: No. 936753 Sgt. Maxfield C. S., No 104 Squadron.

To: Officer Commanding, 'B' Flight, No. 104 Squadron.

Date: 15th July, 1942.

Crash landing of Wellington II Z.8520 in Enemy Territory on the night of 8/9.7.42.

Sir,

I have the honour to submit the following report in respect of the crash landing of Wellington II Z.8520 in enemy territory on the night of 8/9th July, 1942.

We took off from Kabrit at 21.47 hours in aircraft Z.8520 with a load comprising 5 X 500 lbs, and 1 Can of Incendiaries. We were also carrying one overload containing 70 gallons as a precaution against high petrol consumption; that of the starboard engine being an unknown quantity – a new engine on which no consumption test had been done. We did our preliminary climb to 2,500 feet on wing tanks, and then I ordered Overload to be turned on. Allowing a good safety margin I expected to run for 45 minutes on this. After 40 minutes I sent the 2nd Pilot back to stand by the cocks, but before he got into position, both engines cut. Both picked up again when Wing tanks were turned on. The 70 gallon Overload had lasted approximately 43 minutes.

After 1 hour 20 minutes flying I noticed the Starboard oil pressure needle beginning to oscillate rapidly between 65 lbs. and 50 lbs., and gradually the pressure dropped until the oscillation was between 55 and 45 lbs. I ordered the Navigator to pump half a gallon of oil to the Starboard motor and this had the effect of raising the pressure to 65 lbs, and steadying the needle. During all this everything else had remained constant, i.e. Oil Temperature 78°, Radiator temperature 95°. Within five minutes the same thing happened again and after a total interval of twenty minutes, with Oil Pressure again at 45 lbs. I ordered another half gallon to be pumped. The Navigator asked if I intended turning back, but as Tobruk was only some half hour distant, and we could already see flares ahead, I decided to go on, keeping the pressure up by pumping oil every twenty minutes. I took this decision because it appeared that while the oil pressure could be kept up, everything else remained normal. There was no signs of overheating either in Oil Temperature or Radiator Temperature.

At 00.55 hours, however, I noticed a definite flicker on the Port radiator gauge which at the time was reading 92°. The reading became constant at that figure again immediately, but I decided to turn back and bomb Mersa Matruh if everything was still O.K. then. The Second Pilot was at the controls and I ordered him to turn back and asked for a course. We had barely set course when the Port Oil pressure dropped quite suddenly to 45 lbs. I ordered one gallon of oil to be pumped to each engine. This had no effect on the Port engine pressure, and almost immediately the Port radiator needle went up and continued right round the gauge. The Second Pilot immediately throttled back that motor. I leaned over, opened the bomb doors, and jettisoned at 01.00 hours approximately from 9,000 feet. Thinking it might merely be the gauge which was unserviceable I instructed the Second Pilot to open up the port motor again. We got normal boost and revs but the radiator Gauge needle still wandered all round the clock.

At approximately 01.05 hours the Port engine packed in altogether and began to belch blue flame from the exhausts. We began to lose height rapidly, having originally been at 9,000 feet. At this point I took over from the Second Pilot and succeeded in gaining some sort of control by 6,000 feet. The aircraft which was practically unmanageable was now heading North and the Navigator warned me that to maintain the heading for any length of time was risking a crash in the sea. I slowly brought the aircraft round on a heading of 180° – this procedure taking 15 minutes. Meantime we had been losing height fairly rapidly. I had throttled back, feathered and stopped the Port engine, and now, at 3,000 feet, I attempted to jettison some of the petrol. The Wireless Operator had been trying to get through a W.J.R. message, and I later instructed him to alter this to W.V.P. I did not find time to order an S.O.S., however, as it took both hand to hold the aircraft and I could not use my microphone. I motioned the 2nd Pilot to go to the rear of the aircraft and at the same time, the Navigator, seeing a crash landing was inevitable, warned the crew to prepare for same. He then took up a position by the Astro dome and with 1,000 feet on the altimeter he still reported no sign of the ground. I flashed the landing light, still in the retracted position and could not see anything. I kept the light off and had just lowered the landing lights when I saw the ground no more than three feet below. I was flying at 75 m.p.h. in a more or less stalled position. Indicated height was 800 feet. I could not get any more power from the Starboard engine, and I just had time to centralise the aileron controls before we crashed. I did not use flaps or landing light. The machine remained intact though the ground was very rough. The primary impact had been taken under the front turret and Pilot's cabin, and then, as the aircraft settled down, we skidded the last few yards on the bomb beams. I was uninjured and everyone else reported no damage except the 2nd. Wireless Operator who cut his face on some obstruction. The starboard engine had a few tongues of flame licking around the region of the airscrew hub. The Navigator handed out the fire extinguisher and I put out the fire.

We could see lights on the horizon North and North East so hurriedly began to remove necessary equipment from aircraft. I climbed back into the cockpit and pressed the I.F.F. Detonator button. I then went into the rear of the aircraft where the Navigator and 1st Wireless Operator were passing out stores. I enquired about the I.F.F. and the Wireless Operator went back to inspect it. He reported that there were no signs of it having detonated and I proceeded to destroy it with the axe. At 02.10 hours everything was assembled and the question of destroying the aircraft arose. Most of the aircraft was still intact, and I was in favour of destroying it, but the crew pointed out to me that the latest Middle East order was to the effect that aircraft were not to be destroyed. This, combined with the fact that we had had no lights on landing and therefore may not have given away our position decided me in favour of leaving the aircraft whole. Our kit at the outset was as follows: Four Water Bottles and one Thermos Flask, Iron rations and Special Dinghy bag from Aircraft fuselage, 2 parachutes, 1 Navigator's 02 Compass, 1 Axe, 2 First Aid Kits, Verey Pistol, 30-40 cartridges, 2 torches.

The Secret documents were given to me and as we walked I tore them into shreds and eventually buried them in three separate places en route.

Our first course was due South – away from the lights, and the first halt was called at 03.00 hours in order that those with cuts might have them attended to. The Navigator acted as Medical officer and at 03.10 hours we continued on course. Everyone went very strongly in spite of rough ground and at 05.10 hours we decided to rest. All slept except the Navigator and self. We investigated a large mound of stones which turned out to be an underground water cistern containing very filthy water. Much signs of transport having halted here and decided to move on. We had no definite idea of our position except that we were South East of Sidi Barrani. We since have decided that this well must have been Bir el Darwel. We discussed out best means of regaining our lines and decided to head roughly 120° so as to hit the Qattara Depression. Our reasoning being that on the way we should cross the Siwa road and probably have the opportunity of giving our selves up if things were not going well. The contents of the Dinghy bag were useless except for six tins of tomato juice and a signalling mirror, so we abandoned it taking these articles only.

We began walking (120°) at 09.30 hours and decided to rest 5 minutes every hour. At 10.25 hours I saw what looked like a line of telegraph poles on the horizon ahead. We pushed on expecting to get within striking distance of the road within two or three hours. However, by 12.15 hours the poles were no longer visible and as the heat was over-powering we had to rest. There was no shade and we lay with helmet and jackets over our heads and one of the parachutes spread over us.

By 14.00 hours the heat was definitely unbearable and everyone was weakening visibly. Up to this stop, no one had had water so I allowed one mouthful every hour. At 15.00 hours we decided that we simply must move and picked out as our objective a pole which we could see on top of a rise about two miles North. We thought this must indicate something as it had what appeared to be a round disc on top of it. Before setting out we cut up our first parachute for foot bandages and head protection. The remains we spread out and left as a ground signal. Our progress was very slow and we were well straggled out. Flight Sergeant Evans (Navigator) and myself were the first to arrive in the vicinity of the pole and found at the foot of the rise on which it was situated a shaft, at the bottom of which was water. We lowered a beer bottle found at the well and Flight Sergeant Evans tasted the water and pronounced it filthy.

This well had a huge board giving the name and grid reference. The place was Bir el Qattrani, our first definite pinpoint. Everyone being assembled we drank quite a considerable amount of the water, trusting to luck that it wasn't poisoned. The well was surrounded on two sides by mounds of stones and we sheltered in the shadows until 18.00 hours when I set the crew to gather wood and scrub for a fire. We boiled 7 gallons of water and made three pints of tea. Sergeant Hepworth (Rear Gunner) was immediately violently ill – vomited and finally collapsed and had to be carried into the shade. He looked extremely ill and we applied cold water bandages to [his] forehead which revived him considerably. Flight Sergeant Evans dosed us all with Quinine tablets, and we retired for the night at 19.30 hours using the parachute as a blanket.

At 01.30 hours, 10th July, 1942, I awoke to hear aircraft overhead and fired a total of nine verey cartridges at them.

At 06.00 hours we awoke and whilst some proceeded to bottle boiled water, Flight Sergeant Evans and myself decided on days plan of action. Our alternative appeared to be either (i) head east to Siwa road or (ii) head for nearest well in search of good water. The former was a distance of thirty miles, with the risk of not finding a well immediately, and also of being picked up by the enemy. The second alternative meant a trek of twenty miles, the risk being that if we did not hit the well we should definitely be short of water. We decided in favour of this course, however, because firstly it brought us into the track of our bombers, and secondly, in the event of missing the well, the railway was only two miles further on and offered a possibility of supplies. So at 08.00 hours, having had our first meal consisting of one can of bully beef among the six and three biscuits each, we set out for Bir Bethmeyl steering course of 005° and carrying in addition to original water supply a two gallon drum of boiled water, three bottles of boiled water and five bottles unboiled.

By 11.40 hours the sun was again overpowering and we stopped by a small cairn of stones hoping to have protection from the sun. There was no shadow whatever through the heat of the day and from 12.00 hours until sundown we lay under the parachute gradually weakening until by 16.00 hours we were unable to stand but could just crawl weakly around. The ration of water I still kept at one mouthful per hour, but two members, 2nd W/Op. and Rear Gunner, became so very low and weak that their ration had to be doubled. Our speech was almost unintelligible through swollen tongues and cracking lips. We were still only half way to the well and I was in grave doubt whether we could cover the remaining ten miles during the night. However, at sundown spirits began to rise, but everyone remained very weak. At 20.00 hours I distributed one can of tomato juice diluted in three quarters of a bottle of water amongst six and then at 20.30 hours I allowed another whole bottle of water to be consumed. This had a very refreshing effect. We were able to break camp and continue on course at 21.00 hours. For an hour we pushed on very slowly and probably completed two miles before the Rear Gunner stopped and said he could not go another step. I ordered two hours sleep. During this period numerous aircraft passed overhead going West, we fired on nine separate machines and flashed S.O.S. on torch. Positive we must have been seen. At midnight we proceeded forward again, but could only maintain effort for twenty minute spells on account of rear gunner who was very weak. So, walking 20 minutes and resting 10, we went on until 02.00 hours. Again a prolonged halt became essential and we slept for a further two hours.

At 04.00 hours we continued once more and at 05.00 hours called a halt. Taking the 2nd Pilot I set off to do a reconnaissance and found a small but steep escarpment and on top a circular wall approximately five feet high. This turned out to be a strong position, but there were no signs of water. However, it was obvious that we had to have shelter by sunrise so we went back and brought everyone to the compound. Here we rested until first light intending to do a reconnaissance of the area before the sun became too strong. First light brought a thick fog so, being unable to leave the Camp, we decided to eat. I opened one tin of sardines and issued three biscuits each. None of us ate the full meal. I found a petrol can containing about half a pint of sandy water. Filtering this through the parachute silk we found it very fresh and had it with breakfast.

While waiting for the fog to clear we discussed the situation and decided that the well must be within a two miles radius of our present position. Working on this assumption, F/Sgt. Evans, Sgt. Morgan and Sgt. Jobson volunteered to strike North towards the railway. I was to recco some wrecked transport about half a mile away and Sgt. Booth was to go across to a nearby mound. Sgt. Hepworth was too weak to take part in these operations and stayed behind. Across at the transport I collected about one pint of water and several cans of bully. Sgt. Booth came across and reported that he had found a petrol can containing approximately one pint of fresh water beside a deep shaft in the ground. We went back to the Camp by which time the heat was overpowering. Very shortly after the remaining three members returned, unable to stay out in the heat. On hearing about the shaft, however, Sgt. Jobson volunteered to go over with Booth and inspect it. The rest of us meanwhile erected a cover across the compound using blankets and tent canvas found there. Before this was complete, however, Booth came back saying Sgt. Jobson had gone down the shaft, found a huge cavern containing three water pools. We immediately pounced on our remaining fresh water and had a good drink each. I then ordered everyone over to the shaft and one by one we went down into the cavern by means of a twenty five foot knotted rope. We stripped and bathed and then had a conference to review the situation. The points arising from this were (i) obviously we were much too weak to proceed further (ii) here we had plenty of good water, sufficient bully beef over at the transport to last two weeks and lastly, protection in well from the sun by day.

It was decided that in the event of not being picked up, we should stay there until we had sufficient strength to make another attempt to regain our lines. All I insisted on was that in the cool of the day, morning and night everyone must put in plenty of walking. All agreed to this scheme and we settled to try and get some sleep. It was very damp in the well and at noon Sgt. Morgan and Sgt. Jobson said that they would go over to the compound and bring the blankets. Jobson, however, had not the strength to swarm up the rope, so Morgan continued alone. Shortly afterwards we heard Morgan at the mouth of the well saying "saheedah". The greeting was returned in chorus by what appeared to be quite a number of Arabs. Morgan called down for an "escape chit" and this was sent up. Then I went up, being the only member of the crew to know a little colloquial Arabic. I exchanged the usual greetings and asked the most intelligent looking what he thought of the proposals on the chit. He immediately began to read it again and then read it aloud for the benefit of those who could not read. I asked him if he would take us and he countered by asking us if we <u>were</u> English. This was rather surprising considering the statement and official looking seal on the chit. I finally succeeded in persuading him we were in good faith and he then proceeded to question me closely on the War situation in the Western Desert. Firstly it was necessary to describe where the front line was, and I explained that our troops were in El Alamein and the enemy El Dhaba. He then asked about each of the main coastal towns in turn – Tobruk, Sidi Barrani, Mersa Matruh, etc. I had to tell that they were all in enemy hands. He asked why the English had retreated, I said that I didn't know. He asked if the English were coming back – I replied in the affirmative. He then tried to pin me down to the length of time which must elapse before the English returned. I told him "very soon". He wanted to know how far we should advance, I told him probably to Benghazi. Eventually his curiosity appeared to be assuaged and I came back to the question of our escape. I asked him how many camels he could supply – he replied two only. I asked how many Arabs would come with us and again the answer was two. He asked me the distance to El Alamein and I said approximately 200 Kilos. In answer to further enquiries he said that a camel could travel approximately 30 miles a night, so we should do the trip in five days. He could guarantee fresh water every day and after the first night was fairly certain he could avoid meeting the enemy. He asked me about food and I replied that we had sufficient rations for ourselves and that if they liked "bully" there was plenty across by the wrecked transport. He said that they would bring their own supplies and all he asked from us was to have water ready for his camels. All this having been agreed upon, we all retired into the shade of the well where very friendly relations were established, the Arabs brewing tea for us and also supplying us with dates and "V" cigarettes. In the course of conversation we established the fact that this was the well for which we had set course, and we felt extremely pleased at having come twenty miles over desert to a pinpoint. The Arabs also informed us that the water that we had had from Bir El Quattrani was definitely bad and undrinkable. They took a great fancy to much of our kit and the parachute in particular. We promised them everything as a gift when we should be safely handed over to our own troops. They expressed hearty dislike for the Germans and a decided preference for the English. Eventually they all began to leave and I extracted a final promise that they would return after dark. Back in the well again I found that I was the only one who had any confidence in their return and perhaps this was natural since I was the only one who had fully understood what had been going on. However, when we discovered that they had already appropriated the parachute even I had some misgivings which I did not voice.

I instructed everyone to sleep, but being unable to sleep myself I began to fill our water bottles and preparing our stores for the trip. At 18.00 hours I roused the others and sent F/Sgt. Evans and Sgt. Hepworth up the rope to haul up the stores so as to be ready for an immediate start, when the Arabs arrived. We were about to haul up the final load when I heard Sgt. Hepworth shout that he could hear a machine and immediately I heard the engines which appeared to be very near. I heard F/Sgt. Evans fire off a Verey Cartridge and a second later another one. I went up the rope. The machine, a Baltimore, was circling our position very low and had seen us. I held up a blanket to act as a windsock and after another circuit the machine landed and began to taxy [sic] towards us.

I went to meet it and exchanged very warm greetings with the crew. They were in a great hurry to get away, and when I explained that I still had two men in the well who were too weak to get out they came across to give us a hand. On the way over they were looking for a crew who had gone down the previous night. I assured them that they had got the wrong crew and told them that we had been out three days. Sgt. Jobson and Sgt. Booth having been hauled from the well we were instructed to leave everything and get into the machine. When I saw the nature of the ground I had grave misgivings about being able to get off safely, but the Captain, F/Lt Griffiths, did a marvellous job of work and returned us safely to his Base – Wadi Natrun. The Unit was 1437 Strat/R Flight. We had a marvellous reception. After being greeted by the Commanding Officer, S/Ldr. Ault, and having made arrangements by telephone for my Unit to be informed of our safety we all retired to the Mess. Here I have only the word of my crew that a marvellous reunion was had by all as unfortunately I relaxed a little too quickly and was removed to Sick Quarters.

I have the honour to be,

Sir,

Your obedient servant,

(Sgd) C. S. Maxfield Sgt.

RAF FIGHTER COMMAND LOSSES OF THE SECOND WORLD WAR

Norman Franks

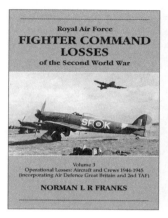

ROYAL AIR FORCE BOMBER COMMAND LOSSES of the SECOND WORLD WAR

W R Chorley

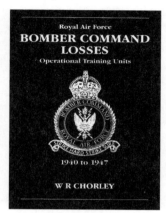

We hope you enjoyed this book . . .

Midland Publishing titles are edited and designed by an experienced and enthusiastic team of specialists.

Further titles are in preparation and we always welcome ideas from authors or readers for books they would like to see published.

In addition, our associate company, Midland Counties Publications, offers an exceptionally wide range of aviation, military, naval and transport books and DVDs for sale by mail-order around the world.

For a copy of the appropriate catalogue, or to order further copies of this book, and any of the titles mentioned on this or the following page, please write, telephone, fax or e-mail to:

Midland Counties Publications
4 Watling Drive,
Hinckley, Leics,
LE10 3EY,
England

Tel: (+44) 01455 254 450
Fax: (+44) 01455 233 737
e-mail: midlandbooks@compuserve.com
www.midlandcountiessuperstore.com

Following the Battle of France and the retreat through Dunkirk, Britain stood alone awaiting the inevitable onslaught from Germany. At the forefront of the UK's defence was Fighter Command and it was their Hurricanes, Spitfires, Blenheims and Defiants that became the world-famed 'Few' that managed to repulse the Luftwaffe in 'The Battle of Britain' during the summer of 1940.

Germany's failure to overcome the RAF and the decision to attack Russia, allowed Britain to consolidate, rebuild, go on the offensive, and after D-day, battle across Europe to the bitter end..

Between 1939-45 Fighter Command, ADGB and 2nd TAF lost over 5,000 aircrew. This work examines on a day-to-day basis the sacrifices made by these men during the desperate years of the war. The reasons and circumstances for the losses are given as crucial campaigns are enacted.

Available in 234 x 156mm sbk format:

Volume 1: 1939-41
Details 1,000 aircraft losses; 168pp
40 b/w pics 1 85780 055 9 **RP UC**

Volume 2: 1942-43
Details 1,800+ aircraft losses; 156pp
53 b/w pics 1 85780 075 3 **£12.95**

Volume 3: 1944-45
Details c.2,450 acft losses; 200pp
83 b/w pics 1 85780 093 1 **£14.95**

This highly acclaimed series identifies, on a day-by-day basis, the individual aircraft, crews and circumstances of each of the 10,000+ aircraft lost in the European Theatre of operations during the Second World War.

Appendices include loss totals by squadron and aircraft type each year; Group loss totals; Squadron bases, bomber OTU losses by unit and type, PoWs, escapers and evaders and the like.

Available in 234 x 156mm sbk format:

Volume 1: 1939-1940
160pp 0 904597 85 7 **£12.99**

Volume 2: 1941
224pp 0 904597 87 3 **£14.99**

Volume 3: 1942
318pp 0 904597 89 X **£16.99**

Volume 4: 1943
496pp 0 904597 90 3 **£18.99**

Volume 5: 1944
576pp 0 904597 91 1 **£23.99**

Volume 6: 1945
224pp 0 904597 92 X **£14.99**

Volume 7: OTUs 1940-1947
384pp 1 85780 132 6 **£18.99**

Volume 8: HCUs 1940-1947
272pp 1 85780 1563 **£16.99**

BRITISH SECRET PROJECTS

Tony Buttler

A huge number of projects have been drawn by British companies over the last 50 years, but with few turned into hardware, little has been published about these fascinating 'might-have-beens'. This series makes extensive use of previously unpublished primary source material, much recently declassified. It gives an insight into a secret world where the public had little idea of what was going on, while at the same time presenting a coherent nationwide picture of military aircraft development and evolution. Each book includes many illustrations plus specially commissioned renditions of 'might-have-been' types in contemporary markings.

Available in 282 x 213mm hbk format:

Volume 1:
Jet Fighters since 1950
176pp, 130 b/w photos, 140 dwgs, 8pp of colour. 1 85780 095 8 **£24.95**

Volume 2:
Jet Bombers since 1949
224pp, 160 b/w photos, 3-view dwgs, 9pp of colour. 1 85780 130 X **£24.99**

Volume 3:
Fighters & Bombers 1935-1950
240pp, 228 b/w photos, c192 dwgs, 6pp of colour. 1 85780 179 2 **£29.99**

FARNBOROUGH: 100 YEARS OF BRITISH AVIATION

Peter J Cooper

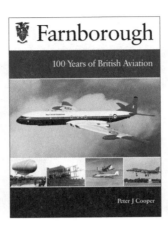

Home to the famous biennial Farnborough Air Show, this Hampshire town has had a pivotal role in the history of British aviation from 1905 when flying first commenced there.

In 1908 His Majesty's Balloon Factory was set up. This was replaced by the Royal Aviation Factory, later renamed the Royal Aeronautical Establishment to differentiate it from the Royal Air Force. The RAE rapidly expanded and was the scene of many significant developments in British aviation for many decades. After the Second World War it played host to a considerable variety of aircraft, including a number of Axis types captured during the war. Farnborough's role as a development base continued after the war, although the name 'RAE' was to disappear when this part of Britain's defence establishment was reorganised. This led to the creation of DERA which was later partially privatised as QinetiQ. This is a fully illustrated history of Farnborough from 1905 onwards. It portrays in words and over 400 illustrations the airfield and the aircraft associated with it. In the course of his research, the author has unearthed a large number of previously unpublished images which appear in the book.

Hbk, 282 x 213 mm, 208 pages
173 colour, 200 b/w photos
1 85780 239 X **£24.99**

RAF COASTAL COMMAND LOSSES Volume 1
Aircraft and Crew Losses 1939-1941

Ross McNeill

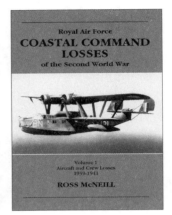

When war broke out in September 1939, the UK's armed forces were ill-prepared. RAF Coastal Command was little more than a reconnaissance force, with less than 300 aircraft (only 170 being operational) with which to combat the menace of the German cruisers, U-boats and magnetic mines that posed a real threat to Britain's very existence.
The invasion of Norway and the low countries, the need to provide 'weather' flights, photo-recce and air-sea rescue from Iceland to the Azores, almost stretched resources to breaking point, but improvements in armament, aircraft, training and U-boat detecting methods began to turn things around, and eventually closed the 'Atlantic Gap'. These were costly times for Coastal Command, by the end of 1941 its constituent units had lost 1,006 aircraft and suffered 2,026 fatal casualties.
This book records the losses on a day-by-day basis, listing the units, crews, aircraft types and service serial numbers, unit code letters, and circumstances behind each loss, where known. Appendices include summaries of losses by type, group and squadron, as well as details of unit bases, PoWs, escapers, evaders, and internees.

Sbk, 234 x 156 mm, 208 pages
32 b/w photographs
1 85780 128 8 **£16.99**